THE ROUGH GUIDE TO

WITHDRAWN

Gangster Movies

ROUGH GUIDES

www.roughguides.com

Credits

The Rough Guide to Gangster Movies

Editor: Matt Milton
Layout: Diana Jarvis and Matt Milton
Picture research: Michele Faram
Proofreading: Derek Wilde
Production: Julia Bovis

Rough Guides Reference

Series editor: Mark Ellingham
Editors: Peter Buckley, Duncan Clark, Daniel Crewe, Matt Milton, Joe Staines
Director: Andrew Lockett

Publishing Information

This first edition published September 2005 by
Rough Guides Ltd, 80 Strand, London WC2R 0RL
345 Hudson St, 4th Floor, New York 10014, USA
Email: mail@roughguides.com

Distributed by the Penguin Group:
Penguin Books Ltd, 80 Strand, London WC2R 0RL
Penguin Putnam, Inc., 375 Hudson Street, NY 10014, USA
Penguin Group (Australia), 250 Camberwell Road, Camberwell, Victoria 3124, Australia
Penguin Books Canada Ltd, 10 Alcorn Avenue, Toronto, Ontario, Canada M4V 1E4
Penguin Group (New Zealand), Cnr Rosedale and Airborne Roads, Albany, Auckland, New Zealand

Printed in Italy by LegoPrint S.p.A

Typeset in Bembo and Helvetica Neue to an original design by Henry Iles

336 pages; includes index

A catalogue record for this book is available from the British Library

ISBN 13: 978-1-84353-423-5

ISBN 10: 1-84353-423-1

1 3 5 7 9 8 6 4 2

THE ROUGH GUIDE TO

Gangster Movies

by
Lloyd Hughes

Contents

Introduction   vi

Say Hi To The Bad Guy:
the origins   1

Once Upon A Crime:
a history of gangster cinema   21

The Canon:
50 essential gangster movies   67

A bout de souffle	69	The Getaway	95
Angels With Dirty Faces	73	Get Carter	97
The Asphalt Jungle	75	Gloria	99
A Better Tomorrow	77	The Godfather	101
The Big Heat	79	The Godfather Part II	104
Black Caesar	80	Goodfellas	107
Bonnie And Clyde	82	Gun Crazy	111
Brighton Rock	85	Heat	113
Bullets Over Broadway	87	High Sierra	117
City Of God	89	Infernal Affairs	119
Cyclo	92	Key Largo	121
Force Of Evil	93	The Killing	123

King Of New York	125	*Pulp Fiction*	153
Little Caesar	127	*Reservoir Dogs*	156
The Long Good Friday	128	*Rififi*	159
Mean Streets	130	*The Roaring Twenties*	161
Menace II Society	133	*The St Valentine's Day Massacre*	163
Miller's Crossing	135	*Salvatore Giuliano*	165
Night And The City	137	*Le samourai*	166
Once Upon A Time In America	138	*Scarface*	168
On The Waterfront	141	*Scarface* (1983)	170
Pépé le Moko	144	*Sonatine*	172
Performance	145	*They Live By Night*	173
Point Blank	149	*White Heat*	175
The Public Enemy	151	*You Only Live Once*	177

The Icons:
dons of gangster cinema 179

Tools Of The Trade:
the archetypes 213

The World Is Yours:
global gangsters 245

Wiseguy Wisdom:
the information 290

picture credits 313

index 315

Introduction

Every book about gangster movies has to have a working definition of what a gangster movie actually is. And each will disagree with the other. For the purposes of the *Rough Guide To Gangster Movies*, it is one in which the gangster is the protagonist, not the supporting player or *bête noir* of the long-suffering cop hero.

There are, of course, exceptions to the rule. The most obvious here is the inclusion of **Fritz Lang**'s *The Big Heat* (1953) in the Canon chapter, picked largely because of the performance of Gloria Grahame as Debbie, the most luminously bittersweet of all molls. Even the definition of a gangster, let alone a gangster movie, is itself a moot and much chewed-over point. For example, Britflick icon **Ray Winstone** has always made a clear distinction between a thief and a gangster when he's discussed the parts he's played. According to him, the Speedo-clad Gal in *Sexy Beast* (2000) is a robber whereas his nemesis, Ben Kingsley's nerveless Don, is a mobster. However, this book flies in the face of both logic and Winstone. It includes thieves, bandits, heist-merchants and even the occasional dandy. Organised crime, in other words.

To explain the reasons for the continuing popularity of the genre would be to deal in generalisations and only the most foolhardy of writers would attempt such a thing. So here goes… There seems to be a two-faced pleasure in watching a gangster movie. There's a distinctly vicarious thrill in seeing the criminal in action, gleefully transgressing our buttoned-up societal norms and getting away with it. But it's also a guilty pleasure. And our consciences are salved with the death of the gangster, as order is restored. The earliest movies articulated this tension, often under orders from self-appointed moral guardians such as the Hays-Breen Office, but even modern directors with no beady-eyed censor breathing down their necks have played with this Manichean complexity.

Martin Scorsese, for instance, has claimed that he had two career options when he was growing up in New York – to be a priest or a gangster. And it's easy to read the same conflict in his movies, which are fables of redemption as much as gangster flicks. Similarly, the Christian iconography in **John Woo**'s work is not just there for aesthetic effect. And even Quentin Tarantino has shoehorned-in religious redemption, albeit in a typically comic book manner, when **Samuel L. Jackson**'s Jules decides to walk the earth in *Pulp Fiction* (1994) after having a miraculous near-death experience.

However, some recent gangster flicks have missed the point. There have been movies that have followed the likes of *Lock, Stock And Two Smoking Barrels* (1998) in being practically live action cartoons which lack the emotional sucker-punches that result from the clash of two competing forces: right versus wrong, society versus the individual, or the super-ego versus the id. It's all a laugh… or rather a "larf". They have no dynamic, and therefore appear one-sided, one-dimensional and superficial.

There is also a curtain-twitching aspect to the gangster genre's appeal, and some movies are practically gossip sheets on celluloid. As explained in the first two chapters, movies such as *Little Caesar* (1930) and *Scarface* (1932) had narratives based on real-life events, merrily stealing from Al Capone's CV. But the genre has had a curious on-off relationship with contemporary reality, its source material, and something odd happened in the late 1950s. The films seemed to leave reality behind altogether. Paradoxically, this occurred with the advent of biopics like *Baby Face Nelson* (1957) and *The Rise And Fall Of Legs Diamond* (1960), which were less concerned with retelling the lives of their real-life subjects than remaking the Hollywood classics of the 1930s. In other words, they were movies about other movies.

This postmodern moment was crystallized in the 1959 release *A bout de souffle*, which was the first truly self-conscious, self-reflexive gangster movie. Since then films have ceaselessly referred to other films, culminating in the work of **Quentin Tarantino**, possibly the one modern artist who has come closest to writer Walter Benjamin's stated desire to create a text entirely composed of quotations. But the relationship of the gangster flick to contemporary reality has bizarrely come full circle, as anecdotal evidence suggests that the movies have given criminals a new sense of self, or a new series of role models. It has certainly made them dress better. Hordes of Triad members rushed out to buy duster coats after seeing **Chow Yun-Fat** in *A Better Tomorrow* (1986). Meanwhile, FBI agents have reportedly claimed that **Marlon Brando**'s Don Corleone gave two-bit mobsters a misplaced, grandiose idea of who they really are – *The Godfather* (1971) sold an image back to the Mafiosi that they were men of honour. It's a point that the cross-referencing TV series *The Sopranos* jokingly but eloquen-makes – pop culture has eaten itself.

This book is designed to help you get a grip on the century-long, world-wide narrative of gangster film. It will take you back to the bloody real-life roots of the genre – the hardmen, corrupt cops, shysters and hoods of early twentieth-century America. It will strongarm you, decade by decade, through the history of gangster cinema, and you'll see film trends and fads rise and fall, almost as dramatically as the career of Tony Montana. And it will show you how every era bled into the one following it, yet nonetheless managed to find a fresh angle.

Of course, the genre's history has been shaped by many different filmmaking nations. The US and the UK are by no means the only homes of the gangster movie. Wherever there is organized crime and a film industry, there are films about organized crime: Japan, Hong Kong, France, Italy, Thailand and South Korea are just some of the different countries covered within this book.

At the book's core lies the Canon. Here you will find fifty of the greatest gangster movies ever made. Inevitably, there will be some readers who disagree with the selection. It's a testament to the plasticity of the gangster film that it has regularly flown in the face of film snobbery and transcended its B-movie/exploitation-flick reputation to produce so many masterpieces.

Say Hi To The Bad Guy: the origins

Al Capone enjoys a cigar en route to the penitentiary
in Atlanta where he will begin an eleven-year sentence

Say Hi To The Bad Guy:

the origins

"Snatched from today's headlines" is how Warner Brothers advertised their gangster movies in the 1930s, and it's a fair indicator of the origins of the genre. "Today's headlines", however, is a bit of an exaggeration – "last decade's headlines" would be more accurate.

The criminal activity on the streets of Chicago in the 1920s – gun battles, drive-by shootings and bomb attacks – was in fact replayed in the movies, novels and plays of the 1930s. Despite this time lag, gangster films were at least more or less contemporaneous with their subject matter, a synchronicity that Westerns, of course, no longer enjoyed. As such there were relatively few literary or theatrical antecedents. The gangster genre was genuinely ripped – or ripped off – from the headlines.

There were gangsters in the US before the 1920s, of course. Most were street gangs who were in the pay of companies, unions and politi-

cians such as **William "Boss" Tweed** of New York in the latter half of the nineteenth century. Played by **Jim Broadbent** in Martin Scorsese's *Gangs Of New York* (2002), Tweed was a corrupt politician, a man who, aided by his "Tweed Ring", leeched between $75–200m from New York between 1865 and 1871. Tweed became Commissioner of Public Works in 1870, and his method was to instruct contractors to massively overcharge the city for their services. He and his gang pocketed the difference. When he was finally brought to trial, evidence such as records of bills for $42,000 brooms and $7500 thermometers (all charged to the city of New York) saw the light of day. His motto of "something for everyone" appeared to extend to the bribing of juries, judges and policemen.

Then there was the **Black Hand Gang**, an extortion racket who brought the old ways with them from Sicily in 1898. Founded by **Ignazio "Lupo" Saietta** (aka Lupo The Wolf), it was New York's first Mafia family, taking its name from the symbolic black hand depicted in extortion letters in Sicily. It printed its mark onto the silver screen a few decades later, in the form of *Black Hand* (1949), a thriller in which Gene Kelly played an Italian-American seeking revenge on the Mano Nera, reponsible for the murder of his lawyer father.

But the gangster of the 1920s was different. The Prohibition era not only made the gangs more money and gained them more power, it saw them get organized. It also made them popular, bringing them into contact with respectable society – often high society. Opera lover **Al Capone** fashioned himself as a businessman who was simply performing a public service: meeting demand with supply. And because he was so vocal and so conspicuous, he also brought the gangster into popular mythology, rendering him very distinct from his nearest outlaw predecessor, the Wild West gunslinger. The gangster was a man of the city, who exploited everything that the city had to offer: cars, clothes, nightclubs and Tommy guns.

Most of his battles were fought on the streets: Capone, **Johnny Torrio**, and **Little Hymie Weiss** were all gunned down (if not always killed) in the public arena. And for those who didn't happen to be on the right sidewalk to see it, the newspaper – that other essential organ of the city – carried the reports the next day.

Almost everything that happens in the classic gangster movie of the 1930s had a counterpart in real life, but the influence didn't just end there. The classic movie, developed over the course of that decade, wrote the rules for the genre *in perpetuum*: the narrative themes, tropes, characters, dialogue, dress codes and more. Even films of today, which may seem a world away from *Little Caesar*, still operate with a template set in 1930, and a bloodline can be easily traced from, say, the Hong Kong action cinema of the 1980s back to the classic model. **John Woo** paid homage to **Jean-Pierre Melville**, who himself paid homage to the archetypal American gangster movie.

Thus the origins of the gangster movie, the first tangible links of the chain, are to be found on the streets of Chicago, hidden somewhere about the personae of Al Capone and his self-mythologizing brethren. But of course the gangster film has taken different directions over the years. The heist movie, the bank-robbing lovers on the run, the syndicate flick, and the caper movie may all vary in their gradations of "gangsterity", but they are all cut from the same organized criminal cloth. With this in mind, here are some of the key people and events that have been the formative influences on the gangster movie genre.

The Mob

Al Capone

It's fair to say that the life story of Al Capone provided the basic rise-and-fall narrative of the classic gangster film. Well, certainly the *rise* part of it. And the fall of Capone has also been alluded to: while no fictional gangster has ever been completely brought to his knees by the taxman, in both *The Untouchables* and the De Palma *Scarface* it's the accountants, and the bad old IRS (Internal Revenue Service), who are the fly in the mobster's ointment – tax evasion being the only thing that will stick to the teflon dons. Al Capone was, famously, convicted for income-tax evasion, prompting his astonished and outraged exclamation "This is preposterous! You can't tax illegal money!"

Born in Brooklyn in 1899, Capone left school after he beat up a teacher, and joined the juvenile **James Street Gang** run by **Johnny Torrio**. He acquired the nickname "Scarface" when he worked as bouncer and bartender at the Harvard Inn; Capone made a disparaging comment to hoodlum Frank Galluccio about his sister, and was cut three times across the face by Galluccio's pen-knife. He was only dubbed "Scarface" by the press, and to his friends he was always known as "Snorky". In 1919 he skipped town to join Torrio in Chicago, who was working for his uncle "Big

Jim" Colosimo, a café-owner and union leader who also ran a prostitution ring. According to Capone biographer John Kobler, Colosimo's café was well known for its wide range of cheeses.

By the time Capone arrived in Chicago it was generally considered that Jim Colosimo was going soft – he had fallen in love with a singer called **Dale Winter**, dedicated all his time to her career and had even capitulated to the extortion demands of the Black Hand Gang. A version of their story is told in *Hell Bound* (1931), the basic facts of their love affair used as springboard for a tale of unrequited love and self-sacrifice. But worse, as far as Torrio was concerned, Colosimo had no interest in bootlegging, didn't see the opportunities that Prohibition brought, and therefore was a hindrance to progress. Whether Capone killed Colosimo on his nephew's orders is a matter of much cinematic conjecture. The two Capone biopics both have him at the scene of Colosimo's murder, while *Scarface* (1932) begins with the Capone-a-like Tony Camonte killing a Mob boss in his club.

However, both Capone and Torrio had stone-clad alibis, and it's likely that they employed a hitman to do the job, probably New Yorker **Frankie Yale**. Big Jim was buried on May 14, 1920, and Torrio and Capone immediately began to build their criminal empire. Chicago at the time was riven by warring factions: the **O'Banion** gang on the North Side, the **O'Donnell Brothers** on the West Side, another set of (unrelated) O'Donnells on the Far South side and in the South itself the Sicilian **Genna family**. Like "Louis Ricarno" in *The Doorway To Hell* (1930), Johnny Torrio managed to bring the gangs together and they carved up Chicago between them, with Torrio giving himself the biggest slice of the pie. The reason that Torrio could do what he wanted in Chicago was that he had the mayor, **Big Bill Thompson**, in his pocket; half the Chicago police force was in the pay of the gangs, as were most of the politicians. And when a reforming mayor, William Dever,

Prohibition, speakeasies and bootlegging

The Volstead Act, named after the Republican senator who introduced the bill, came into force on January 17, 1920. The "noble experiment", in which manufacture, sale, and consumption of alcohol was banned, was already under way in several states, but now the whole of America was going to go dry. At least, that was the plan.

The first crime, according to biographer John Kobler, occurred 59 minutes after the bill became law when a truck carrying medicinal spirits was hijacked. This set the course for the next thirteen years. Prohibition gave gangsters wealth, power, prestige and popularity and introduced a new leisure facility: the speakeasy. The nightclub, with its jazz and dancing girls, is of course a requisite of the gangster genre, but there are plenty of other consequences of Prohibition that have found their way into movies.

Bootlegging has been the subject of a number of films (*Thunder Road* (1958) and *The Moonshine War* (1970), for instance), which show gut-rot whisky being produced in home-made stills in farmhouses or remote rural locations. These films have more than a grain of truth: in 1926 a farmhouse in Williamson County, Illinois, was revealed to be a vast distillery when it was bombed by a plane flown by a rival group of moonshiners. But that's only half the story. The breweries themselves were still producing alcohol, even though they could only legally produce "near-beer". In *The Public Enemy* an upper-class brewery-owner is shown doing a deal with gangster Nails Nathan to continue making real beer. That fictional brewer was based on **Joseph Stenson** who went into partnership with hoods **Terry Druggan** and **Frankie Lake**. Hijacking other gangs' beer trucks was a commonplace crime, also featured in *The Public Enemy*, as was the practice of strong-arming bar-owners into taking your beer. This method, apparently invented in Chicago by **Spike O'Donnell**, was to walk into a speakeasy, look the owner straight in the eye and tell him to take your wares – "or else". The "or else" was pictured in *The Untouchables*, when a bomb is left in the bar of a refusenik; and in *The Public Enemy*, James Cagney simply drains all the competition's beer from the taps of a drinking establishment.

Franklin D. Roosevelt made the repealing of the act an election promise in 1932; on December 5, 1933 he kept his word. But by then it was too late. The national syndicate had been formed two years earlier and the Mob was an immoveable object.

was voted into office in 1923, Torrio moved his whole operation to the satellite town of Cicero, which never knew what hit it. Cicero became a gangster's paradise.

The peace between the rival factions lasted three years, until the Genna family fell out with the O'Banions when the Sicilians broke the territorial agreement and started to move their cheap whisky into the North Side. O'Banion involved Torrio in the war with the Gennas, and practically signed his own death certificate when he tricked Torrio into buying a brewery that was about to be raided by the cops.

In a scene that was re-enacted in *Underworld* (1927), O'Banion was murdered in his flower shop (he was florist to the gangs, and did a roaring trade in funeral decorations) on the orders of Torrio. In retaliation, O'Banion's lieutenant, **Little Hymie Weiss**, attempted to kill first Capone, in a drive-by shooting in January 1925, and then Torrio a fortnight later. The gang boss was shot at close range in the chest, jaw, arm and groin by two men and only survived because the hitmen ran out of bullets when they were about to tap him through the temple. Torrio made a full recovery after only three weeks, but decided to quit the business and handed his empire over to Capone.

Officially an antiques dealer, Capone looked very much the part of a Mob boss and cemented the popular image of the gangster as Dapper Dan: he had hundreds of expensive suits, silk underwear, an armoured limousine, a large yacht and soon added a mansion in Miami to his portfolio of conspicuous consumption. He built up his empire along the same business lines as Torrio, with a board of directors and an estimated annual revenue of $100 million. After Big Bill Thompson's re-election in 1926, his power and profits increased even further.

However, these were also the years of the bloodiest crime war in Chicago's history. All the scene-setting we see in the movies, often in montage, actually happened on the streets of the city: bombs in restaurants, car chases, summary executions and drive-bys were all conducted in the public arena. One of the gangster movie genre's key set pieces had its genesis on September 20, 1926 when Little Hymie Weiss made his most audacious attempt on Capone's life. It's a scene that's been replayed in countless movies. Capone was dining in his restaurant, the Hawthorne Inn, when a convoy of sedans drove past, firing thousands of bullets at its target, tearing up the restaurant and wounding a passer-by, but completely missing Capone.

From that moment on, Weiss was a dead man. He was killed on October 11 as he walked towards his headquarters, shot by two gunmen from the window of a boarding-house across State Street. Ten bullets entered his body and he died almost instantly. On October 21 the warring factions agreed to a peace treaty; one of the points of contention included a promise not to gossip about each other.

But the peace didn't last long. Under new leader **Bugs Moran** the O'Banion gang started hijacking Capone's trucks and blew up six of his saloons. The attempt to rub out Moran is now part of mythology, a singularly bloody event that's become synonymous with Al Capone. On February 14, 1929 two hoods dressed as policemen entered the SMC Cartage Co warehouse, the centre for Moran's operations, and told the seven men present to line up against the wall. With the men's backs turned, the "cops" unlocked the doors and let in two men armed with machine guns, who methodically sprayed their victims with bullets from top to toe.

However, Moran was not amongst them. He'd left the building minutes earlier and was returning to the warehouse when he saw the policemen. The man the killers thought was Moran was an optometrist called **Reinhardt H. Schwimmer**, who'd just dropped by on his way to work. Unfortunately for him, he was wearing

The horse

When dandy gang boss **Nails Nathan** dies after being thrown from a horse in *The Public Enemy*, his loyal employees Tom (James Cagney) and Matt (Edward Woods) walk into the stables and, in a typically pedantic instance of wiseguy retribution, shoot the horse.

Gangster **Samuel J. "Nails" Morton** died after being thrown from his horse in Lincoln Park. According to John Kobler, in his biography *Capone*, the O'Banion gang kidnapped the horse from its stables, took it to the exact spot where their colleague had been killed, and shot it. They then rang the stable manager and informed him that they'd taught his horse a lesson.

the same hat and coat as Capone's deadly enemy. Bugs Moran left Chicago soon afterwards.

Even though he was in his Miami mansion at the time of the massacre, so could not have taken part directly, it was obvious to everyone that Capone had ordered the hit. He was already a well-known figure before 1929 (a play based on his exploits, *The Racket*, had been a Broadway smash two years earlier) but the St Valentine's Day Massacre made him a worldwide celebrity: he graced the cover of *Time* magazine in 1930; his opinion was asked about the state of the nation by one journal, and about the "modern woman" by another; reporters were sent from Paris to interview him; and he was afforded a hero's reception at baseball games. But all this publicity was bad for his career, finally bringing him to the attention of the federal government. **Elliot Ness** of the Treasury Department organized a task force of nine agents who started to seize trucks and close down distilleries (immortalized in the TV series, and of course movie, *The Untouchables*). And a businessman called **Colonel Robert Isham Randolph** set up a vigilante group dubbed The Secret Six (they got their own movie made about them in 1931) to combat the corruption in City Hall. It also transpired that three of Capone's employees – Scalise, Anselmi and Giunta – had been conspiring against him. The boss invited them to a banquet at the Hawthorne Inn, and over dinner he beat them to death with a baseball bat, in a scene that was fictionalized in both *Party Girl* (1957) and *The Untouchables*.

Capone was arrested in May 1929 for "being a suspicious character and carrying concealed weapons". He was sentenced to twelve months, and served ten. But it wasn't, of course, as a suspicious character that Capone got the jail term that finished him off. In June 1931 he was indicted for income-tax evasion; on October 17 he was found guilty of several of the charges, and on October 24 he was sentenced to eleven years. He served the first part of his sentence in Leavenworth prison, where he made an audacious bid for freedom, offering his services to track down the kidnapper of **Charles Lindbergh**'s baby (the American hero and aviator's child had been abducted), on condition that he was granted his liberty. There was even a popular press campaign to free the gangster, but the authorities did not cave in to public opinion or media pressure, and the whole bizarre story was fictionalized in *The Penalty Of Fame* aka *Okay, America* (1932). Capone was moved to the Atlanta Penitentiary and then in 1934 to Alcatraz; it was here he stayed until 1939, when he was released on psychiatric grounds. The venereal disease that he'd caught in the mid-1920s during a visit to a brothel had developed into neuro-syphilis, though the press claimed he'd gone mad because of "the horrors of Alcatraz". He spent the rest of his life in his Florida mansion, mentally disorientated, until his death from a brain haemorrhage on January 9, 1947, age 48.

John Dillinger

John Dillinger has been the subject of three biopics, with *Reservoir Dogs*' **Lawrence Tierney**, **Warren Oates** and **Mark Harmon** all having playing the bank robber. He's also cropped up as a cameo character in *Baby Face Nelson* (1957), *The FBI Story* (1959), *Ma Barker's Killer Brood* (1960), *Kansas City Massacre* (1975) and *The Lady In Red* (1979). The Dillinger mythology has also found its way into *Public Hero No.1* (1935) and *The Petrified Forest* (1936) but, most importantly, his last days were the inspiration for *High Sierra* (1941), which heralded the new *noir* hero of the

Four big-screen Al Capones

It goes without saying that both of the *Scarface* movies got a few ideas from the dramatic life of Mr Capone. But there are four key films in which Al is a major player, named, and under no stand-in pseudonym or in no disguise:

Al Capone
dir Richard Wilson, 1959, US, 103m, b/w

The first biopic gets much of the story right but gives Capone a new moll, the ex-wife of one his first victims, Marie Flannery. She is, however, a complete invention: Capone was married to a woman called Mae from 1918 until his death in 1947. As the Mob boss, Rod Steiger gives it the full hand-wringing, barking Method histrionics, certainly, but it's genuinely chilling in his quieter moments.

The St Valentine's Day Massacre
dir Roger Corman, 1967, US, 99m

Why the long face? The thin-as-a-rake Jason Robards was genuinely miscast; he was due to play Bugs Moran while the appropriately corpulent Orson Welles was to play Capone, but the studios rejected the great man. Robards plays the feared, psychotic mobster as

nothing worse than slightly tetchy. The rest of the film is, however, cinema's most forensic, accurate account of Capone's life (see p.163 for the in-depth movie review).

Capone
dir Steve Carver, 1975, US, 101m

Ben Gazzara plays Al Capone like a *Thunderbirds* puppet, all jerky movements and shoulder shrugs. From the very first scene, which gets the origins of the scar all wrong, we know we're not in Chicago any more. Mrs Capone is nowhere to be seen and the Mob boss gets another new moll, a blonde society girl who is mown down by Bugs Moran and thus sparks the St Valentine's Day Massacre. Typical exploitation hokum.

The Untouchables
dir Brian De Palma, 1987, US, 120m

In order to get inside Capone's head, Robert De Niro got inside his pants: in an instance of Method acting gone mad, De Niro wore the same brand of silk underwear Capone did. But no amount of pant-matching could camouflage the fact that, by 1987, De Niro was such a huge star and recognizable face that Capone was absorbed into De Niro rather than the other way around. The movie builds up a good deal of tension, though, largely courtesy of Sean Connery's genial, rough diamond of a veteran cop.

40s: the dead man running.

Of all the Public Enemy No.1s, John Dillinger was arguably the most famous – the No.1 of Public Enemy No.1s – not least because he broke out of jail twice. After he busted the **Pierpont Gang** out of prison, they returned the favour a few months later when Dillinger was arrested. The gang dressed as policemen and escorted the bank robber from the jail, but Dillinger was seized four months later after a string of robberies, for which he became celebrated as a modern–day Robin Hood. An indicator of Dillinger's fame is the photo call that the Crown Point sheriff's

department organized to show off their celebrity prisoner; the newsreel of the swarthy, charismatic armed robber only added to the romantic image of the modern bandit.

As did his next escape, when he famously, or apocryphally, whittled a wooden washboard into the shape of a pistol and convinced his guards that he was carrying a loaded weapon (**Woody Allen** parodied this scene in 1969's *Take The Money And Run* with a bar of soap). To add insult to injury, Dillinger escaped in the sheriff's car. He hid for a while in his father's house (the police never thought of looking there), robbed a few more banks and killed a few more police-men, but was finally undone by a prostitute called **Anna Sage**, the so-called "lady in red", who was given her own biopic in 1979. She tipped off G-man **Melvin Purvis** (he got *his* own biopic in 1974), the federal agent who also captured **Machine Gun Kelly** and killed **Pretty Boy Floyd** (years later, Purvis committed sui-cide with the very same gun that shot Floyd).

On July 22, 1934, when Dillinger left the Biograph Theatre in Chicago after watching the gangster film *Manhattan Melodrama,* seventeen FBI agents were waiting outside for him. In attempting to escape, he managed to make it to the alley at the side of the cinema, where he was finally slain. Or was he? The body on the marble slab in the morgue didn't look like Dillinger, but that, according to the FBI, was because he

Warren Oates (in front passenger seat and floppy hat) in John Milius's *Dillinger* (1973)

had had a facelift and his hair dyed. However, according to conspiracy theorists the Feds got the wrong man, a hood called Jimmy Lawrence, and the real Dillinger lived happily ever after.

Dillinger
dir John Milius, 1973, US, 107m

Warren Oates uses all his seedy charm to play Dillinger in the last year of his life. All the major events are present and correct, from the jail break to the events outside the Biograph Theatre, and G-man Melvin Purvis gets a lot of attention (writer/director John Milius wrote the script for the Purvis biopic a year later). This was Milius' debut, in which he displayed all the virtues and failings of his subsequent career: he's nowhere near as good a director as he is a writer.

Charles "Lucky" Luciano

Like all famous gangsters, Charles Luciano has been the subject of a film, *Lucky Luciano* (1974), and he has also been played by **Joe Dallesandro** in *The Cotton Club* (1984) and **Stanley Tucci** in *Billy Bathgate* (1991). His extradition from the United States in 1946 formed the basis for the plot of *Key Largo* in 1948.

But his greatest contribution to crime, and therefore crime movies, was the setting-up of the national crime syndicate. Since the 1950s, in films such as *The Phenix City Story* (1955), *Underworld USA* (1960), and *Point Blank* (1967), the locus of crime has not been an individual, conspicuous gangster, but rather a shadowy syndicate or organization (sometimes just known as "the organization") run by a corporate entity – or an elusive "Mr Big" (aka "The Man", as in 1958's *The Line-Up*). In real life, this move from the old-school crime boss to the new business model happened in 1931, the year Al Capone, the most famous gangster of the twentieth century,

was put in prison.

Lucky Luciano was born Salvatore Luciana in Sicily in 1897. He moved to New York in 1906, was first arrested in 1907 (for shoplifting), became a member of the notorious Five Points Gang by 1916 and by 1920 had formed the powerful **Broadway Mob** with **Frank Costello**, **Joe Adonis** and **Arnold Rothstein**. Luciano's big idea was to get away from the insular, old-school ways of the traditional Mafia, according to which only Sicilians could be trusted, and to bring together mobsters irrespective of their nationality or religion. In other words, he was an equal opportunities employer.

In 1931 he was responsible for the death of one Sicilian *capo*, **Giusseppe Masseria**, and he followed it up with the slaying of his rival, the "boss of bosses" **Salvatore Maranzano** on the fabled Night Of The Sicilian Vespers. The film *Lucky Luciano* depicts these bloody events, in which not just Maranzano but forty other Mafiosi were all executed on the same day. Author **Carl Sifakis** disputes the legend, claiming that most of the so-called victims had already died of old age. But whatever the circumstances really were, the fact is that a national syndicate was formed, one which controlled bootlegging, narcotics, prostitution and gambling right across the United States. The "board of directors" included **Meyer Lansky**, **Dutch Schultz** and **Louis Lepke**; unofficially, Lucky Luciano was chairman of the board.

His corporate success, however, is not why he got his nickname: apparently it was acquired after he survived an attempt on his life in 1929. His luck ran out in 1936 when he was sentenced to thirty to fifty years for his involvement with prostitution. He was released in 1946, thanks to his "services during the war", and **Francesco Rosi**'s film *Lucky Luciano* speculated as to just what those services were. The movie suggests his instrumentality in alleged collaboration between the USA and the Sicilian Mafia (in fighting the Italian fascists) – a partnership that infamously continued after the war.

Luciano was deported to Italy, but moved to Cuba briefly where he took charge of the **Havana Conference**, a meeting of most of the important *capi* of the United States, at which **Frank Sinatra** was present, to carve up US territories and businesses between them. He eventually returned to Italy, from where he continued to conduct his business operations in America until his death in 1962.

 Lucky Luciano
dir Francesco Rosi, 1973, Fr/It, 115m

As with his classic, *Salvatore Giuliano*, Rosi has little interest in the psychology of the lead character, but rather in the political forces that supported him. Focusing on the reasons why Luciano was freed after just ten years of his jail sentence, the film nevertheless has some requisite genre thrills, such as the Night Of The Sicilian Vespers murder spree. Possibly because of the post-*Godfather* effect, this is the one Rosi movie that made it out of the arthouse cinemas and into the multiplexes and mainstream TV.

Arnold Rothstein

Rothstein has been a boon to literature as well as cinema, being the inspiration for the Meyer Wolfsheim character in *The Great Gatsby*. Arnie, inevitably, had his own biopic in the early 1960s, *The King Of The Roaring Twenties* (1961), starring **David Janssen**. He's also been played by **Robert Lowery** in *The Rise And Fall Of Legs Diamond* (1960), **George Di Cenzo** in *Gangster Wars* (1981), **Michael Lerner** in *Eight Men Out* (1988) and **F. Murray Abraham** in *Mobsters* (1991). He was the basis for Nathan Detroit in the musical *Guys And Dolls*, as played by **Frank Sinatra** in the 1955 film. Discreet versions of his life story were told in *The Czar Of Broadway* (1930), *Street of Chance* (1930), *Now I'll Tell* (1934) with **Spencer Tracy**, and *King Of The Gamblers* (1948).

"The spiritual father of American crime", as author Carl Sifakis dubbed him, was also known as "Mr Big". Arnold Rothstein oversaw his criminal empire largely in the shadows, and was a mentor to Meyer Lansky and Charles Luciano, who took their inspiration for a national crime syndicate from him. The New York crime lord made his own money from bootlegging, gambling and diamond smuggling, to name but a few of his felonious interests; most importantly he had politicians and the police in his pocket.

And it's really as a fixer that he's best known. He fixed hundreds of court cases against bootleggers, ensuring "not guilty" verdicts or no trials, but most famously he fixed the baseball World Series in 1919. Several players from hot favourites the Chicago White Sox were bribed to throw the game against underdogs Cincinnati Reds; Rothstein cleaned up at the bookies. The scandal became the subject of the film *Eight Men Out* (1988), directed by **John Sayles**.

As the title of the 1948 film suggests, Rothstein was "King of the Gamblers". But this position was also his downfall, a point all the 1930s movies about him make quite bluntly. In 1928, he played a game of poker that lasted an entire two days, from 8 to 10 September. At the end of it, he'd lost $320,000, which he refused to pay, claiming that he'd been cheated. On November 4 he was shot dead, possibly by the two people he owed money to, although there were rumours that this was a succession killing ordered by **Dutch Schultz**, who coveted the Rothstein empire.

Dutch Schultz

Dutch Schultz has been played by at least fifteen different actors (maybe it's the violence of his character that appealed to Hollywood) and had his own biopic, *Portrait Of A Mobster* (1961), starring Jennifer Jason Leigh's dad, **Vic Morrow**. More recently, **Dustin Hoffman** played him in *Billy Bathgate* (1991) as the King of New York, a man possessed by messianic rages, while James Remar portrayed him in *The Cotton Club* (1984) as just another hood with a violent temper.

Remar's portrayal seems closer to the truth, because Schultz was always a loose cannon amongst professional killers. Genuinely homicidal, he was the most unpopular gangster of his time, both feared and loathed by his peers. Dutch was the mobster who managed to kill **Legs Diamond**, the hood dubbed "clay pigeon" because of the number of times he was shot at ("You can't kill me, I'm Legs Diamond" are the gangster's final words in 1960's *The Rise And Fall Of Legs Diamond*). **Mad Dog Coll** was another victim of Schultz's and he too had his own biopic in 1961, and was played by **Nicolas Cage** in *The Cotton Club*. Coll was an even looser cannon, who made his living by holding members of the criminal underworld to ransom. It was thought that he was untouchable but, after Coll abducted one of Schultz's lieutenants, he was filled full of holes in a phone booth. Another infamous execution by "The Dutchman" is recalled in *Billy Bathgate*: ex-colleague Bo Weinberg (**Bruce Willis**) betrayed Schultz while he was awaiting his trial for income-tax evasion; Schultz filled Weinberg's boots full of concrete and pushed him into the Hudson River.

Born Arthur Flegenheimer, the gangster apparently changed his name so that it would fit in the front-page headline space. Like Bogart in *The Roaring Twenties* he violently took over the numbers racket in Harlem, and also the booze trade in the Bronx. In *Billy Bathgate* Schultz is very much the Dapper Dan, when in fact he was known to dress "like a pig", in the words of one contemporary. Dutch was a member of the original national crime syndicate, and one of its first major victims. His fate was sealed when he demanded the assassination of prosecutor **Thomas E. Dewey**; when the organization refused, Schultz declared that he was going to do the hit himself. The outfit immediately voted to put a contract out on Dutch, knowing that the murder of a prosecutor would be the downfall of the syndicate. On October 23, 1935, he was shot in the toilet of a New Jersey restaurant, and died two days later.

Meyer Lanksy

Lanksy was the co-founder and brains of the national crime syndicate (also known as "the outfit" or "the combination"), and once declared that they (the Mob) were bigger than US steel. He has been played in eight films under his own name. But it's as the inspiration for Hyman Roth in *The Godfather Part II* (1974) that he's most famous. Like Roth, Lansky set up gambling operations in Cuba, and like Roth he tried to retire to Israel and failed (Prime Minister Golda Meir famously said "No Mafia in Israel"). However, unlike Roth he wasn't assassinated on his return to America; instead he was indicted for income-tax evasion, and acquitted.

 Lansky
dir John McNaughton, 1999, US, 114m

It's a made-for-cable-TV job, so no one's expectations should be high. It's baggy, in need of rigorous editing, and has an uncharacteristically disappointing David Mamet script. But a reasonable turn from Richard Dreyfuss (one of four actors who play Lansky at different stages of his life) makes this just about worth renting if you're a Mob-movie fiend.

Warren Beatty (left) as a dapper Bugsy Siegel and Joe Mantegna as George Raft (a case of art imitating life imitating art imitating life) in 1991's *Bugsy*

Billy Bathgate
dir Robert Benton, 1991, US, 107m

A fictional account of the last months in the life of kingpin Dutch Schultz as seen through the eyes of eager protégé Billy Bathgate. The script by Tom Stoppard, a chilling turn by Dustin Hoffman and direction by Robert Benton are all unfortunately slightly hampered by an anonymous performance by the forgettable (and now forgotten) Loren Dean, who is in almost every scene of this period drama.

Bugsy Siegel

Bugsy Siegel has featured in very few films, considering he was a gangster intimately connected with Hollywood. Maybe that in itself is the reason why. Siegel has only featured in three movies, including the biopic, *Bugsy* (1991), starring Warren Beatty, and four TV adaptations, including *The Virginia Hill Story* (1974) in which Harvey Keitel took on his part.

A founder of the Bug and Meyer gang,

Benjamin Siegel was involved in bootlegging, hijacking, white slavery, rape, burglary, extortion and murder. Particularly murder. Whereas most gang bosses got others to do their dirty work, Bugsy liked to be personally involved. A leading board member of the national crime syndicate, he moved to Los Angeles to take over operations there in the 1930s. And this is where he found his calling: his undeniable charm was an instant hit amongst the Hollywood glitterati, and Bugsy, or Ben to his friends, could count Jean Harlow, Clark Gable, Cary Grant and Gary Cooper amongst his acquaintances. One of his many mistresses was the actress **Wendy Barrie**, but it was with George Raft that he had a particular affinity and he was a frequent house guest of the actor. Different accounts tell of different origins of their friendship. Some claim that Siegel identified with Raft's character in *Scarface*, others that it was Siegel who taught Raft his famous coin-spinning trick when they were both young hoods in Hell's Kitchen in the 1920s. Meanwhile, Bugsy was making his living by extorting money from the moguls by threatening the non-appearance of film extras if the gangster wasn't given his dues.

Bugsy Siegel's greatest contribution to American culture was Las Vegas, which was previously nothing more than a rest stop in the desert. He persuaded the syndicate to stump up two million dollars to build the Flamingo (the nickname of mistress no.1, Virginia Hill), but the costs at least trebled. When the casino opened, it quickly became a financial black hole, not least because Siegel was skimming money off the top. A death sentence on the "thief" was passed by his best friend Meyer Lanksy in the 1946 Havana Conference of Mafiosi and it was carried out on June 20, 1947 in **Virginia Hill**'s living room. The bullets went through Bugsy's face. His right eye was discovered fifteen feet from his body.

Bugsy
dir Barry Levinson, 1991, US, 136m

In which Hollywood gets seduced by Bugsy Siegel all over again. Even though Barry Levinson's film doesn't avert its eyes from Bugsy's violence, Warren Beatty is so naturally charismatic and his affair with Virgina Hill represented in such a classic Hollywood romantic fashion that the result, from the historically accurate perspective, is not so much nuanced as confused.

Little Hymie Weiss

A bit-part player in the Capone biopics, Little Hymie Weiss cemented his place in folklore when he became the inspiration for *The Public Enemy*'s Tom Powers, the definitive James Cagney gangster – the man who shoved a grapefruit in his moll's mush. In the real-life occurrence, the grapefruit was an omelette, and history hasn't recorded the name of the unfortunate recipient.

Like Cagney's Tom Powers, Weiss was small and pugnacious, and earned his money by building up the bootlegging business. In the words of author John Kobler, he was "thin and wiry with hot black eyes set far apart, tense, tempestuous, vindictive … the brainiest member of the gang and the cockiest". Cagney certainly got the cockiness and temper right. Weiss was also a devout Catholic, and always carried a rosary as well as a gun. After the murder of his boss Dion O'Banion, he tried to kill Al Capone in a drive-by shooting on January 12, 1925; he failed and on September 20, 1926 he tried and failed again. On October 11, 1926 Capone got his own back. *He* didn't fail.

Weiss has bequeathed to crime and crime movies two mythical anecdotes that became archetypal: "taking someone for a one-way ride" and "the motorcade of death". In 1921 Weiss took Steve Wisniewski, who had previously hijacked one of Weiss' beer trucks, for a drive. Weiss returned. The Hymie manoeuvre was to sit the victim in the front seat of the car with the killer seated behind; the cerebellum was, apparently, the ideal target because the bullet wouldn't miss any vital areas.

The "motorcade of death" technique was famously used by Weiss against Capone in 1926, and was much repeated both on the streets and in the movies. It involves a convoy of cars driving by a restaurant or business and spitting out thousands of bullets from the windows of the sedans. It's an imprecise way to carry out a murder, however: a passer-by was struck, while not one of the many bullets even so much as grazed its intended target.

The outlaws

Ma Barker

Ma Barker, the woman who led her sons in a murderous orgy of bank-robbing and kidnapping in the 1930s, was the model for the "big bad mama" character of many an exploitation movie. She was the inspiration for Ma Grissom in *No Orchids For Miss Blandish* (1948), Ma Grissom in *The Grissom Gang* (1971), and Ma Jarrett in *White Heat* (1949).

Shelley Winters famously played her in Roger Corman's *Bloody Mama* (1969), and before her there was **Jean Harvey** in *Guns Don't Argue* (1957) and **Lurene Tuttle** in *Ma Barker's Killer Brood* (1960). But none of the films, not least the biopics, gets the facts right. All have the family die together. In fact, Ma Barker was shot dead in an FBI shoot-out in 1935, with only her son Fred by her side. Her other sons had already left her – one, Herman, committed suicide while the other two, Arthur and Lloyd, were already in jail. The movies also added a few inches to the height of Fred and Arthur, neither of whom were much over five foot tall.

Kate "Ma" Barker's brood began their career trajectory with petty theft before arcing upwards into stealing cars, bank robbery, murder and kidnapping. The then director of the FBI, J. Edgar Hoover, described the Barker-Karpis crew as "the toughest gang of hoodlums the FBI ever has been called upon to eliminate" and professed himself "repeatedly impressed by the cruelty of their depredations".

But it's significant that the name Karpis crops up as often as Barker in referring to the gang. **Alvin "Creepy" Karpis** is thought by many to have been the brains of the bunch. At any rate, it was Karpis and Fred Barker who were the kernel of the crew – the pair met in prison and began to put together the gang when both were free in 1931. Karpis is one of many voices who claim Ma Barker's role within the gang was limited to the domestic.

Ma's posthumous on-screen celebrity would, leaving aside veracity and characterization, doubtless have tickled her pink, for she was an avid moviegoer. Alvin Karpis once said of her, "We'd leave her at home when we were arranging a job, or we'd send her to a movie. Ma saw a lot of movies."

 The Grissom Gang
dir Robert Aldrich, 1971, US, 128m

Irene Dailey plays Ma Grissom like Norman Bates' mother

come back to life, albeit barely; with a club foot and faint moustache, she's the mother of all nightmares. She orders her sons to kill their hostage Miss Blandish, but her plans go awry when her dim-witted son takes a shine to the heiress in this typically lurid, unsubtle Robert Aldrich production. Not the greatest film in the world, but certainly the sweatiest.

Bonnie and Clyde

The life and death of the 1930s bank robbers Bonnie and Clyde had its most obvious influence on the 1967 movie starring **Warren Beatty** and **Faye Dunaway**. In *Bonnie And Clyde*, Clyde is impotent. He "ain't much of a lover boy" until Bonnie coaxes it out of him, and the two become feted and fated outlaw lovers. In truth, the entity popularized by the media as "Bonnie and Clyde" wasn't so much a couple as a trio, a *ménage à trois*.

In the film, there's only one other real member of the gang, C.W. Moss, though Clyde's brother and sister-in-law pitch in. Different accounts have different members of the Barrow gang, but Moss is probably a composite of Raymond Hamilton, W.D. Jones and Henry Methvin. According to John Toland in his tome *The Dillinger Days*, Bonnie was a lover of first Hamilton and then Jones. who later claimed that his sole purpose in the gang was to satisfy Parker's nymphomaniacal needs. However, this raises the hackles of author Miriam Allen De Ford who in her confidently-titled book *The Real Bonnie And Clyde* says that when Clyde heard these allegations, "he laughed his head off." Whatever the truth of the situation, the threesome tag has stuck, though Clyde Barrow's role in this has never been fully determined. Most histories have depicted Clyde as homosexual, bisexual or just celibate. What we do know is that Arthur Penn "worried that this sexual deviance would throw the film off kilter", according to Lester D. Friedman in his BFI book on the film, and that "Beatty was equally adamant that audiences would never accept him in this role and ... that it was not particularly good for his image."

The genesis of the Barrow gang came in 1932, when chicken- and car-thief Clyde Barrow left jail, met cigar-smoking waitress and prisoner's wife, Bonnie Parker, and formed the Barrow gang, comprising Hamilton, Jones, Methvin, and Clyde's brother Buck and sister-in-law Blanche. They robbed banks and gas stations across the South West of the United States, in Texas, Louisiana, and Oklahoma. They weren't the most successful bandits the West has ever seen, never netting all that much cash, but their notoriety grew as their body count increased. They were blamed for the deaths of eighteen people, several of them police officers, and at least two of which were killings in cold blood. However, like Eddie and Jo in *You Only Live Once* (1937), they were blamed for murders and robberies they couldn't possibly have committed. Unlike Jo and Eddie, Bonnie and Clyde were unrepentant killers.

Semi-successful bank robbers who were ruthless cowards would seem to be unlikely models for the "last romantic couple", as Godard once dubbed the lovers in *You Only Live Once*. It is of course not the tawdry reality but the outlaw *myth* that the movie genre bought into, the genesis of which is a piece of shameless self-mythologizing by Parker, who wrote frequent letters and poems to the newspapers, most famously *The Ballad Of Bonnie And Clyde*, the last lines of which read:

> *"Some day they will go down together*
> *And they will bury them side by side*
> *To a few it means grief*
> *To the law it's relief*
> *But it's death to Bonnie and Clyde"*

Here is the essence of the doomed-love scenario that came to define the couple-on-the-run genre: the marriage of love and death, the romantic purity of partners who know they will die before their love does. The genre begins with the *Ballad Of Bonnie And Clyde*, rather than the reality of Bonnie and Clyde. It's a death wish that casts a spell over almost all the screen couples who have taken to the road. Especially Bowie and Keechie in *They Live By Night,* which begins with a close-up of the tender outlaws in soft focus, and titles that read: "This boy and this girl were never properly introduced to the world we live in…" Like Romeo and Juliet and all the other star-crossed lovers who have died before them, their love is neither understood nor tolerated by society, which, of course, only adds to their romantic cachet.

Ironically the section of *Bonnie And Clyde* that drew the sting of critics was the most realistic – possibly the only incursion of reality into Arthur Penn's romp. The deaths of real-life Bonnie and Clyde were just as bloody and bullet-riddled as their beautiful stand-ins, Dunaway and Beatty. Four agents of the law waited three days and three nights in bushes beside a country road, pumping dozens of bullets into the outlaws' car when it eventually arrived. Some bullets even passed through both Bonnie and Clyde and came out the other door, and within hours souvenir-hunters had cut the dress and hair from Bonnie's corpse.

It was a gruesome reminder that the bandits were not just celebrities, but in the dustbowl of the US, during the Great Depression, the gang had become heroes. Like the similarly feted John Dillinger, they were robbing the banks that had robbed the people of their farms and homesteads. Thousands came to mourn at Clyde's funeral.

The writers

W.R. Burnett

Adaptations of **William Riley Burnett**'s novels have changed the course of the gangster film three times – W.R. being the man who wrote the novels *Little Caesar*, *High Sierra* and *The Asphalt Jungle*. He also wrote *The Great Escape*. And yet he's still relatively unknown.

Born in 1899 in Ohio, Burnett studied journalism and moved to Chicago in 1927, where he worked behind the desk of the Northmere Hotel, becoming acquainted with gangsters and gathering material for his novels. He was among the first to arrive at the warehouse where Capone's goons had machine-gunned seven unarmed men – the scene of the St Valentine's Day Massacre – although Burnett refused to look at the carnage. His debut, *Little Caesar*, the first genuine gangster novel, was an instant bestseller, a *roman à clef* which appealed to a public who'd spent the last decade reading newspapers featuring gangsters in the headlines on an almost daily basis. The story of a minor hood, the Machiavellian Rico Bandello, who rises, Capone-like, through the underworld to become Mob boss, Burnett's prose was typified by a reliance upon slang and an economy of narrative. One chapter consists of merely one paragraph, describing Rico combing his hair. It ends "He loved but three things: himself, his hair and his gun. He took excellent care of all three."

With its pace, attention to detail and chapters that could be mistaken for scene directions, *Little Caesar* was practically a blueprint for a screenplay and Warner Brothers snapped it up. Who actually bought the rights is a matter of conjecture. Burnett himself said that **Jack Warner** only wanted the novel because the character Rico hailed from Warner's home town of Youngstown, Ohio. Historians such as Carlos Clarens claim it was actually Darryl F. Zanuck, Warner's chief of Production, who astutely bought the novel to fill a clear gap in the market for gangster movies.

Whoever was responsible, the film adaptation was a phenomenal success. In effect it invented, or at least defined, a whole new genre, and Burnett was rewarded with a contract as a scriptwriter. He worked, sometimes uncredited, on numerous movies, including "*Capone à clefs*" *The Finger Points* (1931), *Beast Of The City* (1932) and *Scarface* (1932), as well as John Ford's *The Whole Town's Talking* (1935) and an adaptation of Graham Greene's *This Gun For Hire* (1942).

In 1941 he brought the genre both back to life and back to reality with the adaptation of his morbid, lyrical, melancholic novel *High Sierra*, in which the gangster is no longer king of the city, but the last of his generation, an outcast and outlaw "rushing to death" – a theme that prefigured *film noir*. Burnett adapted the novel with **John Huston** after star **Paul Muni** was unenthusiastic about the initial script. Muni wasn't happy with Burnett's draft either and dropped out of the project altogether, giving **Humphrey Bogart** his big break.

Then, in 1950, Burnett made his third significant contribution to Mob cinema when Huston adapted *The Asphalt Jungle* – the prototype heist flick. The story of a group of disparate individuals who come together to pull off a safe-cracking job, this extremely faithful adaptation of his hard-boiled/soft-hearted novel provided the plans for hundreds of other wannabe thieves and criminal masterminds, from the sharp-suited lotharios of *Ocean's 11* to

Gangsters on stage

There are three key plays from the time which deal directly with gangsters, and a Capone clone starred in two of them. **Edward G. Robinson** played "Nick Scarsi" in *The Racket* which successfully toured most of the United States (with the exception of Chicago), while **Crane Wilbur** played "Tony Perelli" in *On The Spot* by **Edgar Wallace**. John Dillinger was given the theatrical treatment in 1936 in the original stage version of *The Petrified Forest*, with Humphrey Bogart playing "Duke Mantee" on Broadway (and on film).

Of course, gangsters – defined in the broadest sense – have been a constant throughout theatre history: from Shakespeare's *Richard III*, through Bertolt Brecht's Mack The Knife in the *Threepenny Opera*, to the displaced and bewildered hitmen in limbo of Harold Pinter's *The Dumb Waiter*. But perhaps the most "Scarfacean" of all the stage gangsters is the titular villain of Brecht's 1957 play *The Resistible Rise Of Arturo Ui* – a monomaniacal psycho who is part Adolf Hitler, part Al Capone.

the weasely tough nuts of *Reservoir Dogs*.

Despite all these achievements – creating the classic narratives for gangster and caper movies, as well as writing 36 novels and amassing sixty screenwriting credits – he never won an Oscar or a major literary award. John Huston once pronounced him "one of the most neglected American writers" – an understatement and a half.

Jake Lingle and the press

Gangsters and their exploits provided the sensationalism needed to sell newspapers, and for a decade they made the US front-page headlines almost every day. Capone would even give informal press conferences – *The Untouchables* (1987*)* has a scene in which needy hacks laugh sycophantically at Capone's jokes. He was good copy and often available for a quote, delivering self-important observations such as:

"Everybody calls me a racketeer. I call myself a businessman. When I sell liquor, it's bootlegging. When my patrons serve it on a silver tray on the Lake Shore Drive, it's hospitality."

His opinions were sought by the press about a variety of subjects, including what was wrong with the country and what it needed at that particular moment in time. His answer was "an American Mussolini".

Despite the horrified headlines condemning mobsters, it's fair to say that some journalists had a very good relationship with Capone and his ilk. Columnist **Walter Winchell** would often conduct soft-soap interviews with gangsters such as **Frank Costello** and believed them when they told him there was no such thing as the Mafia. Two other journalists, **Ben Hecht** and **Mark Hellinger**, became Hollywood scriptwriters who, according to Carlos Clarens, regarded gangsters as "the legitimate heirs to the robber barons of the nineties, to be cultivated and enjoyed and not too reluctantly admired". As Clarens pointed out, "A gangster pal was both a badge of sophistication and a way of asserting that all Americans met at the top." Allegedly Hellinger was one of the beneficiaries of **Dutch Schultz**'s will.

But one journalist had a deeper, and more profitable, relationship with Chicago's criminal fraternity. **Jake Lingle** was a police reporter for the *Chicago Tribune* who frequently enjoyed big scoops from both sides of the law. He officially earned $65 a week, and yet had two houses and a chauffeur and would frequently blow $1000 a time on the horses. The reason that he could afford such luxuries on a reporter's salary was that he moonlighted as Capone's go-between with police commissioner **William F. Russell**, Lingle's golf partner. The journalist had such influence on Russell that he was known as "Chicago's unofficial chief of police".

But Lingle was also in debt to the tune of $100,000. This is probably the reason – noone knows exactly why – he was shot dead at a racetrack on June 9, 1930, though there were suggestions that he unwisely tried to play off Capone against Moran. At first he was regarded as a martyr to press freedom, and thousands attended his funeral, but the truth soon emerged about his dealings with Capone and his financial interests in brothels, gambling joints and the careers of certain politicians. There followed articles which exposed other journalists who had extorted money from bootleggers and brothel-keepers to keep them *out* of the newspapers: a kind of blackmail racket for journalists.

A version of Jake Lingle's story is told in *The Finger Points* (1931) and *Dance, Fools, Dance* (1931). His name is changed to Keeley in *Al Capone* (1959). But the truth did little to dent the still-active movie cliché of the reporter as a crusader against crime.

Once Upon A Crime: the history

Daniel Day-Lewis (left) and Leonardo Di Caprio as early

gangsters in Martin Scorsese's *Gangs Of New York* (2002)

Once Upon A Crime:
the history

Gangster movies have existed for almost as long as cinema itself. Once they entered the public consciousness there was no stopping them, and they swiftly became a Hollywood staple. Many sub-genres later, today's mobsters and hitmen have come a long way. Yet all of them remain ultimately cut from the same hoodlum cloth, recognizable descendants of a long tradition of dirty, yellow-bellied rats.

1910–29: silent gangsters

The silent period is in many ways the prehistory of the gangster genre, never quite producing the classic movie. They are films populated by street gangs, muggers, bank robbers and even hat manufacturers, who have more in common with the characters of a Charles Dickens novel than Al Capone. They're the distant ancestors of *Scarface*. Even in the 1920s, the age of Prohibition, screen criminals were never bootlegging or opening nightclubs, but were instead engaged in the less ambitious gangsterous activities of holding up banks or breaking into jewellers. They were "characters in search of a genre", as writer Carlos Clarens put it in his book *Crime Movies*, neatly summing up the era.

Many people assume that **D.W. Griffith**'s fifteen-minute film *The Musketeers Of Pig Alley* (1912), is the first gangster movie. It wasn't. As

Kevin Brownlow points out in his excellent book *Behind The Mask Of Innocence*, Griffith's *Musketeers* is simply the first gangster film of any importance *to survive*. And it is hardly a gangster film as we know it. It concerns a Dickensian street gang who loiter with intent, mug an innocent musician and conduct a shoot-out with another gang. Similarly, in *Regeneration* (1915) made three years later by **Raoul Walsh**, we never see the gang involved in any organized criminal activity: they just play cards and shoot craps (though one of them does at one point stab a police officer).

However, Carlos Clarens makes big claims for *The Musketeers*, declaring that Griffith had created a new icon of cinema with his character The Snapper Kid (the mugger): "with a cigarette dangling from his lips, wearing his hat at an aggressive angle, and tugging at his trousers with a boxer's behavourial reflex, he represented a new addition to the gallery of film types. His gangster was a rough, urban, back-alley Huckleberry Finn." But you have to look very closely to see the iconoclastic moments that Clarens describes, and to the untrained eye The Snapper Kid looks

D.W. Griffith's *The Musketeers Of Pig Alley* (1912): villainy was still very vaudeville back then

nothing less than a pantomime villain, mugging in every sense of the word.

We'll never know how revolutionary *The Musketeers* really was, because all the gangster films made before 1912 have been lost, probably for ever. Marilyn Yaquinto lists some of the missing one-reelers in her book *Pump 'Em Full Of Lead*. Some have tantalizing titles like *The Moonshiners* (1904), *Desperate Encounter Between Burglars And Police* (1905) and *The Black Hand* (1906), named after the notorious Sicilian extortion racket. Who knows how many back-alley Huckleberry Finns starred in these films? The claims D.W. Griffith made about himself should always be taken with a pinch of salt: this was a man who literally advertised his achievements in a newspaper, and listed innovations that weren't strictly his own.

What *The Musketeers Of Pig Alley* and *Regeneration* do share with the genre proper is that they featured real-life gangsters among their cast. Throughout the genre's history, works as diverse as *Scarface* (1932), *Performance* (1970), *Reservoir Dogs* (1991) and *Lock Stock And Two Smoking Barrels* (1998) have all recruited the genuine article (or close associates of). Griffith's studio was near what Brownlow described as New York's "nerve centre of gangsterism", Tammany Hall, and the publicity for *The Musketeers* boasted that genuine hoods "Kid" Broad and "Harlem Tom" Evans were amongst the cast. Raoul Walsh, in turn, actually made it a policy to seek out underworld characters for *Regeneration* in the drinking dens of the Bowery district. As a result, it is a rogues' gallery of gnarled and twisted faces, most memorably the old man with large mushrooms of flesh growing on his nose.

Regeneration is an early example of another staple: the gangster biopic. (Most classic gangster movies are *films à clef*, cannily drawing on real life for their stories, characters and iconography.) Walsh's movie is based on the life story of **Owen Kildare**, a gang leader in the 1890s who went straight thanks to the love of a good woman, schoolteacher **Marie R. Deering**. His best-selling autobiography, *My Mamie Rose*, was adapted into a hit stage play before getting the screen treatment in *Regeneration*. The only difference between Kildare's life and the one depicted in Walsh's film is that his sweetheart and saviour is murdered by his old gang in the latter, whereas in actual fact Marie died of a cold.

A more extreme example of the fact/fiction blur was *The Wages Of Sin* (1913), which starred three notorious criminals, **Sam Schepps**, **Harry Vallon** and **Bald Jack Rose**. They had been involved in the murder of Herman Rosenthal, the owner of a New York gambling den, but, sensationally, they got off scot-free. The controversy was the biggest crime story in newspaper history and *The Wages Of Sin* exploited their new-found fame, with adverts for the film pronouncing that "millions of persons are anxious to see them". The three-reel drama was not about the case itself, but, purportedly, about the dangers of gambling. As Bald Jack Rose said in the same ad, "I have tried in *The Wages Of Sin* to make plain the risks to which young men are subjected in their daily business lives and how they can be changed from law-abiding citizens into police-hunted criminals by the machinations of soulless capitalists. The picture well fulfils its intent to teach a strong moral lesson."

This cut no ice with many critics who were worried about the morals of the nation. *The Wages Of Sin* was "a disgusting film", claimed *Moving Picture News*, which worried that "all the worst elements in the youth in our cities will flock to see this film". Moral panics are another constant in the gangster genre's history.

WILLIAM FOX
PRESENTS
ROCKCLIFFE FELLOWE
& ANNA. Q. NILSSON
IN
"REGENERATION

A TENSE MOMENT

Perhaps it's a measure of *Regeneration*'s staginess that this "Tense Moment" required a little extra signposting...

With the benefit of hindsight, it makes historical sense that the films of the 1910s bore little relation to their 1930s counterparts. After all, the classic gangster himself did not really come into being, or power, until **Prohibition** and the Volstead Act of 1920; what *is* surprising is that the gangster films of the 1920s did not reflect this new reality. Bootlegging is never featured, and gangsters tend to be either thieves or blackmailers. In the case of *The Penalty* (1920), the lord and master of the underworld runs a sweatshop that makes hats – "thousands of hats".

If this sounds like a bizarre business interest for a gangster, its oddity is in keeping with *The Penalty*'s overall gothic strangeness. Its villain, a man named Blizzard (**Lon Chaney**), had his legs amputated by mistake when he was a boy and he plans to have new ones grafted on by the doctor who made the initial error. Then he will be able to lead the under-

world in a revolt and take over San Francisco. To ensure that the doctor complies, Blizzard ensnares the doctor's artist daughter by answering her advertisement for a model to pose as Satan, for her new sculpture. When the surgeon finally does the operation, rather than adding the legs he removes a tumour that has been pressing on Blizzard's brain and, apparently, making him evil.

The gangster's source of income has become a crucial factor among film critics in deciding which was the first classic genre picture. Many writers cite **Joseph Von Sternberg**'s *Underworld* (1927) as the first real gangster movie. In fact Carlos Clarens boldly states that it's "unanimously regarded by cinema historians as the first gangster film with modern credentials". Others, notably Colin McArthur, disagree.

Underworld concerns a love triangle between a gang boss named **Bull Weed**, his best friend "Rolls Royce" and his moll, Feathers McCoy. Based on a story by a Chicagoan former journalist, **Ben Hecht**, it boasts some authentic moments, such as the scene when Bull Weed's rival is shot dead in his flower shop – just like real-life gangster Dion O'Banion, Capone's deadly rival, who ran his operations from a florist's shop. *Underworld* has some generic ingredients: the best friend, the moll, the jealous gangster, the tommy-gun-toting shoot-out with the cops at the finale. But Colin McArthur is not convinced. He points out that bootlegging never gets a look-in, that the gangster is actually a *thief* and that there is little of the iconography we have come to expect. There are few guns, fast cars or fedoras. Even Von Sternberg commented that when he made *Underworld*, he did not know anything about gangsters.

Kevin Brownlow nominates *The Racket* (1928) as the closest silent cinema came to the real thing but, as no one has seen it since its initial release, there's no real way for anyone who wasn't around at the time to corroborate him. (It resides today in one of producer **Howard Hughes'** vaults.)

The Racket, however, does have an interesting history. The film had its origins in a play about a character called Nick Scarsi, a thinly-veiled Al Capone, which toured the US with **Edward G. Robinson** in the starring role. When it came to the movie, director **Lewis Milestone** – for reasons best known to himself – replaced Robinson with the long-forgotten actor Louis Wolheim and missed an opportunity to create a screen legend. Robinson had to wait until *Little Caesar* to play a Capone clone in the cinema, and thus give the gangster movie the icon it deserved. *The Racket* had another problem: real crime bosses weren't so keen about seeing themselves on screen, and threatened the star of the film. When that didn't work, they lent on obliging politicians to have *The Racket* banned in some cities and censored in others. Over forty years later the Mafia made a similar move with

The Godfather, ensuring the words "Cosa Nostra" never appeared in the finished script.

In many ways gangster films only properly got started with the invention of sound: silent films always, of course, lacked the screeching tyres, the snarled dialogue and the rat-a-tat-tat of machine-gun fire. Cinemas always did their best though: a crack on a drum in the orchestra or the crash of piano chords would often stand in for a gunshot. The first all-talking picture, *The Lights Of New York* (1928), was a gangster film, and many followed in the next two years, including *Me Gangster* (1928), *Dark Streets* and *Thunderbolt* (both 1929), but it wasn't until 1930, eighteen years after *The Musketeers Of Pig Alley*, that the first classic gangster movie was produced, in the (rather squat) shape of *Little Caesar*.

Lon Chaney (with legs strapped behind back) as Blizzard in *The Penalty* (1920)

The Musketeers Of Pig Alley
dir D.W. Griffith, 1912, US, 17m

Even gangster movie expert Kevin Brownlow admits he couldn't figure out what D.W. Griffith's film was all about. A convoluted tale of a musician and his girl (played by Lilian Gish), gang war, and a mobster. Griffith's studio, Biograph, admitted that the plot was not very strong. Ultimately the film is only of historic interest.

Regeneration
dir Raoul Walsh, 1915, US, 72m

Brownlow has described it as an inventive movie, pointing to the sophisticated use of tracking shots. But it's hard to spot much more. Everything about this film is stagey. Some of this is down to the primitive techniques of early cinema, but what can't be explained away is the lack of invention in the story. It's a hoary old melodrama about a hoodlum who falls for a society girl. Tragedy strikes, as tragedy tends to, when she's abducted by his own gang.

The Penalty
dir Wallace Worsley, 1920, US, 70m

The presence of Lon Chaney in the lead role only adds to the sense that this is more of a gothic horror than a gangster flick. He plays Blizzard, the kingpin criminal of San Francisco, The Lord And Master Of The Underworld, who enslaves women in his den to make "thousands of hats". *The Penalty* is as screwy as it sounds. In some ways it's a shame that the nascent gangster genre never went in this direction.

Underworld
dir Josef Von Sternberg, 1927, US, 80m

Bank robber Bull Weed picks up an alcoholic vagrant, spruces him up, and turns him into the gangster's little helper. Together with moll Feathers McCoy the trio enjoy the high life until it starts to fall apart. Based on a Ben Hecht story, many elements of *Underworld* would reappear in Hecht's script for *Scarface*, of which this now seems like a dry run.

1930s

The golden age of the gangster film only lasted three years, until the forces of "good" won. The movies' popularity had a meteoric rise until they themselves became Public Enemy No. 1, brought down by the Legion Of Decency and the Hays Office. When screen gangsters first appeared the world was theirs, but they ended the decade on the run and – temporarily – on the way out.

There were over sixty gangster films shot in the US between 1930 and 1933, including the three classics which set the template and the standards of the genre: *Little Caesar* (1930), *The Public Enemy* (1931) and *Scarface* (1932). This triumvirate defined every trope, every icon, and every theme of the classic model: the rise and fall of an immigrant, the allusions to **Al Capone**, the honour killings, the moll, the cars, the tommy guns, the gang war, the significance of clothes, the best friend, the loyal mother, the father figure who must be killed and usurped, the shoot-out in the streets, and the pathetic death of the protagonist, usually apotheosized by some famous last words.

The classic gangster story goes something like this. A small-time hood and his best friend rise ruthlessly through the ranks of the Mob; the boss becomes wary of his ambition and tries to rub him out. The attempt fails and the gangster exacts revenge by removing and replacing him. The world is now his: he has the clothes, the girl, the power and, of course, enough money to look after his mother, who thinks only good of him. But this point is the beginning of the end, and a psychological flaw will be his undoing. He becomes jealous of his best friend, whose dedication is compromised by a woman; the friend is killed, most likely by the gangster, which leaves him vulnerable to attack by rival gangs and/or the police. He is shot dead in the street.

There's always another shadowy hood wanting to become the guy at the top of the staircase: big trouble in *Little Caesar* (1930) for Edward G. Robinson

There were many variations on the classic theme. The innocent drawn into the criminal world by the prospect of easy money is one well-worn archetype used in *Bad Company* and *City Streets* (both 1931). The unlikely pairing of the gangster and the society girl is another, as in *A Free Soul* (1930), *Ladies Love Brutes* (1930) and *Night After Night* (1932). Then there are the female gangsters of *Madame Racketeer* (1932) and *Blondie Johnson* (1933); the Mob lawyers of *The*

Mouthpiece, Lawyer Man and *Attorney* (all 1932); and the "vigilantes versus the Mob" model, typified by *The Secret Six* (1931), *The Star Witness* (1931), *Beast Of The City* (1932) and *This Day And Age* (1933). (Even cowboys took on the Mob in 1931's *Gun Smoke*.)

Future clichés were minted, templates set, and icons created: the stars of *The Public Enemy, Little Caesar* and *Scarface* – James Cagney, Edward G. Robinson, Paul Muni and George Raft – became collectively known as "Murderers Row". The epithet also intimated that the four actors were prisoners of the studios – a sense they seemed to share, as it was something they would all carp about during their careers. Only Muni won a reprieve, going on to play the prestige roles that Robinson openly coveted. The others never shook off their gangster stereotypes, possibly because they were unknowns before they played the gangster parts that made them famous, and movie-going audiences never got over the typecasting.

However, the inmates of Murderers Row weren't the only fresh faces to play mobsters. **Clark Gable** had a cameo as a hood in *The Finger Points* (1931), a major role as a crime boss in *A Free Soul* (1931) and was the star of *Manhattan Melodrama* (1934). (The latter movie was the last one that the gangster **John**

Dillinger ever saw: the bank robber was shot outside the Biograph Cinema in Chicago after seeing it.) **Spencer Tracy** played a trucker running a protection racket in *Quick Millions* (1931), aided and abetted by George Raft. Even **Gary Cooper** joined the gang, unconvincingly, in *City Streets* (1931).

But the genre typecasting never stuck to Gable, Tracy or Cooper as it did to Cagney and Robinson. Both were under contract to Warner Brothers, whose policy was to give actors similar roles in similar films until the law of diminishing box-office returns eventually kicked in and the cash cow keeled over. In a typical Warners move,

The *Smart Money*'s on James Cagney spoiling cigar-chomping Robinson's big plans by messing around with a moll

Cagney and Robinson's lucrative screen personas were immediately exploited by the studio, bringing them together in 1931's *Smart Money* (a possible reference to the box-office potential) – the first, and last, time the two would ever work together. Robinson took the lead as a barber with big dreams of owning his own casino, and Cagney played his best pal, whose friendship ends tragically when a moll gets between them (doesn't it always?).

1934 was the year when everything changed. The golden age came to an end for a number of reasons: the Legion Of Decency was set up by the Catholic Church who threatened eternal damnation on those unfortunates who saw "condemned" films. There was pressure from the FBI, and J. **Edgar Hoover** in particular. Prohibition, by which gangs and gangster movies symbiotically thrived, had ended in 1933. But most importantly, the Hays Code was stringently enforced on all American productions. The Motion Picture Production Code, which had been in place since 1930, stated that "the sympathy of the audience shall never be thrown to the crime of wrong-doing, evil or sin".

The code was initially regarded more as a word in the ear to directors than a hard-and-fast rule. That all changed when the Legion Of Decency threatened a nationwide boycott of all cinemas in the summer of 1933. Keen not to alienate Catholics and their cash (they represented 30 percent of the audience), Hollywood complied with their demands for greater censorship by requiring that all films be given a seal of approval by the Hays-Breen Office. The law was laid down: movies must not make criminals seem heroic, teach methods of crime or inspire imitation.

However, the studios got around the prohibitive code with an ingenuity worthy of a bootlegger. In *G-Men* (1935) and *Bullets Or Ballots*

(1936), Cagney and Robinson changed sides. Both were now working for the law, though they acted as if they were still gangsters. Literally so in Robinson's case: in *Bullets Or Ballots,* he played a cop who pretends to have quit the force and joined the Mob, but for much of the film the audience isn't let in on the act. As Robert Warshow wrote, "we gain the double satisfaction of participating vicariously in the gangster's sadism and then seeing it turned against the gangster himself". The appeal of the gangster film has always worked on two levels. *Bullets Or Ballots* recognized the appeal of that double satisfaction, understanding that there's a duplicitous pleasure in watching a gangster movie, and exploited it by creating its own Janus, a mobster who turns out to be a cop. In other words, *Bullets Or Ballots* let us have our cake and eat it.

In *G-Men*, Cagney played a two-fisted FBI agent with all the vigour and the potential for violence that he brought to his bad guys, and he still wielded a tommy gun. Cagney's role, Brick Davis, was a maverick with gangster connections who becomes a G-man in order to avenge the murder of a Fed friend. *G-Men* was personally supervised by J. Edgar Hoover, who assigned agents to the film to make sure the story came out the way he wanted; it eventually got the FBI seal of approval which was shown before the credits. The 1949 re-release even begins with a new scene at the FBI's training division in which a seasoned Fed tells his class that they're about to watch "the daddy of all FBI pictures", but warns that "the cars are old and you won't see women wearing the new look". It is not just the clothing and the cars that make *G-Men* a product of its time: it's a 30s gangster flick in cunning disguise.

Another way to get around Hays was to pair the gangster with a good person as his foil, in what author Thomas Schatz terms the Cain and Abel scenario. Previously he had been the lesser of two evils, a gangster who would typically choose love over money, and whose life would be threatened or lost once he's made that decision (eg *Little Caesar, The Public Enemy*, and *Scarface*). The best friend character was now a redeeming influence. True to the Cain and Abel scenario, the best friend was a priest in *Angels With Dirty Faces* (1938) and a lawyer in both *The Roaring Twenties* (1939) and *Manhattan Melodrama* (1934).

The latter post-Hays parable was about two orphans who are saved from drowning in an acci-

Fritz Lang presses his camera's "apocalyptic expressionist proto-*noir*" button for the doomed lovers on the run of *You Only Live Once* (1937)

dent that killed their parents, and who are brought up as brothers. The sibling played by Clark Gable becomes a professional gambler, while William Powell turns into the DA who prosecutes him and ultimately puts him in the electric chair. Father Pat O'Brien did the same for his best friend James Cagney in *Angels With Dirty Faces*.

Both Cagney and Gable are redeemed by their visit to "Old Sparky". Cagney pretends to die a coward, while Gable, miraculously, agrees to take the death penalty to help his pal's career. This was the revenge of the good son: redemption was only available for the bad one through his own death. In fact, the Cain and Abel scenario can be regarded as the logical conclusion of Warshow's "double satisfaction" theory, as the audience identifies with both the good and the bad seed. And in many ways the gangster was going to the chair to pay for our sins, our guilty vicarious pleasure in enjoying his villainy.

Robbing the gangster of his powers by making light of him was another way to elude the new censorship laws. Gangster comedies had been made before, but after 1934 they came thick and fast. Cagney made *Jimmy The Gent* in 1934, a comedy of social manners in which a wide boy from the East Side of Manhattan enters high society to win back his girl. Robinson duly played it for laughs in *A Slight Case Of Murder* (1938), *Brother Orchid* (1940) and *Larceny Inc* (1942). He played two roles, a violent crime boss and a humble accountant who is his exact double, in **John Ford's** *The Whole Town's Talkin'* (1935) – thus playing both Cain and Abel.

Humphrey Bogart heralded a new kind of criminal when he made his debut in *The Petrified Forest* (1936): the gangster on the run. Hunted by the law, holed up in a gas station, Bogart's Duke Mantee is waiting for a girl who will ultimately betray him. This character type, the displaced hoodlum, a man out of time, reappeared a year later in Julien Duvivier's *Pépé Le Moko*. Jean Gabin's crime boss is more debonair than Duke Mantee, but exhibits the same air of melancholy: trapped in the Casbah, dreaming of the Paris he knows that he can never return to. Another melancholic loser, Henry Fonda, was also on the run in 1937, and like Gabin and Bogart, his fate was determined by forces that were out of his control: the criminal was turning into an existential hero, a role he would play all through the next decade. The difference with Fonda is that he was *with* his lover, thus kick-starting a whole new genre: love on the run, or the killer couple on the road. Fritz Lang's *You Only Live Once* (1937) started a trend that has included *They Live By Night* (1949), *Gun Crazy* (1949), *Badlands* (1974), *Natural Born Killers* (1994) and *Bonnie And Clyde* (1967).

What's remarkable about Fritz Lang's film is how much attention is given to the social origins of crime. Society is to blame for the criminals' plight, and Fonda's cry "they made me a murderer" is the movie's key line. These concerns also crop up in *Angels With Dirty Faces* and *The Roaring Twenties* in which Cagney, like Fonda, only turns to crime because he can't get a job. This interest in contextualizing crime, according to Colin McArthur, was a result of the "increased interest in sociology during the Depression, and in particular to the Chicago school of sociology". In the early 1930s gangsters were born and not made, but by the close of the decade bank robbers and bootleggers were no longer sociopaths but the socially excluded. And no matter how much they tried to go straight, their paths were set: death by electric chair, being hunted down in the woods, or dying on the steps of a church. Thus the decade ended not with the gangster being feared or glamorized, but being pitied. The last line of *The Roaring Twenties* sums it up: "he used to be a big shot".

The Doorway To Hell
dir Archie Mayo, 1930, US, 78m

One of the sixty gangster films of the golden age that has never attained classic status despite its popularity at the time. When crime lord Louis Ricarno (Lew Ayres) quits the business and leaves his lieutenant (James Cagney) in charge, the organization falls apart. One gang decide to bring Ricarno back by kidnapping his little brother and Ricarno returns to the city to wreak a terrible revenge. The casting of doe-eyed Lew Ayres as Ricarno is the main reason for the film's forgotten status: preppy and boyish, he doesn't scare anybody.

G-Men
dir William Keighley, 1935, US, 86m

With its hoodlum milieu, montages of hold-ups, car chases and newspaper headlines hurtling into focus, this is a 30s gangster flick disguised as a police procedural. The machine-gun shoot-outs between men in hats are indistinguishable from the gang wars that graced *Scarface* et al a few years earlier. Cagney is essentially Cagney – all Puckish charm and tightly-coiled energy – single-handedly taking on his enemies as he had done in *The Public Enemy*.

The Petrified Forest
dir Archie Mayo, 1936, US, 83m

Bogart's screen debut was the movie that heralded a new direction for the gangster: he plays a deadly armed robber who's holed up in a gas station in the middle of a desert with wandering intellectual Leslie Howard and waitress Bette Davis. Bogart doesn't turn up until two-thirds of the way through, and the film isn't about gangsterism at all, but is figuratively (and literally) about the death of the intellectual. Its roots as a stage play show through, with its incessant but sonorous speechifying.

Bullets Or Ballots
dir William Keighley, 1936, US, 82m

Edward G. Robinson plays the maverick cop dedicated to bringing down the Mob; he is fired by the new police commissioner so swaps his stripes and joins his nemesis, Kruger, whose right-hand man Humphrey Bogart is not at all convinced by Robinson's change of career. It all ends in the first, but by no means last, shoot-out between Bogie and Robinson.

Alan Ladd and Veronica Lake get to know each other in *This Gun For Hire* (1942)

1940s

The 1940s were the decade of *noir*, when women turned bad, and gangsters were out on a limb, severed from the organization that had defined them. They weren't just killers, they were killers with complexes, who had loved their mother a little too much or their father not enough. They were men who were fated to repeat the same mistake over again (generally by getting involved with unsuitable women). If the 1930s were about

society, the 1940s were about the individual, and the criminal's behaviour was explained via psychological rather than sociological reasons.

One year in, a film set out the stall for the next ten years. *High Sierra* (1941) starred Humphrey Bogart in his last great gangster role as Roy "Mad Dog" Earle who has been let out of jail to do one more job, a heist on an expensive hotel resort. Earle is referred to as the last of his generation – who are now either "dead or in Alcatraz". He spends much of the movie complaining about the younger generation, particularly the young "jitterbugs" he has to work with. And to underline his sense of dislocation, he spends all his time not in his natural habitat, the city, but in a secluded cabin in the country. This was a key motif of the following years, in which the gangster went rural and became a bandit of sorts. More importantly, though, in the last third of the film he is a hunted man.

Many hitmen or gangsters would follow suit over the next decade, moving from town to town, traversing the states, never being able to trust anyone they meet, in films such as *They Live By Night* (1948), *Raw Deal* (1948) and *Gun Crazy* (1949). Famously, in *Key Largo* (1948) Edward G. Robinson played Johnny Rocco, an underworld kingpin who has to leave America because he was double-crossed by a politician who was previously in his pocket. Although he claims that he will be back, bigger than ever, there is a real sense that this is a swansong for the classic gangster. In a more typical movie of the decade, *This Gun For Hire* (1942), Alan Ladd played a psychotic hitman who is double-crossed by his employer and who spends the whole movie on the run from the cops. His loneliness and psychosis is crystallized and emphasized in the first scene, when Ladd slaps a cleaner in the face because she has chased his beloved cat out of his boarding room.

Towards the end of the film, Ladd talks about seeing a doctor who can get rid of his dreams. This is a sure sign that Freud had arrived in Hollywood. *Citizen Kane* (1941) was the first classic Freudian tale, and it set the narrative template, whereby one key event in a character's life, often their childhood, is the key to their entire personality. It turns out that Raven, the hitman Ladd plays, was beaten by his aunt every day for most of his childhood, even breaking his wrist with an iron, until he finally slit her throat with

a knife. Ellen Graham (**Veronica Lake**), who's listened to his story, concludes that he's been "killing his aunt ever since" and that's the reason he's become a contract killer.

This is but one of a number of on-screen diagnoses in 1940s films. In *White Heat* (1949) a police officer informs us that Cody Jarrett (James Cagney) has a psychotic attachment to his mother, and that's why *he's* a killer. *The Dark Past* (1949) is a movie-length analysis of the gangster's state of mind, following William Holden's break-in to psychiatrist Lee J. Cobb's house; Cobb eventually concludes that Holden is suffering from an Oedipus complex, responsible for his father's death when he sold him out to the cops.

More psychoses unravelled in *Gun Crazy* (1949), in which the couple of protagonists are literally crazy about guns. **John Dall** is obsessed with firearms, while **Peggy Cummins** just wants to kill people. This is very different from the couple in the movie's two couple-on-the-run precursors, *You Only Live Once* (1937) and *They Live By Night* (1949). In the former, the fugitive lovers were essentially good people who had been treated badly by society. In *They Live By Night* (1949), the couple were also basically decent, but they are let down less by society than by their own foolishness and the machinations of fate. Here Farley Granger plays a victim of circumstance and his own soft head. It marked an almost perfect transition from the sociological to the psychological.

So, whilst in all three movies the couples are criminals who appear to have little control over their actions, in *Gun Crazy* it's the characters' crippled psyches, an uncontrollable mania for guns, that sets them on their path. In the first two films, the couple want a normal life, to be like other people; in *Gun Crazy* they just want to rob banks and possibly kill a few people. There's

John Dall and Peggy Cummins just wanna have guns

gangster movie and the *film noir*, though there's a very blurry line between the two genres.

Criss Cross (1949) had an equally duplicitous seductress in the shape of Yvonne De Carlo, who persuades her ex-husband (**Burt Lancaster**) to rob his own armoured truck so that they can both escape the clutches of her new, crime-boss hubby (Dan Duryea). Lancaster had previously played another sap in *The Killers* (1946), an ex-boxer drawn to crime by the love of a bad woman, a gangster's moll played by Ava Gardner. She, naturally, double-crosses him and he mournfully accepts his fate, shot by two hitmen without a fight. In *Kiss Of Death* (1947) a thief played by Victor Mature turns over evidence to the DA after his wife cheats on him while he is in jail, only to be hunted down by the man he's just informed on, a psychopathic Richard Widmark.

one more significant, qualitative difference. Cathy O'Donnell and Sylvia Sidney play never-been-kissed innocents, whereas Peggy Cummins in *Gun Crazy* is one of the all-time great *femmes fatales*.

Of course, it's often an alluring woman who draws the protagonist into the gangster's sphere of influence in the classic *noir* of the times. In *Out Of The Past* (1947), ex-private eye **Robert Mitchum** is called out of retirement by rich gangster **Kirk Douglas** to track down his girl, Jane Greer; she double-crosses both of them and all three end up dead. The transition of the female character from the loyal moll who cradles her dying lover in her arms to the *femme fatale* who's actively responsible for his death is, with the odd exception, the biggest difference between the

Meanwhile in Britain, a new character emerged: the spiv. War rationing was Britain's equivalent of Prohibition, when ordinary people became involved with criminals who supplied them with goods they were being denied by the government. Rather than alcohol, the contraband tended to be everday staples such as nylons, meat, petrol, and so on. Rationing continued after the war, and according to Donald Thomas in his excellent book *An Underworld At War*, the spiv became a popular figure: "a licensed jester at the government's expense, 'Flash Harry' or 'Jack The Lad'". Comedians such as **Frankie Howerd** and **Arthur English** impersonated spivs in their music hall acts, and the character often turned up in film comedies, such as Ealing Studios' *Passport To Pimlico* (1949) and *The Ladykillers* (1955), and continues to this day in the form of Del Boy in the TV series *Only Fools And Horses*.

Ealing Studios and an Ealing acolyte were responsible for two of the best spiv thrillers. *It Always Rains On Sunday* (1947), made by the studios, concerned the efforts of Rose (Googie Withers) to help her former fiancé and jailbird Tommy Swann (John McCallum) escape from the authorities, and was set in an East End almost exclusively populated by chancers, fight-riggers and black marketeers. *They Made Me A Fugitive* (1947) revealed even more about the workings of the London underworld. **Trevor Howard** played an ex-RAF pilot given work by a gang of spivs who use a funeral parlour as a cover to trade in black-market nylons, cigarettes and New Zealand mutton, as well as drugs. The portrait the film paints of post-war Britain is grim: "sometimes I don't know what England's coming to" and "you never know who's up to what these days" are two telling lines. The gang use a "coaxer", a large studded belt, to beat information out of their victims; and their leader, played by Griffith Jones, is the daddy of Mockney villains, delivering the now-familiar injunction "just you keep your trap shut" with unbridled menace. But this isn't recommended for just sociologists or film historians. *They Made Me A Fugitive* is a cracking thriller, handsomely directed by documentary-maker **Alberto Cavalcanti**, who was responsible for the famous episode in *Dead Of Night* (1946) where ventriloquist Michael Redgrave's dummy comes chillingly to life. And he brings the same kind of fevered, nightmarish atmosphere to bear here in his gloomy vision of Britain through the looking glass.

Both films are part of a tradition that has been referred to as the postwar spiv cycle. Starting with *Waterloo Road* (1944), in which soldier **John Mills** tries to rescue his wife from flash racketeer **Stewart Granger**, it continued with films such as *Night Beat* (1947), *Noose* (1948), *Good Time Girl* (1948) and Jules Dassin's *Night And The City* (1950). Even though the criminal in Dassin's thriller is American, **Richard Widmark** is in many ways the ultimate spiv: he's a garishly dressed, smooth talking, double-dealing, pipe dreamer. His checked coat marks him out as a wide boy; he's got a new get-rich-quick scheme every month; he's desperate to be somebody, and he's doomed to fail. The London that the film portrays is as bleak as the one in *They Made Me A Fugitive*: it's a city covered in the sticky web of a criminal network from the West to the East End, and Widmark discovers that there's nowhere to hide when he makes a run for it. Probably the most famous spiv, however, is Orson Welles' Harry Lime in **Carol Reed**'s *The Third Man* (1950). Set in post-war Vienna, it showed that the spiv wasn't just a denizen of the UK, and that the ultimate victors of World War II included black marketeers all over Europe.

Brighton Rock (1947) is often thought to be the pinnacle of the spiv cycle, but it's debatable how much it's actually part of the genre. The novel was written before rationing was introduced in 1938 and the film, as it's keen to tell us, is set before the war. The author, Graham Greene, insisted that gang leader Pinkie and his associates were based on Brighton race gangs (so-called for their fighting near the racecourse) that were becoming extinct even when he was writing the novel. But, despite the film's opening disclaimer, it would have been obvious to its contemporary audience that these were actually a gang of spivs, that they were representatives of the new breed of screen villain. As was Dirk Bogarde, the juvenile delinquent who killed PC Dixon (of the spin-off TV series *Dixon Of Dock Green*) in *The Blue Lamp* (1949), thus ushering in the rebel teen movie. Though that's a subject for another book altogether.

All these films were criticized at the time for their cheap sensationalism, but none received quite as much vitriol as was hurled upon British gangster movie *No Orchids For Miss Blandish* (1948). Based on James Hadley Chase's novel, it tells the story of the kidnapping of heiress Miss Blandish by a small-time gang who are themselves knocked off by the Grisson Gang, led by Ma Grisson and her son Slim. He soon takes a shine to the captive, and his interest is reciprocated; when he is shot dead by the police, she commits suicide by throwing herself out of a window. This B-movie caused one of *the* moral panics in British film history. It was banned in some areas, censored in others, and it led to questions being asked in the Houses of Parliament. Critics called it "the most sickening exhibition of brutality, perversion, sex and sadism ever to be shown on a cinema screen", and pronounced that it had "all the morals of an alley-cat and all the sweetness of a sewer". It was remade 25 years later as *The Grissom Gang*, and caused no controversy at all.

In America, the 1940s were the decade of the private eye, a transition marked by the fact that **Humphrey Bogart**, who had played possibly more gangsters than anyone else in the 30s, was now the archetypal gumshoe, playing roles such as Sam Spade in *The Maltese Falcon* (1941) and **Philip Marlowe** in *The Big Sleep* (1946). There were few out-and-out gangster movies, though there were some interesting variations, such as *Lady Scarface* (1941), with **Judith Anderson** as a bank robber, and *Angel On My Shoulder* (1946), in which a dead gangster does a deal with the devil and comes back as a judge. When we do

see the gangster, his modus operandi is now gambling rather than bootlegging, such as **Kirk Douglas'** role in *Out Of The Past* (1947). How the numbers game works is forensically explored in *Force Of Evil* (1949) in which writer/director Abraham Polonsky presents us with a near-as-damn documentary on where the racket operates and how the money is made.

But the film that really pointed the way to the next decade was a cheapie called *Dillinger* (1945) with *Reservoir Dogs'* **Lawrence Tierney** playing the eponymous gangster. Sufficient time had passed for the gangsters to be named but *Dillinger* was the first out-and-out biopic, and had many of the hallmarks that were to define the genre: it was cheap, it was sensationalist and it never let the truth get in the way of a good story. The success of the film led to other treatments in the next decade – *Baby Face Nelson* (1957), *Machine Gun Kelly* (1958), *Al Capone* (1959), and *The Rise And Fall Of Legs Diamond* (1960).

Ball Of Fire
dir Howard Hawks, 1941, US, 112m, b/w

If Gloria Grahame gets the gold, and Gena Rowlands gets the silver, then Barbara Stanwyck definitely receives the bronze medal in the Moll Olympics. She went on to play the *femme fatale* of all *femmes fatales* in Billy Wilder's *Double Indemnity* (1944). But in this comedy, written by Wilder and Charles Brackett, she's the perfect wisecracking moll, hiding from her gangster boyfriend in a house full of absent-minded professors, including Gary Cooper who, of course, falls for her worldly ways. Who wouldn't?

This Gun For Hire
dir Frank Tuttle, 1942, US, 80m, b/w

Alan Ladd plays contract killer Raven who is hunting down the employer who double-crossed him. *This Gun For Hire* spins a web of changing loyalties, foremost among them Raven's questionable loyalty to his country, and the movie rightly made Alan Ladd a star. With his stiff bottom lip and piercing eyes, he somehow succeeds in being hard-bitten, psychotic and sympathetic.

It Always Rains On Sunday
dir Robert Hamer, 1947, UK, 92m, b/w

Written and directed by the lost genius of British cinema, Robert "*Kind Hearts And Coronets*" Hamer, the main story is incidental to the pleasures of a parallel tale of three spivs who try to offload a haul of nicked rollerskates, one of whom rejoices in the name Dicey Perkins. Everyone is on the make, and even small children resort to extortion.

Out Of The Past
dir Jacques Tourneur, 1947, US, 97m, b/w

Tourneur's classic is an almost perfect *film noir*, with its play of light and shadows, a flashback structure that imposes a sense of predetermination on the fate of the progatonists, and a *femme fatale* who seduces and double-crosses almost every man she meets. Robert Mitchum plays an ex-private eye pulled out of retirement by a wealthy gangster (Kirk Douglas), who employed him years earlier to track down his moll (Jane Greer). Mitchum soon finds himself ensnared, the dupe caught in the crossfire.

They Made Me A Fugitive
dir Alberto Cavalcanti, 1947, UK, 103m, b/w

Trevor Howard plays Clem Morgan, an ex-RAF pilot who starts to work for a gang of black marketeers led by Narcy (Griffith Jones), but falls out with them when they start dealing drugs. It's not just the portrait of the London underworld that's convincingly grim; the whole of the country seems to be in the grip of a moral malaise. One of the few great British *noirs*.

Criss Cross
dir Robert Siodmak, 1949, US, 87m, b/w

Most of *Criss Cross* is told in flashback as Burt Lancaster prepares to rob his own armoured truck, which is filled with dollar bills. In voice-over he explains how he fell back in love with his ex-wife, sultry janus Yvonne De Carlo, the spouse of crime boss Dan Duryea. *Criss Cross* has all the ingredients of classic *noir* – *femme fatale*, flashbacks, voice-over and hapless sap – plus it boasts an impressive heist sequence that was the shape of things to come for the gangster movie.

The Third Man
dir Carol Reed, 1949, UK, 104m, b/w

Orson Welles plays the ultimate spiv in the postwar cycle of British gangster films. He is not only amoral but regards his amorality as a form of superiority, famously arguing that war produces great art and that centuries of peace (in Switzerland) only produced the cuckoo clock. It's entirely appropriate that he first emerges from the shadows and finally dies in the sewers. The film is a product of three great talents – Welles, Graham Greene and Carol Reed – and the director's contribution has, grossly unfairly, been the one least acknowledged.

1950s

If the 1940s were about the individual, then the 1950s were about team-work, in the form of heists and syndicates. The heist movie was usually concerned with the lives and personalities of the thieves, the syndicate film with the shadowy henchmen throwing stool pigeons off high buildings, the anonymous voice making threatening phone calls, or the Red Menace. Both were about forces beyond the control of the protagonist: one was fate, the other political. And in this decade the real-life gangster at last emerged from the shadows, finally given his real name (if not an accurate portrayal of the facts of his life).

The decade began with the genesis of a new sub-genre, the heist movie. Movies had had heists before, such as *Criss Cross* and *The Killers*, but *The Asphalt Jungle* (1950) was the first film to be entirely about one robbery – about the process, the procedures, but above all about the characters. The heist itself, a safe-cracking job, takes up less than ten minutes of screen time. More important was the characterization of the thieves: the lordly Mob lawyer who's providing the funds, the working-class hooligan, the German eccentric

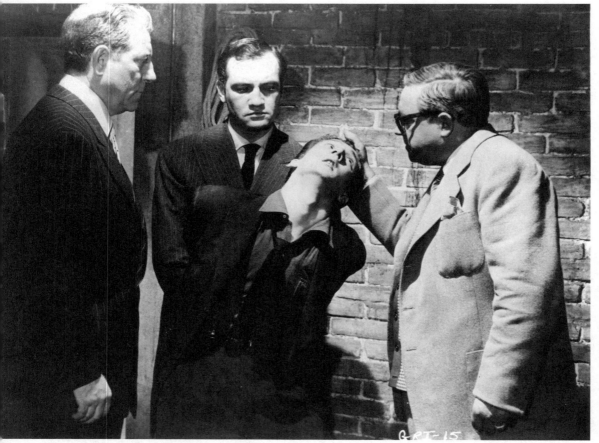

Debonair melancholic Jean Gabin (left), in cold and impassive mode, takes care of business in *Touchez pas au Grisbi* (1954)

who's the brains behind the operation and the rest of the motley crew. The fact that they are a cross-section of society – albeit an unlikely one – is important, and became a key component of subsequent films. The diverse backgrounds of the gang signal a changing attitude towards crime. It was endemic throughout society: cinema's orga- nized criminals were no longer just working- class immigrants on the make, no longer just the Ricos and the Tony Camontes of this world.

There followed a whole slew of heist mov- ies. *Armored Truck Robbery* (1950) was released at the same time as *The Asphalt Jungle* but hasn't stood the test of time, unlike **Stanley Kubrick's**

The Killing (1956) which played narrative fun and games with time by showing its race-track robbery from different perspectives. *Touchez pas au grisbi* (1954) was a post-heist movie focusing on an ageing villain (Jean Gabin) who has to deal with the fall-out from his gold bullion robbery. Jean-Pierre Melville's *Bob le flambeur* (1955) concerned a casino robbery, and ended with a neat twist. Jules Dassin's *Rififi* (1955) put the mechanics of the heist right at the centre of the heist movie, with an uninterrupted 25-minute *coup de cinéma* which had no dialogue or music and featured the ingenious use of an umbrella to break in through the ceiling of a jewellery shop. Robert Wise's *Odds Against Tomorrow* (1959) added a racial dimension to the social mix, as **Harry Belafonte** joined forces with bent cop Ed Begley and ex-con Robert Ryan to pull off a bank robbery; inevitably, for the time, it's the matter of race that brings about their mutual destruction.

The second significant shift of the 1950s was the Mob syndicate flick. Between 1950 and 1951, Senator Estes Kefauver's investigations of organized crime were televised and revealed to an unsuspecting public the extent to which crime was not just organized, but corporatized: how criminals had head offices, hierarchies, and branches nationwide.

Hollywood was not slow to capitalize on this new-found interest. After all, the hearings played out like the plot of a movie. *The Enforcer* (1951) was arguably the first syndicate film, starring Humphrey Bogart as a DA who tries to bring a syndicate boss to justice, his only witness falling to his death on the night before the trial. It was loosely based on the story of New York DA Burton Turkus who smashed a nationwide murder syndicate, dubbed Murder Inc, in the 1940s, and who also had a similar problem with the sudden deaths of important witnesses. With the workings

of the Mob now public knowledge, it became an obviously juicy subject matter for movies, and the floodgates duly opened: *Appointment With Danger, The Racket, The Mob, Captive City, The Strip* (all 1951), *Hoodlum Empire, Narrow Margin, Turning Point* (all 1952), *The Big Heat* (1953), *Miami Story* (1954), *New York Confidential, The Big Combo, Phenix City Story, When Gangland Strikes* (all 1955) and *Chicago Confidential* (1958) were all concerned with the long arm of the Mob. *The Big Heat* was the blueprint for the syndicate movie: a lone hero, a cop or DA, fighting a personal battle against a crime lord which results in the death of a loved one, soon discovers that the Mob's malevolent influence extends almost everywhere, even to the police force.

There were other well-publicized Senate hearings taking place in addition to the Kefauver investigations. The HUAC hearings into Communist Party members and sympathizers in the entertainment industry began in October 1947. Their full impact was felt in the 1950s: many left-wing writer/directors such as **Abraham Polonsky** and **Jules Dassin** were blacklisted, the content of Hollywood movies was carefully scrutinized, and of course "Red Menace" paranoia swept the United States.

The result was a series of right-wing movies which dominated the decade and took many forms. The most obvious bore hysterical titles such as *I Was A Communist For The FBI* (1951), but the best of these propaganda thrillers was Sam Fuller's *Pick Up On South Street* (1953). Fuller takes typical gangster-film tropes – the plot, the underworld milieu and hoodlum icon Richard Widmark – and gives the film an anti-Communist twist by making the crime syndicate a Communist conspiracy. Widmark plays one of his usual cocky lowlifes, a pickpocket who unknowingly steals a microfilm containing government secrets that was destined

Mickey Rooney (left) and Leo Gordon wielding Tommy guns in *Baby Face Nelson* (1957)

Terry Malloy, the "gang" member who decides to talk to the crime commission about the illegal activities of the union. The parallels between the House Un-American Committee and the crime investigation of the movie were clear in Kazan's mind: the left were a criminal syndicate whose crimes were against America.

On The Waterfront now has the status of a classic, and is regarded as a one-off that stands outside genre, let alone the gangster genre. In fact, it's the most well-known example of the unions-as-gangsters movie that was a feature of the 1950s. *The Mob* (1951), *Slaughter On Tenth Avenue* (1957) and *The Garment Jungle* (1957) are but three examples, although the most bizarre is *Never Steal Anything Small* (1959), a ludicrous James Cagney musical about union racketeering amongst longshoremen in the docks of New York, which included the perky number, "I'm Sorry, I Want A Ferrari".

for a Red spy ring, and is caught between the law and the Commies. He must decide whether he'll work for a country that keeps on putting him in jail. In Britain the film was disparaged as McCarthyite propaganda and in France the dialogue was changed, with all mention of Communists lost in translation and the spy ring suddenly becoming a drug operation.

However, the film that conjoined the two hearings – Kefauver and McCarthy – was *On The Waterfront* (1954). Written and directed by two men who had named names at HUAC investigations – **Bud Schulberg** and **Elia Kazan** – its subtext was about the importance and the moral rectitude of informing on colleagues. Kazan admitted in his autobiography that he thought of himself as

The third significant development of the 1950s was the biopic. Not only had sufficient time passed for it to be safe to name the criminals involved, but the films could now be made as period pieces. This, however, didn't mean that the Production Code approved; Section 13 still forbade the historical depiction of gangsters. But the films got made anyway and, importantly, they were shot by independent companies who were less worried about censorship than the major studios. And they made the films a lot quicker, which was a significant factor. *Baby Face Nelson* (1957) was made so fast – nineteen days – that no one noticed that it had broken the rules of the code. J. Edgar Hoover sent a letter of protest to the studios but to no avail. *Baby Face Nelson* was released in cinemas and set a precedent.

Hot on its tail were *Machine Gun Kelly* and *The Bonnie Parker Story* (1958), *Al Capone* and *Pretty Boy Floyd* (1959), *Ma Barker's Killer Brood* and *The Rise And Fall Of Legs Diamond* (1960); a trend which reached its pinnacle in 1967 with *The St Valentine's Day Massacre*. The irony is that after years of fictionalizing real-life gangsters and giving them false identities, such as "Rico Bandello" and "Tom Powers", when Hollywood could finally tell the truth, and when Al Capone's henchmen could no longer come knocking, 1950s biopics turned out to be even greater works of fiction. Director **Budd Boetticher** was told that he could do anything with the life of Legs Diamond except tell the truth. The biopics of the 1950s abandoned the facts to be more like their 1930s counterparts, possibly because reality wasn't enough like a movie. The 30s classics became the prism through which true stories were refracted. They provided the blueprint, set the tone and influenced characters' behaviour. The men died glorious deaths – Micky Rooney played Baby Face Nelson like James Cagney, going out heroically in a hail of gunfire, when in real life Nelson died ignominiously in a ditch. And the women were almost always molls rather than unglamorous housewives – the 1959 Capone biopic made Mrs Capone significantly younger and more genre-appropriate.

The Enforcer
dir Bretaigne Windus, 1951, US, 87m

The first film to exploit the appeal of the TV phenomenon of the Kefauver hearings was based on an earlier case that equally shocked America, the Murder Inc trials. It creaks like an old house, and Assistant DA Humphrey Bogart seems stiff and uncomfortable in his role as a buttoned-up official of

the law, a starchy world away from the maverick private eyes and lone wolves Bogart had made a career out of.

Pick Up On South Street
dir Sam Fuller, 1953, US, 80m

Although it may seem like a spy film, this is very much a gangster movie, not least because of another sterling Richard Widmark performance as a spiv-like, smooth-talking, cocksure operator called Skip McCoy. And Thelma Ritter almost steals the movie from him as eccentric Mo The Stoolie, who sells silk ties and information in return for "happy money". The only people she won't sell to are Commies, and thus she dies a heroic American death in Fuller's idiosyncratic exercise in flag-waving.

Touchez pas au grisbi
dir Jacques Becker, 1954, Fr/It, 94m

Jean Gabin plays a debonair melancholic, a criminal nearing his retirement. He wants to leave the profession on the proceeds of his last job – a gold bullion heist. But first he has to deal with the loot, the attentions of a rival gang and his feelings for dancer Jeanne Moreau. *Grisbi* is in many ways the least typical of the 1950s heist cycle, not least because we don't see the heist, and because the focus is on the individual and not the team.

Bob le flambeur
dir Jean-Pierre Melville, 1955, Fr, 98m

Melville was about to make a full-blown heist movie until he saw *The Asphalt Jungle* and changed course. Dismissed at the time for its amateurishness and continuity errors, *Bob* emerged from the critical wilderness thirty years later with its reappraisal in 1986: its raw moments, particularly of Parisian streetlife, were no longer regarded as embarrassing mistakes but as major influences on Godard, Truffaut and the *nouvelle vague. C'est la vie.*

The Ladykillers
dir Alexander Mackendrick, 1955, UK, 97m

Mostly regarded as a farce, occasionally seen as a heist movie, only one man considers *The Ladykillers* to be a political allegory. That man is Professor Charles Barr who claims that the gang can be seen as the postwar Labour government, using a façade of respectability as a cover for a more radical plan to redistribute wealth. What stops them is the "paralysing charisma of the governing class". Incidentally, star Herbert Lom has heard of this theory but doesn't think much of it.

The Phenix City Story
dir Phil Karlson, 1955, US,100m

A potent fusion of the quasi-documentary and the syndicate flick. Karlson's thriller about a vice ring in Alabama has all the ingredients – a ripped-from-the-headlines story, a crusading DA whose father was killed by the Mob, newsreel footage of the actual events – and bundles them into a devastating political critique of a town formerly known as "Sin City". It also helped its subject, DA John Patterson, in his campaign to become Governor of Alabama.

Baby Face Nelson
dir Don Siegel, 1957, US, 85m

It's appropriate that the first gangster film to follow the groundbreaking *Dillinger* was a biopic of one his gang. One of the few true-to-life elements in the film is Dillinger's death, as much of the hoodlum's career is tailored to suit genre expectations. Mickey Rooney, cast superbly against type, continues where Cagney left off in *White Heat* – all psychosis and simmering paranoia, while Siegel shows the promise that would make him one of the great action directors in Hollywood history.

Machine Gun Kelly
dir Roger Corman, 1958, US, 80m

Corman takes the life of the robber and kidnapper and turns his story into a psycho-sexual drama, a Tennessee Williams B-movie. Charles Bronson plays the seemingly fearless gunman whose domestic life takes a turn for the Freudian when it's revealed that "without his gun he's yellow". The film certainly has its moments, though it has fewer of the scurrilous B-movie thrills that we expect from director Corman and producer Arkoff.

1960s

In the 1960s all sorts of developments took place in the world of gangster cinema. The heist movie went all light-headed and turned into the caper flick; in Japan, the Yakuza replaced the samurai; and in America a film about two bank robbers from the 1930s helped to destroy the power of the very studios that had produced the classics it paid homage to.

Paradoxically, the 1960s really began in 1959 with the release of *A bout de souffle*, which changed the course of film history, invented a new syntax for cinema and liberated directors from the shackles of cause and effect by the invention of the jump-cut. Godard created a cinema about cinema, which divorced film archetypes from social connotations or context. The most successful exponent of this new pure cinema was **Jean-Pierre Melville**, who'd appeared in *A bout de souffle* as a novelist. Melville's *Le doulos* (1962) and *Le samourai* (1967) were set in a no-man's-land which was neither France nor America, but a hybrid of the imagination. His gangsters dressed in fedoras and trenchcoats not because it was what contemporary hoodlums wore but because it was Alan Ladd's uniform in *This Gun For Hire*. And how they wore them was just as important as what they said or what they did: clothes took on a new meaning with Melville. Like Godard, Melville played games with narrative structures, but with very different intentions from Godard who wanted to make the workings of cinema transparent, to let light in on the magic. Instead, with his final-act twists, Melville set out to obfuscate and conjure more illusions. Both *Le doulos* and *Samourai* boast acts of "misdirection" that any magician would be proud of.

Many critics have pointed out the connection between the French *nouvelle vague* of the early 1960s and the American new wave of the late 1960s and early 1970s. There is a very real connection between the two, between *A bout de souffle*, the start of the French cinematic revolution, and *Bonnie And Clyde*, the beginning of American cinematic independence. In the mid-1960s two Americans in Paris, **Robert Benton** and **David Newman**, were so enamoured with the *nouvelle vague* that they wrote a script for **François Truffaut**. Their screenplay, based on the infamous careers of Bonnie Parker and Clyde Barrow, piqued Truffaut's interest; he added two scenes of his own but was unable to finish the project because he was already scheduled to make *Fahrenheit 451* (1966), so he passed it on to **Jean–Luc Godard**.

The director apparently liked the script and wanted to make it in America. The tantalizing prospect of Godard making an American movie was stymied when Jean-Luc fell out with the producers. The project was forgotten until a chance dinner in Paris between Truffaut and actor **Warren Beatty**. The French director told the American star about the script, and when Beatty read it, *he* wanted to direct it. But eventually he opted to act as producer instead and brought in **Arthur Penn**. The rest wasn't quite history; the film came out to horrified reviews, and was only saved by a famous reconsideration of the movie's worth in *Newsweek* magazine, helped by the powerful backing of critic **Pauline Kael**, and by Warren Beatty going down on his knees in front of studio boss Jack Warner.

Bonnie And Clyde was a phenomenon on its wider release in September 1967. The film played to an audience who had been radicalized by the Vietnam War, who had to face the very real possibility that if they burnt their draft cards they would have to live outside the law and head for the Canadian border. The beautiful outlaws who cocked a bloody snook at society and had a good time doing it became symbols of the counter-culture, as iconically potent as Che Guevara. Testament to the film's popularity among radicals was that many of them began dressing in fedoras and double-breasted suits. The "Bonnie Look"

became an international trend – women cut their hair like Faye Dunaway, lowered their hem-lines and donned berets. In fact, so many berets were bought in America that the small factory in France that was making them ran out of stock within a month. *Bonnie And Clyde*'s success at the box office made it clear to studios that there was a new audience out there which wasn't going to be satisfied with their big budget-musicals.

The decade also did strange things to the heist movie. It began with two films about ex-servicemen using their military skills to pull off the perfect robbery. However, the pair couldn't have been more out of step with one another. The jaunty Rat Pack comedy *Ocean's 11* (1960) starred **Frank Sinatra**, Dean Martin, Sammy Davis Jr and Peter Lawford as sharp-suited ex-GIs who swoop on Las Vegas's five big casinos. It heralded a 1960s that was all set to swing, whereas *The League Of Gentlemen*, made the same year, harked back to the early 1950s and postwar, *noir*-inflected cynicism. Jack Hawkins brought together seven disillusioned ex-army officers, among them a black marketeer and a dodgy padre with a suitcase full of muscle mags and a criminal record for public indecency.

As in *The Asphalt Jungle*, love is just another commodity, as shown by the men's disastrous personal lives: one is a cad who sells his body and services old ladies, while another is a cuckold who keeps his unfaithful wife in the lap of luxury. In another telling scene a young woman is salaciously compared to the latest model of a car which will eventually be traded in. Hawkins essentially black-mails the men into taking part in a robbery which is an act of revenge for him on an army that made him redundant after 25 years of dedicated service. The unrelenting, breathtaking misanthropy occasionally gives way to misogyny and homophobia, and concludes with Hawkins' mournful observation that "the party's over".

I smell a rat (pack), suavely heralding the caper movie in *Ocean's 11* (1960)

In fact the party had only just begun, and, of the two, it was *Ocean's 11* that set the tone for the rest of the decade. The heist flick turned into the "caper" movie – light, larky, roguish robberies played for laughs rather than for tension or thrills. The characters became little more than ciphers for snappy dialogue; happy endings replaced gloomy denouements; and the bleak fatalism of earlier movies such as *The Asphalt Jungle*, *Rififi* and *The Killing* was replaced by hip, glib comedy. **Jules Dassin** even parodied his own *Rififi* with the decadent international production *Topkapi* (1964) about an audacious attempt to nab a jewelled dagger from an Istanbul museum. This became par for the caper course as plots often involved outrageous ways to steal a priceless artefact from a well-guarded museum, such as the valuable statue in *How To Steal A Million* (1966) and the crown jewels from the Tower of London in *The Jokers* (1967).

There was one British movie that combined the best of the heist and caper formulae: *The Italian Job* (1969). This **Michael Caine** comedy thriller had all the light-heartedness of the caper – the car chase over the roof of the football stadium, the oft-quoted dialogue ("you were only supposed to blow the bloody doors off"), and a turn from comedian **Benny Hill**, playing a boffin with a fixation on big women. But it also had an essential ingredient of the heist film: diverse members of society coming together for one big payday. The gang in *The Italian Job* has a representative, or stereotype, from a broad spectrum of the late 1960s British social milieu: Jack The Lad (Caine), a West Indian, a gay dandy and, pulling all their strings, the upper class (in the form of **Noel Coward**).

However, John Patterson argued in *The Guardian* in 2003 that *The Italian Job* was both racist and xenophobic: "if it voted, it would vote for Enoch Powell," he opined. Racist because it's the black character who fouls up, driving the bus off the road and almost over a cliff, and xenophobic because *The Italian Job* was a celebration of Little Englanders taking the mick out of the continentals, their Euro-scepticism rambunctiously expressed with the triumphalist chorus "The Self Preservation Society". The film certainly manifests anxiety about Britain's place in Europe and fears about the Common Market, but Patterson's analysis is crude. *The Italian Job* is a last romp for a Britain which was at the centre of pop culture, which even had a national cinema that was cool; a Britain now teetering at the edge of a precipice, with no real ideas of what to do next. Whether or not it's a paean to that era is another matter entirely.

In Japan, Yakuza movies began to replace samurai films. In many ways the Yakuza were seen as postwar samurai – even parodies of samurai – with the same adherence to codes of silence, loyalty and obedience. Hundreds of Japanese gangster movies were made between 1963 and 1973, but according to Mark Schilling, they all followed the basic pattern, revolving around "the age-old theme of *giri-ninjo* – the dilemma of the hero forced to choose between his own interests and an obligation that may cost him his life". Recommended viewing would have to include *Pale Flower* (1963) about the friendship between a young gambler and a gangland killer, and almost anything by director **Seijun Suzuki,** whose films *Tokyo Drifter* (1966) and *Branded To Kill* (1967) were so bafflingly idiosyncratic that he was sacked by his studio and wasn't allowed behind a film camera for ten years. The genre died out in the early 1970s because the times had changed. According to author Donald Richie in *A Hundred Years Of Japanese Film*, "the sacrifice of individuality for the sake of the group, the message inherent in the ritualistic Yakuza film was of little interest to a more permissive, younger audience".

The League Of Gentlemen
dir Basil Dearden, 1960, UK, 113m

Jack Hawkins invites a motley crew of crooked ex-army officers, including Richard Attenborough and Bryan Forbes, to pull off a robbery. They set up a thieves' boot camp, steal a cache of arms from an army base and rob one million pounds in used notes from a city bank. Unstinting in its cynicism and directed with tight military precision, it is one of the best bona fide heist movies in British cinema.

Ocean's 11
dir Lewis Milestone, 1960, US, 127m

Fans often talk about the Rat Pack's effortless cool, and it's certainly on show here. In a disappointingly over-literal sense: Sinatra, Martin and co are undeniably cool and they clearly

put no effort into making this turgid, lazy dog of a comedy.

The Rise And Fall Of Legs Diamond
dir Budd Boetticher, 1960, US, 101m

Budd Boetticher's biopic takes a few facts from the life story, such as Legs' Rasputin-like ability to remain alive after being shot several times, but it ultimately owes more to the 1930s films it pays homage to (even using the same Warner Brothers sets). It neglects the fact, however, that Diamond was the most barbarous of hoods, who would torture his victims by lighting matches underneath their bare feet. His last words "You can't kill me, I'm Legs Diamond!" are, apparently, authentic.

Underworld USA
dir Sam Fuller, 1960, US, 99m

Fuller's punchy B-movie classic is very hard to find – a VHS edition was once available in the US – but well worth keeping an eye out for in the TV listings. A young boy witnesses the murder of his father by some hoods and, when grown up, infiltrates the gang in order to exact revenge. *Underworld USA* ushered in the modern era of revenge narrative, the most famous exponent being *Point Blank* (1967). *Underworld* is not as stylish or as opaque as John Boorman's thriller, but delivers a different kind of minimalism: tabloid realism.

Robin And The Seven Hoods
dir Gordon Douglas, 1964, US, 123m

In a sad farewell to his gangster past, Edward G. Robinson crops up in a cameo in the Rat Pack's homage of sorts to the Prohibtion era. Playing a version of Rico, Robinson is mercifully killed early on by a rival gangster. His friends, Robbo (Frank Sinatra), Little John (Dean Martin) and Will (Sammy Davis Jr) take up their cudgels, while Robbo romances Jim's daughter, Marian. You may enjoy the sight of Sammy Davis Jr doing a song and dance routine with a machine gun.

Topkapi
dir Jules Dassin, 1964, US, 120m

A sure sign of the switch from heist to caper movie is Dassin's own light-hearted treatment of a genre he helped to create. Again the emphasis is on the robbery itself:

Caine and co. end a Brit-movie era with *The Italian Job* (1969)

Mercouri, Schell and Ustinov go in through the roof of the Topkapi museum in Istanbul; but this time it's not fate, human weakness or misplaced affection that undoes all their hard work.

 ### Le deuxième souffle
dir Jean-Pierre Melville, 1966, Fr, 144m

Melville's *Deuxième Souffle* is rarely celebrated, or even seen, outside France. This is a shame, as this thriller is a typical Melville mélange of duplicity, honour, stoicism, long silences and groovy nightclubs, as Lino Ventura seeks his revenge on the cop who tricked him into betraying his best friend. It also boasts one exemplary set piece: a hold-up of a bullion van on a sinuous mountain pass that's perfectly executed (by both director and thieves) and is the superbly-crafted equal of any classic heist movie.

 ### Robbery
dir Peter Yates, 1967, UK, 114m

The only British film from the 1960s to address one of the major crimes of the decade, the so-called Great Train Robbery. Even then the names of the participants were changed and certain events were glossed over, not least the savage assault on an unarmed train guard who later died of his injuries. However, it doesn't stint on the pedal-to-the-metal action, which is what we've come to expect from the underrated director of *Bullitt* and *The Hot Rock*.

 ### The Brotherhood
dir Martin Ritt, 1968, US, 96m

The film that time forgot. The first movie by a major Hollywood studio about the Mafia has been lost in the midst of film history and *Godfather* hype. Unlike Coppola's masterpiece, it was brave enough to call the Cosa Nostra by name as it told the tale of a New York don (Kirk Douglas) who clashes with an ambitious young upstart. There's one very good reason why history has not been kind to *The Brotherhood*: it's not very good.

 ### The Thomas Crown Affair
dir Norman Jewison, 1968, US, 102m

An indicator of how the heist movie had changed since *The Asphalt Jungle* is the presence of Steve McQueen's gentleman thief who doesn't even do his own thievery, but employs others to do it for him. The modish split-screen techniques give this movie an antique curio appeal, though the chess game between McQueen and Faye Dunaway still contains one of the most unlikely erotic *frissons* in mainstream cinema history.

 ### The Italian Job
dir Peter Collinson, 1969, UK, 112m

Still one of the best comedy thrillers that Britain has produced, though admittedly the competition isn't that stiff. The testimony to its success is just how much of it is easy to recall: the nifty dialogue; the traffic jam in Turin; the Mini Cooper chase through the streets, over the stadium roof and down in the sewers; the bus swaying over the cliff edge; and Caine's final tantalizing line.

1970s

The early 1970s were a golden age for American cinema and the gangster movie in particular: *Mean Streets* and *The Godfather* were the best Mob movies since *Scarface*. Even British films, briefly, were as good as their 1940s counterparts, with East End gangland dons the notorious Krays twins replacing spivs as the new role model for the screen villain.

The Godfather, of course, changed the gangster movie forever, and altered people's perception of gangsters in general. A fairly low-budget epic with low expectations, it became one of the most commercially successful films ever made, and reignited Hollywood's interest in bona fide gangsters (as opposed to heist merchants).

It showed the Mob as a family affair. **Francis Ford Coppola** was not the first person the studio wanted to direct it – he wasn't even the tenth – but he made Mario Puzo's novel his own, and as much of *The Godfather* is about Coppola's family as it is about Don Corleone's. The mistake many make, however, is to assume that *The Godfather* was the first film to document the life of the Mafia. There had been other attempts, such as *The Black Hand* (1949), starring an unlikely Gene Kelly as a young Italian who comes to New York at the beginning of the twentieth century to revenge his father's murder by the Black Hand Gang, and *The Brotherhood*. One of the many reasons that *The Godfather* is head of the family while *The Brotherhood* sleeps with the fishes is the latter's choice of Don – Kirk Douglas is quite simply not very convincing as the head of the syndicate who clashes with his younger brother about the future of the Mafia.

The success of *The Godfather* meant that there was no problem naming the Mafia in the sequel, and it soon became open season in Hollywood.

Films like *Charley Varrick* (1973) nonchalantly used the Cosa Nostra as a framing device for a tale in which armed robber **Walther Matthau** accidentally steals Mafia loot from the small, rural bank they were using to launder money. There were of course *Godfather* clones such as *Honor Thy Father* (1972) and *The Don Is Dead* (1973) in which **Anthony Quinn** did his best Brando impersonation, but the only real Mafia movie of note – the best film about the Mafia, according to **Norman Mailer** – was Francesco Rosi's *Lucky Luciano* (1973). As was typical of Rosi, he was less interested in Luciano himself than in the political corruption that made him the man he was.

Besides *The Godfather*, the other movie-brat classic of the time was, of course, Martin Scorsese's *Mean Streets* (1973) – see p.130. It was a very personal film and largely sui generis, and in many ways the director's previous effort, *Boxcar Bertha* (1972), was more typical of the times.

About a gang of outlaws who hold up trains and are ruthlessly hunted down by the railroad company, *Boxcar* was part of the post–*Bonnie And Clyde* interest in 1930s banditry. *Bloody Mama* (1969), *The Grissom Gang* (1971), *Big Bad Mama* (1973) and *Dillinger* (1973) all had the same, often interchangeable, combination of jaunty ragtime music, Art Deco title sequences, jalopies, dirt roads and low budgets. It's notable too just how many of the movie brats turned to the outlaw couple as subjects for their films. Both **Steven Spielberg** and **Terence Malick** made their cinematic debuts with lovers on the run in *The Sugarland Express* (1974) and *Badlands* (1973), in which, respectively, Goldie Hawn helped William Atherton to bust out of jail, and Sissy Spacek's simpleton accompanied Martin Sheen's psychopath in his cross-country murder spree. **Robert Altman** went back to the source material of Nicholas Ray's *They Live By Night* to make

Thieves Like Us (1974) with **Keith Carradine** and **Shelley Duval** as the star-crossed lovers. There is, of course, a good commercial explanation for this influx of rural outlaws – they all coveted the box-office returns of *Bonnie And Clyde*, and at the time Altman was even accused by one critic of ripping off Arthur Penn's classic.

But there is another reason. The criminal as anti-hero fell in with the mood of the new Hollywood. There were two distinct cycles in early 70s cinema. On the one hand were, broadly speaking, left-leaning films in which criminals are romanticized (as above), or in which the law is corrupt and incompetent (*Chinatown*, *The Long Goodbye*). On the other, were right-wing films such as *Dirty Harry* (1971) and *Death Wish* (1974) in which the law is too liberal, criminals are psychopaths, and only one man with a powerful handgun, a cop or a vigilante, can prevent society going to hell in a handcart.

A movie that much more radically set cop/criminal representations on its head, though, was **Melvin Van Peebles'** *Sweet Sweetback's Badass Song* (1971), the first film in which a black man kills a cop and manages to get away with it. The film took ten million dollars in its first year, making it the most successful independent film ever. The studios, of course, took notice and the blaxploitation genre came into its own. The gangster movies of blaxploitation were often Afros-and-flares make-overs of classics. *The Asphalt Jungle* became politicized in the form of *Cool Breeze* (1972), in which the proceeds of a robbery will fund a black people's bank. *Hit Man* (1972) was a speedy remake of *Get Carter*, which had been made only a year earlier. *Black Caesar* (1973) wasn't a remake as such, but pastiched every element of the classic genre, from *Angels With Dirty Faces* to *The Godfather*.

It also boasted a score by **James Brown**. The soundtrack was a core component of blaxploitation; as Carlos Clarens says, "the scores by Isaac Hayes for *Shaft*, Curtis Mayfield for *Superfly* and James Brown for *Black Caesar* had a genuine hard-hitting energy that the films either lacked or faked". This is very true, particularly of *Superfly* (1972), which featured Ron O'Neal as the drug pusher/hero. Despite its excellent score, garrulous clothing, frequent nudity and amusing facial hair, it is dull, pedestrian and has few pleasures, even ironic ones.

Meanwhile, in Britain, the film industry finally caught up with the truths behind the UK's own bona fide gangland monsters, the **Kray twins**. It's astonishing that in the 1960s, a decade of conspicuous crime, the British were making flim-flam like *The Jokers* (1967). The Great Train Robbery of 1963 was documented in Peter Yates' *Robbery* (1967), but the names were changed to protect the guilty. (It was not until the sentimental *Buster* in 1988 that the heist was addressed directly, and even then in compromised form.)

But thanks to their photographs, taken by **David Bailey**, their well-groomed hair, their Savile Row suits and their monogrammed shirts, the Kray twins became style icons, mingling with celebrities in their London nightclubs. And if any of the British public weren't *au fait* with their exploits, they soon were when all came to light in the twins' trial for the murder of Jack "The Hat" McVittie in 1969.

The classic Brit flick *Performance* was made in 1968 and scheduled for release that year, but two years of interference by Warner Brothers meant that the film was delayed until the Krays had been locked up. But that hadn't been a factor in the studio's meddling – the execs were more concerned by the dirty water in **Mick Jagger**, Anita Pallenberg and Michèle Breton's bohemian *baignoire à trois*. The screenplay of *Performance*

Style-over-substance(s); Ron O'Neal (right) takes on the pusher-men of *Superfly* (1972)

There's another connection between Carter and the Krays. The villain's lair in *Get Carter* had recently been the home of nightclub-owner Vince Landa, who had mysteriously disappeared after the murder of his right-hand man, Angus Sibbet. The Krays had recently become acquaintances of Landa and had started to take an interest in the North East, hoping to expand their empire, leading to speculation that the twins may have had something to do with Sibbet's death.

Certainly this murder, and the Krays' well-publicised trial for that of McVittie, were the impetus behind *Carter*, as writer/director Mike Hodges admitted. "British criminals never did anything we saw in American film noir; nothing really unpleasant or sadistic. Then it all changed with the Krays and the Richardson trials. Suddenly one realized there was a whole other game going on." That a whole stratum of British underworld life was now visible gave *Get Carter* a confidence and credibility Hodges compounded with his own documentary-style techniques, honed during his time on the TV series *World In Action*.

Villain (1971), made the same year as *Get Carter*, took Ronnie Kray as its role model for the mother-loving, gay East End crime boss. An agonized **Richard Burton** took a typically histrionic lead role (with Ian McShane as his unlikely love interest) as the Oedipal criminal whose empire begins to crumble after an armed robbery goes

gained considerable authenticity from the input of **David Litvinoff,** an underworld face who was an associate of both the Krays and South London gangster **Charlie Richardson,** as well as being friends with the writer and co-director Donald Cammell. The modus operandi of Harry Flowers' gang in *Performance* is certainly based on the anecdotal behaviour of the Krays, though unfortunately a sizeable part of the Flowers gang footage was cut by the studio, who wanted more Mick Jagger and less James Fox. East End criminals weren't yet the new rock'n'roll back then.

An unmistakeably post-Krays criminal surfaced in Michael Caine's starring role in *Get Carter* (1971). Jack Carter paid close attention to sartorial detail, with a crisp blue suit and cufflinks, while his nose drops revealed that the London hardman was in touch with his inner dandy.

badly wrong. Written by Dick Clement and Ian La Frenais, *Villain*, like its protagonist, was an uneasy mix of cloying sentimentality and narky aggression. And after that renaissance, the British gangster movie disappeared as quickly and as mysteriously as Vince Landa. Its place in the British film industry was taken by the sad spectacles of the soft-porn *Confessions Of A...* series and the like. There was a brief comeback in 1977 with Michael Apted's squalid *The Squeeze*, featuring Stacy Keach as a washed-out cop amid a motley cast including David Hemmings, Edward Fox and comedian Freddie Starr.

The French Connection
dir William Friedkin, 1971, US, 104m

They got the wrong man. The filmmakers, that is. Friedkin had wanted Francisco Rabal, one of the stars of Buñuel's *Belle de jour* to play the part of the Marseilles Mob boss. But producers hired Fernando Rey by mistake. He couldn't even speak a word of French. However, it's hard now to imagine anybody else playing the role. Rey's European sophisticate is the diametric opposite of Gene Hackman's crude blue-collar cop, and his presence adds the dimension of class conflict to their rivalry.

Badlands
dir Terence Malick, 1973, US, 94m

Though hardly a gangster film – Martin Sheen plays a psychotic killer rather than a professional robber – *Badlands* is essential viewing as it was the high point of the 1970s outlaw cycle. Based on the real-life case of Charles Starkweather and Caril Fugate, Malick's elliptical, hypnotic elegy perfectly carries off the tricky balancing act of preserving the audience's distance from but interest in the delusional couple.

Charley Varrick
dir Don Siegel, 1973, US, 111m

Throughout his career, director Don Siegel maintained an interest in characters who live by their own, often sociopathic, moral code. *Charley Varrick* continued this trend with a breezily amoral tale of an ageing bank robber, Walter

Matthau, on the run from the Mafia. There is no honour amongst thieves, loyalty is always misplaced and the Mafia are above and more effective than the law – these are the messages of this incongruously upbeat, cynical caper.

Chinatown
dir Roman Polanski, 1974, US, 131m

Reptilian monster Noah Cross (John Huston) is the leader of the Mob and the city in Roman Polanski's masterpiece. Cross is the embodiment and repository of political and moral corruption, draining water from drought-ridden Los Angeles. One of the great detective movies in cinema history.

The Taking Of Pelham 1-2-3
dir Joseph Sargent, 1974, US, 104m

The film that gave *Reservoir Dogs'* colour-coded criminals their names. Leading the investigation is Walter Matthau, reminding us that he was more than just Jack Lemmon's grumpy stooge. This ingenious thriller was photographed by Owen Roizman, whose hallmark was shooting NYC in a low-tech graininess – as in *The French Connection* and several other early 1970s rough diamonds.

Bugsy Malone
dir Alan Parker, 1976, UK, 93m

A real oddity of British cinema, Alan Parker's debut movie was a daft musical for kids. Young children play 1930s gangsters. Tommy guns squirt some sort of foamy gunge and their victims are "splurged" rather than shot. A tiny Jodie Foster plays Talulah, a vampy moll, and the plot concerns a turf war between rival gangsters Fat Sam and Dandy Dan, into which Bugsy (Scott Baio), our hero, is drawn.

The American Friend (Der amerikanische Freund)
dir Wim Wenders, 1977, Ger/Fr, 125m

Another Dennis Hopper take on the gangster role. That is, if Ripley can really be described as a gangster – criminal Ubermensch might be a better term. In the Ripley novels he's urbane and educated, whereas Hopper plays him more like a ranch-hand. But it works – his laid-back manner masks his malevolent intent, of embroiling terminally ill Bruno Ganz in the assassination of a Parisian gang leader.

The Squeeze
dir Michael Apted, 1977, UK, 107m

A deliberately grubby British film that succeeds too well in rubbing the audience's face in its squalor, especially when Carol White is forced to strip in front of her captors (and us). *The Squeeze* is a rare beast: a film with all the grit of British TV drama which doesn't seem out of place on the big screen.

1980s

In the 1980s, America looked back to the 1930s, while Hong Kong looked to the future. **Al Pacino** introduced us to his little friend and British cinema had yet another of its new (false) dawns with *The Long Good Friday*.

The problem with dividing films into decades is that trends don't always fit neatly into them:

Robert Shaw and a big gun spells unavoidable delays and terrified commuters in *The Taking Of Pelham 1-2-3* (1974)

take for instance Hollywood's renewed interest in the Prohibition era, which began in the mid-1980s and ended in the early 1990s. In seven years Hollywood added contemporary colour to the golden-age template with *The Cotton Club*, *Johnny Dangerously* (both 1984), *The Untouchables* (1987), *Millers Crossing*, *Dick Tracy* (both 1990), and *Billy Bathgate*, *Bugsy* and *Mobsters* (all 1991). But the movie that set the trend was *Once Upon A Time In America* (1984). **Sergio Leone**'s masterpiece, over a decade in the planning, was conceived as a redressing of the ethnic balance of the American dream from the perspective of Jewish immigrants. There were powerful Jewish gangsters in the 1920s, such as Meyer Lansky, Bugsy Seigel and Arnold Rothstein, but the Hollywood gangster tradition hadn't really reflected this. Leone set out to throw off the "shadow of the two *Godfathers*", to end the myth that all American gangsters were either Italian-American or Irish-American.

Once Upon A Time In America failed to establish the Jewish gangster film as a serious subgenre. After all, it was easy to miss the ethnic origins of Max and Noodles. Instead it heralded a return to the classic gangster pic. Some played post-modern games by placing fictional characters in historical circumstances, exhibiting a selective memory, and merrily cherry-picking their facts. In *The Cotton Club* Dutch Schultz and Lucky Luciano are among the dizzying number of historical figures of the time who are portrayed; Duke Ellington, Charlie Chaplin, James Cagney and Cab Calloway all crop up. Yet the "George Raft" character – the lead role, played by **Richard Gere** – was given the name "Dixie Dwyer" and a trumpet to play, as opposed to being the dancer Raft was before his screen break.

The Cotton Club and its brethren failed because they were hopelessly reverential in their re-creation of the 1920s and 1930s milieu: too in love with their props, a procession of fedoras, Ford Ts, and tommy guns. To quote Uma Thurman in *Pulp Fiction,* they were wax museums with a pulse. More successful were the movies which updated the classic gangster movie, or at least dressed it in modern costume, as in *Scarface* (1983). **Brian De Palma**'s overblown/operatic (take your pick) take on Howard Hawks' 1930s masterpiece is surprisingly faithful to the original plot, replacing bootlegging with drug trafficking but keeping the rise-and-fall narrative, the protagonist's violent usurping of his boss, and his dubious feelings for his sister, which lead to him murdering his best friend. More tellingly, the representation of women hadn't changed over fifty years; if anything it had got worse, as Karen Morley never quite had the quality of a passive-aggressive doormat that characterized **Michelle Pfeiffer**'s Elvira, the terminally bored, ultra-cynical bitch with an unfathomable lack of interest in anything at all. Ultimately *Scarface* was a 1930s film set in a 1980s disco.

De Palma's next foray into the genre was *Wiseguys* (1986), a lame comedy in which Mafia foot soldiers **Danny De Vito** and Joe Piscopo are ordered by their aggrieved boss Dan Hedaya to bump one another off. It was proof (if proof were needed) that De Palma should lay off the comedies (just think of *The Bonfire Of The Vanities*) and stick to drama. He wasn't the only major director to come a cropper when making fun of the Mafia – **John Huston** didn't have the necessary directorial chutzpah in *Prizzi's Honor* (1985) to give the farce the pace it so desperately needed.

Jonathan Demme fared better with *Married To The Mob* (1988), in which Michelle Pfeiffer showed a little more life than her previous screen moll in which she possessed the bloodless pallor and lifeless demeanour of the undead. Here she's a vivacious, if taste-free, widow of a hit-man who sets up a beauty salon, and who has to face the advances of both FBI agent **Matthew Modine** and Mob boss (and hubbie-killer) **Dean Stockwell**. Meeting with critical indifference at the time of its release, *Married To The Mob*, with its depiction of mobsters as suburbanites and their women as desperate housewives, now seems like an early prototype of *The Sopranos*.

The Long Good Friday (1981), *The Hit* (1984) and *Mona Lisa* (1986) were the only significant blips for the British gangster, while *McVicar* (1980) started an unlikely trend that still con-tinues to this day, with a pop star playing the part of a real-life criminal. In this instance, it was The Who's **Roger Daltrey** taking on the role of armed robber John McVicar. Focusing on the his break-out from jail and attempts to avoid recapture, *McVicar* suffered from the British complaint: small-scale and visually unimaginative, it could have been made for TV. Sting contin-ued his ill-advised acting career in **Mike Figgis'** *Stormy Monday* (1988) as a Newcastle nightclub-owner who fights off an unfriendly takeover by US mobster **Tommy Lee Jones**. The subtext of Figgis' debut focused on one of the main planks of Margaret Thatcher's policy: the special rela-tionship with America (though *The Long Good Friday* had already made capital from this con-nection earlier in the decade, more potently and pertinently). Figgis' political points seemed to get lost in the fog of his moody neo-*noir*.

The other 1980s film which made use of the genre for symbolic currency was *The Cook, The Thief, His Wife And Her Lover* (1989), which none-too-subtly but nevertheless effectively made the connection between gangsterism and free-market late capitalism. Taking the 1980s mantra that greed is good to its logical and literal

conclusion, **Peter Greenaway**'s self-conscious art movie starred Michael Gambon as a glut-tonous, bibulous gangster who gorges himself on a series of magnificent feasts which are the epicurean epitome of conspicuous consumption. The Thatcherite mobster ultimately (and signifi-cantly) turns to cannibalism when, in an act of revenge for the murder of her bookish lover Alan Howard, his wife feeds Gambon her dead lover.

In Hong Kong, **John Woo** rejuvenated the gangster genre, with *A Better Tomorrow* (1986) and *The Killer* (1989). Fittingly for a postmodern age, many of his changes have been stylistic, on the surface. Style isn't *everything* with Woo – there are recurrent themes of brotherhood and redemp-tion – but most of what makes a John Woo film distinctive is its highly individual mix of expert choreography and stylized iconography. *A Better Tomorrow* was a surprise hit, resurrecting Woo's then flagging career, making **Chow Yun Fat** not just a star but a fully-fledged idol and launching a genre all of its own: heroic bloodshed. Many producers subsequently cast Chow Yun Fat in thrillers such as *Rich And Famous* (1987), *Tragic Hero* (1987), and *God Of Gamblers* (1989) in the hope of reproducing *A Better Tomorrow*'s box-office gold. The director who most successfully replicated the Woo/Chow alchemy, though, was **Ringo Lam**, who collaborated on five movies with the star, including *City On Fire*, which had an influence on American cinema that is argu-ably greater even than Woo's. That's largely due to the last fifteen minutes of his movie being "borrowed" by Quentin Tarantino for the basis of the plot of *Reservoir Dogs*. It resulted in a Mexican stand-off that would last well into the nineties.

In Japan, actor **Takeshi Kitano** took over the directorial reins on *Violent Cop* (1989) from **Kinji Fukasaku** when the veteran director was taken ill. It was a significant moment that crystallized the shift in generations and heralded a new aesthetic for the Yakuza movie. Kitano seemed to find his métier straight away with his meditative, almost transcendental, style. Another sign of things to come was *Circus Boys* (1989), about two boys brought up in a circus (hence the does-what-it-says-on-the-tin English title) who go their separate ways but both end up in the hands of the Yakuza. Director **Hayashi Kaizo**'s monochrome meditation often wandered lyrically into the surreal and set the tone for the following decade – in which the in-your-face realism that Fukasaku was an exponent of would give way to philosophical contemplation, gross-out horror or occasionally science fiction. Basically, the Yakuza movie was set to go more than a bit weird...

Atlantic City
dir Louis Malle, 1980, Can/Fr, 105m

A tender character study of an ageing numbers-runner (Burt Lancaster), who falls for his neighbour (Susan Sarandon). Louis Malle's film is less concerned with plot than it is with the theme of flux: the shift from the old days and the old ways, as typified by Lancaster, to the new, corporate super-casinos, a legal way to take people's money. The movie's eponymous location, a seaside resort out of season, complements Lancaster's displaced gangster perfectly.

Breathless
dir Jim McBride, 1983, US, 100m

Typically contrarily, Quentin Tarantino prefers Jim McBride's gaudy remake to Jean-Luc Godard's original. This pop-art cover version isn't actually half bad, but Richard Gere's preening narcissism doesn't compare to Jean-Paul Belmondo's implacable stubbornness, and Valerie Kaprisky is definitely a poor woman's Jean Seberg.

The Hit
dir Stephen Frears, 1984, UK, 100m

John Hurt and Tim Roth are the hit men who have to bring back ex-gangster and supergrass Terence Stamp from Spain to face the music. On the journey back, Stamp refuses to play the part of the fearful victim; his zen-like calm begins to unhinge the killers and a captivating power game plays out between the three of them. Frears' first film for the cinema since his private eye parody *Gumshoe* (1973) was a genuine curio.

Prizzi's Honor
dir John Huston, 1985, US, 129m

Huston returned to familiar territory with this tale of a contract killer (Jack Nicholson), who falls for a fellow professional (Kathleen Turner), while betrothed to a Mafia boss's daughter (Anjelica Huston). All sorts of knockabout comedy abounds, although *Prizzi's Honour* is slow with its punches. Huston has never been known for his pace, which unfortunately is exactly what a black comedy like this needs.

Blue Velvet
dir David Lynch, 1986, US, 120m

"Why does there have to be people like Frank in the world?" asks Kyle MacLachlan midway through the movie. But there's nobody quite like Dennis Hopper's Frank, an oxygen-inhaling pervert with a penchant for 1950s crooner tunes. When Hopper read the script, he excitedly told director David Lynch that he *was* Frank; Lynch was very happy for the film, but deeply concerned about actually having to meet him. Hopper here kick-starts the modern eccentric gangster performance, of which Christopher Walken is surely the master.

Colors
dir Dennis Hopper, 1988, US, 120m

Controversial at the time because of the then-alarming presence of hip-hop on its soundtrack, it now seems both pedestrian in its pacing and a little retrograde in its decision to focus on white cops (Sean Penn and Robert Duvall) rather than the black inhabitants of South Central LA. At least director Dennis Hopper was far-sighted enough to take the problems of South Central seriously, rather than adopting the usual Hollywood isolationist policy of ignoring its neighbours.

Stormy Monday
dir Mike Figgis, 1988, UK/US, 93m

Sting goes toe-to-toe with Tommy Lee Jones who's trying to muscle in on his territory. Jazz trumpeter Mike Figgis' debut impressively turns Newcastle into a bona fide *noir* location, but is less sure with the plotting and the subtext about Anglo-American relations and the free market.

The Killer (Da sha shou)
John Woo, 1989, HK, 93m

The film that brought John Woo to international attention, it's a refinement of the themes of *A Better Tomorrow* that still play out in his Hollywood movies, most obviously *Face/Off*: the cop and the criminal who appear to be opposites but are really mirror images of one another. Chow Yun-Fat plays the hitman and Danny Lee plays the policeman who stalk and circle each other but ultimately unite when Chow befriends a nightclub singer he accidentally blinded.

1990s

Looking back and counting the number of classics made over the decade, the 1990s now seem like a golden age (despite the presence of *Lock,* *Stock And Two Smoking Barrels*). They were the age of Tarantino's wordy hoods, Kitano's silent Yakuza, the LA ghetto's gangstas jacking the very spelling of their epithet, killer couples hitting the road and heists inevitably going wrong.

In the US, it was by some distance the decade of Quentin Tarantino, the postmodern nerd-auteur who fused almost all the elements of the gangster genre to make *Reservoir Dogs* and *Pulp Fiction*. With a pinch of Godard, a large helping of Hong Kong action films and the lexicon of blaxploitation, he redefined the language (or at least the dialogue) of cinema while reintroducing the cool of *Le samourai*. After the impact of Tarantino it seemed that every American indie film had to have a scene in which characters discussed the various merits of superheroes or the varying qualities of fast food. But his influence extended in other directions, briefly reinvigorating both the heist movie and the couple-on-the-

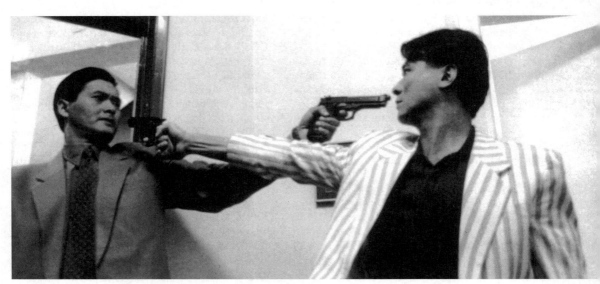

The Mexican stand-off that Quentin Tarantino universalized, as demonstrated by Chow Yun-Fat (left) in *The Killer* (1989)

run genre.

The "failed heist" movie, rejuvenated by *Reservoir Dogs*, was a gift to low-budget film-makers, with most of the action confined to one set. It was also a boon to actors because the long takes meant they tended to have dialogue-heavy scripts. *Reservoir Dogs* has often been described by critics as a Jacobean tragedy, and there is definitely something theatrical about it (inevitably it was adapted into a play for the Edinburgh Fringe Festival). So it's not surprising that **Kevin Spacey**, an actor who freely admits to preferring the stage to the screen, made his directorial debut with a failed heist movie. In *Albino Alligator* (1996) three robbers take a bar-load of drinkers hostage after a job goes wrong; the results are intermittently interesting, but the film is ultimately, and predictably, too stagey. A better example is the knowingly quirky *Palookaville* (1997), in which a gang of losers accidentally break into a doughnut shop rather than the jeweller's next door which they had intended to rob. This is the first of a number of incidents in a film that unfortunately gradually runs out of steam and invention.

Playwright **David Mamet** found the genre suited his stylized dialogue and his interest in the unravelling of male assertiveness in *Heist* (2001). The thought of **Gene Hackman** going to work on Mamet's chewy demotic was almost as tantalizing as the prospect of what the writer would do with the genre's obligatory twists. This is after all a director who had expertly pulled the rug from under the audience in *House Of Cards* and *The Spanish Prisoner*. In both these films the audience never saw the twist coming, whereas in *Heist* everyone was expecting to be surprised, waiting to be impressed, almost synchronizing their watches for the moment of revelation. And when it finally came, it was a tad underwhelming.

More twists than a bowl of fusilli were served up by *The Usual Suspects* (1995), which spun a labyrinthine multi-faceted shaggy-dog story from the germ of a heist-gone-wrong, whilst *Killing Zoe* (1997), by *Pulp Fiction* co-writer **Roger Avary**, was a nasty, cynical movie about nasty, cynical bank robbers in Paris.

Tony Scott's film of Tarantino's script, *True Romance* (1993), with Christian Slater and Patricia Arquette, heralded a renewed interest in another crime-cinema staple: the couple on the run. (Although Nicolas Cage and Laura Dern had beaten them to it, hitting the road in 1990 with David Lynch's *Wild At Heart*.)

Juliette Lewis went for a trip with serial killer Brad Pitt and hostages David Duchovny and Michelle Forbes in *Kalifornia* (1993). Obviously not learning her lesson, Lewis went on another journey the following year with another psycho-path, Woody Harrelson in *Natural Born Killers* (1994), based on a Tarantino script, which director **Oliver Stone** made his overblown own. Trailing in their dust were Renée Zellweger and Gill Bellows in the deservedly little-known *Love And A 45* (1994).

In all of them there's a distinct visceral pleasure in the leads' psychotic reactions for the audience. Characters are replaced by archetypes, psychology replaced by psychopathology and unlike other road movies – *You Only Live Once*, *They Live By Night*, *Bonnie And Clyde* – the 1990s models had nothing to say about the society they were passing through, only about the other movies that had travelled the same journey. This is especially true of *Kalifornia* and *Natural Born Killers*, which both had satiric pretensions of holding up a mirror to modern culture's vicarious fascination with psychopaths and murderers. However, neither was deft enough to pull off the sleight of hand needed to make a satire about the media obsession with serial killers without themselves becoming a part of the same media obsession. The depressing failure of both films only compounded the sense that cinema's lovers on the run had entered a hermetically sealed universe which they could not leave, and that the road movie was travelling in ever-decreasing circles.

Tarantino's pop-culture references were new to cinema but not to anyone who'd read the novels of **Elmore Leonard**. Tarantino was once caught trying to shoplift a copy of Leonard's novel *The Switch* from a Los Angeles bookshop and in 1997 Tarantino acknowledged the debt by adapting his novel *Rum Punch* in the form of *Jackie Brown*. You could argue that, as a screenwriter, Tarantino's shoplifing days never ended. But Tarantino's championing of Leonard led to a renewed interest from other writers and directors: Barry Sonnenfeld directed a post-*Pulp Fiction* **John Travolta** in *Get Shorty* (1996), while Steven Soderbergh rescued his own career and finally made **George Clooney** a bona fide film star in *Out Of Sight* (1998). The connection between that film and *Jackie Brown* is unmistakeable: Michael Keaton played the same character, a cop called Ray Nicolette, in both films.

With **Pam Grier** playing the title role, *Jackie Brown* briefly brought blaxploitation back into focus. Black cinema had long since emerged from blaxploitation's shadows, with Spike Lee leading the way for a new generation of African-American filmmakers in *She's Gotta Have It* and *Do The Right Thing* back in 1989. But it was not until 1991 that Hollywood made an authentic movie about "gangstas". *Boyz N The Hood*, written and directed by lifelong resident John Singleton, was the first authentic look at South Central. It featured the debut performance of ex-NWA rapper **Ice Cube** among its all-black

cast, and also had a mainly black crew. The most profitable film of 1991, its phenomenal success at the box office was overshadowed, albeit temporarily, by reports of shootings at cinemas that screened it.

With their criminal instincts for a quick buck, Hollywood studios rapidly bankrolled a number of movies set in the 'hoods or the projects: *South Central* (1991), *Straight Out Of Brooklyn* (1991), *Juice* (1992), *Menace II Society* (1993), *Sugar Hill* (1994) and the curio *Hoodlum* (1997), in which Larry Fishburne revisited his role of 1930s Harlem gangster Bumpy Johnson from *The Cotton Club,* this time taking on **Tim Roth**'s Dutch Schultz and **Andy Garcia**'s Lucky Luciano.

Menace II Society has since been deemed the best of that wave of the new black cinema. It's certainly the toughest. Set in Watts, it tells the story of Caine (Tyrin Turner) a drug dealer who becomes an accessory to the murder of two Korean shopkeepers, and who is himself wounded in a car-jacking in which his cousin is shot dead; Caine makes his reprisals, but finds that the cycle of violence doesn't come full circle with the act of revenge. *Boyz N The Hood* would seem to be an obvious influence, but writer/directors the **Hughes Brothers** hardly have a kind word to say about Singleton's territory-staking, genre-defining work. According to author Marilyn Yaquinto, they would refer to it as "Toyz N The Hood" and claimed that the film was a joke amongst real gangstas as it was all about the "good guys going to college". Their film, in contrast, was unapologetically about the bad guys. The siblings have also dismissed the similarly iconoclastic *New Jack City* (1991), in which Wesley Snipes played a Harlem drug baron whose operation had been infiltrated by undercover cops **Ice T** and **Judd Nelson**. They claimed that Mario Van Peebles' film had a "comic book look", and it's certainly

Larenz Tate as the nihilistic, violent O-Dog in the Hughes Brothers' *Menace II Society* (1993)

stepfather's baronial mansion in Shropshire is not insignificant; this was a period in which middle- and upper-class young men adopted the speech and mannerisms of East End wide-boys – or rather their mediated idea of them. As writer Mark Simpson has perceptively commented, "envy of the working class lad's imagined lack of self-consciousness, his sexy physicality and ease-in-the-world, his unshakeable sense of who and what he is, and above all his authenticity, had become the dominant cultural trend in Britain".

The "New Lad" was born and *Lock, Stock* became

true that its flashy MTV visuals get in the way of a powerful story, sacrificing the *frisson* of authenticity for the thrill of a fairground ride.

On the other side of the world, and on a whole different planet stylistically, the UK went all mockney following the success of **Guy Ritchie**'s *Lock, Stock And Two Smoking Barrels* (1998). Its characters bore little resemblance to any real gangsters and the whole was a compendium of clichés from *The Italian Job*, *Performance*, *Get Carter* and *The Long Good Friday*. Its overall feel was akin to some kind of action cartoon. The phenomenal success of the film demonstrated that it had tapped into an unfortunate Zeitgeist in which criminals were celebrated in lad mags, biographies and autobiographies. The fact that *Lock, Stock* was written and directed by an ex-public schoolboy who was brought up in his

more than just a movie, it was a style guide. It was quickly followed by the director's own *Snatch* (2000) as well as *Shooters, Love Honour And Obey, Shiner, Circus, Gangster No. 1, Sexy Beast, Essex Boys, Rancid Aluminium* (all 2000), *Charlie* (2003) and *Layer Cake* (2004). Most were witless combinations of tricks such as Tarantino's riffing monologues and Scorsese's voice-overs, featuring RADA graduates doing embarrassing turns as drug pushers and gun dealers; in all, a new low for British cinema. Perhaps the nadir was the pop group **All Saints**' vanity project, *Honest* (2001), directed by Dave Stewart of Eurythmics fame.

Of all the turn-of-the-century Britflicks only three are worth watching. *Face* (1997) was at least a serious attempt to examine the success of Thatcherism and the death of socialism via an analogous bank robbery and the fallout from it.

A heist-gone-wrong movie, it also benefited from a Britflick dream partnership of **Robert Carlyle** and **Ray Winstone**. *Gangster No. 1* only partially succeeded, and this was down to a typically charismatic performance by Paul Bettany (although it's ultimately a very accurate impersonation of James Fox in *Performance*). *Sexy Beast* was a Pinteresque take on the genre, but flags a little when the protagonist, played by Ray Winstone, leaves Spain and returns to Britain, to come face to face with none other than Brit gangster icon James Fox.

In Japan, stand-up comedian and TV presenter **Takeshi "Beat" Kitano** did something that no British director had managed to do: he took an old genre and made it vital and original. His take on the Yakuza in *Sonatine* (1993), *Kids Return* (1996) and *Hana-bi* (1997) was very much his own. Eschewing the formula of 1960s movies for a meditative atmosphere that is zen-like, his pictures focus on the "still lives" of characters: cops and gangsters who are pushed to the margins. Often literally so, as Kitano frequently favours seaside locations for his movies, which have some indefinable end-of-the-world feel about them.

While Kitano's movies played in art houses in Japan, a new market opened up: so-called "V cinema" films made with the intention of going straight to video. The king of V was guerilla film-maker **Takashi Miike**. *The Third Gangster* (1995) is officially his first film, but *Shinjuku Triad Society*, made the same year, is often regarded as the first distinctly Miike movie. The first of his Triad trilogy about the relationship between Chinese and Japanese gangsters, it was completed by *Rainy Dog* (1997) and *Ley Lines* (1999). However, *Dead Or Alive* (1999) is usually considered to be the best of his early work, not least because of its opening montage of buggery and bloodletting.

Pop goes the gangster

The pop star and the gangster movie have had an on/off relationship ever since since Truffaut cast French crooner and ladies' man **Charles Aznavour** in *Tirez sur le pianiste* (*Shoot The Pianist*, 1960). Perhaps the greatest meeting of the two was the Mick Jagger/James Fox face-off in Donald Cammell's *Performance* (see Canon entry).

But we've also seen Sting playing bar-owning hardmen in both *Stormy Monday* and *Lock, Stock And Two Smoking Barrels*. **Phil Collins** starred as a "great train robber" in *Buster* (1988), Gary and Martin Kemp from pop fops Spandau Ballet were unlikely choices as *The Krays* in 1990, while the producers of *Charlie* were really 'aving a larf when they cast ex-Bros pin-up **Luke Goss** as South London bone-cruncher Charlie Richardson.

This incongruous casting, however, became increasingly appropriate in the 1990s, when criminals like Frankie Fraser received rock-star treatment. Fraser, who used to pull out his victims' teeth with pliers, was celebrated on the covers of style magazines, conducted a very popular tour of his old East End haunts, and, inevitably, appeared in a British gangster movie, *Hard Men* (1996).

Of course, Francis Ford Coppola also made *Godfather III* in this decade. But we'll swiftly draw a veil over the subject.

The Grifters
dir Stephen Frears, 1990, US, 110m

Frears brings the panache of his *Dangerous Liaisons* (1988) to the table, while some scenes, notably the shocking violence of the denouement, clearly have Scorsese's fingerprints all over them. John Cusack is the con man with nimble fingers and an Oedipus complex. His domineering mother, Anjelica Huston, is also in the game, as is Cusack's new belle, Annette Bening. When mother and lover don't get on, Cusack's house of cards falls apart – spectacularly.

Boyz N The Hood
dir John Singleton, 1991, US, 107m

The simple plot follows four friends from childhood to their late teens. Their lives are turned upside down when Ricky is shot dead in a drive-by shooting (rather predictably, it's on the day that he receives his successful exam results). Despite its melodramatic moments, its authenticity rings true, not least in the banter between the impoverished and frustrated young men sitting in front of their houses all day long, shooting the breeze and drinking cheap liquor from plastic bottles.

Carlito's Way
dir Brian De Palma, 1993, US, 145m

De Palma and Pacino reunite for the first time since *Scarface* to very good and quite surprisingly low-key effect. Pacino plays a hood who leaves jail and tries to go straight but is compromised, calamitously, by the scheming of his lawyer. Sean Penn is unrecognizable in a curly wig, as the nervy, nerdy, coke-fuelled shyster with big plans for himself and his client. The deftest criminal activity in *Carlito's Way* is in fact Penn's stealing of the film from under Pacino's nose.

Natural Born Killers
dir Oliver Stone, 1994, US, 119m

Loosely based on one of Tarantino's early scripts, Oliver Stone made it his own. The changes horrified QT so much that he asked to have his name removed from the film's credits. A satire on the media's influence on crime, *Natural Born Killers* is complicit in the very phenomena it was satirizing by satisfying the same vicarious appetite for destruction.

Shinjuku Triad Society
dir Takashi Miike, 1995, Jap, 100m

One of Miike's earliest films, this has less of the sexual or indeed textual perversity that we know and love him for. The surprisingly coherent plot concerns a trade in human organs, which presages Miike's interest in (if not obsession with) the removal of body parts.

The Usual Suspects
dir Bryan Singer, 1995, US, 108m

More of a detective story than a gangster flick, with the viewer doing the detecting. Five criminals meet at a line-up and join forces to pull off various heists, finding themselves caught in an increasingly Kafkaesque bind. The tale is told us in flashback and it becomes less and less clear who is pulling the strings. But does it really make sense? Just who is the near-mythological Keyser Sose really?

Get Shorty
dir Barry Sonnenfeld, 1996, US, 105m

Loan shark Chilli Palmer (John Travolta) tracks a client down in Los Angeles and discovers that Hollywood is the perfect place for sharks like him. He carves his way through the film industry with unsavoury producer Gene Hackman and egomaniacal actor Danny De Vito in Sonnenfeld's jaunty comedy. The combo of John Travolta and Elmore Leonard source material is Tarantino-as-tapas for those who can't stomach a whole helping of Quentin.

Donnie Brasco
dir Mike Newell, 1997, US, 127m

A sort of cinematic karaoke, in which Pacino and Johnny Depp replay the hits of the 1970s – *Mean Streets* loudest of all. Pacino plays the real-life ageing New York wiseguy and Depp, with unseemly facial hair, plays the protégé who's actually an FBI agent. A *tour de force* of acting, but a cover version is rarely as good as the original.

LA Confidential
dir Curtis Hanson, 1997, US, 138m

The gangster – slick, suave Pierce Patchett (David Strathain) – is very much in the background, pulling the strings in Curtis Hanson's adaptation of James Ellroy's excellent novel. His power is eventually exposed by three cops with widely different methods and no love lost between them, who are drawn into a web of police corruption, scandal sheets, women cut to look like famous stars, and male prostitution. The moral turpitude becomes so endemic that not even the crusading Guy Pearce is incorruptible.

Lock, Stock And Two Smoking Barrels
dir Guy Ritchie, 1998, UK, 105m

As easy (and frankly as fun) as it would be to hate it for all the harm that its woeful legacy has done to British cinema, Guy Ritchie's film is actually not bad. It's like a live-action cartoon in which four chancers plot to rob a neighbourhood drugs operation to pay off Harry The Hatchet. Their plans soon spiral out of control. If it doesn't actually seem to make total sense, that's possibly because actress Laura Bailey had all her scenes excised and the ending was re-shot – hence the sudden appearance of a hat on Jason Flemyng's head: his hair had unhelpfully grown back since the original shoot.

Out Of Sight
dir Steven Soderbergh, 1998, US, 123m

George Clooney, in a career-making role, plays a robber who breaks out of jail with US marshal Jennifer Lopez in tow. Smitten by his charms and the twinkling Clooney Smile™, Lopez has to decide whether to take him in or take him on. Somehow Soderbergh seems to have hit upon the secret formula for on-screen sexual chemistry.

The Limey
dir Steven Soderbergh, 1999, US, 91m

Terence Stamp flies to America to avenge the death of his daughter at the hands of record-producer Peter Fonda. Steven Soderbergh's casting of two 60s icons is achingly poignant, as is the use of footage from the 1968 film *Poor Cow* for the flashback to Stamp's youth, when he was at his most criminally handsome. *The Limey* is not just clever but packs an emotional wallop, especially in the last revelatory scene, a real *coup de théâtre*.

2000+

Even in the 21st century, Martin Scorsese's influence still works its magic on films around the world. Unfortunately, his own recent work has been far more hit-and-miss. His *Gangs Of New York* (2002) could have been the *ne plus ultra* of gangster films, as it went all the way back to the very roots of gangsterdom in the US. Its setting, New York's Five Points district, can arguably be called *the* site of modern crime in America: it's where many of the all-time villains came from, notably **Al Capone**. However, Scorsese's film is about the gangs that existed before the Italian-Americans moved in, the predominantly Irish gangs from the middle of the nineteenth

century. Thirty years in the incubation, it could have been both the first and last word on gangsters, but problems in the script and casting made *Gangs* one of the great disappointments of recent times. At one point in the project's thirty-year genesis, Scorsese had De Niro in mind to play Amsterdam, the young man intent on killing Bill The Butcher to avenge the death of his father. De Niro has proved he can handle an epic – *1900*, *Godfather Part II* and *Once Upon A Time In America*, for example – and would, in his prime, have given the movie a lead it deserved.

Ironically it was a film that was hugely indebted to Scorsese – *City Of God* (2002) – which overshadowed *Gangs*. **Fernando Meirelles** and **Katja Lund**'s kaleidoscopic epic set in the slums of Rio had all the vibrancy and cinematic chutzpah that we still hope and pray that Scorsese can produce, but which he has singularly failed to do since *Goodfellas*. Perhaps it is simply that it has an urgency of subject matter that Scorsese's films no longer have; Italian-American gangsters now seem all played out, and it's hard to get past the well-worn clichés. But *City Of God* – like the dog-fighting scenes in Alejandro Iñárritu's *Amores Perros* (2000) and like Aleksei Balabanov's Russian movie *Brat* (*Brother*, 1997) – has the *frisson* of a connection with the society it's depicting: the same topicality that classic 1930s gangster flicks had in their day, that *The Asphalt Jungle* had, and that *The Long Good Friday* had.

And which a film like *Road To Perdition* (2001) conspicuously lacked. A collection of beautifully photographed gangster iconography, particularly of Tommy-gun-toting men in hats, **Sam Mendes'** film would have worked better as a series of stills (it was based upon a graphic novel). At least Steven Soderbergh's "films about films" have a wit and a flair that stylize their lack of profundity: *Out Of Sight* (1998) and *Oceans 11* (2001)

Daniel Day-Lewis (left) and Leonardo DiCaprio wait impatiently for gangster couture to hurry up and get stylish; *Gangs Of New York* (2002)

were empty but elegant and sassy, and *The Limey* (1999) had an unexpected emotional punch that belied its unforgivable jokes about cockney rhyming slang.

But if we want true innovation, we have to look east. The Japanese director and actor **Takashi Miike** has become possibly the most original filmmaker on the planet – so much so that no one else knows quite what he's doing. Best known in the West for his horror movie *Audition*, he averages almost five films a year and has dabbled in musicals and comedies, but mostly turns out Yakuza movies which always contain some hard-to-stomach moment of ultra-violence.

Each one is very different from anything you've ever seen before. *Fudoh: The New Generation* (1996) is about a gang entirely made up of children and teenagers, but is certainly no *Bugsy Malone*. *Ichi The Killer* (2001) begins with ejaculated sperm forming the words of the credits and is so violent that it's one of the few recent films to receive major cuts by the British censor. *Gozu* (2004) features a Yakuza hitman who enters an underworld of a different kind – of spirits – and is ultimately destroyed by a vagina.

At the end of the twentieth century Hong Kong cinema seemed to be on its last legs, eclipsed by the tiger economies of Thailand

and South Korea. The phenomenal popularity of the gangster film *Dang Bireley And The Young Gangsters* kick-started the Thai film industry in 1997, while *Friend* had a similarly rejuvenating effect on Korean cinema in 2001. It was followed by works such as *Bad Guy* (2001), *Guns And Talks* (2001), *My Wife Is A Gangster* (2001), *Marrying The Mafia* (2002), *My Wife Is A Gangster II* (2003) and *Mokpo: Gangsters' Paradise* (2004), which offered the same transgressive thrills that made Hong Kong films so exciting in the 1980s. However, the ex-colony wasn't through yet. Arguably *Infernal Affairs* (2002) is the definitive gangster film of the decade so far. Directed by **Andrew Lau** and **Alan Mak**, it's an ingeniously, fiendishly plotted thriller about a cop who infiltrates a Triad and a Triad member who infiltrates the cops. It has been so successful internationally that it was remade in America by none other than Martin Scorsese.

City Of Lost Souls
dir Takashi Miike, 2000, Jap, 103m

The usual Miike sick alchemy of outré violence, bizarre images and scatological humour. Witness: a cockfight between two cartoon birds; a midget on a toilet; a loo's-eye view of a man's head; immolation and eye-gouging. With more ideas than a dozen Hollywood action movies, it's a typical Miike battle between Triads and the Yakuza, and it's all bathed in vogue-ish electric blues and radioactive greens.

Sexy Beast
dir Jonathan Glazer, 2000, UK/Sp/US, 88m

Old East End thief Ray Winstone is enjoying his retirement in Spain, soaking up the sun in his tiny yellow swimming trunks, but his life with his wife (Amanda Redman) is disturbed by news of the imminent arrival of a former associate (Ben Kingsley). The first half of Glazer's debut works a treat, with words and pauses deployed like artillery fire, as if Harold Pinter had turned his pen towards the Mob genre. But when Winstone goes back to London, the film loses its way and the plot takes a bewildering direction.

Oceans 11
dir Steven Soderbergh, 2001, US/Aus, 116m

A pretty, vacant remake of a pretty awful caper movie, which just preserves the basic setup: a group of well-groomed, youngish men steal a lot of money from a casino. In the original there were five casinos and more in-jokes, but its lackadaisical pace reflected the actors' attitudes. At least George Clooney and Brad Pitt make an entertaining and spirited effort, while director Steven Soderbergh applies a gloss finish.

The Good Thief
dir Neil Jordan, 2002, UK/Fr/Ire, 109m

Neil Jordan certainly picked a more interesting heist movie than Soderbergh to remake – Melville's *Bob le flambeur*. There's a lot of knowing, winking dialogue about copies and originals, as junkie and safe-cracker Nick Nolte is called out of retirement to break into a vault full of Picassos and Van Goghs. *The Good Thief*'s thriller elements succeed, but – as in all good heist movies – the real concern is with the people not the plot.

Road To Perdition
dir Sam Mendes, 2002, US, 117m

Legendary cinematographer Conrad Hall's last job, *Road To Perdition* is more a testimony to him than to Mendes. It's like a series of stunning, often rain-drenched *tableaux vivants*, but the story suffers a little amidst all the beauty. Tom Hanks and son go on the run, doggedly pursued by a very believable Jude Law as a merciless hitman. The film aims for a *Godfather*-like solemnity, particularly in the Paul Newman/Hanks face-offs, but ends up overblown and empty.

Gangs Of New York
dir Martin Scorsese, 2002, US, 168m

Spectacular set pieces (the battles, the knife-throwing incident) can't hide the fact that DiCaprio's shoulders are too slender to carry an entire epic. As it is, Daniel Day-Lewis steals the film, even though he sails too close at times to a very passable impersonation of Desperate Dan. If only *Gangs Of New York* had been made twenty years earlier...

Sympathy For Mr Vengeance
dir Park Chan Wook, 2002, South Korea, 121m

The trade in body parts is now one of the major profit centres for organized crime, and cinema has not been slow on the uptake. This grisly story concerns a deaf-mute whose sister requires a new kidney; he kidnaps the daughter of his former boss and events spiral viciously out of control. Predating *Old Boy*, it boasts a similar blend of delirious invention, torture and gore that really tests the audience's ability to hold onto the contents of their stomachs.

Infernal Affairs II
dir Wai Keung Lau/Siu Fai Mak, 2003, HK, 119m

A prequel which explains the labyrinthine back-story to the original, and which throws in material about Triad families and the hand-over of Hong Kong. Self-consciously epic, it lacks the pacing and plotting that distinguished its predecessor, while trying that little bit too hard to be a masterpiece.

Infernal Affairs III
dir Wai Keung Lau/Siu Fai Mak, 2003, HK, 118m

The Hong Kong film industry certainly knows how to cash in on a hit. Here the theme of doubles extends to the narrative structure, which is both a prequel and a sequel to the original, as it nimbly cuts between two time zones. Breathless and inventive, it certainly brings the trilogy back up to speed and occasionally displays the moments of sheer narrative nerve and aplomb that made the original such an audacious pleasure.

Ong-Bak
dir Prachya Pinkaew, 2003, Thai, 108m

Advertised as a return to the traditions of martial-art movies before the use of wires and CGI, *Ong-Bak* is about the clash of two cultural forms – the old chop-socky film versus the urban gangster movie. The movie would like us to think it's on the side of the old, purist traditions, but prefers to have it both ways, clearly relishing the crime-movie elements, the venal underworld of drug addicts, street fighters and other nocturnal creatures, sweaty dives and human cesspits and a gangster with voice-box who smokes cigarettes via a hole in his throat.

Bullet Boy
dir Saul Dibb, 2004, UK, 89m

A whole decade after Hollywood made *Boyz N The Hood*, UK cinema finally came to grips with gangsta culture. Using the *Mean Streets* template of a young man who wants to go straight but is pulled back into a life of crime by his reckless, mercurial friend, *Bullet Boy* is a little rough around the edges in a singularly British way – it's a bit naff. But it boasts a star-making performance by Ashley Walters, who possesses the brooding, hypnotic stillness that cameras just love to dwell upon: he's got a face that was born to be photographed.

Layer Cake
dir Matthew Vaughn, 2004, UK, 104m

"Layer Cake" refers to the various strata of criminal society, which coke dealer Daniel Craig has to make his way through to track down the unruly daughter of a powerful and dodgy businessman (Michael Gambon). Directed by *Lock Stock*'s producer, who stepped in when Guy Ritchie turned the script down, the result is a more mature affair than *Lock, Stock* was. But that's not really saying much.

The Canon: 50 essential gangster movies

Shades and cigar maketh the gangster in Roger
Corman's *The St Valentine's Day Massacre* (1967)

The Canon:
50 essential gangster movies

A bout de souffle
(Breathless)

dir **Jean-Luc Godard, 1959, Fr, 90m, b/w**
cast **Jean-Paul Belmondo, Jean Seberg, Daniel Boulanger, Jean-Pierre Melville, Henri-Jacques Huet** *cin* **Raoul Coutard** *m* **Martial Solal**

A bout de souffle was a revolution in cinema, rewriting film grammar and introducing the jump-cut into the lexicon of moving pictures. As historian David Thomson says in his *Biographical Dictionary Of Film*, director **Jean-Luc Godard** was "the first filmmaker to bristle with the effort of digesting all previous cinema and to make cinema itself his subject". The reason that *A bout de souffle* is in a book about gangster movies at all, let alone the canon, is because American cinema, in particular the gangster movie, was the subject of Godard's debut. As an influential critic for legendary film magazine *Cahiers Du Cinéma*, Godard expressed "vital admiration of the beauty of American action cinema, and of the way it expressed character, emotion and universal meanings within rigid genres". To extend Thomson's digestion metaphor, *A bout de souffle* is a gangster movie in pieces. Or rather, chunks.

The first few shots tell us that we're in gangster territory. Michel Poiccard, aka Laszlo Kovaks (**Jean-Paul Belmondo**), is reading a paper, wearing a Humphrey Bogart fedora almost over his eyes, with a Gauloise dangling arrogantly from his lips. He certainly looks the hoodlum part, and we witness him hotwire a

The chain-smoking poseur Laszlo Kovaks (Jean-Paul Belmondo) seeing if he's made the papers in Godard's masterpiece *A bout de souffle* (1959)

car. He drives through the countryside, providing a running commentary on the action, and refuses to give some hitch-hikers a lift because, apparently, they're too ugly. When his car breaks down and a traffic policeman investigates, Michel shoots him. Or rather, we assume he does, because the murder features one of the most famous jump-cuts in cinema history. We see a close-up of a gun, hear a shot and then the film cuts to the cop sprawling backwards into some bushes. We have to fill in the details for ourselves, not least the psychological motivation – no reason or explanation is given for the crime, and none is ever offered. Michel makes a run for it; he has to get to Paris to collect money that's owed to him so that he can leave the country. In the city – and, indeed, throughout the film – he shows no remorse. He's still playing Bogart, strutting through the streets, lighting cigarettes from previous cigarettes. When someone asks him for a light he tells them to buy a box of matches. And then he comes across Patricia (**Jean Seberg**) selling the *New York Herald Tribune* in the middle of the street. With her striped T-shirt and gamine haircut Seberg started a fashion that lasted longer than she did. (She committed suicide in 1979.) She is an American signed up for the Sorbonne and it's not long before Michel and Patricia end up in bed together. Cue one of the interminable scenes that feature in almost every Godard movie: two people endlessly talking in an apartment or hotel room. Some of the dialogue is interesting, most is banal. She asks if he prefers her eyes, her mouth or her shoulders. He's like an awkward child, trying to remove her top.

When she finds out that he's a killer, Patricia has a strange reaction. She wants him to steal a Cadillac. It seems that we are about to be thrust into the killer-couple-on-the-run sub-genre that the director so admired. Both Godard and **François Truffaut** (credited as writer of *A bout de souffle*) championed American gangster movies when they were critics for the magazine *Cahiers Du Cinéma*: Godard once called the lovers in *You Only Live Once* (1937) "the last romantic couple" and went on to claim that "all you need to make a film is a girl and a gun". But this is *A bout de souffle*, in which Godard doesn't so much deconstruct the genre as utterly thwart our expectations.

So, instead of the hijinks on the road that we might be hoping for, the film returns to the four walls of a room. Seberg has decided to turn him in to the cops; Belmondo makes one last run for it, but in one of the great tracking shots of cinema, he's gunned down in the streets. She follows after him and hears his bathetic dying words: "C'est vraiment dégueulasse!" (literally "This is really disgusting!", though "What a drag!", or "This is a real bitch!" could equally apply). Whether this is some existential pronouncement about life or a wonderfully laconic understatement about the pain of being shot is uncertain. She asks a policeman what he said, who replies – perhaps having misheard him – "T'es dégueulasse" ("You're disgusting"). "Qu'est-ce que c'est, 'dégueulasse'?" ("What's 'disgusting'?") she enquires. *Fin*.

If Godard borrowed from the gangster genre, then he paid the genre back with interest. The director's fingerprints are everywhere: all over *Bonnie And Clyde*, which he was due to direct, and which was written as a homage to the *nouvelle vague*; also visible in the dazzling technical innovations of Scorsese's *Mean Streets* and in the work of **Quentin Tarantino**, who named his company A Band Apart, after Godard's other unique foray into the genre, *Bande a part* (1964).

As Phil Hardy has written, "Godard tore the genre apart in *A bout de souffle*. That film drew on American models but in its presentation of teenage delinquency as existential angst, added a new dimension that all subsequent gangster films would to some extent incorporate." Above all Godard made the hoodlum cool. Or rather he let the hoodlum *know* that he was cool. Michel is probably the first self-aware gangster, he realizes that he's playing a part. He knows how a movie gangster should act – he's learnt his lessons from the cinema – and, as importantly, he knows how a movie gangster should dress.

He's different from all the dandies who preceded him – Cagney and Robinson wore expensive threads to look good; they wanted to fit into high society, whereas Belmondo wants to look like a mobster. You could say that he dresses to kill. Director **Jean-Pierre Melville**, who played the part of a novelist in *A bout de souffle* took that notion to its logical conclusion in *Le samourai*, in which Delon's fedora and raincoat are deliberately anachronistic and unfashionable, and function mainly as a film reference. *Le samourai* was also an influence on both Tarantino and **John Woo**, whose characters are similarly marked by their movie-conscious dress sense and existential angst; Woo's work has subsequently fed back as an influence into American and Asian cinema. In other words, if there was a gangster family tree, *A bout de souffle* would be one of its strongest roots.

Angels With Dirty Faces

dir **Michael Curtiz, 1938, US, 97m, b/w**

cast **James Cagney, Pat O'Brien, Humphrey Bogart, Ann Sheridan, George Bancroft** cin **Sol Polito** m **Max Steiner**

The most didactic, moralistic, sermonizing movie in the gangster canon, this film is saved from its own preachiness by a performance of real potency and urgency from **James Cagney**. *Angels* tells the tale of two childhood friends whose paths are set by one incident: when Jerry Connolly (Pat O'Brien) and Rocky Sullivan (Cagney) break into a freight wagon (to steal some fountain pens!) and are spotted by the cops. Rocky is caught but never reveals the name of his accomplice and is sent to an institution for juvenile delinquents. A classic montage of excited newspaper headlines informs us of Rocky's subsequent turn to a life of crime, whilst Jerry joins the priesthood. Now a gangster, Rocky, returns to his old haunt after another stint inside, this time covering for his lawyer, Frazier (**Humphrey Bogart**). As critic Richard Schickel has pointed out, Rocky must be the nicest gangster in cinema history – he's always the fall guy for his friends. The deal is that Frazier will take the money, set up a business, and they will share their spoils when Rocky gets out. However, when Frazier does make it to the big time, running a casino with crime lord Keefe, he doesn't want another partner and reneges on his deal. The pair of them try to bump off Rocky and when the attempt fails, he takes their incriminating notebooks "that will tear the whole town wide open", detailing their crooked deals and including the names and numbers of the most important people in the city. Realising they can't touch him so long as he has that information, they make an uneasy truce.

Meanwhile Rocky has become a hero to the street kids that Jerry is looking after. Although Rocky is trying to do the right thing, he's leading them further into a life of crime. Concerned, Jerry leads a press campaign against Rocky, Keefe and Frazier.

Panicked, Frazier and Keefe try to ambush Rocky, but he kills them both and is captured by the cops.

And this is the moment when the sermonizing really kicks in. Rocky is about to be executed, and Jerry asks him "to go to the chair yellow" – to pretend that he's scared so that the kids won't glorify him as a hero, to give them a chance he never had. Rocky refuses. Defiant to the last, he takes on the guard that's marching him to the chair. But then, at the moment of his death, he kicks, screams and cries out that he doesn't want to die. Jerry silently prays, and looks up, a light shining in his eyes – it's clear to him that a miracle has occurred. But the story doesn't end there. Back in the boy's den, they're reading the newspaper headline "Rocky dies yellow: killer coward at end." They can't believe it, but Father Connolly assures them it's true, and asks them to "say a prayer for a boy who couldn't run as fast as I could." He takes them out of their dark basement and into the light: as religious symbolism goes it doesn't get much cheesier.

This really is a movie of two halves – the pleasure of one undercutting the message of the other. It's not difficult to see why Cagney's charismatic bad boy is more appealing to the kids than O'Brien's worthy priest. It's Jimmy's film, and his performance is notable not least for the appearance of the Cagney shoulder-shrug that everyone does when they impersonate him. He claimed he only ever did it once, and that he took the gesture from a pimp he observed when he was growing up on the streets of New York. "He had four girls working for him " Cagney remembered, "and this is all he did all day long. The extent of his activity."

But credit must also be given to **Michael Curtiz**, notwith-standing the laying–it–on–a–bit–thick ending, A Hungarian émigré with an infamously bad grasp of English, his phrase "Bring on the empty horses" provided **David Niven** with the title of his auto-biography. Curtiz also directed *Casablanca* (1942) but he has never been granted the auteur status conferred upon other directorial salarymen such as **Howard Hawks**; all his successes have generally been credited to the "genius of the system" (as Thomas Schatz's study of the studio era put it). What Curtiz brought to *Angels* was a sense of place. The neo–Dickensian slums teem with life: grubby urchins, street vendors, neon signs, and washing hanging over bal-conies. It has cinematography that prefigures *noir*, as shadows begin to encroach slowly upon the faces of the characters.

The Asphalt Jungle

dir John Huston, 1950, US, 112m, b/w

cast Sterling Hayden, Louis Calhern, Jean Hagen, Sam Jaffe, James Whitmore, Marilyn Monroe *cin* Harold Rosson *m* Miklós Rozsa

The Asphalt Jungle was the heist movie that launched a thousand capers. Widely regarded as the first of its kind, it started a genre that includes *Rififi* (1955), *Ocean's 11* (1960) and *Reservoir Dogs* (1991), and has itself been remade three times, as *Badlanders* (1958), *Cairo* (1963) and *Cool Breeze* (1972).

An eccentric criminal mastermind, Doc Riedenschneider (**Sam Jaffe**), has planned a robbery that will net one million dollars' worth of jewels. To do it he needs $50,000, and he approaches Mob lawyer Emmerich (a lordly **Louis Calhern**), a man who "uses his brain to circumvent the law". Doc requires three men for the job: a "box-man" (a safe-cracker), a driver

Louis Calhern and a young Marilyn Monroe in Huston's prototype heist movie *The Asphalt Jungle* (1950)

and a "hooligan". The hooligan is Dix Handley (**Sterling Hayden**), a stick-up artist who's addicted to betting on the horses. What the gang don't know, and what we subsequently learn, is that Emmerich doesn't have any money. He's broke and is going to double-cross them. He'll pretend to fence the loot, stall for time and leave the country with the bounty. The robbery is a success but it all goes wrong when Emmerich's real intentions are dramatically uncovered by the rest of the gang.

One of the remarkable things about **Ben Maddow** and **John Huston**'s screenplay is its scrupulous attention to detail. All the characters are fleshed out with a life beyond the caper and their own back story, whether it's Emmerich's relationship with his young lover (a first screen appearance by **Marilyn Monroe**) or Doc's eye for the women which will eventually bring him down. Characters reminisce about riding a horse, or talk about their worry over their 9-year-old child's temperature. Even minor players such as Gus, a hunchbacked café-owner, are rigorously well drawn. (As well as being sourced from a pristine print, the 2004 Region 1 DVD has audio archive of James Whitmore, the actor who played Gus.)

Fundamentally, all relationships in *The Asphalt Jungle* are determined by economics: Dix owes money to a bookie, who pays off a corrupt cop, who is himself in the pocket of the corrupt lawyer Emmerich, who himself is steeped in debt because of the rising costs of keeping a mistress (Monroe). The screenplay is extremely fastidious in filling us in on the accountancy of a heist: we find out that a fence never gives less than 50 percent of the loot's worth; and that a box-man should be paid $25,000, a driver $10,000 and a hooligan $15,000. When Doc tells a taxi driver that he'll give him a $50 tip if he drives to Cleveland, the cabbie informs him that for a $50 tip he'd take him to the North Pole. And that seems to sum up the guiding principle of the universe in which *The Asphalt Jungle* takes place: money changes everything.

A Better Tomorrow
(Yingxiong bense)

dir **John Woo, 1986, HK, 95m**

cast **Chow Yun-Fat, Leslie Cheung, Ti Lung, Emily Chu, Waise Lee** *cin* **Wong Wing Hang** *m* **Joseph Koo**

This is not John Woo's first film – that was made thirteen years earlier in 1973 – but this is the first film by John Woo as we know him: the John Woo who choreographs action scenes with all the painstaking precision, care and attention to detail of classical ballet or a golden-age Hollywood musical. His previous two films had been unfunny comedies that hardly anyone was interested in, so the success of *A Better Tomorrow* was all the more surprising. Its phenomenal box-office takings relaunched Woo, making him Hong Kong's most famous film director. It also made **Chow Yun-Fat**, hitherto best known as a Hong Kong TV actor, into a global superstar and started a sub-genre of gangster movies known as "heroic bloodshed".

Ho (Ti Lung) is a successful Triad gangster who has two brothers: his surrogate brother Mark (Chow Yun-Fat), a deadly member of his gang, and Kit (**Leslie Cheung**), who is a police officer. Ho is ambushed and imprisoned in Taiwan as part of a gang war which leads to his father's murder. When he gets out of jail he discovers that the world is not his anymore. Mark is also down on his luck, while Kit is obsessed with catching Shing, the new big crime boss. Ho tries to go straight, and get a new job, but finds out that "it's easy to become a gangster but it's more difficult to get out" – especially when Shing is prepared to do anything to bring him back into the fold. After being beaten to a pulp by the Triads, Mark and Ho realize the error of their criminal ways and take on Shing and co in a suitably bloody shoot-out.

Although Chow Yun-Fat is by no means the lead character in *A Better Tomorrow*, he is indisputably the star. He has a laconic cool and an impeccably good dress sense, which was much imitated in

Hong Kong. Teenagers and Triad members alike adopted his long duster coat, dark glasses, matchstick-munching, and even some of his dialogue. Although Mark dies at the end of the film, the producers knew they were onto a good thing, and brought Chow back in the sequel, as his identical twin.

A Better Tomorrow is the first of his movies to use the classic Woo hallmarks: two protagonists who would appear to be complete opposites (often, as here, a cop and a criminal) who have more in common than they care to admit; cold-eyed killers who operate by a strict code of honour and loyalty; heavily stylized slow-motion shoot-outs; and guns which have an apparently endless amount of ammunition. Being low-budget, it lacks the slick visuals of later Woo, nor does it have his usual religious symbolism or trademark flocks of doves. If you want baroque-period Woo try *The Killer* or *Hard Boiled*.

Chow Yun-Fat in the career-making, epoch-defining *A Better Tomorrow* (1986)

The Big Heat

dir Fritz Lang, 1953, US, 90m, b/w
cast Glenn Ford, Gloria Grahame, Jocelyn Brando, Lee Marvin, Carolyn Jones *cin* Charles Lang Jr *m* Daniele Amfitheatrof

Strictly speaking this is a "cop movie" rather than a gangster pic, but this gets into the canon because it features the best moll in film history: Debbie Marsh, a lush with a big mouth played by **Gloria Grahame**.

However, the ostensible main focus of Fritz Lang's film is **Glenn Ford**'s downbeat, dogged Sergeant Dave Bannion. He has a happy home life, with a lovely daughter and a wife who cooks him steak. It is torn apart when he starts to investigate the apparent suicide of policeman Tom Duncan. Bannion discovers Duncan's connections with crime lord Mike Lagana (**Alexander Scoursby**), but he gets too close and his wife is blown up by a car bomb intended for him. Bannion leaves the force when the police won't go after the culprit – the Police Commissioner is in the pay of the Mob – and goes it alone. The trail leads him to Debbie Marsh, the loose cannon girlfriend of psychopathic gangster Vince Stone (**Lee Marvin**), Lagana's right-hand man. Vince finds out about the pair having met and, in the most memorable moment of the film, throws a pot of boiling coffee in her face. Disfigured, she joins forces with Bannion to bring the syndicate down.

The coffee-in-the-face scene is the one thing that everyone remembers about *The Big Heat*; and it's a measure of how powerful the scene is that many viewers have "remembered" more than is actually shown in the film. Like the ear-removal moment in *Reservoir Dogs* (1991), the disfigurement happens off-screen. Debbie is applying lipstick in the mirror (looking at herself is Debbie's favourite pastime). Vince is asking where she's been, laughing at her one-liners, flirting with her, and complimenting her as a "real pretty kisser". But there's always a hint of a threat with Vince. With his high temples, oiled-back quiff and long, lupine face, Lee Marvin looks like a cartoon wolf about to blow someone's house down.

Gloria Grahame and Glenn Ford tussle
in Fritz Lang's *The Big Heat* (1953)

He suddenly snaps, forces her arm behind her back, and demands to know where she has been. He knows that she's just been with Bannion, but she won't admit it and pleads with him to let her go. Big mistake. His eyes dart around the room, and fall onto a pot of coffee bubbling away. The camera cuts to the percolator, an arm stretches for the handle and takes the coffee pot out of the frame; we hear a whoosh or a splash and then a sharp cry. A quick cut to men playing cards in the next room before Debbie runs in, screaming "My face, my face."

Gloria Grahame is the life force of the film – the perfect foil to Ford's introspective, emotionally churned-up cop. In many ways she's a little girl, "cracking wise" whilst hopping around a room like a drunken pixie. Yet she has an adult wit, her sharp tongue delivering such zingy one-liners as "you're as romantic as a pair of handcuffs", "we're sisters under the mink", "I guess a scar isn't so bad when it's on one side. I can always go through life sideways" and, commenting on the decor of Ford's sparse hotel room, "I like this – early nothing." And just when we think we have the measure of her character, her final moments in the movie reveal a few profound hidden depths: a genuinely redemptive scene in a cinema history littered with phoney ones. It's probably Grahame's greatest performance and – if her spontaneous, headstrong and difficult reputation is accurate – the closest to how she was in real-life.

Black Caesar

dir Larry Cohen, 1973, US, 96m
cast Fred Williamson, D'Urville Martin, Gloria Hendry, Art Lund, Val Avery, Minnie Gentry *cin* Fenton Hamilton *m* James Brown

As the title suggests, *Black Caesar* is a version of classic gangster movies that bears all the hallmarks of the blaxploitation genre: the clothes, the sass, the politics, the low budget and the soundtrack by a funk legend, **James Brown**. Although it customizes the gangster model for its own funky ends, it's also been a source of inspiration to the genre proper, not least in its scene of ear removal.

Tommy Gibbs, a young black shoeshine boy, delivers protection money to a bent cop, McKinney (**Art Lund**), who claims that $50 is missing and beats him with a yardstick until his leg breaks. Years later, Gibbs (**Fred Williamson**), is back on the street in a sharp suit and Homburg hat after spending most of his young life on the inside. He gains his entrée into the Sicilian Mafia by taking it upon himself to kill a gangster who has a contract on his head. Tommy removes his victim's ear with a razor (sound familiar?) and presents it as proof of his deed to the capo of the neighbourhood. Although he's informed that the organization "doesn't employ niggers", he tells him that he only wants a block to call his own.

Soon Tommy's running his own section of Harlem, and when he gets hold of documents which detail the crimes of the rich and famous he gets real power, and puts McKinney on the payroll. He also employs a lawyer, buys the lawyer's house and all its contents, and presents them as a gift to his mother, the lawyer's maid. Hell-bent on power, Tommy goes to war with the Mafia, but they hit back – it should be pointed out that the plot is not the strongest part of *Black Caesar* – and he's betrayed by his ex-girlfriend, who tells the Mob where he hides the documents. One by one the organization snuffs out his men, and eventually hunts him down.

Black Caesar makes reference to almost every classic gangster movie you can think of, including a low-budget remake of the wedding scene from *The Godfather* (which features a suitably tacky parody of **Nino Rota**'s music). However, in *Black Caesar*, of course, the Italian family are wiped out by the brothers from Harlem. As in *Angels With Dirty Faces*, the protagonist's best friend is a priest, and just like Cagney in the earlier film, Tommy steals documents which hold the secrets of the Mob and thus the key to power.

Black Caesar was written, produced and directed by "whitesploitation" director **Larry Cohen**. A true cult auteur, he created the TV series *The Invaders*, directed *The Stuff* (1985 – about a killer blancmange), made **Bette Davis**'s last film, *Wicked Stepmother* (1988) and directed *Black Caesar*'s sequel, *Hell Up In Harlem* (1973) as well as returning to the blaxploitation genre with *Old Gangstas* in 1996. Cashing in on the success of *Jackie Brown* (1997), *Old Gangstas* united icons **Pam Grier**, **Richard Roundtree** and **Fred Williamson** as vigilantes who take on the new order of "gangsta".

All Cohen's films have the same originality, inventiveness, poor production values, intentional and unintentional humour, as well as a political edge: even though *The Stuff* is a B-movie horror about a deadly dessert, it's also an astute critique of consumerism. Similarly, *Black Caesar* is more than just a pastiche. In its own exploitation-movie way, it draws an unusually complex picture of race relations in 1970s America: when Tommy gives his mother his lawyer's expensive apartment, she claims that she would be lynched for living there. Although Tommy seems to be the top dog, his power is only a chimera. It is McKinney, and white people like him, who are really pulling the strings. In the ironic and poignant ending Tommy isn't killed by mobsters, but is mugged by black street kids from his old tenement and left for dead, a premonition of the black–on–black violence that would be a depressingly mundane feature of life in US ghettoes over the following decades.

Bonnie And Clyde

dir **Arthur Penn, 1967, US, 111m**
cast **Warren Beatty, Faye Dunaway, Michael J Pollard, Gene Hackman, Estelle Parsons** *cin* **Burnett Guffey** *m* **Charles Strouse**

Bonnie And Clyde changed not just American films but American culture. Along with *Easy Rider* (1969), it made Hollywood execs realize there was a new youth audience who were not being catered for by their big-budget extravaganzas like *Dr Doolittle*. *Bonnie And Clyde*'s success heralded the new wave of movie-brat cinema, in which film school graduates such as **Steven Spielberg**, **Francis Ford Coppola** and **Martin Scorsese** wrested control from the studios, and made films with a personal, rather than corporate, vision. Bonnie and Clyde, as portrayed in the movie, became icons of the counterculture.

The initial inspiration for **David Newman** and **Robert Benton**'s script was Benton's memories of his father regaling him with folk tales of Bonnie Parker and Clyde Barrow's exploits: his dad was one of the thousands of people who went to Clyde

Barrow's funeral. Intended as a project for **François Truffaut** (he even rewrote a couple of scenes), it passed into the hands of first **Jean-Luc Godard** and then **Warren Beatty**, who was going to make the project his directorial debut. He eventually and wisely decided to star and produce instead, and brought in Arthur Penn to direct.

Bonnie (Faye Dunaway) and Clyde (Warren Beatty) meet when Clyde steals her family's car. She decides to go with him and, after a false start, they become bankrobbers. Their relationship remains strictly professional (until near the film's end) because Clyde is impotent. She remarks to him, "your advertising is just dandy. Folks just never guess you didn't have a thing to sell." Soon joined by a sweet but dim garage hand, C.W. Moss (**Michael J. Pollard**), Clyde's brother Buck (**Gene Hackman**) and his grouchy wife Blanche (**Estelle Parsons**), they form the Barrow Gang, and become instantly notorious. Or rather, heroic: in a time (the Great Depression) when the banks robbed the people, the bank robbers became folk heroes. It all goes well – in fact it's something of a hoot – until the police catch up with them at a motel. Hunted down the next day, Buck is killed and Blanche

Faye Dunaway and Warren Beatty engaging in some authentically hillbilly target practice in *Bonnie And Clyde*

83

captured. C.W. takes the barely-alive Bonnie and Clyde to his father's house. Dismayed at how the couple have turned his boy into thieving trash, he turns them in, and they are ambushed and gunned down at a roadside.

It was this ending – the iconoclastic death in slow motion, Bonnie and Clyde's bodies writhing and dancing as they are perforated by bullets – as well as the glamorization of cold-blooded killers which led most critics and even the studio boss, Jack Warner, to condemn the film. In fact it wouldn't have lasted a week, according to Robert Benton, if critic **Joe Morgenstern** hadn't decided to see it again, this time with his wife. Morgenstern was one of the critics who had excoriated the film in his initial review, but after seeing it again he made cinema history by publishing a retraction in *Newsweek* magazine. This swung critical and public opinion, especially when the *capo di tutti capi* of film critics, **Pauline Kael**, got behind the film, and after Beatty literally dropped to the floor and begged Warner to give it a proper release, the movie became a major hit.

Its classic status is deserved. It still works, even though (perhaps even because) it's very much a product of its time. (Sometimes quite literally so: the slow-motion death scene is a visual echo of the Zapruder footage of **President Kennedy**'s head being blown apart.) Even though neither Truffaut nor Godard directed it, their influence is constantly felt. As Beatty said at the time, Newman and Benton had written a French film, and Penn gave it a *nouvelle vague* edginess: arrhythmic editing, cameras put in the "wrong" place and the deliberate use of anachronistic back projection in the driving scenes. All of these elements deliberately jar. We're constantly reminded that we're watching a film and yet we're simultaneously seduced by the film's jaunty, jagged energy and the charisma of the too-beautiful stars. The phenomenon of the "Bonnie look" in the late 1960s – young women lowering the hems of their miniskirts and wearing berets – is a testimony to the success and the seductive power of the movie, and indeed of the cultural sway of movies in general.

Brighton Rock

dir John Boulting, 1947, GB, 92m, b/w
cast Richard Attenborough, Carol Marsh, Hermione
Baddeley, William Hartnell, Harcourt Williams *cin* Harry
Waxman *m* Hans May

Until *Perfomance* and *Get Carter*, *Brighton Rock* could easily have been described as the greatest British gangster movie. At the time, however, the *Daily Mirror* preferred to see it as "false, cheap, nasty sensationalism". Located in prewar Brighton (a different Brighton from 1947, the film insists) it follows the fortunes of Pinkie (**Richard Attenborough**) and his gang. Pinkie has killed a snitch who had found his way back to the coastal town, and he's now trying to cover his tracks. There's only one witness who can destroy his alibi – naïve waitress Rose (Carol Marsh). Pinkie seduces and then marries her, on the grounds that a wife can't testify against her husband. Meanwhile his gang, and Spicer in particular, are getting nervous because some-one is on their trail – big, brassy Ida (Hermione Baddeley), who befriended the victim only hours before his death and is convinced that he was murdered. Pinkie is also getting a little aggravation from a rival gang, the Colleonis, and tries to arrange for Spicer to be killed. When this fails he does the job himself.

Rose is unaware of all this, blissfully ignorant, and totally besot-ted with Pinkie. In a stand-out scene, he records a message for her in a booth and gives her the disc as a gift. What she doesn't know is that it's a testimony of hate. "What you want me to say is 'I love you', but here's the truth: I hate you, you little slut" he snarls while Rose, with luminous innocence, gazes at him in almost religious adoration through the glass.

When Ida gets too close for comfort, and it looks as if it is the end of the line, Pinkie tries to get rid of Rose by talking her into a "suicide pact". The pair will kill themselves by leaping from Brighton pier together – with Rose going first, of course. But the police get there in time and Pinkie, in a bid to escape, dives into the sea and drowns. Back home, Rose is left alone with the record. She puts it on the turntable, it starts to play, but gets stuck just at the moment he says "I love you". This refrain repeats endlessly as the camera pans to a cross on the wall above her. Is it a miracle?

In Graham Greene's novel, Rose, possibly pregnant, goes home with the record in her bag, "towards the worst horror of all". That's where many feel the film should have ended. In **Terence Rattigan**'s original script, she heard *all* the message. According to film historian **David Thomson**, Graham Greene hated this ending and was allowed to rewrite it. *He* put the scratch on the record, arguing that "Anybody who wanted a happy ending would feel that they had had a happy ending. Anybody who had any sense would know that the next time, Rose would probably push the needle over the scratch and get the full message." And it has to be said, except for the heavy-handed Catholic symbolism, this version is just as horribly ironic as the novel, and seems even more like God's little joke.

Greene, together with Rattigan, did a great job of adaptation – clearly the years of being a film critic had paid off. And

Richard Attenborough as the sadistic murderer Pinkie, in John Boulting's cruel Brit *noir Brighton Rock* (1947)

he makes many changes to the novel to render it cinematic – not least a murder in a ghost train which is both thrilling and imaginative, and made at a time – the late 1940s – when British cinema was both of those things. Credit here must go to producers and directors the **Boulting Brothers** (John directed and Roy produced) who have been largely forgotten. When Roy died in 2001 he was living on his own in a small shabby flat surrounded by cardboard boxes full of mementoes from his glory days. Their evocation of squalid locations (you can almost smell the damp in Pinkie's boarding room) and expressionistic composition make this a genuine British *noir*, as good as its American counterparts.

But the real star is Richard Attenborough. Unrecognizable from the cuddly, darling Dickie we all know and love, he's a psychotic, dead-eyed, baby-faced assassin. He was so good that after *Brighton Rock* he was only offered Pinkie-clone roles, and he soon became typecast. "It was a curse," he said, and retired from acting to take up directing. Still, it's impossible to read the novel now without thinking of him; he made the character his own, which is probably the greatest accolade an actor can earn.

Bullets Over Broadway

dir **Woody Allen, 1994, US, 99m**

cast **John Cusack, Jack Warden, Chazz Palminteri, Tony Sirico, Joe Viterelli, Dianne Wiest** *cin* **Carlo Di Palma**

1994 was an *annus horribilis* for Woody Allen, during which he was accused of molesting one of his adopted children, and actually started dating Mia Farrow's adopted daughter, Soon-Yi Previn. The controversy and acrimony was so bitter that it seemed as if nobody would ever want to produce or see another Woody Allen film again. Instead Woody changed producers and made a minor classic, *Bullets Over Broadway*, about actors and gangsters in 1920s New York – the last great film he has made.

"I'm an artist" are the first words of the movie. They're uttered by neurotic, hypochondriac, precocious writer David Shayne, who is played by **John Cusack**, possibly the best of all the on-screen Allen-manqué protagonists. David is prone to making great statements about the integrity of his art, but is forced to make changes when his play, *God Of Our Fathers*, is bank-rolled by a hoodlum who'll only stump up the cash if his moll, Olive, gets a big part. Played by **Jennifer Tilly**, she's a gauche, garrulous ex-dancer whose act involved picking up nickels with an unlikely part of her body. She's accompanied at all times by a minder called Cheech (**Chazz**

Palminteri) who soon gets bored watching the rehearsals every day, and begins to make suggestions. His alterations work and soon he's rewriting the play. It turns out that Cheech has a natural gift – a greater talent than the play's writer – but he's happy for David to take the credit because "where I come from, nobody squeals". But the more involved Cheech becomes, the more he realizes that Olive is "killing [his] words" and that he can't have her ruining his show. So he takes her to the docks and bumps her off. Cheech, it turns out, is really the artist who cannot compromise.

At the end of the film, David goes back home, realizing that he is not a true artist. And this echoed Woody Allen's own self-doubt at the time. When the film was released he announced that he'd given up trying to make thoughtful movies about weighty issues, and that he was going to return to what he did best – making comedies. The irony is that this light comedy is as profound in its themes – the definition of an artist and the constitution of artistic integrity – as his "serious" films.

The film wouldn't work were it not for Chazz Palminteri's performance: his role could easily have been a one-note one-joke affair, but he makes the character real and three-dimensional. He somehow manages to convey a human warmth even when describing how he stabbed someone in the back forty times with an ice-pick. Lending more screen-gangster weight was **Joe Viterelli**, as gang boss Jack Valenti. Viterelli was a businessman who got a break in films when **Sean Penn** asked him to play a gangster in *State Of Grace* in 1990. He enjoyed a career spanning fourteen years, largely playing the same thick-set, bovine hoodlum roles in films such as *Mobsters* (1991), *Analyse This* (1999) and *Mickey Blue-Eyes* (1999)until his death in 2004.

The success of *Bullets* coincided happily with Woody's public rehabilitation. Allen was forgiven by the press, the child-molestation charges were dropped, and his relationship with Soon-Yi was accepted. The film was nominated for seven Oscars, getting Dianne Wiest Best Supporting Actress. And the film is a success because it's genuinely funny – arguably the last Woody Allen to be consistently so. Working in a genre distinct from the brand of metropolitan-sophisticate comedy he had made his own paid dividends, because the dictates of the formula don't allow for ninety minutes of navel-gazing.

City Of God
(Cidade de Deus)

dir **Fernando Meirelles/Katia Lund,
2002, Braz, 135m**
cast **Matheus Nachtergaele, Seu Jorge, Alexandre
Rodrigues, Leandro Firmino da Hora, Phelipe
Haagensen** *cin* **César Charlone** *m* **Antonio Pinto**

The film that made the front pages in Brazil, *City Of God* showed
the realities of life in the *favelas* of Rio to the rest of the country,
and then the rest of the world. The nation's president, **Luiz Ignatio
Luiz de Silva**, even wrote a political article about the movie.

An adaptation of **Paulo Lin**'s novel, the movie's authenticity
stems from it being shot mainly in the "Cidade de Deus" itself,
one of the most dangerous, run-down slums in Rio. All the actors
under the age of thirty were boys from the *favelas*: two thousand
children were interviewed, two hundred were eventually chosen.
Workshops took place for six months in which scenes were shaped
and dialogue improvised before the cast was chosen and four
months of rehearsals began.

However, *City Of God* is not filmed using the traditional
methods of realism, and this is clear from the very first scene.
Symbolically, a chicken runs away from a pot in which it's about to
be cooked. Some street kids with guns chase it through the streets
until it runs into a passer-by. He's about to catch it when the cops
arrive and he suddenly finds himself caught in the middle of a
stand-off between armed police and the gun-toting street kids. The
camera spins 360 degrees around the unfortunate boy. It spins and
spins, signalling a flashback to the 1960s, when the story begins.
The boy is in the same pose but this time he's catching a football
rather than a chicken. A voice-over introduces us. This is Rocket
(**Alexandre Rodrigues**), the film's protagonist.

Through chapter titles such as "The Story Of The Tender
Trio", "The Story Of The Apartment" and "A Sucker's Life" it

Lil' Ze (Leandro Firmino) – *City Of God*'s very own Joe Pesci

tells the story of these gangsters in T-shirts, from the start of their careers as hoodlums in the 1960s, sticking-up trucks and robbing whorehouses, into the 1970s, when gun-crazy Lil' Ze and his loyal lieutenant Benny end up controlling the "City Of God" via their drug-dealing racket. They eventually go to war with a rival gang, resulting in daily battles which turn the slums from purgatory into hell. And always in the middle is keen photographer Rocket, documenting it all through his camera lens.

Director **Fernando Meirelles** deploys every camera trick he knows and uses every device in the digital-editing manual: freeze-frames, split-screen, time-lapse, slo-mo, fast-mo, dissolves, screen wipes, montage, hand-held, and Steadicam. It's all very giddiness-inducing and, held together by excellent samba music, it can sometimes come across as an advert for the gangster life-style. Especially in the quick-fire montage that adumbrates Lil' Ze's seizing control of the "City Of God": he fires his gun as if it was a toy, and we feel the same visceral pleasure that he evidently does. At moments like this there's little distance between movie audience and on-screen killer.

Meirelles has denied that he glamorized the violence of his *favela* gangsters and claimed that the difference between his film and *Goodfellas* (which would seem to be an obvious influence) is that "when you leave the theatre the last thing you want to do is to be friends with that gang. When I see *Goodfellas* it looks great to be part of the Mafia because they look so cool. I don't have the same feeling watching *City Of God*."

It is important to note that Meirelles is not the only director of the film; a co-direction credit goes to **Katia Lund**, who was report-edly unhappy that Meirelles alone received *City Of God*'s nomina-tion for the Best Director award at the Oscars. Having previously made a striking documentary about the *favelas* called *Noticias de uma guerra particular* (*News from a Private War*, 1999), she was able to introduce Fernando, a middle-class advertisement-director from São Paolo, to the boys of the "City Of God". The received wisdom is that Meirelles was responsible for the visual side of things, while Lund worked closely with the cast, developing the script with them. She was on set every day supervising the crew, and attended and contributed to the edits.

City Of God won Oscar nominations, worldwide attention, record-breaking box-office takings, and a subsequent spin-off TV series, *City Of Men*. But more importantly it got many people in Brazil talking. Meirelles took part in countless debates up and down the country and, interviewed at the time of the film's British release, he was optimistic that something would finally be done about the *favelas*: "The film really helped people think about the problem. Now it seems that our government finally realize that this is the moment to work on it. So things are changing, hopefully."

Cyclo (Xich lo)

dir Tran Anh Hung, 1995, Fr/Vietnam, 129m
cast Le Van Loc, Tran Nu Yen Khe, Nguyen Nhu Quynh,
Tony Leung, Nguyen Hoang Phuc *cin* Benoit Delhomme
m Ton That Tiet

This is what happens when two worlds collide: art cinema's take on the gangster movie. **Tran Anh Hung**'s award-winning follow-up to his equally award-winning debut *The Scent Of Green Papaya* (1993) is painterly, leisurely, anthropological, languorous and hypnotic. The film is just as interested in the life around its cyclo protagonist, in the poverty of his family and with the streets that teem with the incessant hubbub of perpetual traffic, regular accidents and minor riots, as it is in the crime story.

Le Van Loc plays a young "cyclo", who carries passengers on his pedal-cab in modern-day Ho Chi Minh City. Most of his money goes to the Boss Lady (**Nguyen Nhu Quynh**), from whom he rents his bike. When it is stolen he finds himself deep in her debt and she orders him to join The Poet (**Tony Leung**) and his gang. The Poet is also employing the cyclo's elder sister as a prostitute, albeit a prostitute whom clients are forbidden to have sex with, as the bizarrely lovelorn gangster wants to preserve her purity. One satisfied customer, for instance, pays to watch her pee. All this may make *Cyclo* seem like a cold, hard, pitiless film. Instead, it boasts a ravishing series of tableaux, with a sumptuous palette, an application of rich colours and skilful hatching of shadows across faces. Urination has never looked so beautiful.

Too beautiful, some critics have carped. Journalist Richard Gott claimed in *The Guardian* newspaper that Vietnam had been "unrecognizably transmogrified into an oriental theme-park of the imagination", complaining particularly about "the romantic decay of the back streets in aesthetic colour ... everything here is sanitized and de-odorized". There is undoubtedly a whole art gallery's worth of arrestingly extravagant images in the movie: a boy paints himself yellow; the cyclo plunges his head into a tank of goldfish and, after taking some pills, he paints his face bright blue and inserts a goldfish into his mouth. Fish are an ever-present in *Cyclo* and take on a puzzling significance. *Sight And Sound*'s Tony Rayns has advanced the credible theory that the orphaned, lonely cyclo is associated with fish because of "the silent need expressed so eloquently by a fish's jaw movements".

The young cyclo's criminal career begins fairly modestly when he lobs a Molotov cocktail at a rival cycle garage, but he descends into ferrying drugs carefully planted in carcasses from an abattoir, and is eventually trained to be a killer. The violence, when it comes, shocks and awes because the beauty of the preceding scenes has had a hypnotic hold on the viewer. The bloodletting seems to belong in a different movie, and to acknowledge this fact the music changes dramatically, recalling **Bernard Herrmann**'s scores for **Alfred Hitchcock**, or indeed for *Taxi Driver* (1976) – Scorsese's masterpiece is an acknowledged influence. This discordant, disturbing effect is at its most extreme in a particularly gruelling execution scene. A gang boss called Mr Lullabye has a victim tied to a chair. Sticky tape is wound around his arms and legs and across his face. He cannot move or speak, and can barely breathe. Mr Lullabye sings him a comforting song, before puncturing his jugular with a switch-blade. It is, of course, shot immaculately beautifully.

Force Of Evil

dir **Abraham Polonsky, 1948, US, 78m, b/w**
cast **John Garfield, Beatrice Pearson, Thomas Gomez, Howland Chamberlain, Roy Roberts** *cin* **George Barnes** *m* **David Raksin**

"What do you mean 'gangsters'? It's business!" A key line in *Force Of Evil* succinctly sums up its major theme: this was the first film to emphatically and unambiguously make the connection between crime and business, capitalism and gangsterism.

Joe Morse (**John Garfield**) is a crooked lawyer who helps run a numbers racket for the mob. This numbers game, we are informed by a voice-over, is an illegal lottery, a network of "banks" situated behind pool halls and in slum apartments and lofts, in which punters go to bet on what that day's lucky number will be. Morse has cooked up a plan to take over, or rather merge, the small banks.

As his boss Ben Tucker (**Roy Roberts**) says: a few years ago the Mob would have taken control of the banks with guns and threats, but now they're doing it through brains and business. Every 4 July, almost all the punters tend to bet on 776, because it's the "liberty number". Should it come up, all the banks will lose their money and be vulnerable to a merger. Morse is going to fix the winning number. The only problem is that his older brother Leo (**Thomas Gomez**) runs one of those banks, and it would kill him if he lost his money. Joe desperately tries to persuade Leo to close down his business before it's too late, but things get complicated when Joe falls in love with one of his brother's workers, Doris, and has to decide just whose side he's on.

None too subtly, but nevertheless effectively, *Force Of Evil* makes the point that there is little or no difference between gangsters and businessmen. Different means, but the same result. Similarly, when Leo's wife, despairing, complains that he used to run a *proper* business, he scoffs and tells her that all business is about thieving: when he ran a garage he would add "three cents on every gallon, two cents for the chauffeur and one penny for me".

The drama of the film's climax revolves around a wire-tap on a phone – something writer/director **Abraham Polonsky** knew all about. During the making of *Force Of Evil*, his own phone was being tapped by the FBI, who believed him to be an influential member of the **Communist Party**. Polonsky was one of the Hollywood Ten who refused to testify to HUAC (see p.216), and who was blacklisted after *Force Of Evil* was released. He didn't direct another film for twenty years, eventually returning with *Tell Them Willie Boy Is Here* (1969). Consequently, *Force Of Evil* has become legendary, lauded by critic Andrew Sarris as "one of the great films of modern American cinema". It's not *that* good – it's too didactic and doesn't have the narrative complexities of the very best *noir* – and it's hard not to suspect critics are overcompensating Polonsky for the injustices he suffered. For, although he continued to turn out screenplays under a pseudonym, or used a non–blacklisted writer as a front, such as John O. Killens for the heist movie *Odds Against Tomorrow* (1959), Polonsky was robbed of a career, and American cinema was robbed of a forensic intelligence.

The Getaway

dir **Sam Peckinpah, 1972, US, 122m**
cast **Steve McQueen, Ali MacGraw, Ben Johnson, Sally
Struthers, Al Lettieri** *cin* **Lucien Ballard** *m* **Quincy Jones**

Ali MacGraw and Steve McQueen making their getaway

When critics talk about director Sam
Peckinpah they usually mention *The Wild
Bunch* (1969) or *Straw Dogs* (1971), or even
Bring Me The Head Of Alfredo Garcia (1974).
The Getaway hardly ever gets a look-in.
Which is odd − it has a script by Walter
"*48 Hours*" Hill based on a **Jim Thompson**
novel, and it stars **Steve McQueen**. But
even Peckinpah didn't like it when he first
saw it. McQueen had the final say on the
cut and when the director saw the results,
he stood up and pissed on the screen,
shouting "This is not my film!"

McQueen plays Doc McCoy, a bank
robber who's halfway through a ten-year
stretch when he is paroled by a corrupt
prison official and Mob boss Beynon
(**Ben Johnson**), after McCoy's sultry wife
Carol (**Ali MacGraw**) pays him a "special
visit". Johnson wants the couple to do one
last heist − a small-town bank − but they
have to do it with two of his men, Rudy
(**Al Lettieri**) and Frank (**Bo Hopkins**).
Inevitably, it goes wrong. Frank gets trig-
ger-happy and kills a guard; he in turn is
killed by Rudy. At a disused farmhouse
Rudy tries to double-cross McCoy, but
Doc is quicker on the draw and leaves
Rudy for dead. Rudy survives, however, and enlisting, at gun point, the help
of a timid veterinarian and his all-too

accommodating wife, Rudy follows them across country to El Paso. Meanwhile Doc and Carol get into some trouble of their own when delivering the loot to Beynon. McCoy discovers exactly what Carol had to do with Beynon to get him out of jail. When *she* kills Beynon they now have the Mob, the police and Rudy on their trail.

Jim Thompson was originally hired to adapt his own novel for the movie. Thompson wrote a screenplay that was very close to his novel, and kept the extraordinary, surrealistic ending where the couple end up in the magical kingdom of El Rey, a hell run by gangsters where, it's suggested, people eat each other. Steve McQueen thought the script was too dark and had Thompson replaced by the up-and-coming screenwriter Walter Hill, who had the thieves get away scot-free. (Screenings in Spain had an additional sequence tacked on in which McCoy is captured and returned to prison, because Franco declared that it was bad for the "moral health of the people" to show that criminals can escape from paying their debt to society.)

As well as Peckinpah's trademark slow-motion gun fights, *The Getaway* has many memorable set pieces: McQueen and MacGraw hiding in a garbage truck which is getting dangerously fuller by the minute and being tipped out with all the rubbish into a dump; Rudy taking a leak next to the hanging body of the vet, who has committed suicide after being continually tormented and cuckolded; the poetically destructive climactic shoot-out in the El Paso hotel; and a long Hitchcockian scene on a train in which McCoy has to track down a con man who has stolen the couple's swag-bag. There are also some very tender moments between the two leads – like Bogart and Bacall in *To Have And Have Not* (1944), the pair fell in love on set – in which they have to become reacquainted, rekindle their intimacy, and learn how to trust each other again. The first shot of this tough, amoral film is a freeze-frame of a cute deer, which is somehow bizarrely appropriate.

Get Carter

dir **Mike Hodges, 1971, UK, 112m**
cast **Michael Caine, Britt Ekland, John Osborne, Ian Hendry, Bryan Mosley** *cin* **Wolfgang Suschitzky** *m* **Roy Budd**

Dismissed at the time, compared to "a bottle of neat gin swallowed before breakfast", *Get Carter* is now regarded as the greatest British gangster movie ever made. And quite rightly so. As **Michael Caine** has said, British movie gangsters before Jack Carter were mainly stupid, silly or funny. And Caine knew what real gangsters were like. Brought up in the Elephant and Castle area of South London, he based Carter on the characters he grew up with. With his cufflinks, his nose drops, and his sharp blue suit, Caine's Carter echoes both the classic dapper gangster of 1930s movies and the 1960s Savile Row cool of the **Kray Twins**.

Jack Carter is a London gangster who travels to Newcastle to avenge the murder of his brother, after the police have shown no interest in the case. His investigations lead him to the lair of crime lord Cyril Kinnear (played by the playwright and ex- "angry young man" **John Osborne**) and to crooked businessman Cliff Brumby (*Coronation Street*'s Alf Roberts, aka **Bryan Mosly**), a "big man" in "bad shape". Everywhere that Carter goes he leaves a trail of destruction and broken bones, until he eventually stumbles upon the truth: his brother was murdered when he discovered that his daughter had been coerced into making a blue movie for Kinnear's porn empire. Armed with that knowledge, Jack destroys everybody who had any part in it.

It took over twenty years for *Get Carter* to be properly appreciated. But the real tragedy of the film has been its unwitting and unlooked-for influence on British film and culture. In the 1990s, thanks largely to the success of **Guy Ritchie**'s homage (of sorts), *Lock Stock And Two Smoking Barrels* (1998), *Get Carter* produced several Britflick bastard children: *Shooters* (2000), *Snatch* (2000), *Sexy Beast* (2000), and *Essex Boys* (1999). It was also remade in America, with **Sylvester Stallone**, of all people, reprising Caine's role. All the

The Carter car park

The car park where Jack Carter memorably throws Brumby off a parapet was never actually used as a car park because of health and safety regulations. It's regarded as an eyesore in Gateshead, but every attempt to knock it down has been resisted by The Twentieth Century Society and by *Get Carter* fans – although not all are happy with it. One appreciation society has organized pilgrimages to it, while another group agrees with many locals that it's a big car park, but it's in bad shape, and it has to go.

recent copycats took the style and swagger of Caine's character, but missed the pathos and morality. Carter was amoral; *Get Carter* wasn't. Many people – fans and critics alike – have mistaken the character for the film: with his long lens and documentary approach, writer/director Mike Hodges is clearly *observing* his protagonist. Sure, he's not judging him but he's no cheerleader either. *Get Carter* is a subtle indictment of municipal corruption and misogynistic machismo. Which made it all the more ironic that Jack Carter became the poster boy for *Loaded* magazine's generation: the lads' mag even had a *Get Carter* cartoon amongst its galleries of tits and bums – spectacularly missing the fact that the film was an attack on the corrosive nature of pornography.

Get Carter succeeds because it's one of those rare films where every element works, and works to serve the whole. The script, the performances and the locations are all tied up by **Roy Budd**'s score – a simple, evocative, memorable refrain – and refracted through cinematographer **Wolfgang Suschitzky**'s lens. Hodges worked on ITV's award-winning documentary series *World In Action* before making *Carter* (his debut feature film), and it shows. It feels like a documentary, but is framed like a movie: every millimetre of film is perfectly composed. If only all British films could be like this.

The film's producer, **Michael Klinger**, went on to form a production company, The Three Michaels, with Caine and Hodges. Their next film, *Pulp*, was a self-indulgent comedy, and Hodges' promise materialized only sporadically throughout his career. This is the man who made *Croupier*, *Flash Gordon* and *Morons From Outer Space*. He never lived up to the impeccably high standard he set with his debut. Then again, neither have most other British films.

It's well worth picking up *Carter* on DVD, as it has one of the few multi-track audio commentaries that actually works, courtesy of Caine, Hodges and Suschitzky. Though they were not recorded at the same time, at least they're watching the film, and the audio track cuts between them like a radio documentary. (Often multi-track commentaries are off-cuts from a "featurette" and bear no relation to what's on the screen.) Caine talks about the Jack Carters he knew, his childhood in the Elephant and Castle, and how nobody messed with his family. Hodges points out the film's often quite literal symbolism ("it's curtains for Caine"), insider secrets (Carter's killer is sitting with him in the train carriage in the very first scene) and alludes to the genuine animosity between Caine and actor Ian Hendry.

Gloria

dir John Cassavetes, 1980, US, 121m
cast Gena Rowlands, John Adames, Buck Henry, Julie
Carmen, Lupe Guarnica *cin* Fred Schuler *m* Bill Conti

Gena Rowlands shows why this is no "cute kid" movie

Director John Cassavetes' most commercial film was possibly his best work. And that's largely due to the performance of his wife, **Gena Rowlands**, in the title role as the hard-bitten ex-lover of a Mob boss – a performance that vies with Gloria Grahame's in *The Big Heat* (1953) for the position of the greatest gangster's moll in cinema history.

It's a simple enough story: ex-gangster's moll Gloria is asked by her neighbour to look after her six-year-old boy, Phil (**John Adames**), because she fears that something might happen to the family. The response is typical Gloria – "I hate kids. Especially yours." But when the boy's parents are executed by the Mob, Gloria takes the boy under her wing, against her better judgement. We learn that his father was the mob's accountant, and that he kept a book of all the deals and the people involved. His son now has the book, and the Mafia want both him and the evidence. Rather than go to the police, they zigzag across New York, seeking sanctuary in slophouses and late-night bars that are the very definition of the word seedy, looking for a place where the gangsters can't find them, that doesn't have Mob connections. Which is difficult, as the Mafia seem to be everywhere. It all comes to a dramatic, violent head when Gloria has a summit meeting with her former lover Tony Tanzini and tries to barter the book for their freedom.

John Cassavetes has been dubbed the "patron saint of American independent cinema" by expert Ray Carney, because his films were self-financed and therefore free from studio control, which was revolutionary at the time of the 1950s and 1960s. With films like his ground-breaking debut *Shadows* (1959) and *Faces* (1968), Cassavetes often eschewed script for improvisation and plot for characterization in order to make films seem less like films and more like real-life.

But *Gloria* is different. It's a studio film, made for Columbia and as such was Cassavetes' least favourite, though this was not

The Cassavetes technique

According to Ray Carney in his book *Cassavetes On Cassavetes*, the director's penchant for naturalism came to the fore in *Gloria* when he "rounded up actual gangsters and various street people for the scene in Tony Tanzini's apartment. Cassavetes solicited their opinion about whether this was the way things would really happen. The man Gloria shoots on her way to the elevator, for example, was an actual professional hit man with fifteen years' experience."

true of the critics, many of whom argued that working within the confines of a genre instilled some much needed narrative discipline in a director prone to self-indulgence. In fact, he only wrote the script in an attempt to rake in some cash, as his last two films had been commercial failures and he was virtually broke. However, the studio bought the screenplay on one condition – that he would direct it. The film benefits from Cassavetes' presence behind the camera: his gritty *cinéma verité* style precludes any cheesiness, which is always a dangerous possibility when a film centres around a six-year-old kid.

But above all, what Cassavetes' documentary approach allowed was freedom of expression for actors, and no one benefited from that more than his wife, Gena Rowlands.

Gena starred in most of her husband's films, famously giving a raw, gutsy performance in the shout-fest *A Woman Under The Influence* (1974) as an alcoholic undergoing the breakdown of both her sanity and her marriage. If that was Rowlands' best performance, then *Gloria* comes a close second. There is an extraordinary scene in which her old friends catch up with her and ask her to hand over the boy. With an alacrity that stuns both the audience and her victims, she whips out a gun and fires with an intuitive accuracy, almost as if it's a behavourial reflex. We realize that Gloria is a woman who likes to shoot first and answer questions later. The intention according to Cassavetes was to show that "there's still something deep in them [women] that relates to children and this separates them from men in a good way. This inner understanding of kids is something very deep and instinctive … Gloria doesn't know why she's doing any of these things." Mercifully, there's no big scene so typical of Hollywood soft-corn in which characters open their hearts to each other and learn life lessons; no getting-to-know-all-about-you montage. It's one of those rare instances in Hollywood history – *The Godfather* being another good example – where we see a character genuinely, hesitatingly transform before our eyes.

And part of the reason that she's so believable, according to Ray Carney, is that Rowlands never came out of character between takes, believing it would only confuse John Adames and possibly ruin their scenes together. *Gloria* would never have been a success without Gena Rowlands, as Sharon Stone demonstrated when she took on the role in 1999's fatuous remake.

The Godfather

dir **Francis Ford Coppola, 1971, US, 175m**
cast **Marlon Brando, Al Pacino, James Caan, Richard Castellano, Robert Duvall, Sterling Hayden, Diane Keaton, John Cazale** *cin* **Tonino Delli Colli** *m* **Nino Rota**

The contenders for "Greatest Gangster Movie Ever Made" are usually *The Godfather* and its first sequel. *The Godfather* changed the genre forever and became the yardstick by which all gangster movies are now judged. Though it seems surprising now, Francis Ford Coppola was in fact a long way down the list of directors that Paramount Studios approached to make the film: although Coppola's independent movie *Rain People* (1969) had been a success, Coppola had just made the disastrous musical *Finian's Rainbow* (1968) with a very old **Fred Astaire**. And even when Coppola was eventually hired, the studio considered sacking him after a few weeks and replacing him with the editor **Aram Avakian** when Avakian claimed that many of the shots the director had filmed would not cut together. Producer Robert Evans was also dismayed at **Marlon Brando**'s now-famous mumbling and wondered aloud if the film would need subtitles.

But that wasn't the studio's only problem. Both the Italian-American Civil Rights League and the Mafia were upset that a film was being made of Mario Puzo's novel. According to Peter Cowie's *The Godfather Book*, the League sent a letter to Paramount claiming that the book "unfairly stigmatizes all Americans of Italian descent" by linking them to organized crime. In 1970 the League organized a rally in Madison Square Gardens headed by **Frank Sinatra**, in which $600,000 was raised to help the campaign halt the production. The Mafia, for their part, sent death-threats to producer Al Ruddy. A compromise was eventually settled upon with the League, by which it was agreed that the words "Mafia" or "Cosa Nostra" would never appear in the film, replaced instead by the euphemism "the Five Families".

In one of the more compelling DVD audio commentaries, Coppola reveals the suitably Mafiosiacal battles for power and position behind the scenes and his own Michael-style victory

The Godfathers that could have been...

Before Coppola was asked to direct the movie, Paramount approached Peter Yates (*Bullitt*), Arthur Penn (*Bonnie And Clyde*), Sidney J. Furie (*The Ipcress File*), Otto Preminger (*The Man With The Golden Arm*), Elia Kazan (*On The Waterfront*), Fred Zinnemann (*High Noon*), Franklin J. Schaffner (*Patton*), Larry Peerce (*Goodbye Columbus*) and, most unlikely of all, British director Lewis Gilbert – the director of *Alfie* and Bond movie *You Only Live Twice* – who even signed a contract to direct, but backed out when he saw how low the budget was.

over colleagues who had betrayed him. Thirty years later he still remembers the exact day (and the scene he was shooting) when he thought he was going to be fired.

It's impossible now to conceive of *The Godfather* having been directed by anyone but Coppola. His stamp is on the movie from its very first scene. The opening, at a wedding, introduces us to the main characters: to Michael (**Al Pacino**) and Kay (**Diane Keaton**), who both want nothing to do with the family business; to the hot-head Sonny (**James Caan**), who wants to hump bridesmaids and take on the FBI; to Michael and Sonny's dumb brother Fredo (**John Cazale**); to the patient, sharp lawyer Tom Hagan (**Robert Duvall**); and to Don Corleone himself (Brando), operating in the shadows and pulling the strings. The scene sets the tone of what's to come – the magisterial sweep, the stately pace, the themes of family and business – but also on display are the finely captured minutiae of all the rites and rituals, such as the bride gathering up the long trail of her dress to receive gifts from the guests.

The film is peppered with acute details from Coppola's own memories of life in an Italian-American family – physical gestures and family recipes – as well as actually featuring members of his own family: his father wrote the incidental music; his sister plays the bride; his daughter, Sofia, is the baby being christened in the film's famously bloody climax (in which all of Michael's enemies are ruthlessly wiped out whilst he is at the ceremony). As Coppola has said, it's a film about a family made by a family. As such, it's hardly surprising that he cut out much of the novel's story (including a sub-plot about a young girl with unfeasibly large genitals) and concentrated on the family aspects. It's almost cinema as anthropology.

Coppola's problems didn't end with the filming. He had hundreds of hours to edit, and when he finally cut it down to a manageable 126 minutes, he was told by producer Bob Evans that the film was too short – "you shot a saga and turned in a trailer". And it was the only time Coppola got it wrong – he duly went back to the editing suite and restored whole scenes and chunks of dialogue to beef it up to 175 minutes – in everything else he was proved correct. The film became the most commercially successful movie of all time, as well as winning Oscars for Best Screenplay and Best Film.

But is it better than *Godfather Part II*? The first film certainly contains the most famous lines – "make him an offer he can't refuse" and "Luca Brasi sleeps with the fishes". It also has the most memorable scenes – the horse's head in the bed, and the bullet-riddled assassination of Sonny at a tollbooth. Not forgetting Brando's iconic, much-imitated, Kleenex-in-the-cheeks performance, as well as **Nino Rota**'s haunting score (which the studio also disliked). And *Part II* doesn't have a scene comparable to the first film's last shot: the door closing on Kay and her relationship with her husband Michael, which crystallizes Pacino's transformation from idealistic young man to hard-hearted, hollowed-out Mafia boss, a modern-day Mephistopheles. It's one of the most bone-chilling moments in cinema history.

Vito Corleone (Marlon Brando) commands respect in Coppola's masterpiece

The Godfather Part II

dir Francis Ford Coppola, 1974, US, 200m
cast Al Pacino, Robert Duvall, Diane Keaton, Robert De Niro, John Cazale, Talia Shire *cin* Gordon Willis *m* Nino Rota, Carmine Coppola

Often cited as one of the few – and sometimes even as the only – example of a sequel being better than the original. This film has one crucial thing that the first one doesn't: **Robert De Niro**. Neither was it plagued by any interference from the film studios or the Mafia. Coppola was allowed to use the words "Mafia" and "Cosa Nostra" and had complete control over the script, the shooting and the editing. This freedom allowed him to play with a more complex narrative, cross-cutting between time zones and between two parallel lives. As Coppola has said, it's about "two generations, two men at the same point in their life – they both have young children, and they are learning to deal with power". There's the young Vito Corleone (**De Niro**) in 1917, a Sicilian immigrant who is ruthlessly building up his criminal empire; and Michael Corleone in the 1950s trying to consolidate that empire in the face of Senate hearings into Mob activities and the revolution in Cuba, which destroys the Mafia haven of casinos and drinking dens. Michael wins the battle, but loses everything else. He kills all those who conspire against him, such as fellow crook and longtime family associate Hyman Roth (**Lee Strasberg**), and those who could testify against him, such as Frankie Pentangeli (**Michael V. Gazzo**), an old-time gangster who used to work for Michael's father. But his mother dies, Kay and his children leave him, his brother Fredo betrays him, and Michael consequently orders his execution.

Part II definitely has the edge over its predecessor in the sense that it has two of the greatest actors of their generation in one film (but not in the same scene – we had to wait until **Michael**

Like father, like son: Michael Corleone (Al Pacino) in the seat of power in *The Godfather Part II*

The Godfather Part III
dir Francis Ford Coppola, 1990, US, 162m

A sequel too far – if any film didn't need another instalment it was *Godfather Part II*, which rounded off the saga perfectly. Francis Ford Coppola has practically admitted that he did it for the money and, although critics didn't like the overall movie much, they threw most of their vitriol at Coppola's daughter, Sofia. A late replacement for Winona Ryder, her performance – particularly in the pasta-making/lovemaking scene with **Andy Garcia** – had the critics reaching for their revolvers. But Sofia wasn't all that bad. The problem lay mostly with Garcia. Brought in as a De Niro type, he has neither the charisma nor the energy to pull off the part of the mad, bad and dangerous-to-know nephew.

The only critic who preferred *Part III* to *Part II* was the late **Alexander Walker**, who regarded it as a searing indictment of the Vatican's connections to the Mafia. It's true that *Part III* based its events on the headlines (the mysterious deaths of "God's Banker" Roberto Calvi and **Pope John Paul I**), but as part of *The Godfather* saga it simply doesn't work. And the last scene, showing Michael Corleone's rather anti-climactic death from a heart attack, ends the trilogy not with a bang but a whimper.

Mann's *Heat* in 1995 to finally see De Niro and Pacino on screen together). It won more Oscars – as well as Best Film, Coppola was given Best Director and his father shared Best Score. The most deserved Oscar – for Best Art Direction – went to **Dean Tavoularis**, the production designer, and a vital contributor to the *Godfather* trilogy. It's his eye for detail and period pieces that fully realized Coppola's vision on screen. Another unsung *Godfather* hero, cinematographer Gordon Willis, was nicknamed "Prince Of Darkness" due to his fondness for placing characters in inky black shadows, though even he admitted that he went too far in a couple of scenes in which Michael is almost completely enveloped in gloom.

The first film changed the genre forever, and *Godfather Part II* also made cinema history, albeit in a more prosaic way. It was the first movie sequel to be titled as such – christened simply by the addition of a II – thus starting a trend that has led to *Halloween VII* and *Friday The Thirteenth Part X*. Perhaps this hasn't been the film's greatest legacy.

Goodfellas

dir **Martin Scorsese, 1990, US, 145m**
cast **Robert De Niro, Ray Liotta, Joe Pesci, Lorraine Bracco, Paul Sorvino** *cin* **Michael Balhaus**

Three men are driving in a car. They hear a knocking sound coming from the trunk. They pull over, open the boot, the tail-lights bathe them in a hellish red, and we see the bloody body of a man, still breathing, looking up at them. One of the men takes a kitchen knife and stabs him repeatedly. When he is finished another man fires a few bullets into the trunk for good measure. Freeze-frame. A voice says: "As far back as I can remember, I always wanted to be a gangster."

Goodfellas on DVD

The *Goodfellas* DVD has a veritable Italian-American feast of tasty extras. The cast and crew commentary has ten speakers, including Scorsese, his editor Thelma Schoonmaker, and stars such as Ray Liotta and Lorraine Bracco. Their comments are cleverly cut together to form an almost seamless whole. Sometimes they don't refer to what's on screen, other times there's an analysis of a scene (such as Pesci's terrifying "what's funny about me ?" monologue). Author/co-writer **Nicholas Pileggi** provides an instructive history lesson and explains the derivation of the term "wop".

The so-called "cop and crook" commentary features an amiable conversation between **Henry Hill** himself and the FBI agent who prosecuted him, Edward McDonald. They reveal the truth behind the "true story" of *Goodfellas*. For instance, Joe Pesci's character Tommy was actually 6'2', built like a prizefighter and very handsome. What's most chilling is the mundane nature of their good-humoured chat about psychopaths, beatings and murders.

There are also two superficial documentaries, half with recent interviews, half from the archive, which discuss the making of the film and the life of a wiseguy. Another featurette has directors **Richard Linklater**, the Hughes Brothers, Frank Darabont, Antoine Fuqua, Jon Favreau and Joe Carnahan breathlessly enthusing about *Goodfellas'* influence on them.

Pasta *alla Mafiosi*

Goodfellas is one of the few gangster movies to supply handy tips and recipes which you can try at home. In prison, the convicts make pasta sauce, and we see Paulie cutting up a clove of garlic with a razor blade, apparently to make the garlic so thin that it would "liquefy in the pan". *Goodfellas* also teaches us to watch how many onions you put in the tomato sauce. Scorsese had previously given us his mother's recipe for meatballs over the credits of his quickie documentary *Italianamerican* (1974).

Another film that has its culinary uses is *The Godfather*, in which Luca Brasi tells Michael Corleone the perfect recipe for pasta sauce with sausages: "you start out with a little oil, you fry some garlic, then you throw in some tomatoes, some tomato paste, you fry it, you make sure it doesn't stick, you get it to a boil and you shove in all your sausage and your meatballs, add a little bit of wine and a little bit of sugar and that's my trick." In his initial script Coppola wrote "you brown some garlic". **Mario Puzo** read it and immediately corrected the director, informing him that "gangsters don't brown, they *fry*".

Coppola has said that he would like to include a recipe in every one of his films, because even if the movie is no good at least the audience will get something out of it.

This is the voice of Henry Hill (**Ray Liotta**) and this scene both begins the movie and recurs in the middle. Director Martin Scorsese described his method thus: "You take the tradition of the American gangster film and deal with it episode by episode, but you start in the middle and move backwards and [then] forwards."

After this opening we flashback to the beginning of a traditional rise-and-fall narrative. A young Henry follows his childhood dream of becoming a "wiseguy" (Mafia slang for gangster). He comes under the tutelage of the neighbourhood Mafia boss Paulie (**Paul Sorvino**) and at age 13 makes enough money to buy a suit, tie and a pair of shiny shoes – he's made it. We follow Henry as he goes to work for Paulie's hit man, a local legend named Jimmy Conway (**Robert De Niro**). We watch Henry serve his brief first jail sentence, marry a local Jewish girl called Karen (**Lorraine Bracco**), and fall back in with Jimmy and the violent Tommy De Vito (**Joe Pesci**).

They make their money mostly by hijacking trucks and selling their contents on the black market, but when one job goes wrong, they end up in jail. It's the beginning of the end for Henry. Against Paulie's advice he starts dealing drugs and, inevitably, taking them. This is after all the classic downfall of the modern gangster – getting high on your own supply. On his return to the outside world, success goes to his head. He takes a mistress and even more drugs and – together with Conway – pulls off the biggest heist in US history. But one by one the members of the gang end up in the morgue. Tommy is killed by the Mob in a revenge shooting and, when the Feds arrest Henry for possession and supply, he knows that he will be next. So he testifies against Paulie and Jimmy in exchange for a new identity on the Witness Protection Program, to "live the rest of his life like a schnook".

Goodfellas has many parallels with *Mean Streets* (1973), not least the fact that we follow events from the perspective of the calmest, most rational character in the whole film. Or, as some critics have claimed, the most boring. Certainly the movie becomes dangerously exciting every time Joe Pesci appears – he is to *Goodfellas* what De Niro was to *Mean Streets*. This is certainly the case in the famous "How am I funny?" scene, in which Henry makes the mistake of calling Tommy a funny guy. Pesci refuses to let it lie, taking offence, repeatedly demanding to know in what way he is funny, and becoming more and more heated. Both Hill and the audience recoil, sensing that he could explode spectacularly at any moment. The reason that the scene works so well is the same reason that similar scenes in *Mean Streets* do: it was a result of improvisation.

Goodfellas has many lovely, mordant touches, such as the three gangsters' drawn-out disposal of Frank Batts' body: stopping off at Tommy's mother's house to get a shovel, and being waylaid by Mrs De Vito and henpecked into eating a massive meal (before borrowing her kitchen knife, which will prove handier than they realize). But even though *Goodfellas* is semi-biographical (based on Nicholas Pileggi's book *Wise Guy: Life In A Mafia Family*), it is of course not *autobiographical*. Scorsese does not invest it with direct moments from his own life: Henry Hill is not Italian-American and there is more of a distance between protagonist and director than in his earlier gangster movie.

However, Scorsese fills that distance with some dizzying, dazzling formal innovations. He moves the narrative through time and space, compacting years into seconds and stopping the action to comment on it, with bravura cinematic displays such as the one-shot scene as the camera glides elegantly through a club, tracking Henry and Karen's VIP entry. Whether you prefer this to *Mean Streets* depends on how you like your movies: pyrotechnical or personal.

Three *Goodfellas*, hard at work: (left–right) Joe Pesci, Ray Liotta and Robert De Niro

Gun Crazy

dir **Joseph H Lewis, 1949, US, 87m, b/w**
cast **Peggy Cummins, John Dall, Berry Kroeger, Morris Karnovsky, Annabel Shaw** *cin* **Russell Harlan** *m* **Victor Young**

From the very first shot we know we're in *noir* country. It's raining hard. In the distance, a neon hotel sign flickers. Shadows fall across the screen. Into the frame walks a young boy. He looks lovingly and longingly into a shop window. It's full of guns. He smashes the glass and grabs one but falls over as he hoofs it, directly into the path of a police officer. Cut to a courtroom. His sister Ruby is pleading with the judge. Apparently Bart isn't a bad boy, he just loves guns. He loves to shoot, not to kill. The judge is sympathetic but sends him to reform school.

Years later, after a stint in the army, Bart (**John Dall**) returns home, older and wiser but with his obsession for firearms intact. At a carnival he meets a feisty, flirty sharpshooter named Annie (**Peggy Cummins**), someone who's just as "gun crazy" as him. As he remarks, they "go together like guns and ammunition go together" (did we mention he's rather fond of guns?). He joins the circus to be with her, but her boss, an ex-lover, becomes jealous and, like the weapons the pair fetishize, they are both fired. So they head out onto the highway, get hitched, and start sticking up banks and stores to pay their way. Annie, the crazier of the pair, is always pushing Bart further, hoping that they'll actually be able to use their guns and kill somebody.

Made as another B-movie cheapie, it was championed by critics and filmmakers of the 1960s. Its greatest influence was upon **Jean-Luc Godard**, manifest in *A bout de souffle* (1959), and probably because of one shot – one *very long* shot. In amongst the familiar device of a montage of stick-ups and bank heists is a remarkable instance of a quasi-*cinéma verité* style. The camera is positioned on the back seat of a car. We have a view of the back of Dall and Cummins' heads as they are driving through a town, which they are doing for real (no back projection). At one point he tells her to

Lewis' other gangster masterpiece

In Joseph H. Lewis' second classic, *The Big Combo* (1955), policeman Leonard Diamond (Cornel Wilde) spends his own money trailing creepy, venal crime boss Mr Brown (Richard Conte). But Diamond's interest is not strictly professional. He's obsessed by Brown's trophy girlfriend, Susan Lowell (Jean Wallace). As the gangster says, "the only problem with you is that you want to be me", and it's clear that they are two sides of the same sick coin.

Like *Gun Crazy*, *The Big Combo* has some brilliantly imaginative touches. Just before a rival gangster is to be executed, Brown takes away his hearing aid. Suddenly the soundtrack stops, we hear nothing, and all we see is the flash of machine-gun fire coming straight at us. It only lasts a few seconds, but it's difficult not to think of Godard's similar tricks with sound a few years later in *A bout de souffle* and *Pierrot le fou*.

Combo belongs as much to John Alton, the movie's cinematographer, and one of the people most responsible for creating the shadows and fog of *noir*. Alton wrote the textbook on the subject, *Painting With Light*, and was the cinematographer on many B-movie classics such as *He Walked By Night* (1949). He also famously worked with director Anthony Mann on *Raw Deal* (1948) and *T-Men* (1947). All bear Alton's imprimatur of faces veiled by shadows, scenes lit by one source (often an overhead desk lamp), figures emerging from an inky blackness, and long shots that look like Edward Hopper paintings come to life.

There are few shades of grey in Alton's films; they are mostly black and white. *The Big Combo* has all of this and its last shot has become iconic in its genre. A third of the screen is blocked out by the doors of an airport hangar. Outside everything is shrouded in fog, and nothing is visible. There's only one light, a revolving searchlight. In the middle of the frame are two silhouettes, the walking shadows of Leonard and Susan. It's a moment of pure abstraction.

watch out for a rock in the road and worries about finding a parking space. He really meant it, according to director Lewis, who later explained "they didn't know where to park. I wanted it to be that realistic. It so happens a car pulled out as they drove up. Otherwise she was going to double park."

The camera holds still as Dall gets out of the car, walks past some unsuspecting bystanders, and enters a bank; it only moves when she gets out to talk to a policeman, before returning to its original position as Dall gets back in with the loot. The shot is held as they make their getaway. Altogether it lasts three minutes, twenty seconds. In 1949 it was unheard of in Hollywood cinema for one shot to last so long, for dialogue to be improvised so freely, and for reality to intrude into a genre movie.

The pioneer responsible was director **Joseph H. Lewis**. The fact that he could do this sort of thing on the one hand and so many unremarkable films on the other is a testimony to the strengths and weaknesses of Hollywood's studio system. He was free to experiment in cheap movies but had to churn them out, and he never had, as David Thomson says, "the chance to find out if he was an artist".

Cinematic innovations aside, *Gun Crazy* is well worth tracking down simply to marvel at the performance of Welsh actress Peggy Cummins. She's one of the best bad girls of US *noir*. Not "the type that makes a happy home", she is by turn coquettish, romantic, vampish, full of pouting attitude, demonically-possessed, filled with blood lust, and girlish: never the same woman twice.

Heat

dir Michael Mann, 1995, US, 103m
cast Robert De Niro, Al Pacino, Val Kilmer, Jon Voight, Amy Brenneman *cin* Dante Spinotti *m* Elliot Goldenthal

The moment we'd all been waiting for: Al Pacino and Robert De Niro together on screen. After first appearing in the same film in *Godfather II*, they finally share a scene – three in fact – 21 years later. But in one of the most frustrating directorial decisions of recent years, we don't actually see both of their faces on screen at the same time, which has led many to openly wonder whether they're really in the same scene at all.

The two godfathers of screen acting play mirror images of each other, two men so dedicated to their jobs that they can't form lasting relationships. De Niro plays Neil McCauley, a professional armed robber whose mantra is to "have nothing in your life that you can't walk out of in thirty seconds flat if the heat is around the corner". Pacino plays obsessive cop Vince Hanna whose maxim is "all I am is what I'm going after". He's already been through two failed marriages and his third one to Justine (**Diane Venora**) doesn't look too steady.

Neil and Vince's paths cross when McCauley and his crew (**Tom Sizemore** and **Val Kilmer**) hold up a security van containing millions of dollars' worth of bonds. One of the gang, a psychopath named Waingro (**Kevin Gage**) kills two of the guards. McCauley executes a third because he doesn't want to leave a witness. Despite the senseless waste of human life Hanna seems to be impressed by the man who planned the job, and starts to track him

The two most charismatic screen actors of the late twentieth century square off in an oft-debated scene in *Heat* (1995)

down, with the nickname "Slick" being his only clue. Thanks to an informant, Hanna and his men are soon onto McCauley, but the tables are quickly turned, and, in keeping with the movie's theme of mirror images, the surveillants become the surveilled.

Realizing that Neil now probably knows as much about him as he knows about Neil, and that he hasn't got enough evidence to arrest him, Vince invites him for coffee in *that* scene. The cop and the robber discuss their personal lives, displaying a mutual respect but conclude that they will have to take each other down if it comes to it. Michael Mann shoots the entire scene without De Niro and Pacino – two of the most powerful and charismatic actors in cinema history – ever properly engaging with each other. Instead, when one talks we see the back of the other's head. It's like watching two monologues cut together.

Mann used three cameras to shoot the scene simultaneously, but only used footage from two of them, leaving out the master shots of the talking heads together in the same frame. No one has given a totally satisfactory explanation as to why Mann decided on this perverse course of action, although Nick James, in his *BFI Modern Classics* book on the movie, argues that it makes the two characters seem as if each one is looking at his reflection. In his review for *The Guardian*, Jonathan Romney offered another theory, that "Mann's ploy is to capture the dynamic of the meeting yet stress their separateness."

Of course the film reignited the old debate: who is the greatest, Pacino or De Niro? Neither is in his prime here, their best years behind them. The Pacino we see here is the Mach II version, having gone over-the-top in *Scarface* (1983) and never come back down again. Pacino briefly quit screen acting after the disaster of *Revolution* (1985) and, when he returned, he seemed to have a different voice – much deeper and much, much louder. In *Heat*, he doesn't do the full "Hoo-hah!" routine that plagued *Scent Of A Woman* (1992), but he does break into song, get a few regulation shouting scenes (this surely must be in his contract by now) and bulge his eyes a lot. And, for the most part, De Niro does his "regular Joe" act (albeit a slick, high-rolling master criminal of a regular Joe): the quiet De Niro performances typified by *Night And the City* (1992), *Flawless* (1999) or *Men Of Honor* (2000), which, in their most subdued moments, dissolve into a screen absence. But, of course, this is only judging the greatest screen actors of their generation by their own uniquely high standards.

Iconic stars aside, this is very much a Michael Mann movie: scenes bathed in shades of blue, the glass-fronted house by the ocean (à la *Manhunter*), and occasionally portentous dialogue (Diane Venora's complaint to Pacino, for example: "You don't live with me, you live with dead people! You sift through the detritus!"). But, above all, the Mannliness of *Heat* lies in its obsession with design. Mann was after all the creator of the Armani-clad designer cop TV show *Miami Vice*, and his adherence to matters of style in *Heat* extended to Robert De Niro's haircut, the minimalist interior decor and even the coat hangers. According to actress **Ashley Judd**, who played Val Kilmer's wife, "he brought specially designed hangers into the hotel room for the scene between me and Mr De Niro". As she told the *New York Times* in 1995, "he wanted the hangers to have this certain look – a sort of wire-brushed, stainless steel sheen – and he wanted them to make a certain noise when Mr De Niro knocked them out of the way". It's this meticulous attention to detail and control freakery of Kubrickian proportions that distinguishes the director's work. Almost everything, whether it's the fabric of the characters' clothes or the houses they inhabit, has to conform to the Mann total design concept.

Mann is, however, at his most impressive in his direction of *Heat*'s second robbery – a bank heist that results in urban warfare on the streets of Los Angeles. He brought in ex-members of the SAS to help stage it (including author Andy McNabb, it's said), and it took all of twelve days to film, with hours devoted to getting the sounds exactly right, of bullets ricocheting in "a concrete canyon" as Mann put it. In fact the heist was so impressive that it has been copied twice by real gangsters. The first was an unsuccessful attempt in LA on March 1, 1997 by five armed robbers who came out of a bank and started a running battle with police on the city streets. "These guys were ready for war," a local store-owner was reported as saying, and despite their military hardware, their M16 assault rifles, it was a war they lost.

More successful were the self-styled "Dream Team" who operated in Spain in 2001 and used the same cars, names and modus operandi as the characters in *Heat*. They netted the equivalent of fifteen million pounds, until they too were captured. This is quite fitting, as the film itself was inspired by a real-life case. The paths of detective Chuck Adamson and bank robber Neil McCauley crossed in the early 1960s. The two had coffee together, discussed personal issues and, even though they left as friends, their next meeting was not so convivial. According to a *Time Out* interview with Mann in 1996, "Chuck was called to an armed robbery, saw McCauley coming out and there was a chase: Chuck came round a corner, McCauley came up with his gun but it misfired, and Chuck shot him six times."

High Sierra

dir **Raoul Walsh, 1941, US, 100m, b/w**
cast **Humphrey Bogart, Ida Lupino, Alan Curtis, Arthur Kennedy** *cin* **Tony Gaudio** *m* **Adolph Deutsch**

After his years of playing second fiddle in B-movies, *High Sierra* finally made **Humphrey Bogart** a star. True, he's playing another gangster, but at least he's no longer James Cagney's stooge.

He plays Roy "Mad Dog" Earle, who's been granted a pardon after receiving a life sentence for armed robbery. He's been sprung by crime boss Big Mac (**Donald McBride**) to pull off a job at an expensive resort in the Sierra mountains. He has two punks and a moll, Marie (**Ida Lupino**), as his accomplices, and the trio are obliged to wait uneasily in a nearby wood cabin until they get the go-ahead. Earle becomes infatuated with a young local girl called Velma (**Joan Leslie**). She has a club foot, and he pays for her operation to have it corrected, but she rejects his proposal of marriage and abandons him. So he returns to Marie, but makes her aware that she means nothing to him.

When the gang eventually stage the robbery, it goes wrong. A guard and Earle's two hoods are killed, and Roy and Marie go on the run. It all ends famously on the Sierra mountains – no studio backdrop here – with Earle isolated and alone, hunted down by police sharpshooters.

In many ways, the plot is secondary to the characters and theme. Roy Earle is one of a dying breed, among the last scions of the Dillinger generation. In a telling exchange between Earle and his boss, Big Mac laments the fact that all the old guys have gone – either "dead or in Alcatraz"– and that times have changed, to which Roy replies "sometimes I feel like I don't know what it's about anymore". Before the film gets too maudlin, writers **John Huston** and **W. R. Burnett** inject a note of comedy, as The Mob's doctor enters and reminds Roy that the last time they met he was "pulling slugs out of Lefty Jackson's chest … those were the times!"

There is a palpable moral disapproval of the younger generation, who are described as "screwballs, young twerps, soda jerkers, jitterbuggers", and everything we see in the movie reinforces this opinion. Velma, who's a beacon of virtue when she has a club foot, becomes a different person after the operation: she's transformed into a good-time girl now she can dance all night. It's not the first or the last time in the twentieth century that music will be blamed for one of society's ills: long before punk and rock'n'roll there were the harmful effects of trad jazz for the elders-and-betters to worry about.

The movie was also the last real gangster Bogart played; soon after *High Sierra*'s success he could choose his roles. He very nearly didn't get this one. **Paul Muni** was signed to star but he rejected the script; so **George Raft**, another member of the so-called "Murderer's Row" (Robinson and Cagney were the others), was offered the part, and he asked Bogart for advice. Bogie advised him not to take it, telling him that "Roy Earle is just another heavy who gets shot."

What Raft didn't know was that Bogie wanted the role for himself – he had read an abridged version of W.R. Burnett's original novel and telegrammed the producer Hal Wallis asking to play the part. But even when Raft turned them down they still didn't give it to Bogie. Cagney, Robinson and John Garfield were all approached until they finally let him have it. And it is a star-making role, a combination of the Bogart we knew, the tough who thinks nothing about killing, who doesn't think or flinch when taking a human life, and the Bogart to come, the Bogart of *Casablanca* and *Key Largo*, the tormented man caught in the crossfire between his head and his heart in the battle to do the right thing.

Infernal Affairs
(Wujian dao)

dir **Andrew Lau & Alan Mak, 2002, HK, 100m**
cast **Andy Lau, Tony Leung, Anthony Wong, Eric Tsang, Sammi Cheng** *cin* **Andrew Lau, Lai Yiu-Fai, Christopher Doyle** *m* **Chan Kwong-Wing**

Just when Hong Kong action cinema seemed to have finally run out of energy, *Infernal Affairs* came along in 2002 and broke all domestic box-office records. Rather than being a revival of the form, it's probably better to regard *Infernal Affairs* as the ultimate – though of course not the last – Hong Kong action movie, taking the style and substance of directors John Woo, Ringo Lam and Wong Kar Wai to their illogical conclusion.

Triad boss Hon Sam sends several of his protégés to the Hong Kong police academy as spies. Among them is Lau Kin Ming (**Andy Lau**), the owner of surely the sharpest cheekbones ever committed to celluloid. One of Lau's fellow cadets, Chan Win Yang (the marginally less chiselled **Tony Leung**), is recruited by Superintendent Wong to infiltrate the Triads. Ten years later, Lau is Hon Sam's mole in the police force, while Chan is Wong's informer in Sam's gang. Both Chan and Lau are living a lie, and neither really seems to know who he is anymore.

Both are in purgatory, as the movie's original-language title imparts in its direct reference to the Buddhist concept of the Eighth Hell. We're informed in the film's preface that this is a place of eternal suffering. If this was a **Wong Kar Wai** movie, the next ninety minutes would be all alienation, longing and pouting. Instead, *Infernal Affairs* has a plot that moves briskly and with brio: in a tautly edited, edge-of-the-seat set piece, the police dragnet is about to fall on Hon Sam when Chan alerts him, just in time, that his drug deal is about to be busted. Both Wong and Sam realize that they have a mole problem, both know in advance the other's actions. And in a delicious irony, Chan and Lau are each given the task by their respective bosses of unmasking the informer. This is just the first of a number of outrageous twists. Just when we think directors **Andrew Lau** and **Alan Mak** can't possibly twist again, they produce a killer blow, the final turn of the screw. Furthermore, *Infernal Affairs* has two endings, one for mainland China, where criminals must be seen to punished, and one for the rest of the world; both can be seen on the DVD.

The movie shouldn't work but it does. This is down to the pace and precision injected by directors Lau and Mak, who realize that speed is of the essence if the audience is to believe all this hokum; the camera rarely settles, while scenes are cut asphyxiatingly tight. Somehow it all seems so fresh. As Jonathan Romney acutely observed in his review for *The Independent On Sunday*: "it's so-seen-it-all-before that you feel you've never seen it before". It's easy to identify the films that inform *Infernal Affairs*: the theme of the cop and criminal who are mirror images of each other is from **John Woo**'s *The Killer*, the police mole trope is from **Ringo Lam**'s *City On Fire*, and the visual stylings are from Wong Kar Wai. In fact, Andrew Lau was the cinematographer on Wong's debut *As Tears Go By* before taking up the directorial reins himself, notably with the phenomenal *Young And Dangerous* series (more of which in the Hong Kong section); all of Lau's films are Kar Wai-lite, retaining the steely surface sheen but lacking Wong's philosophical depth.

Indeed, most of the major players in *Infernal Affairs* would be handy in a game of Six Degrees Of Wong Kar Wai (if ever anyone felt like inventing the game).

Mirror-image moles in *Infernal Affairs* (2002)

Andy Lau starred in *As Tears Go By*, but was soon eclipsed by Tony Leung as the director's leading man in subsequent films such as *Chungking Express* (1994) and *In The Mood For Love* (2000). The cinematographer on those films, **Christopher Doyle**, was *Infernal Affairs*' visual consultant, and his crucial and defining contribution to Hong Kong cinema becomes more celebrated every year.

A sign of *Infernal Affairs*' phenomenal success is that two sequels were rushed out in a year. *Part II* is a convoluted, self-regarding prequel, whereas *Part III* is half prequel, half sequel, set six months before and ten months after the events of the original, but it thankfully harnesses the first film's kinetic energy. Then there's the matter of the inevitable Hollywood remake, *The Departed*, scheduled for a 2006 release. It's a little more prestigious than the usual cheap knock-off copy, starring Leonardo Di Caprio and Matt Damon as the moles, and is directed, appropriately enough, by the don of the modern gangster movie, **Martin Scorsese**.

Key Largo

dir **John Huston, 1948, US, 101m, b/w**
cast **Humphrey Bogart, Edward G Robinson, Lauren Bacall, Lionel Barrymore, Claire Trevor** *cin* **Karl Freund** *m* **Max Steiner**

A film symptomatic of disillusioned, postwar American cinema, *Key Largo* showed euphoric idealism being increasingly soured by the experience of civic corruption and continuing organized crime. Its tacit, persistent question is "Is this what we fought the war for?"

Humphrey Bogart plays Major Frank McCloud, a jaded World War II veteran of no fixed abode, who visits Nora (**Lauren Bacall**), the widow of a friend who was killed in the Battle of Cassino. Nora runs a hotel in the storm-swept Florida Keys with the help of her wheelchair-bound father, played by Lionel Barrymore. The hotel has been taken over by the gang of Johnny Rocco (**Edward G. Robinson**), a crime boss whose "rule extended over beer, slot machines, the numbers racket and a dozen other enterprises". The Feds are on his tail because he was ratted out by a mayor who was previously in his pocket, and he is waiting for a boat to take him to Cuba. When the gang take hostage Frank, Nora, her father and a policeman, Frank refuses to do anything about it – he will "fight nobody's battles but [his] own", even when the policeman is killed. But, pricked by his own conscience and the gentle pleadings of Nora, he realizes that he has to re-enter the fray.

The power of the film comes from the chemistry between Bogart and Robinson, rather than Bogart and Bacall – she is given little more to do than make doe-eyes at him. Robinson, in his last great gangster role, is magnificent. Sweaty, sadistic, oily, anxious and devious, he is vaingloriously half gangster, half toad. Bogart, on the other hand, is in perpetual moral torpor, physically articulating the discomfort of a man skewered on the horns of a dilemma.

And even if the dialogue is a little stagey, it nonetheless remains on-the-nose because, sociologically, it's fascinating. *Key Largo* is one of the many films of its era that voiced the disappointments of the generation that had endured World War II. Movies such as *The Blue Dahlia* (1946) concerned soldiers coming back from the war, ready to take their place in a new society and to reap the rewards of a freedom and democracy they had fought for, only to find that things had changed for the worse. In *Key Largo* the reasons for this disillusionment are clear. Bogart says he went to war to "cleanse the world of ancient evils, ancient ills". Those ancient ills, in the shape of Johnny Rocco, are taking over America again. As Bogart's character says: "Welcome Back, Rocco. America is sorry for what it did to you." And even though Rocco is fleeing the country, he's sure that he will be back, and bigger than ever. He boasts about how easy it was to fix elections, to get his people into power, and how he made politicians "like a tailor makes a suit". All the gangsters agree that Prohibition will be reintroduced in a few years and that then they will join forces rather than fight each other. Bogart's Frank McCloud represents the average Joe who must decide what he's going to do: as Bacall's character says: "Maybe it is a rotten world, but a cause isn't lost as long as someone is willing to go on fighting."

That sentiment could equally apply to all the writers, directors and stars who were at the time fighting anti-Communist witch-hunts. Bogart, Bacall, and director John Huston had publicly protested against the Senate hearings, while Robinson had refused to testify at them. But, unlike his *Key Largo* character, Bogart eventually chose the path of least resistance. When the film was released, Bogie gave an interview claiming that he had had a change of heart, and that his protests were the result of his being duped by the Communist Party.

Robinson was dismayed and continued his stand against the House Un-American Activities Committee (HUAC). He lost work because of it, and when he eventually testified, tried to backtrack by distancing himself from many of the liberal organizations he had been campaigning for. The damage was done however. Robinson's career never really recovered, and because he was born in Romania, his US passport was taken from him. His fate gave a poignant, prescient resonance to one of his Johnny Rocco lines: "they called me an undesirable alien like I was a dirty Red or something!"

The Killing

dir **Stanley Kubrick, 1956, US, 84m, b/w**
cast **Sterling Hayden, Coleen Gray, Vince Edwards, Jac C Flippen, Marie Windsor, Elisha Cook Jr** *cin* **Lucien Ballard** *m* **Gerald Friel**

An almost perfect marriage of director Stanley Kubrick's self-conscious artistry and writer Jim Thompson's pulp sensibilities resulted in a minor *noir* masterpiece. *The Killing* concerns a gang who plan to make a killing by stealing the winnings from a racetrack on the biggest meet of the season. Among their number are the mastermind Johnny Clay (*The Asphalt Jungle*'s **Sterling Hayden**), the track's barman (**Joe Sawyer**), and the racetrack's cashier George (**Elisha Cook Jr**). It's George's task to let Johnny into the office. But George has a gold-digging wife, Sherry (**Marie Windsor**), who's got her hooks into him. She browbeats him into revealing the plans and proceeds to pass them on to her lover, who intends to rob the thieves after the heist.

No punches are pulled in Stanley Kubrick's meticulously-constructed *The Killing* (1956)

NO ADMITTA

The film has become famous for its narrative structure. The heist is told from the perspective of each gang member. We only get so far into the robbery before the movie cuts back to an earlier part of the day. Take the man who's going to cause a diversion by picking a fight with the guards at the track: we see him in the morning, then watch him arriving at the course, and then starting his fight; once his part in the heist is over we cut to another member of the team, seeing *him* in the morning, arriving at the track and so on. It's this breaking down of narrative, withholding information, and giving each character a chapter that directly influenced Quentin Tarantino, and he used similar methods in both *Reservoir Dogs* (1991) and *Jackie Brown* (1997).

But this is hardly the only reason for watching *The Killing*. At the film's core is the relationship between George and Sherry. George is one of the great weasels of cinema history. He's the sap's sap and even when he realizes he has been double-crossed – even when he's gunning his wife down – he tells her that he loves her.

Sherry, on the other hand, is a classic *femme fatale*, with carefully painted face and bottle-blonde hair. Almost every sentence she utters is a put-down, and every one of them is quotable. When George informs her that she's about to come into some money, that he'll give her "cash up to her curls", she replies "Of course you are, darling. And did you put the right address on the envelope when you sent it to the North Pole?" She towers over him, belittling him in every way. When George asks where his tea is, she tells him that it's in the superstore.

This dialogue, and the details of the pair's relationship, come courtesy of **Jim Thompson**, one of the most original of pulp fiction's hacks; many of his novels have been turned into great films, such as **Sam Peckinpah**'s *The Getaway* (1972), **Stephen Frears**' *The Grifters* (1990) and **Bertrand Tavernier**'s *Coup de torchon* (*Clean Slate*, 1981 – adapted from Thompson's novel *Pop. 1280*). Thompson is only credited with writing additional dialogue for *The Killing*, and he almost fell off his chair when he saw the credit on the screen. According to Thompson's biographer, Robert Polito, the writer had adapted the source novel, *Clean Break*, by Lionel White, *with* Kubrick – he'd created new characters and added storylines and dialogue while the director worked on the structure. Apparently Thompson spent the rest of his life telling anyone who'd listen how he'd been cheated by Kubrick. Nevertheless, this didn't stop him working on Kubrick's next film, *Paths Of Glory* (1957). This time, however, he was properly credited.

King Of New York

dir Abel Ferrara, 1989, US, 103m
cast Christopher Walken, David Caruso, Larry Fishburne, Victor Argo, Wesley Snipes, Janet Julian *cin* Bojan Bazelli *m* Joe Delia

"Look at that shot. That's a big-time shot." This is director **Abel Ferrara** talking about his own film on the audio commentary of the DVD edition of *King Of New York*. He may not be modest, but he's right. Shot after shot is exquisitely composed: plays of light and shadow, and orchestrated hues of brake-light reds, marine blues and pale greens. Or as Ferrara puts it, "it's Rembrandted-out".

But it's not just the cinematography (by **Bojan Bazelli**) that gets this film into the Top 50. *King Of New York* boasts a career-best performance by **Christopher Walken** as Frank White, the movie's eponymous gang boss who comes out of jail to discover that his power has waned and his organization has fragmented. As he brutally regains control of his drug-trafficking operations, he's

The Funeral
dir Abel Ferrara, 1996, US, 99m

Ferrara's other foray into the gangster genre is similarly controlled – almost stately in its pacing and composition. A chamber piece set in 1930s New York about two brothers who convene at the funeral of their youngest sibling – a gangster seemingly gunned down by their deadliest rival. When the suspected rival sends a bouquet to the funeral, everything begins to unravel and the truth is slowly revealed in flashbacks. *The Funeral* stars four of the most idiosyncratic actors of their generation – **Christopher Walken**, **Christopher Penn**, **Vincent Gallo** and **Benicio Del Toro**. Mannered and over-wordy at times, it explodes with a cathartic climax which lies somewhere between Greek tragedy and soap opera.

hounded by police detectives played by **Wesley Snipes**, **Victor Argo** and **David Caruso**, who use Frank's own violent means in attempting to bring him to an end. But Frank wants to go legit. He wants to be mayor, regarding himself as a businessman with scruples, and he tries to raise funds for a local hospital whilst putting his rivals in the morgue. It would be corny if it wasn't for Walken's performance. With his gravity-defying hair, staccato delivery and alarming tendency to break suddenly into dancing (!), he skirts close to parody, though he never does the full **Al Pacino** and go way over-the-top.

Instead his spectral appearance reveals a melancholy behind the bravado; described as a "cocksucker who's got no friends", he captures the *Citizen Kane*-like loneliness of a self-made man. Frank says that he has come back from the dead when he's released from jail, and in many ways Walken plays him like a dead man walking (or a "kabuki android", as cult writer **Iain Sinclair** described him).

The film took five years to write and direct and, apart from the religious iconography and theme of redemption, is in many ways untypical of Ferrara's work. Ferrara himself is a frazzled, Keith Richards lookalike whose most infamous films – *Driller Killer* (1979), *Bad Lieutenant* (1992), *Ms. 45* (1980) – have a rough, improvised feel about them. *King Of New York*, by contrast, doesn't have a hair out of place.

It owes much to **Brian De Palma**'s *Scarface* for its operatic bombast. But there is another connection between the two films: hip-hop. Whereas *Scarface* unintentionally became a reference point for many rap artists, *King Of New York* explicitly made the connection between gangster and "gangsta". Frank White is an equal opportunities employer – his number two is a fully-blinged-up **Laurence Fishburne** and the film's music is by rapper **Schooly D**.

Hip-hop repaid the compliment years later, when rapper OC paid musical tribute to the film on his classic track "King Of New York". But it's not just New York's hip-hop cognoscenti who have sung the movie's praises. It found a champion in Iain Sinclair, who nominated the film one of the Top 10 of all time in *Sight And Sound* magazine's critical round-up, arguing that it is an "ambitious piece about the end of ambition" and a neglected classic – possibly *the* neglected classic of Hollywood history.

Little Caesar

dir **Mervyn LeRoy, 1930, US, 80m, b/w**
cast **Edward G Robinson, Douglas Fairbanks Jr, Glenda Farrell, Stanley Fields, Sidney Blackmer** *cin* **Tony Gaudio**

By no means the first gangster movie, it's nonetheless easily the first *classic* gangster movie – the film that set the template for almost every genre flick to follow. *Little Caesar* is about the rise and fall of Catholic Italian immigrant Rico (**Edward G. Robinson**) who with his best friend, Joe (**Douglas Fairbanks Jr**), travels to the city to make it big as a gangster. Rico joins the gang of Sam Vettori and rises ruthlessly and quickly through the ranks until he is running the show himself. Rico has no characteristics other than his stated desire to be somebody, no principles other than Darwin's survival of the fittest.

A dinner is held in his honour by The Mob and this provokes the wrath of rival gangster, Archie Lorch, who decides that Rico has gone far enough. Rico survives the attempt to fill him full of holes, receiving only a scratch, and wreaks revenge on his nemesis by throwing him out of the city and taking over his business. Rico is now only second to "Big Boy", the man who runs the city and who has the clothes and the lifestyle to fit. But he is not happy, and this is the start of the fall. His best friend Joe has left the gang to pursue a career as a dancer and has fallen in love with a fellow hoofer called Olga. When Joe defiantly refuses to come back to the fold, Rico follows him to Olga's apartment. But he cannot bring himself to kill his old friend and, when Olga informs the authorities, Rico is forced to go on the run, penniless. His life ends in a vainglorious shoot-out with the cops.

Is this the end for Rico? Edward G. Robinson is the dapper *Little Caesar*, his empire beginning to fall apart

There is, of course, a great line to end the film and sum up the fall of the criminal. Robinson breathes his last with the words "Mother of God, is this the end of Rico?" or, in the censored version, "Mother of *mercy*, is this the end of Rico?"

Little Caesar portrays the mobster as a Dapper Dan, fussing over his tuxedo. As the original novel states, Rico only cares about three things: himself, his hair and his gun. What the film doesn't have is a moll – there's no love interest for Rico. And this has led many critics to claim that Rico is in fact in love with Joe, and that that is why he's jealous of Olga, why he doesn't kill Joe when he has the chance, and why he's finally undone. As Rico says, "that's what I get for liking a guy too much". Repressed sexuality is certainly a common undertone of the classic gangster movie: the suggestions of incest in *Scarface* and of Oedipal love in *White Heat*, for example. The hoodlum must, traditionally, have a flaw that destroys him, and it's possible to construe Rico's lack of acknowledgment or subconscious disavowal of his sexual urges as being his downfall.

Of course, what *Little Caesar* most palpably gave the world was a screen icon: Edward G. Robinson. A five-foot Romanian, he had made movies since 1923, but this is the film that made him both a star and an archetype. Fights broke out in queues to see the film, and there was at least one minor riot outside a cinema that showed the movie. "I think the popularity of my role can be attributed to the public preoccupation with the American dream of success," Robinson said years later, explaining the appeal of Rico to an audience in the middle of the Great Depression, "Rico made it straight up the ladder and everyone could identify with the climb." Robinson himself exploited that appeal, according to biographer Alan L. Gansberg, by touring the US in 1931 with a sort of vaudeville act. He would go on stage dressed in his *Little Caesar* garb and do a short routine as Rico. It paid well, apparently.

The Long Good Friday

dir John MacKenzie, 1979, UK, 114m
cast Bob Hoskins, Helen Mirren, Dave King, Bryan Marshall, Derek Thompson *cin* Philip Meheux *m* Francis Monkman

As much a premonition as a movie, and made in the year the Conservative Party won the first of their electoral victories under Margaret Thatcher, this eerily predicts what will happen to London's docklands, and to Britain, under Thatcherism. The enterprise, "get rich quick" culture, the special relationship with America, the revival of patriotism, and the "no such thing as society" attitude are all crystallized in MacKenzie's critique of the gangster as ultimate capitalist.

Bob Hoskins plays Harold Shand, a little big man who wants a special "hands across the ocean" relationship with American business, and with the Mafia in particular. He has invited a Mafia *capo* (**Eddie Constantine**) over to sign a deal that will redevelop London's Canary Wharf, make London great again, and turn Shand's criminal empire into a legitimate corporation. Shand has got London sewn up. He has a posh wife (**Helen Mirren**) as a front of respectability, and has a dodgy councillor, Harris, and an even dodgier cop, Parky, on the payroll. He's also got a great line in bons mots.

This is Hoskins' film. He plays a pugnacious, racist British bull-dog, and yet you can just about empathize with him. His sadism and xenophobia are repellent, yet there are the occasional flashes of

Cockney geezer Harold Shand (Bob Hoskins) thinks he's pulling the strings in *The Long Good Friday* (1979)

The wit and wisdom of Harold Shand

"You don't crucify people! Not on Good Friday!"

"We're looking for people who can contribute to what England has given the world: culture, genius, sophistication. Bit more than an 'ot dog, know what I mean?"

Pool attendant: "They're gonna collect the body in an ice cream van." Shand: "There's a lot of dignity in that, isn't there? Going out like a raspberry ripple."

"Bent law can be tolerated for as long as they're lubricating, but you have become definitely parched. If I was you, I'd run for cover and close the hatch, 'cause you're gonna wind up on one of those meat hooks, my son!"

a sympathetic character beneath, such as the dread overwhelming him as he begins to comprehend the bloody mess he has made of his trusted right-hand man.

Hoskins' performance has its crowning glory, however, in the prescient speech Shand makes about making London great again. Standing on his yacht, framed by Tower Bridge, the speech predicts and encapsulates what will happen to Britain over the next ten years. It's a defining moment in British cultural and cinematic history. (According to director **John MacKenzie**, the shot itself was hell to get, especially when the tide changed and the boat went full steam into the bridge.)

MacKenzie has admitted that he and writer **Barrie Keefe** could never have guessed the extent to which their movie would chime with the rise of Thatcherism, for the "full onslaught of Thatcherism hadn't really begun" when the film was made in 1979 – the year Margaret Thatcher came to power. The film was not released until two years later, in 1981, the year of the Falklands War. It was delayed because ITC boss, **Lew Grade**, hated the film, claimed it was unpatriotic and shelved it. And it would have stayed on the shelf had it not been for **George Harrison**'s company Handmade Films, which paid £900,000 for the rights to the movie.

Another reason that Grade didn't release the film is that he was scared that the IRA would blow up cinemas that showed it. He needn't have worried. As MacKenzie found out in a pub in Dublin, the Provisionals quite liked *The Long Good Friday*. "The boys don't mind the film," he was told. "It doesn't make them look stupid and it makes them seem like good planners."

Mean Streets

dir **Martin Scorsese, 1973, US, 110m**
cast **Harvey Keitel, Robert De Niro, David Proval, Amy Robinson, Richard Romanus** *cin* **Kent Wakeford**

Ironically for a film so rooted in New York (of which Little Italy is such a vital part) *Mean Streets* was actually shot in Los Angeles, for budgetary reasons and because of problems with the neighbours. It is Martin Scorsese's most personal film, about the small-time hoods who peopled Little Italy. He described it as "an attempt to put myself and my old friends on the screen".

The "myself" character is Charlie, played by **Harvey Keitel**: a guilt-laden number-runner who always tries to do the right thing. The film opens with a voice-over of his thoughts: "You don't make up for your sins at church, you do it on the streets and at home." Scorsese has always said that he had only two career options when he was growing up: to be a priest or a gangster. And if the connection between director and protagonist wasn't already clear enough, Charlie's inner monologue is read by Scorsese.

Then we're introduced to the other members of the gang, Scorsese's old friends. Tony (**David Proval**) owns a bar, Michael (**Richard Romanus**) is a wheeler-dealer, and of course there's Johnny Boy (**Robert De Niro**). The first time we see Johnny Boy he's blowing up a post box. For fun. Johnny Boy is a natural anarchist, and Charlie regards it as an almost religious duty to keep him from serious harm and debt. However, Charlie's dreams of running a restaurant hinge upon him keeping a distance from both Johnny and his cousin Teresa, an epileptic girl whom he is secretly seeing.

The film is made up of a series of episodes – anecdotal versions of real events Scorsese had seen or heard about, such as the scene in which a man keeps on walking after he's been shot in the chest several times. But mostly the movie is about how men often are with each other: the raucous banter which can explode into violence, the violence which can become comic, and the casual racism. It has an underlying restless tension that will explode cathartically at the film's climax.

Even though Charlie is the main character, it is Johnny Boy's wired, electric energy which both crystallizes and animates the film's nerviness; both the character and the film are always on edge. And this is entirely down to De Niro – when director Sydney Pollack first saw *Mean Streets*, he thought they'd let a psychopath out of the hospital to play Johnny Boy's part. It's possibly De Niro's greatest performance, before anyone knew who he was and before screen audiences became over-familiar with his facial tics and shoulder-shrugs.

The film often gives the impression of being improvised, and some of it was. A key early exchange between Charlie and Johnny

Prime Cut
dir Michael Ritchie,
1972, US, 86m

Forget Takashi Miike or Korean bad boy Kim Ki-Duk. There's really nothing as genuinely, intelligently transgressive as Hollywood cinema of the early 70s. Take *Prime Cut*, whose opening scene is in a meat manufacturing plant where we witness the industrial transformation of cows into hamburger patties. Amongst the cattle to the slaughter is a dead body, which is soon processed into a string of sausages. This human hot dog was once a Mafia hood sent down to Kansas to bring renegade mobster Gene Hackman back into line. So the Chicago godfathers call on the services of genial toughnut Lee Marvin. Whilst getting heavy with Hackman, he comes across Sissy Spacek in a meat market where naked women are displayed in pens for the inspection of prospective buyers. Prime Cut is a potent mix of the visceral and the cerebral, as much about competing modes of capitalism as it as about gang warfare – the old industrial model versus the new service sector offering "dope and flesh". This is epitomized by an unlikely chase sequence involving a potentially fatal combine harvester. It climaxes with a car, the most pertinent symbol of Fordism, being chewed up and spat out by the metal teeth of a threshing machine, a grim reaper.

Harvey Keitel as the troubled but steady Charlie, in a typically moodily-lit and impressionistically-filtered shot from *Mean Streets* (1973)

at the back of the bar was entirely made up on the spot. Scorsese wanted the feeling of Bob Hope and Bing Crosby crossed with **Abbott and Costello**, and he got it. Keitel and De Niro can barely contain their laughter at times, and you don't quite know what or who you are watching – the actors or the characters they play.

Of course, Scorsese – the film world's most inspired movie geek – pays a devotee's homage to the golden age of gangster movies. Although he felt the 1930s gangster flicks were heavy-handed, he loved the way that **William Wellman** had made use of popular tunes in *The Public Enemy* (1931). And *Mean Streets* is full of music from the 1960s that palpably breaks through the texture of the film, adding even more chaotic energy to it. As Scorsese said to Ian Christie and David Thompson, "For me the whole movie was *Jumping Jack Flash* and *Be My Baby*."

If *Mean Streets* showcases De Niro's best performance, it could well also be Scorsese's best film, and for similar reasons. It reveals a Martin Scorsese before form became more important than content, before his work became a catalogue of interesting camera angles and great crane shots. Of course, *Mean Streets* does have genuine technical innovations – a camera was attached to Harvey Keitel to shoot the scene in which a very drunk Charlie staggers woozily through the bar. The bar itself is suffused in a red that suggests hell and references **Michael Powell**'s *Red Shoes* (1948) – Scorsese admitted that it was the look of Powell's film that he was going for here, and piled on the red filters to achieve it. But *Mean Streets* is always as much about people as it is about cinematic virtuosity, which gives it the edge over *Goodfellas*.

Menace II Society

dir **Allen & Albert Hughes, 1993, US, 97m**
cast **Tyrin Turner, Jada Pinkett, Larenz Tate, Arnold Johnson, Samuel L. Jackson** *cin* **Jon Kranhouse** *m* **QDIII**

The first scene in *Menace II Society* bluntly shows us what to expect from the next hour or so. Caine (**Tyrin Turner**) and O-Dog (**Larenz Tate**) visit their local convenience store in Watts, California, to get some beer, and when the Korean shopkeepers presume, volubly, that they are there to steal something, O-Dog whips out a gun and shoots them both in cold blood. This scene prepares us not only for the fact that this will be a grimly violent film, but for the fact that the violence will be random, often out of keeping with what has gone before: don't expect a build-up or a showdown.

It also places us in a morally queasy position: our screen surrogate, Caine, is an accessory to a particularly unnecessary murder, but shows no pained remorse à la Brando in *On The Waterfront*. It is this amorality that bothered some commentators, such as the critic for *Newsday* who called *Menace* "an almost evil film". It is, however, a more subtle film than it was given credit for. Like Charlie in *Mean Streets* Caine has to define his own moral position, and work out his ties to the clearly psychotic O-Dog, who is from the Joe Pesci school of wired, short-fuse malevolence, always a hair-trigger away from committing some sickening act of violence.

Caine refuses to rat on his friend, even in the face of a vicious beating from members of the LAPD. But his doubts about his own drug-dealing lifestyle intensify when his friend Harold is killed as part of a gang war and his girlfriend Ronnie (Jada Pinkett) gets a job in Atlanta, offering Caine a chance of escape.

His muddled ethics are in complete contrast to the uncomplicated morality of Tre, the virtuous hero of *Boyz N The Hood* (1991). Indeed, the directors, the Hughes Brothers, set out to make *Menace* the flip side to **John Singleton**'s ground-breaking debut, telling the *Washington Post* in 1993 that *Boyz* "had nothing to do with bad guys" and that "it had a whole different drive altogether. It had good guys going through this bad city, on their way to college. The gangsters, they hated that thing … They called it 'Toys In The Hood'."

The irony is that if anybody knew about real "gangstas" it was Singleton, who was brought up in the 'hood. The twins, Allen and Albert, on the other hand, were born in Detroit and were brought up in a middle-class suburb of Los Angeles by their Armenian mother. As they admitted to *The Daily Telegraph* in 2002, "We were surrounded by Armenian culture. We were around gangsters as much as Spielberg was around extraterrestrials."

However, at the time of the film's release, they played up their gangsta credentials, telling the *Los Angeles Times* that their mother bought them a video camera when they were 12 to stop them from dealing drugs. The twins graduated from making parodies of their favourite films to shooting videos for rap artists which quickly got Hollywood's attention. When *Menace II Society* was released, they were just 20 years old.

Movies can't be judged by their director's badge of authenticity, however, and *Menace* is by far a better movie than *Boyz*. Singleton's film, at its worst, is a pious soap opera, whereas Albert and Allen realize that the gangster movie is a dubious pleasure, both visceral and vicarious. Like *Little Caesar* and co before it, *Menace* walks the line between glamorization and condemnation of the gangster lifestyle. The brothers clearly learned their lessons from watching Scorsese's films, using *Goodfellas*, in particular, as their acknowledged model, borrowing its voice-over strategy, audacious use of long tracking shots and punchy, kinetic editing techniques. Scorsese seemed to be flattered. In an interview with Woody Allen in 1997 he exclaimed "*Menace II Society*? That's a great picture!"

Miller's Crossing

dir Joel Coen, 1990, US, 115m
cast Gabriel Byrne, Albert Finney, Marcia Gay Harden,
John Turturro, Jon Polito, J.E. Freeman *cin* Barry
Sonnenfeld *m* Carter Burwell

Whether it's James Cagney perching his on the top of his head in *The Public Enemy* or Alain Delon positioning his inch-perfectly in *Le samourai*, the fedora has always had a special place in the gangster movie. In *Miller's Crossing* hats are more than simply a gangster accessory, they are invested with an almost portentous significance. **Ethan Coen** claimed it was a "film about hats" and cinematographer Barry Sonnenfeld said they'd made "a handsome movie about men in hats". The title shot focuses on a fedora gliding through a wood, transported by the wind, and we later learn that this is an image from the hero's dream. The drop of a hat denotes the start of a love scene, a hat suddenly hitting the ground means our hero has been punched out yet again, and a hat sitting unattended on a staircase ominously signposts a murder.

This homage to men in felt was inspired by two **Dashiell Hammett** novels, *Red Harvest* and *The Glass Key* (which **Stuart Heisler** had already directed in his 1942 *noir*). Set in Prohibition-era America (albeit a slightly abstracted Coen Brothers' take on it), **Gabriel Byrne** plays Tom, the loyal lieutenant of Irish gang boss Leo (**Albert Finney**), whose empire is coming under attack from rival gangster Johnny Caspar (**Jon Polito**). They're going toe-to-toe because Caspar wants to kill bookie Bernie (**John Turturro**), who has fiddled the odds on Caspar's fixed fights. But Leo won't give Bernie up because he's the brother of Leo's lover Verna (**Marcia Gay Harden**) who, as it turns out, is also seeing Tom. When Leo eventually finds out, he boots Tom out of the organization and Tom switches to the other side.

To prove his loyalty, Tom has to take Bernie into the middle of the woods and put a bullet in his brain. This is the moment when John Turturro steals the film from the rest of the cast, the Coen Brothers and even the hats. He snivels, "bawls like a twist", prays for

John Tuturro as the weaselly Bernie in the Coen Brothers' tense *Miller's Crossing* (1990)

his life and implores Tom to look into his heart. It's a scene that churns even the hardiest of stomachs and it announced Turturro as a major Hollywood talent; it was his calling card.

The Coens relish playing with the language of the gangster genre, and the dialogue's slang is consistently delightful: "He's an artist with the Thompson" (ie he's good with a gun); "What's the rumpus?"; "Don't smart me!"; and "when we last jawed you gave me the high hat". "The high hat" is an expresion that crops up throughout the movie, and it also features in **Fritz Lang**'s *You Only Live Once*

(1937). What do all these hats mean? It was a question that almost every journalist who interviewed the brothers asked, but not one received a meaningful answer. Poker-faced, the brothers denied all knowledge of the hats' possible symbolism. Joel's response to journalist Jean-Pierre Coursodon was typically unforthcoming: "Everybody asks us questions about that hat, and there isn't any answer really. It's not a symbol, it doesn't have any particular meaning." Unhelpful, but at least it was more enlightening than the answer they gave Gabriel Byrne. Apparently when the leading man asked about the hats' significance, all he got was "Mmm, hmm". In the absence of any clues from the writers and director, critics and fans have advanced their own theories in print and on Internet message boards: Tom's hat in turn equals his sense of security, his love for Verna or his dignity. It's entirely possible, of course, that the Coen Brothers were telling the truth, that the hat signifies nothing and that there's less to *Miller's Crossing* than meets the eye.

Night And The City

dir Jules Dassin, 1950, UK/US, 100m, b/w
cast Richard Widmark, Gene Tierney, Googie Withers,
Francis L Sullivan, Herbert Lom *cin* Max Greene *m*
Benjamin Frankel

London has never been filmed so well as in Jules Dassin's 1950 thriller. It looks and has the feel of a real *noir* location, as oppressively forbidding as Los Angeles or San Francisco. With dank streets, seamy underground clubs and dingy, crepuscular alleyways, it was a London that was rarely shown.

Its atmosphere owes much to Percy Hoskins, a police inspector who took Dassin to areas of the East End that the director claims "very few Londoners knew existed". The director himself prepared for the shoot by doing what he always did – walking. "When you make a film about a city you walk it, and ideas come when you're walking", as Dassin once told this author. The film's other defining force is **Richard Widmark**. He's magnificent as Harry Fabian, a small-time American hoodlum who plans to take control of the wrestling racket away from underworld kingpin Kristo (**Herbert Lom**). The first time we see Fabian he's running away from somebody. "Always in a sweat", he inevitably ends up running for his life. He's never less than desperate, with a new get-rich-quick scheme every month, and will double-cross anybody to be somebody. In other words, he's the quintessential loser. To get money for his wrestling show, Fabian does the dirty on the woman who loves him, Helen (Googie Withers), who is herself doing the dirty on her husband, nightclub-owner Phil (Francis L. Sullivan), who in turn betrays Fabian to Kristo.

Dassin only took on the project and came to England because of the House Un-American Activities Committee investigations (see p.216); directors **Frank Tuttle** and **Edward Dmytryk** had named Dassin as a fellow member of the Communist Party in their testimony to the Senate hearing. Dassin's friend **Darryl Zanuck**, head of 20th Century Fox knew that it was only a matter of time before the director would be called before the committee himself and eventually blacklisted. According to Dassin, Zanuck went to his house in the middle of the night and told him to go to London, make the film, and "start with the most expensive scenes so they won't stop you, because this is the last film you will ever make". And for five years it seemed as if Zanuck was right. There were problems distributing *Night And The City* after the accusations that Dassin was a Communist sympathizer, and he couldn't get a job as a film director in either America or Europe until he was offered *Rififi* (1955).

Britain should be grateful to Zanuck. *Night And The City* is one of the few great London films, although English critics didn't think so at the time. The London that Dassin portrays *is* unremittingly sordid: everyone is on the make, matchbox girls are taught how to fleece and flirt with male clients, Harry easily scams American tourists. As Dassin recalls it, all the critics were asking "who is this foreigner who's doing this to us?"

Once Upon A Time In America

dir **Sergio Leone, 1983, US, 229m**
cast **Robert De Niro, James Woods, Elizabeth McGovern, Treat Williams, Tuesday Weld** *cin* **Tonino Delli Colli** *m* **Ennio Morricone**

A top contender for "Greatest Gangster Movie Ever Made" status, many critics now argue that this is an even better movie than *The Godfather* (1971). Not that anyone would have believed it at the time of the film's release, after the studio had taken it out of the hands of director Sergio Leone and given it to the editor of *Police Academy* to re-cut — or rather butcher.

The fully restored version is not only the last word on the classic gangster movie, it is, as Leone once said, "about time, memory and the cinema". It is set in three different eras — 1923, 1933 and

1968 – but its narrative isn't chronological. Shuttling back and forth through time, it charts the history of four boyhood friends, Max, Noodles, Cockeye and Patsy, who make their way from being hustlers in 1923 to kings of New York in 1933, thanks to police corruption, Prohibition and bootlegging. But running parallel is the story of Noodles' return to New York in 1968, 35 years after his gang met their end in a shoot-out with the cops, to do one last job for the mysterious Senator Bailey. As he revisits his old haunts, Noodles uncovers the events that led to the death of his friends.

It's a sinuous, intricate film, with a style that's best summed up by one early scene. Noodles (**Robert De Niro**) is resting in bed in an opium den. A phone is ringing. There's a flashback to events earlier that day, when his friends were killed. The phone still rings. Another flashback – this time to Noodles and Max (**James Woods**) at a party. Noodles goes to the phone and picks it up. The ringing doesn't stop. He starts to dial. The film cuts to a different phone, belonging to one Sergeant O'Hallohan at a police station. O'Hallohan picks it up, the ringing stops and we are brought back to Noodles in the opium den. He gets up with a start: the ringing was in his head. The memory of one fateful phone call is haunting him, because – as we will later learn – it was the moment he sold out his friends. It's an audacious scene which sets the tone for the rest of the film, but it confused many who saw it at a test screening.

When the film was first re-cut, the sustained phone-ringing was the first thing to go – reduced from 22 rings to one. The flashback structure also went, along with 85 minutes of footage, reducing the movie from 229 minutes to 144. Critics nominated the released version as the worst film of 1984. But the shoddy results of its bowdlerization weren't the only reason the movie was dismissed at the time. There were accusations of misogyny manifest in not just the characters but the film itself. Two scenes in particular were at the centre of the controversy: one in which Noodles rapes his childhood sweetheart Deborah after she definitively rejects him; and one in which, during a heist, a character called Carol clearly enjoys being violated by Noodles – a scene which seems to be played for laughs.

Despite the dubious sexual politics, there is no doubt that the film – Leone's cut, that is – is a masterpiece. Almost two decades in the planning, the movie's screenplay had a first draft written by **Norman Mailer**, but which was apparently so bad the producers

Did *Once Upon A Time In America* kill Sergio Leone?

Sergio Leone died of a heart attack five years after the release of *Once Upon A Time In America*. But biographer Christopher Frayling suggests that the problems with the film's release might have been the beginning of the end for him. In 1982 his doctors told him that he had a heart complaint and should avoid stressful situations, just as he had become involved in a lengthy and stressful legal battle with the studios. *Once Upon A Time In America* was to be his last film.

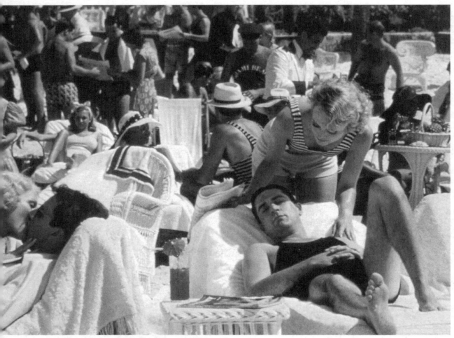

Once Upon A Time, James Woods (left) and Robert De Niro lived the high life in single-piece bathing costumes

tried not to pay him. However, the years of research and rewriting paid off, and are clearly visible on screen. From Leone's legendary eye for meticulous detail, to the wistfully evocative **Ennio Morricone** score (written before the film was made and played on set each day), every piece of the movie's complex mechanism works like clockwork. It's a genuine epic, ambitious in its intellectual, visual, narrative and thematic scope; it's also a treatise on America, immigration, friendship, betrayal, politics, idealism and corruption. So far, so *Godfather*. But what *Once Upon A Time In America* has over Coppola's epic is its second layer, its meta-narrative about memory and cinema. And, quite simply, it's a better story – the film's four hours feel like two.

In interviews, Leone always gave the impression that the whole action of the movie was a drug-induced hallucination of Noodles, as if the American dream depicted in *Once Upon A Time* was not just figurative but "literal": an American dreaming the American dream. The film does end back in 1933, as Noodles takes a drag on an opium pipe and smiles enigmatically. But, as **Christopher Frayling** points out in his book *Something To Do With Death*, how could someone in 1933 dream so accurately about the future, and anticipate exactly what the cars and television sets would look like in 1968?

On The Waterfront

dir Elia Kazan, 1954, US, 108m, b/w
cast Marlon Brando, Eva Marie Saint, Karl Malden, Lee
J Cobb, Rod Steiger, Pat Henning *cin* Boris Kaufman *m*
Leonard Bernstein

This film may seem an odd choice. *On The Waterfront* might strike you as more like a classic melodrama about unions than a mobster movie. But make no mistake – this a gangster film. A very real connection between unions and gangsters has existed in the US since the beginning of the twentieth century, and has been well documented in films such as *Hoffa* (1992) and *Once Upon A Time In America* (1983). And the late 1940s and 1950s saw a whole sub-genre of unions-as-Mob movies, mostly set around the docks, of which *On The Waterfront* is the most famous. And the dilemma faced by the hero is a core concern of the genre. To rat or not to rat, that is the question.

The film was written and directed by two men who had named names at the infamous HUAC investigations (see p.216). Both writer **Bud Schulberg** and director **Elia Kazan** had been members of the Communist Party – Schulberg in 1937–40 and Kazan in 1934–35. They had both testified against fellow members of the Communist Party, and had received threats from colleagues. *On The Waterfront* is accordingly concerned with the morality of informing on your friends. Ostensibly based on the case of real-life long-shoreman, Tony Mike, it also had echoes of Kazan's own recent experiences, as the director pointed out in his autobiography, *A Life*: "I did see Tony Mike's story as my own … When Brando at the end yells at Lee Cobb, the Mob boss 'I'm glad what I done, you hear me, glad what I done!' That was me saying with identical heat, that I was glad that I'd testified as I had."

Malloy (**Marlon Brando**) is a near-permanently punch-drunk ex-boxer who "could've been a contender". He could have taken a shot at the title but instead he took a dive in the most important fight of his life. This was under orders from his brother, Charlie (**Rod Steiger**), the right-hand man for union leader and gang boss

Johnny Friendly (**Lee J. Cobb**), "a butcher in a camel coat". The unions run the New York docks, taking a cut from everything that moves in and out, and they decide who works and who doesn't. They keep hold of power because the workers – the longshoremen, – stay "D and D" (deaf and dumb): they don't rat.

Terry is now working for Johnny, and he plays an unwitting but vital role in the murder of longshoreman Joey, a "canary" who was about to sing to the Crime Commission and implicate Johnny Friendly. Terry is stricken with remorse and is further troubled when he falls for Joey's sister, Edie (**Eva Marie Saint**). Helped by priest Father Berry (**Karl Malden**), she's determined to find out who killed her brother. Love-struck and guilt-ridden, Malloy tells her the truth about his involvement, and realizes that he will

He coulda been a contender. Marlon Brando (right) is the canary of *On The Waterfront*

have to testify, even though it could be the death of him and his brother.

The film is a classic for a number of reasons: foremost among them is the scene featuring Brando and Steiger in the back of a cab, with Brando's immortal "I could've been a contender. I could've been somebody, instead of a bum, which is what I am" and "What did I get? A one-way ticket to Palookaville." Possibly the scene's intensity comes from the fact that it was shot quickly: Brando had to leave by four o'clock and couldn't stay for Steiger's close-ups, and Kazan had to play Brando for part of the shooting. It's the best-remembered of the movie's many great Brando scenes. He has a simple, winning charm, full of child-like contradictions – the hard man who keeps pigeons, a boxer fighting his own kindness.

Part of the film's success is due to its documentary quality, revealing the mundane corruption, the lousy pay and conditions, and the long-term harm of manual labour. It's a feeling that's increased by the use of the bustling docks of Hoboken in New York and the use of real longshoremen as extras. However, this use of actual locations did bring its own problems, in the form of real-life Johnny Friendlys who weren't too pleased with the movie's subject matter, as the director explained to Michel Ciment in the book *Kazan On Kazan*: "Watching me shooting used to be all the gangsters that we described in the picture! And they'd come up – once a guy grabbed me and was going to beat me up. A longshoreman beat him up." As for the parallels with Kazan's post-HUAC experiences, Kazan is, in his autobiography, unequivocal: "I did see [the] story as my own, and that connection did lend the tone of irrefutable anger to the scenes I photographed and my work with actors ... so when critics say that I put my story and my feelings on the screen, to justify my informing, they are right."

The irony – which, one assumes, was either lost on Kazan or bullishly endorsed – is that when Malloy testifies he is told that he will never get work in America again; Kazan and all those who also testified easily found work afterwards and, allegedly, were often able to command larger fees. It was the people who were *named* who found it difficult to work in cinema again. As blacklistee Jules Dassin said about himself, he was one of the lucky ones – only out of work for five years, rather than permanently. Elia Kazan was by no means a victim of HUAC.

Pépé le moko

dir **Julien Duvivier, 1936, Fr, 93m, b/w**
cast **Jean Gabin, Mireille Balin, Line Noro, Lucas Gridoux, Fernand Charpin** *cin* **Jules Kruger, Marc Fossard,** *m* **Vincent Scotto**

Described by Jean Cocteau as a masterpiece, the film is undeservedly more famous for providing the inspiration for the Warner Bros cartoon character Pépé Le Pew. Like *A bout de souffle*, it changed the cinema that had inspired it: a homage to the gangster genre, it influenced the US movies that were to follow.

It's set in the Casbah in Algiers, a honeycomb maze of narrow corridors and vaulted caves where the authorities fear to tread. In the middle of it is Pépé Le Moko (**Jean Gabin**), a gangster who had to leave France in a hurry two years earlier after a bank robbery in Toulon which netted him 2,000,000 francs. Dandyish and charismatic, he "has a smile for his friends and a knife for his enemies", according to his adversary, local inspector Slimane. Although Le Moko has a small empire, he's in domestic purgatory – he's fed up with his gypsy girl Ines (**Line Noro**) and his life in the Casbah, but he cannot leave because at least there he is safe. Enter Gaby (Mireille Balin), a Parisian socialite and social climber. Dripping with diamonds, she's temptation on legs. And it's not just her rocks he has eyes for. She has the glitz and glamour of the Paris for which he yearns.

Behind the scenes and pulling the strings is Slimane, who cannot simply bring the thief to justice, because, as he explains to French and Algerian police chiefs, Pépé would kill him if he tried to arrest him in the Casbah. Instead he has a cunning plan. He ferrets around, playing off characters against each other and using Pépé's obsession with Gaby to entice the gangster out of the Casbah where he can be successfully arrested.

The film was influential on two counts. First and foremost was the model it provided in the portrayal of its lead character, Pépé Le Moko. Displaced, disaffected and poetically doomed, he is the existential loner who will be a common figure in American *film noir* of the 1940s and early 1950s. The influence is particularly acute in the character of the gangster in John Huston's 1948 movie *Key Largo*. Like Johnny Rocco in *Largo*, Pépé has been removed from his power base, but is still a force to be reckoned with. Both Rocco and Moko are trapped, living off their reputations, loathing the woman they're with and waiting for the moment when they can return to the big time. Both will fail and die. Of course, where Rocco is oily, Moko is slick.

The other big influence was director Julien Duvivier's idiosyncratic style. His synthesis of expressionism and crime-movie tropes was to be repeated again and again by directors of *films noirs* a decade later. Two things particularly stand out. One is a memorable shot of Gabin's face covered in shadow, the light falling only on his eyes (a terrible cliché now, but an innovative trick back then). And the other is an exemplary use of Venetian blinds. These have become a key prop of *noir*, especially the self-conscious *noir* of the 1980s and 1990s (see *Double Indemnity* (1944), *Body Heat* (1981) and *Angel Heart* (1987) for sterling blind-work). When light pours in through a Venetian blind, characters appear to be either bisected or imprisoned by the ensuing shadows; it either undermines their authority and sense of self, or is an ominous foretelling of their fate. *Pépé Le Moko* has one of the first and most subtle uses of the "blinds technique": it's one of the many reasons we should be grateful for the film's existence.

Performance

dir **Donald Cammell & Nicolas Roeg, 1970, UK, 105m**

cast **James Fox, Mick Jagger, Anita Pallenberg, Michèle Breton, Ann Sidney** *cin* **Nicolas Roeg** *m* **Jack Nitzsche**

The critical appraisal of *Performance* has had a rocky ride. At the time it was lauded as a kaleidoscopic treatise on the nature of gender, sexuality and identity; now it's sometimes denigrated as a compendium of Brit-flick clichés. It's actually a rare British masterpiece.

Chas (**James Fox**) is the flash right-hand man for London gang boss Harry Flowers (**Johnny Sheehan**). His job is to apply pressure, he likes his job and "that's the half of it". This self-styled Lone Ranger gets into trouble with his employers when he kills bookmaker Joey Maddox. Looking for somewhere to lie low, he overhears a conversation about a room for rent in a house belonging to Turner (**Mick Jagger**), a superstar-turned-hermit, a rubber-lipped rock god who's lost his creative demon and wasted his musical talent. Chas claims – somewhat incredibly – that he is a bohemian juggler, and Turner is uninterested in putting up such a transparently dodgy geezer in his basement, until he divines in Chas some of the energy and ferocity he wants to recapture for himself, and decides Chas is a suitable case for treatment. Aided by his female entourage (played by **Anita Pallenberg** and **Michèle Breton**), and some particularly potent magic mushrooms, Turner plunges the hardman into a psychological maelstrom of bewildering gender-interrogation and role-play, all framed with a suitably psychedelic dazzle. Chas's protestations of his "normality" to his boho hosts become increasingly unconvincing over the course of his stay, and identities blur. Events become more and more dream-

A bloodstained Chas (James Fox) prepares to go into hiding, having just received one

like and unfixed: Chas appears to kill Turner by shooting him in the head, but when Chas's gang finally track him down to take him away, it's Turner, not Chas, who gets carted off.

Although the film was set in Powis Square, Notting Hill, it was actually filmed in Lowndes Square in Kensington. And what happened in that flat has passed into rock and film legend: the apartment became "a psycho-sexual laboratory" in the words of Jagger's then girlfriend, **Marianne Faithfull**. The best rumours include the one about out-takes of Jagger and Pallenberg's sex scenes somehow finding their way to the so-called **Wet Dream Festival** in Amsterdam in 1968 and winning first prize. And that, when **Keith Richards** heard what Jagger and Pallenberg (Keith's then girlfriend) were getting up to, he refused to play on the soundtrack's Rolling Stones feature, "Memo From Turner". At least the latter is definitely true.

It is rumoured that James Fox had a mental breakdown on set, that – like the character he played – he unknowingly took drugs given to him by Jagger and Pallenberg and was teased and tormented by the duo until he didn't know who he was. It's true that after *Performance* Fox gave up acting to sell both vacuum cleaners and Jesus. Fox, however, has always maintained that whatever happened on that set did not lead directly to his decision to quit the business. The movie hit Michèle Breton hardest of all. A young ingénue, her head really was turned by the making of *Performance*: she became a heroin addict and drifted around Europe for decades, missing presumed dead, until author **Mick Brown** tracked her down for his book on the film.

Performance had a very real connection with the gangster world it depicted. The film's *éminence grise* was a character called **David Litvinoff**, whom writer/director Donald Cammell had befriended. Litvinoff was an underworld legend, a charismatic chancer who knew both Charlie Richardson and Ronnie Kray, and it was his stories that gave substance to the script. For instance, Harry Flowers, the East End crime lord with a penchant for muscle mags, is clearly based upon Ronnie Kray. Flowers was played by Johnny Sheehan, who had never acted before – his suitability for the part was noticed while he was giving Fox boxing lessons. And the part of Moody was played by John Bindon. Part actor, part hood, he was the wideboy of British TV and cinema of the 1960s and 1970s (most notably in **Ken Loach**'s *Poor Cow* of 1967). He ran a protection racket in pubs and clubs in Fulham and was put on trial for the murder of South London gangster **Johnnie Darke**. Even though he was found not guilty, the bad publicity killed his career.

Performance was the directorial debut for both **Nic Roeg** and **Donald Cammell**; and while Roeg equalled, if not bettered, it with films such as *Don't Look Now*, *The Man Who Fell To Earth* and *Eureka*, Cammell never quite succeeded in doing so. A brilliant polymath, his ideas never wholly translated, always seeming a little arch in their erudition and knowingness, and he produced a string of interesting failures: *Demon Seed*, *White Of The Eye* and *Wild Side*. The latter was re-cut by the studios against his will, but, despite its traumatic and acrimonious nature, friends dispute that the subsequent battle led directly to Cammell's suicide in 1996. Cammell shot himself through the forehead: he remained alive for 45 minutes, during which time he remained lucid and asked for a mirror so that he could, as far as possible, observe his own death.

Performance is well known for its kaleidoscopic form: its jump-cuts, inserts, flash-forwards and flash-backs. But it didn't start out this way. The original cut was much longer, the early gangster scenes in particular. When the studio executives saw a test screening they were disgusted – not just by the sex and drugs, but also apparently by the dirty water in the bath that Jagger, Pallenberg and Breton are seen in. The execs were also unhappy that Jagger did not appear until some way into the film. Cammell was forced to radically re-edit. Together with editor Frank Mazzola he came up with a strategy for the narrative which leaps between the movie's various milieux with a bewildering abruptness and brevity. Considered both inventive and incoherent on its release, its edginess has been blunted over time, with many of its innovations becoming familiar clichés, especially in rock videos. As Mazzola once told this author, "*Performance* was the first MTV movie."

Like *Get Carter* (1971), *Perfomance* became adopted and co-opted by the new gangster chic of the 1990s film world. *Gangster No.1* (2000), in particular, owed a stylistic debt to Cammell and Roeg's film: Paul Bettany's performance is virtually an impersonation of James Fox. And Fox himself, enough water having passed under the bridge, made a knowing cameo in *Sexy Beast* (2000). Tellingly, it's now Fox's East End flash villain who's the cultural icon and not Mick Jagger's androgynous rock star.

Point Blank

dir **John Boorman, 1967, US, 92m**
cast **Lee Marvin, Angie Dickinson, Keenan Wynn, Carroll O'Connor, Lloyd Bochner, Micheal Strong** *cin* **Philip H Lathrop** *m* **Johnny Mandel**

Dead or alive? That's the question we keep asking ourselves throughout John Boorman's 1967 revenge movie.

When we first see the movie's protagonist, Walker (**Lee Marvin**), he's been left for dead on Alcatraz island. His wife and supposed best friend Mal Reese (**John Vernon**) have double-crossed him after the three of them ripped off some members of a criminal outfit at a money drop on the island: they've shot him (at the titular point-blank range) and taken his money. What happens subsequently could either be the dream of a dying man, or the revenge of a man who has come back from the dead (perhaps even literally).

Walker manages to get off the island, although we are never told how and are reminded, significantly, that no-one has ever swum back to the mainland. One year later, he's being helped by a secretive informant called Yost (**Keenan Wynn**) who tells him that Mal Reese has progressed to the upper echelons of a crime syndicate called The Organisation and that he's living with Walker's wife. Yost gives Walker their address, explaining to him that "you want Reese and I want The Organisation". Arriving at the house, he discovers that Reese has now left his wife for her sister Chris (**Angie Dickinson**), but it transpires that she too has been badly treated, and gladly helps Walker to track down her lover. Even when the plan succeeds, and even after he has thrown Reese off the roof of his penthouse apartment, Walker is not satisfied. He wants his money and decides that he will make The Organisation pay.

There are many hints that Walker is already dead or dying. He's asked at one point if he's still alive, and is later told "you died in Alcatraz alright". The film's structure is not always linear, often shuttling back and forth through time. The depiction of events that Walker recalls is accompanied by a dream-like voice-over, the

The Outfit
dir John Flynn,
1973, US, 103m

Like *Point Blank*, John Flynn's abrasive thriller is based on a "Parker" novel by Donald E. Westlake, and the two films, unsurprisingly, share certain traits. First up, the protagonist undergoes another name change – Parker is now Earl Macklin, played by the ever-dependable Robert Duvall. And the plot rings familiar: Macklin is gunning for the syndicate that killed his bank-robber brother, but is seeking financial retribution rather than revenge per se. But that's where the similarities end: where *Point Blank* was all minimalism and jet-age sheen, *The Outfit* is fleshy, grainy and more concerned with gnarly male relationships than abstract, metaphysical notions. And this difference is best articulated by the protagonists themselves: Lee Marvin's spectral *sang froid* gives way to Duvall's bruised humanity.

Lee Marvin as the impassive force of nature Walker in *Point Blank* (1967)

sound doesn't always match the pictures, and his moments of agony (death?) in Alcatraz are returned to over and over again, as if that is the present, and everything in between is not real.

Walker is a combination of the Lee Marvins we've seen in other movies; there's the preternaturally cool Lee Marvin, a man without emotions, but the psychopath of *The Big Heat* (1953) is never far from the surface, not least when he's shooting holes into the bed of his wife and his best friend. As critics have suggested, the name Walker is perfect for the character (he was called Parker in Richard Stark's source novel *The Hunter*); in one classic scene he's walking along a corridor, the click-clacking of his heels echoing on the soundtrack, and the sound continues even when the scene ends and a new one begins. The name suggests that Walker is someone who's defined by his actions, that he has no defining characteristic other than he wants his money back, and brings to mind Nietzsche's dictum "to do is to be".

There is a fascinating connection between character and actor, Marvin and Walker, as John Boorman revealed in an interview with *The Independent* newspaper in 1998. "When I made *Point Blank* it was to some extent a documentary about him," the director said, explaining that as a Marine during World War II, Marvin and his platoon were ambushed in Saipan. Almost all his colleagues were killed, and he was shot, almost fatally. Boorman believed that Marvin "had guilt about surviving, but he came back. That was what *Point Blank* was. It was about a man who's shot, comes back and is searching for his soul. Lee did that every day."

What Boorman brought to the film was a design aesthetic not

unlike another 1967 movie, *Le samourai*. Everywhere Walker goes he's framed by modernist, elemental architecture marked by its clean lines, as spare of detail as Walker is himself. And the film not only succeeds on visual and metaphysical levels but as a good old-fashioned thriller: it's pacy and taut (again, qualities it shares with Walker). Ultimately *Point Blank* works so well because it unites the tension and plotting of the best Hollywood movies with the sensibility and minimalist style of the best European cinema.

The Public Enemy

dir **William Wellman, 1931, US, 84m, b/w**
cast **James Cagney, Jean Harlow, Edward Woods, Donald Cook, Joan Blondell** *cin* **Dev Jennings** *m* **David Mendoza**

The film that made James Cagney a star and turned the grapefruit into an unlikely and unforgettable weapon, it is one third of the holy trinity of early gangster movies. With *Little Caesar* (1930) and *Scarface* (1932), it set the template for a whole genre.

The *Public Enemy* charts the rise and fall of a gangster, Tom Powers, and his friend Matt (**Edward Woods**). It starts with their early shoplifting days in 1909, then progresses to their robbery of a factory in 1915, and to the start of Prohibition in 1920, the year in which they go to work for dandy gangster Nails Nathan. They become the leaders of his trouble squad, strong-arming bar owners into selling their beer. When Nails is killed, a gang war flares up as rivals fight to take his place; Matt is gunned down in the street and Tom single-handedly wreaks his revenge.

The bare bones of the story hardly begin to suggest just how influential *The Public Enemy* was. So many elements of it have appeared in other movies: the two best friends who are closer than brothers; and the character who is the moral conscience of the movie (in this case Tom's saintly brother Mike) persistently clashing with the bad seed. *The Public Enemy* has a classic confrontation scene. In the age of Prohibition, Tom brings a barrel of beer

Public Enemy Number Two

When we first see Cagney he's strutting into a room like a bantam cock, wearing his hat with attitude, his cap tilted to one side. He doesn't so much speak as snarl, baring his teeth like a dog. What's surprising is that Cagney was actually hired to play Matt – the best friend – and Edward Woods was cast as Tom Powers and the film started being shot that way. It was only when director William Wellman saw the daily rushes that he realized that the actors were playing the wrong parts and swapped them around. His decision changed Cagney and Woods' lives for good; by the end of the 1930s Woods' career was all but over while Cagney was on his way to becoming a big-screen icon.

The grapefruit

According to biographer **Richard Schickel**, it was a grapefruit that made James Cagney a superstar. And that defining citrus makes its impact halfway through the film, during the period of Tom's first flush of success. Bored by his domestic arrangements, sitting at the breakfast table with its bourgeois trappings, Tom is being nagged by his girl, Kitty (**Mae Clark**), and remarks – with irremediably flawed semantics – "I wish you was a wishing well, so I could tie a bucket around you and sink you."

When she replies that maybe he's found someone he likes better, he takes half a grapefruit from his dish, shoves it in her face, and gives it a twist. It's such a startling moment, even in an age of ubiquitous on-screen violence, that everyone involved in the movie wanted to take credit for it – the sceenwriters, producer Darryl Zanuck and director William Wellman (who claimed that the original weapon was going to be an egg, but it was considered too runny to be viable). Legend has it that the scene was based upon an incident involving the real-life gangster **Little Hymie Weiss**, a moll and an omelette. Mae Clark, the victim of the grapefruit, claims the scene and its subsequent notoriety ruined her career. But it was the making of Cagney's.

home, and plonks it on the dining table. No one can see around it while they're eating. The scene veers close to Mel Brooks–style parody until Mike accuses Tom of working for gangsters. He asserts, melodramatically, that the barrel contains "not just beer. But beer and blood!" (the latter being the original title of the movie) and tips over the keg. The mother of course is ignorant of all her sons' goings-on – in most early gangster movies the mother is a naïve bastion of virtue, never wanting to think ill of her offspring.

The Public Enemy has many other archetypal gangster-movie aspects. The gangsters make it big and celebrate by purchasing flashy new threads. And there is that typically Oedipal hallmark of the gangster genre: the killing of the father-figure. (Here it is Putty Nose, the fence who left them in the lurch after a botched burglary five years earlier. They eventually catch up with him and despatch him in a particularly striking honour killing. Putty Nose pleads for his life while sitting at a piano, even going as far as performing a song he used to play to them as children, hoping that it will stir their sympathies. The camera pans away, a shot is fired, and we hear the crashing of chords as Putty's body slumps on the keys.) The movie, of course, has the obligatory platinum-blonde moll. **Jean Harlow**, throughout her brief appearance, towers over Cagney, making him appear small in every way. He's infatuated by her indifference to him: she gives him the run-around and he can't get enough.

What's unusual about *The Public Enemy* is the gangster's death. There is no moment of glory, no climactic shoot-out with the cops. Instead there's something else entirely – a horribly discordant finale. A shoot-out leaves Tom seriously injured and he is taken to hospital, where he is reconciled with his mother and brother. They later hear that he has been kidnapped from the hospital by members of a rival gang, but a phone call allays their fears. Apparently he's on his way home, and his mother excitedly gets his bedroom ready, gabbing on about how good it will be to have her son back again. There's a knock on the door, and Mike opens it. Tom's corpse, trussed up in a blanket like an Egyptian mummy, falls forward towards the camera and towards us. It's a scene more akin to one from a Universal horror movie than a Warners gangster film.

Cagney and Harlow: gangster and moll of *The Public Enemy*

Pulp Fiction

dir Quentin Tarantino, 1994, US, 154m
cast John Travolta, Samuel L. Jackson, Uma Thurman, Bruce Willis, Harvey Keitel, Tim Roth, Rosanna Arquette
cin Andrzej Sekula

The origins of *Pulp Fiction* and its relationship to *Reservoir Dogs* (1991) are as complicated and as cyclical as the narrative itself. The basic idea of *Reservoir Dogs* was originally one of the short stories that was to comprise *Pulp Fiction*, but Tarantino decided it was worth developing into a full-length script and eventually got the financial backing to shoot it. Its success gave him the where-withal to make *Pulp Fiction*, and intended it as a prequel of sorts to *Reservoir Dogs*, chronicling the adventures of gangster Vic Vega, a part Tarantino envisaged being played by Michael Madsen. But

How *Pulp Fiction* was written

Pulp Fiction, according to the credits is "written and directed by Quentin Tarantino", with stories "by Quentin Tarantino and Roger Avary". In fact, Avary did more than just write a story, he was as much responsible for the complex narrative structure as Tarantino. This is how they did it, according to Avary: "Quentin said, 'let's get all of our favourite scenes that we've ever written and put them altogether and see how they fit'. And so I went to my files and he went to his files and we rented a flat in Amsterdam, which supplied us with the creative motivations needed to assemble such non-linear story-telling techniques. And we literally took these scenes and laid them out on the floor, and started moving them around, and pretty soon a movie started to form."

Madsen turned down the role to make *Wyatt Earp* (1994) instead. Tarantino brought in John Travolta and Vic became Vince, Vic's brother, thus raising the possibility, which was often talked about by Tarantino and Madsen, that they could always make a third film – The Vega Brothers. However, there is no overt reference to a brother in either movie, and it's still a scenario that exists only in Tarantino's imagination.

The idea behind *Pulp Fiction*, according to co-writer Roger Avary, was to take stock situations but "instead of turning right where you're used to turning right, turn left" (for a more detailed account of the writing of *Pulp Fiction*'s screenplay see box). So we start with the gangster who has to take the boss's wife out for the evening, with explicit instructions not to touch her (even for a foot massage); in a typical *noir* story they would fall in love and plot to despatch the husband. In *Pulp Fiction*, just as temptation is about to get the better of them, our moll mistakes some grade-A "madman" heroin for cocaine and overdoses. Then we have the story of the boxer (Bruce Willis) who defies orders to throw his fight and, rather than the "doomed flight from the city" scenario, his story ends up in urbanized *Deliverance* territory – held prisoner, alongside the gangster, he crossed in a basement with a gimp. The third part takes the "disposing of the body" trope (see *Goodfellas* [1990] for a classic body-disposal scene) and gives it a twist. And all this is book-ended with a "killer couple" (cf. *Bonnie And Clyde*, *Gun Crazy*, *You Only Live Once*) sticking up a diner.

Tarantino succeeded where most postmodern fiction fails: he took conventions and clichés and rehabilitated them, making them entirely his own. And that's largely due to the potency of his reference-strewn, pop-culture-saturated dialogue: the difference between quarter-pounders in France and America, the taste of five-dollar milkshakes, apocalyptic fire-and-brimstone sermonizing (Samuel L. Jackson's "Vengeance of the Lord" speech), the Pepsi challenge, Kung Fu, obscure TV pilots, and the value of gourmet coffee are all grist to the mill of Tarantino dialogue. After *Pulp Fiction* it seemed as if every hip American movie had to have a scene in which a few characters meditate on the virtues of comic-strip heroes or the qualities of hamburgers. Which is better – *Pulp Fiction* or *Reservoir Dogs* – became an argument as vociferous as the *Godfather I* or *II* debate. Some *Dogs* fans claimed that, with *Pulp Fiction*, Tarantino entered his own alternative universe of cartoonish violence, from which he's never escaped, and that by making movies about movies he has, to quote *Pulp Fiction*'s screenplay, made "a wax museum with a pulse".

If there's one theme that resonates throughout *Pulp Fiction*, it's resurrection: Mia Wallace (**Uma Thurman**) is brought back from the dead after she has overdosed. Thanks to the flashback structure, Vince "comes back to life" after being shot by Butch

Travolta and Jackson: the burger-munching hitmen of *Pulp Fiction* (1994). Note: Vincent Vega is not actually a butterfly magnet; it's a sticker on the glass behind him

(**Bruce Willis**). Jules is saved from certain death by a miracle. It's a theme which appeared to extend beyond the confines of the film itself: *Pulp Fiction* resurrected Travolta's career; Bruce Willis was reborn, in terms of the movie roles he was offered; and Samuel L. Jackson became a superstar. Everyone could quote at least one line of dialogue from the movie, usually "Bring out the gimp!" But behind all the talk of Big Macs, the retro soundtrack, and the casual violence, there are also sly references and in-jokes for afficionados: for instance Travolta (Vince) and Jackson (Jules) start out in classic gangster chic – the *Reservoir Dogs* uniform of sharp black suit, white shirt and black tie – but end up in their shorts and T-shirts looking like a couple of dorks. It's a portent of the end of their gangster careers. Soon Vince will be dead and Jules will leave the profession "to walk the earth".

Reservoir Dogs

dir Quentin Tarantino, 1991, US, 99m
cast Harvey Keitel, Tim Roth, Michael Madsen, Chris Penn, Steve Buscemi *cin* Andrzej Sekula *m* Karyn Rachtman

The film that changed the dialogue of the gangster movie, if not the language of cinema. At the time of its release, many critics remarked how unusual it was for a heist film not to show the heist itself. In fact it had been done before, the most notable example being *They Live By Night* (1948). What *is* unusual about *Reservoir Dogs* is the dialogue: Tarantino was fed up with characters just talking about their schemes "while polishing their bullets". He wanted his gangsters to talk about real things – though in Tarantino's universe, real things tend to be other movies and pop songs.

And so the film starts with the gangsters having a learned discussion about the lyrics of **Madonna**'s song "Like A Virgin" being an extended metaphor about the pleasures of big dicks; then the conversation moves on to the ethics of tipping. Mr Pink – all the gangsters have been assigned simple colour-related aliases by the ageing boss Joe (**Lawrence Tierney**) – doesn't believe in tipping, and nor did Tarantino himself, apparently. The writer wrote the part for himself, and much of Mr Pink's dialogue is based on Tarantino's own prejudices and observations; it was only reluctantly that he conceded it to **Steve Buscemi** and demoted himself to Mr Brown (or "Mr Shit", as he says in the film).

After the iconic title sequence of the "Dogs" walking in slow motion in their uniform of black suits, thin black ties and white shirts to the musical accompaniment of "Little Green Bag" by The George Baker Selection, the film flashes forward abruptly to Mr Orange (**Tim Roth**) in the back of a car, squealing and bleeding. Mr White (**Harvey Keitel**) takes him to the warehouse that is the gang's agreed rendezvous point, where the rest of the movie will play out. Details are revealed, the story is fleshed out in flashback (though Tarantino prefers to call them chapters rather than flashbacks), and that's how we discover that Mr Orange is an undercover cop who has infiltrated the gang and that he tipped off the cops who were waiting at the diamond wholesalers. The survivors of the heist, Mr Blonde (**Michael Madsen**), Mr White and Mr

Recipe for *Reservoir Dogs*

Take the non-linear narrative from Stanley Kubrick's *The Killing*.

Blend in Jean-Pierre Melville's *Le doulos*: one of the thieves has tipped off the police and we only find out twenty minutes from the end who the real informant is (in *Reservoir Dogs* it's thirty minutes).

Add a pinch from *The Taking Of Pelham One Two Three* (1974): a gang who hijack a subway train in return for a ransom refer to each other using colour-related pseudonyms – Mr Blue, Mr Green, Mr Grey and Mr Brown – so that they can't be identified.

Toss in an ear removed from *Black Caesar* (1973): in the blaxploitation flick, gangster Fred Williams slices off his victim's ear with a razor. At least his victim was dead...

Stir in the last fifteen minutes of *City On Fire* (1987): in Ringo Lam's Hong Kong classic, undercover cop Ko (Chow Yun-Fat) infiltrates a gang about to do a jewel heist; the robbery goes wrong, Ko is shot, and is taken to a warehouse where the surviving members of the gang try to work out who ratted them out. It climaxes in a Mexican stand-off.

Dogs on DVD

Aside from a minor glitch – the cast and crew commentary seems to be gleaned from interviews that are included on the second disc – the 2004 special-edition DVD of *Reservoir Dogs* is excellent. There are two informative documentaries, a heavily edited interview with the punctuationally-challenged director which is both exhaustive and exhausting, and Chris Penn divulging the secret of who killed Nice Guy Eddie. There are interviews from 1992, as well as deleted scenes (which reveal that there was once a woman in the cast), and a tribute to Lawrence Tierney, but the real added-value extra is the dry run, shot by the Sundance Lab. It's a sort of filmed rehearsal of scenes, in which Tarantino takes Harvey Keitel's place as Mr White, and doesn't do that badly. No, really!

Pink, know that someone has set them up, that "there's a rat in the house", but they're not sure who the rodent is.

They beat up a policeman to find out. Mr Blonde tortures him, more for his own amusement than for information, in a scene that caused most of the movie's controversy. *Reservoir Dogs* was not released on video in the UK for a few years while the censors worked out what to do about the on-screen violence. What's interesting is that there isn't much. The ear-removal scene is off-camera and, muffled screams aside, left to our imagination, which makes it more disturbing (though its accompaniment by the jaunty "Stuck In The Middle With You" by Stealers Wheel certainly helps). However, the reasons for the off-camera decision may have been practical: footage was shot of the ear being sliced off but apparently the ear wasn't all that impressive – looking too much like a piece of latex glued to the side of an actor's head, as we can see for ourselves in an extra feature on the special-edition DVD.

It all ends, famously, in a Mexican stand-off: Joe shoots Mr Orange, Mr White shoots Joe, and Nice Guy Eddie shoots Mr White, begging the question who killed Nice Guy Eddie? There have been lots of articles, websites, and even T-shirts that have tried to answer the question. There have been theories similar to those about the Kennedy assassination involving magic, zigzag bullets. In the audio commentary for the 2004 special-edition DVD, **Chris Penn** reveals the secret: Harvey Keitel was meant to turn and shoot Penn after being hit himself, but Penn's special-effect squib went off too soon and he fell backwards, covered in fake blood. Instead of re-shooting Tarantino decided to keep the take. He liked the mystery. "Don't worry, they'll be asking us forever," he reputedly prophesized. And they were.

A final word regarding the two actors, Lawrence Tierney and **Eddie Bunker**, who played Joe and Mr Blue. Tierney was an actor and real-life heavy, while Bunker was a career criminal who wrote novels while in jail. Two of Bunker's books have been adapted into movies: the edgy prison thriller movie *Straight Time*, based on his no-holds-barred novel *No Beast So Fierce*, and *Animal Factory* which was directed by Mr Pink himself, Steve Buscemi. One afternoon on set, Bunker stared and stared at Tierney's bald, scarred head. When Tim Roth asked him what he was doing, Bunker said he was trying to remember if it was him who had given Tierney those scars forty years earlier.

Rififi

dir **Jules Dassin, 1955, Fr, 117m, b/w**
cast **Jean Servais, Carl Möhner, Robert Manuel, Perlo
Vita (Jules Dassin), Magali Nöel** *cin* **Philippe Agostini** *m*
Georges Auric

Rififi was the heist movie that put the heist at the centre of the
movie. An audacious 25-minute robbery without dialogue or
music, it set the standard for subsequent screen thievery.

According to writer/director **Jules Dassin**, he was only given
the job because he had been blacklisted in the United States. When
he completed the adaptation, he was called to the home of the
author of the novel it was based on, **Auguste Le Breton**. Le Breton
told him "I've read your screenplay and what I would like to know
is: where is my book?" Dassin explained what often happens to
novels when they're adapted for a movie. Le Breton again asked
"where is my book?" And, just as Dassin was about to go over it all
again, Le Breton pulled out a gun. Dassin burst out laughing, which
broke the deadlock. Le Breton hugged him and they became firm,
but unlikely, friends.

In fact, Le Breton had, perhaps, a legitimate gripe: what survives of his novel is only the bare bones. Parisian thief Tony (**Jean
Servais**) is released from jail and is approached by two friends who
want him to take part in a smash-and-grab raid on the jewellers
Mappin and Webb. Tony decides against it but persuades them to
take part in a more elaborate, more rewarding plan: to go in through
the ceiling and to rob the safe with the help of safe-cracker Cesare
(played by Dassin himself, under the pseudonym Perlo Vita).

The carefully executed plan goes well. They net 240 million
francs' worth of gems, and their heist makes all the front pages. It's
almost the perfect crime until Cesare makes a fatal mistake. He
gives his lover a stolen ring, which comes to the attention of a local
gangster and, under duress, Cesare rats out his accomplices, placing
both their loot and their lives in jeopardy.

The near-silent robbery scene, in which all we hear is the chip-
ping away of the ceiling, is the stand-out moment in the film. It was

To the victors, the spoils: it's all downhill from here for *Riffifi*'s robbers

entirely due to Dassin's genius: he realized that since the thieves were consummate profes-sionals, they wouldn't make a sound during the robbery. Composer **Georges Auric** was not convinced and wrote twenty min-utes of music for the scene anyway. He was only convinced by the merits of dropping it when he saw the final cut. Only then did he agree with Dassin: "pas de musique".

By making the robbery a spectacle *Rififi* changed the heist movie forever, and introduced an element of panache and audacity that was soon imitated in films such as *How To Steal A Million* (1966), *The Thomas Crown Affair* (1968), and Dassin's own *Topkapi* (1964), in which acrobats famously dangle from a rope attached to the roof of a museum in order to steal a jewel-encrusted dagger. However, the brilliance of the 25-minute *coup de cinéma* in *Rififi* overshadows everything that follows in the film, which is a shame as *Rififi* is more than just a glorious set piece. The unravelling of the plot is equally, and very differently, impressive as the gang are remorse-lessly picked off one by one with grim predictability. The unrelent-ing, uncompromising gloom and the vivid evocation of ominous Parisian streets led director **François Truffaut** to declare that *Rififi* was "the best film noir I have ever seen". The film won Dassin the best director's award at Cannes in 1955 but also earned him the reproach of authorities around the world. Everywhere it was shown, copycat robberies ensued: criminals were using the film as a blueprint.

The Roaring Twenties

dir Raoul Walsh, 1939, US, 106m, b/w
cast James Cagney, Priscilla Lane, Humphrey Bogart,
Gladys George, Jeffrey Lynn *cin* Ernest Haller *m* Heinz
Roemheld

The film that has almost everything – Bogart, Cagney and every plot point, stock character and cliché of the 1930s – it is like a compilation album of the genre's greatest hits. Made at the end of the 1930s, the period of classic gangster movies, it feels like a parody or homage to the films that had been made only seven or eight years earlier.

Starting in World War I, the film cuts to a rat-hole on the Western Front in France, where three men are taking refuge in the middle of a battle – tough but tender Eddie Bartlett (**James Cagney**), frightened, vulnerable Lloyd Hart (**Jeffrey Lynn**), and the possibly psychopathic George Hally (**Humphrey Bogart**). When armistice is declared they go their separate ways. Eddie is expecting to go back to his old job but his boss reneges on his promise that he will always have a place for him. After taking a job as a taxi driver he is forced, out of sheer economic necessity, to work for a speakeasy, but his good business sense means that he's soon running his own distillery. His partner in crime is Panama Smith (**Gladys George**), a thinly veiled version of nightclub hostess Texas Guinan, who used to address her clientele with the words "Hello, suckers!" Panama has a similar line in patter, and even though she clearly loves Eddie, he only has eyes for young, wannabe singer Jean (**Priscilla Lane**). The money he makes from his gin empire allows him to employ Lloyd as his lawyer and to pay for an audience to watch and applaud Jean. However, it's not long before he's involved in a turf war with another gangster, Nick Brown (**Paul Kelly**), and it is at this point that he is reunited with George, a booze-runner for Brown, who swiftly, too swiftly, changes sides. Eddie's happiness doesn't last long – Jean has an affair with Lloyd, and Eddie is betrayed by George, who's tired of being his stooge.

With his life and his empire in tatters, Eddie turns both to the bottle and to Panama. And then he's approached by Jean who, in a textbook case of adding insult to injury, begs him to help out Lloyd who's in deadly trouble with George. And Eddie agrees! If Cagney's Rocky Sullivan in *Angels With The Dirty Faces* was the nicest gangster in cinema history, then Eddie Bartlett runs him a close second. Based on real-life underworld kingpin Larry Fay, Eddie comes across more like a good businessman than a gangster, just matching supply with demand. It's a long way into the film before he takes up a gun, and even then there's no sense that he's lost his humanity, or crossed the line.

As for Bogart's George, although Bogie played many psychopathic gangsters, this is by far his most cynical and cold-blooded. When Lloyd refuses to shoot a 15-year-old German during the war, Bogart does the job with relish, adding "well, he won't be sixteen". And he has no compunction about killing his old sergeant years later, even though the man is unarmed. When he does the dirty on Cagney, he laughs "I always said, when you got a job to do, get someone else to do it."

Bootlegger barons: Lynn, Cagney and Bogart

It's these moments of knowing villainy that add to the sense of pastiche in *The Roaring Twenties*. And this is increased by the extravagant montages: many 1930s gangster films have a montage section – of newspapers reporting crimes, of the hoodlum shooting his way to the top, of restaurants being blown up in gang wars – but nothing quite like this. *The Roaring Twenties* tells the recent history of America in overblown, almost camp images that wouldn't look out of place in a **Busby Berkeley** musical. For instance, the Wall Street Crash is denoted by a giant ticker-tape machine towering over a mass of people and spilling out paper like confetti, and then, like a Dalí dream sequence, the stock exchange melts down.

Shooting began under one director, **Anatole Litvanak**, and finished under another, Raoul Walsh, but it is Don Siegel (himself later to be a director) who, as a member of Warner Brothers' montage department, takes credit for the exuberant interludes. Walsh, however, was certainly the man responsible for the last scene, and another memorable Cagney death: falling onto the snow-clad steps of a church, mortally wounded, he dies in the arms of his lover. When a policeman asks what his business was, she replies "He used to be a big shot."

The St Valentine's Day Massacre

dir Roger Corman, 1967, US, 99m

cast Jason Robards, George Segal, Ralph Meeker, Jean Hale, Clint Ritchie, Frank Silvera, Joseph Camanella, Bruce Dern *cin* Milton Krasner *m* Fred Steiner

Corman's movie is a late entry to the gangster biopic era that started in the late 1950s, though it is usually regarded by critics as the pick of the bunch. Critic Phil Hardy even described it as "one of the best gangster films of the decade" – high praise indeed when you consider that the decade gave us *Point Blank*, *Bonnie And Clyde* and *Le samourai*, to name but a few. Corman would appear to agree, describing his film as "the most accurate, authentic gangster movie ever". The director had already made one biopic, *Machine Gun Kelly* (1958) and, to make his screenplay as authentic as possible, he employed **Howard Browne** to write it. Browne was a Chicago journalist who'd actually covered the killings four decades earlier. And the film's documentary intent is signalled right away by the use of a voice-over. The authoritative yet almost tabloid-style intoning of **Paul Frees** harks back to the police serials of the late 1950s/early 1960s, a clear intimation that we are going to get the facts, just the facts.

The movie's credibility is punctured somewhat by the first appearance of Al Capone, who's played by the thin, lanky **Jason Robards**. With his hound-dog face, Robards lacks both the corpu-

The real St Valentine's Day Massacre

There have been at least half a dozen screen representations of the St Valentine's Day Massacre and none really conveys the gruesome reality of the killings. In Corman's film, like in so many, the victims simply fall down in a heap when they're shot, their bodies staying intact. According to Capone biographer John Kobler, however, "the executioners had been systematic, swinging their machine guns back and forth three times, first at the level of the victims' heads, then chests, then stomachs. Some of the corpses were held together in one piece only by shreds of flesh and bone. Yet evidently life had still flickered in Kashellek and May after the machine-gun volleys, for they had been blasted with shotguns at such close range as to all but obliterate their faces."

lence and the terrifying presence that the criminal overlord possessed in real-life. But these shortcomings were neither Corman's nor Robards' fault. The venerable actor was originally employed to play arch-rival **Bugs Moran**, while the role of Capone was to be filled by **Orson Welles**, who had both the requisite weight and gravitas. Unfortunately 20th Century Fox refused to bankroll a film starring Welles, who was by now considered somewhat of a troublemaker in Hollywood. There was one advantage to working with that particular studio however. Corman had access to their backlot, and made typically resourceful use of it. Eagle-eyed viewers may be able to recognize some of the locations: Capone's house was once the manor in *The Sound Of Music* and the rest of Chicago was the set of *Hello Dolly*.

Despite the considerable handicap of having a less than ideal leading man, Corman managed to stick to his intentions and supply all the necessary genre thrills – rubber-burning car chases, tommy-gun battles in the streets, and a satisfyingly high body count – without making truth the first casualty. With a forensic attention to detail, the film depicts the war between Moran and Capone that led to the historic events on February 14, provides biographical details of all the major players, catalogues the painstaking plans that went into the hit, and explains how the main target – Moran – escaped the firing squad because of a case of mistaken identity.

The film is also of historic interest to cinephiles because of an appearance by a young **Jack Nicholson** as a getaway driver, who only has one line in the whole film. According to Corman's autobiography *How I Made A Hundred Movies In Hollywood And Never Lost A Dime*, Nicholson was offered a much meatier part with many more lines, for which he'd get two weeks' pay. To play the driver, he'd get seven weeks' pay. The choice was a no-brainer for Nicholson. "I'm taking the seven weeks' pay" was his response.

Jason Robards: an oddly 60s-looking Capone

Salvatore Giuliano

dir Francesco Rosi, 1961, It, 125m, b/w
cast Frank Wolff, Salvo Randone, Federico Zardi, Pietro
Cammarata, Fernando Cicero *cin* Gianni di Venanzo *m*
Piero Piccioni

Though the film isn't strictly *about* the Mob as such, Francesco
Rosi's masterpiece is one of the few films to be made in Sicily that
addresses the Sicilian Mafia. *Giuliano* is about the eponymous bandit who fought for Sicilian liberation and then for the Cosa Nostra,
and who was ultimately betrayed by them.

The film starts with Salvatore Giuliano's corpse laid out in a
courtyard, surrounded by policemen and onlookers, then it cuts
back to Giuliano very much alive, carrying out his exploits. It
shuttles back and forth between Giuliano's life and the investigation of his death, culminating in a lengthy courtroom scene which
uncovers the shadowy forces at work in contemporary Italy. It's a
curious hybrid of documentary realism and *nouvelle vague* artifice; at
times Rosi himself, in voice-over, explains the background to the
action: how the bandit fought against the Italian army in 1944 as
part of **EVIS**, the liberation movement for Sicily and, when they
were granted autonomy in 1946, how his gang went to work for
the Mafia, kidnapping businessmen and extorting money from
them; and how they were in the pay of political forces who ordered
the gang to fire on unarmed civilians taking part in a left-wing
demonstration on May Day 1947 – the first political massacre in
Sicilian history.

But Rosi also withholds information from us. Most of the film
is silent: we often witness the gang from afar as they swoop down
on isolated army vehicles and return to the cover of the mountains.
We never see Giuliano's face: there's never a close-up, and our view
of him is only of a man in a white coat charging across the hills
and rocky terrain of Sicily like a ghost. The effect is to make him
as elusive to us as he is to the *carabinieri*, though perhaps this was an
attempt by Rosi not to over-romanticize Giuliano – apparently he
was exceptionally handsome.

The movie was shot in Giuliano's home town of Montelpre, and starred people who had experienced (and in some cases supported) his reign of terror. The locals suggested a scene which appears in the film: as all the men in the town are rounded up by the police, the women come running and screaming out of their homes, down the main street into the square, and try to bulldoze their way through armed officers. The bandit's mother, who at one point is obliged to identify Giuliano's corpse, is played by a villager who had only recently lost her own son.

The film's moral ambivalence towards the protagonist is paralleled stylistically and adds to a sense that Rosi is always trying to wrong-foot us. It's not only the complex narrative structure, but the style of the film itself, the neo-realist flow punctuated by moments of abstracted, theatrical artifice in which characters are lit and posed like a painting. There's nothing quite like *Salvatore Giuliano*.

Le samourai

dir Jean-Pierre Melville, 1967, Fr/It, 95m
cast Alain Delon, Nathalie Delon, François Périer, Cathy Rosier, Jacques Leroy *cin* Henri Decaë *m* François de Roubaix

Jean-Pierre Melville took the style and iconography of the gangster genre and made them the substance of the film itself, the results leaving an indelible impression upon the likes of Quentin Tarantino and John Woo. *Le samourai* is considered Melville's masterpiece and is the most extreme example of his craft. Sieving out extraneous elements from a genre that was already spare on details, it is often wordless and mesmeric, simply inviting us to gaze at the fedora-and-trenchcoat-clad **Alain Delon**. The film's star apparently agreed to make the film when he found out that there was no dialogue in the first two reels. He was even more excited when he discovered the film's title. It's said that at the time his bedroom contained only two things: a couch and a samurai sword.

Delon plays the modern-day samurai of the title, whose armour is

the hat and trenchcoat, as worn by **Alan Ladd** in *This Gun For Hire*.
Silently, he steals a car, changes the numberplates, walks into a jazz
club and kills the owner in his office. The only witness is the club's
piano player, and she is asked by the police to view an identity parade
of which he is part. It's significant that the film centres around an
ID parade, because we can only identify the character by his clothes
– there is nothing else to him. Delon is a walking, empty signifier. He's
a brand, as beautiful and as banal as David Beckham, a blank slate for
us to project our own desires and aspirations. In a telling moment, he's
asked "What kind of man are you?" He has no answer.

The piano player claims not to recognize him. We – and Delon
– know she's lying. He – or perhaps it's just us – hopes that she
has fallen in love with him. However, when he goes to collect his
money his employers are unhappy that the police had called him
in for questioning, and attempt to kill him. Wounded, he now has
both the Mob and the cops after him. His room is bugged, he's
constantly watched, but he is nonetheless given one more contract:
to kill the only witness.

The movie finishes with a flourish, a twist that turns it into a
kind of shaggy-dog story told by **Albert Camus**. Melville's work
has been dubbed the "cinema of process", and, in its focus upon
the before and the after rather than the event itself, you can see its
influence on **Quentin Tarantino**. This is a film about surfaces and
action (though you could hardly call it an action movie).

Le samourai has a palette of blues and greys which is supposed
to match Delon's eyes; Melville himself said he wanted to make a
black-and-white film in colour. As in *Point Blank* (1967), the cir-
cumambient look of the movie becomes almost like another character, the external world matching the internal condition of the
protagonist. And like John Boorman's film, the world of *Samourai* is
sleek, minimalist and artificial. The jazz club has futuristic furniture,
bubble chairs and perspex pipes which dangle pointlessly but beautifully from the ceiling. Delon's apartment is a complete contrast,
but no less stylized and alienating, with its washed-out blues and
the unexplained bottles of water on top of the distressed wooden
wardrobe. The first time we see Delon he is asleep, dressed in 1940s
clothing that is out of sorts with his saturated 1960s surroundings,
a Rip Van Winkle about to awake years later into a different world.
Like **Philip Marlowe** in Robert Altman's *The Long Goodbye*, he's a
man out of time.

Scarface

dir **Howard Hawks, 1932, US, 90m, b/w**

cast **Paul Muni, Ann Dvorak, Karen Morley, Osgood Perkins, Boris Karloff** *cin* **Lee Garmes** *m* **Adolph Tandler, Gus Arnheim**

Probably the greatest gangster movie of the early period (1930–33), *Scarface* proved highly controversial, and its release was severely delayed due to problems with the censors. Screenwriter Ben Hecht's concept for the movie was "The Borgias living in Chicago". It stars a wonderfully reptilian **Paul Muni** as Tony Camonte, an immigrant on the make, who has a cross carved into his left cheek. He's the right-hand man of gang boss Johnny Lovo (Anthony Perkins' dad, **Osgood Perkins**), but he has plans to take over the whole operation with his loyal friend Guino, played

Scarface and the censors

Howard Hawks and his boss **Howard Hughes** spent two years fighting the censors over *Scarface*. The film was only released after certain additions were made, one being an apologia at the beginning: "This film is an indictment of gang rule in America and of the callous indifference of the government to this constantly increasing menace to our safety and liberty. Every incident in this picture is the reproduction of an actual occurrence, and the purpose of this picture is to demand of the government: 'What are you going to do about it?' The government is your government. What are YOU going to do about it?" A scene was added in which concerned citizens tell the police and the press about the havoc on their streets – such as children's bellies being filled with lead as they go to school – but Hawks didn't shoot it and didn't even know who did. And finally an alternative ending was inserted, in which Tony Camonte is captured, tried and hanged. Except it isn't **Paul Muni** up there on screen. He wasn't around for re-shoots, so in the last five minutes we only ever see "his" hands and shadow, which gives the scene a surrealistic edge and somewhat detracts from the film's sermonizing. It makes little difference anyway, because *Scarface*'s "war" scenes are so thrilling that no matter how many moralizing messages were book-ended to it, the film cannot help but seem like an ad for gangsterism.

by **George Raft**. A dancer who had been carrying a gun for The Mob in real-life, Raft steals every scene he's in – simply by being there. While Muni acts the gangster, Raft just *is*. It was a method of (non) acting that Raft would repeat in many of his following movies, but here it works to great effect – with his calm, understated menace and signature style of flicking a coin, you can't keep your eyes off him.

Despite the distractions of being a full-time gangster – bootlegging, extorting and wiping out the competition – Tony still has time for his mother and his sister Ceska (Ann Dvorak). His sister in particular. Tony makes sure that no man ever gets close to her and, as she says, he doesn't act like a brother, he acts "more like a…". Exactly what that is she never says, and Tony's borderline incestuous feelings are left as just an intimation for the viewer to pick up. But she's not the only woman Tony has eyes for – he's melting the heart of blonde ice maiden Polly (**Karen Morley**). There's only one problem: she's the boss's moll.

Tony initiates a war with the North side of the city, and this is where the film changes gear and gathers speed with an exhilarating montage of metal-crunching car chases, bullet-flying machine-gun battles and shots of restaurants being torn apart by gunfire, which have been oft imitated but never bettered. But possibly the boldest shot of all denotes the passing of time by showing the leaves of a calendar flying into the air as they're riddled by bullets from a tommy gun.

Bullets fly thick and fast at the climax of *Scarface* (1932)

From then on the film moves at a lick, as Tony wins the war, but draws the jealous wrath of his boss. Tony survives an attempt on his life and kills Johnny. Looking out over his empire he sees a sign for Cooks Tours, saying "The World Is Yours". But that world falls apart when he catches his sister with his best friend Guino; he kills him and retreats to his lair, where he and Ceska take on the cops in a furious but futile gun battle. Tony is eventually mowed down on the street in a hail of police bullets, and above his dead body a neon sign flickers into life: "The World Is Yours".

It's no coincidence that "Scarface" was **Al Capone**'s nickname – the film even features a dramatization of the St Valentine's Day Massacre – and when Capone heard about it he sent two henchmen to pay Ben Hecht a visit. After they had okayed the script, the production went ahead; after the film's release, director **Howard Hawks** was invited to meet the man himself, and they had tea together. Luckily for Hawks, Capone liked the movie – he had seen it five or six times and eventually even bought a print of it for himself.

Scarface

dir **Brian De Palma, 1983, US, 170m**
cast **Al Pacino, Steven Bauer, Michelle Pfeiffer, Mary Elizabeth Mastrantonio, Robert Loggia** *cin* **John A. Alonzo** *m* **Giorgio Moroder**

Depending on your point of view, *Scarface* is either woefully over-the-top or ambitiously operatic. In this "remake" the titular gangster is now from Cuba, his feelings for his sister are clearly incestuous, the guns are bigger, bootlegging has been replaced by drug-dealing, the acting verges even closer on hysteria, and there's a death by chainsaw moment that, so legend has it, became an influence on East End villains. Everything in this film is turned up to eleven.

Al Pacino plays Tony Montana, a cocky, nerveless criminal who doesn't break his balls or his word for anyone, and who has moved to Miami in the exodus from Cuba in 1980. Together with his best friend, Ray Manola (**Steve Bauer**), he starts working for drug lord

Frank Lopez (**Robert Loggia**), but his bristling self-assurance and transparent ambition quickly become a threat to his boss. Montana survives an assassination attempt and murders Frank. He usurps him in both the boardroom and the bedroom, taking charge of his empire and his mistress, Elvira (**Michelle Pfeiffer**). Montana is now living the American dream. He has the fancy cars, the big house with a circular bath, a tiger in the garden and a trophy moll in the bed; he also buys his beloved sister Gina (**Mary Elizabeth Mastrantonio**) her own beauty parlour. But it all goes wrong when he breaks the dealer's golden rule, and gets high on his own supply. He's caught laundering money by the Feds, he catches his best friend with his sister and kills him, and, fatally, he double-crosses the Bolivian drug baron he's been doing business with.

It all ends in an orgy of gunplay and bloodletting that is typical of the film. Director Brian De Palma said he wanted to show violence as it had never been seen in a gangster movie before. And he certainly succeeded – writer Oliver Stone diligently researched the various methods of execution depicted, and all are apparently based on real-life incidents. Interestingly, the most infamously violent scene – Tony being forced to watch as his friend is carved up by a chainsaw, whilst chained to a shower railing – doesn't actually show the gory murder on screen. All we see is the blood splattering on Tony's understandably tense face, while we hear the high-decibel buzzing of the saw, almost drowned out by the victim's agonized screams. This led to the urban myth that the scene had been slashed by censors, and that a director's cut would one day emerge in all its limb-lopping glory. Sadly for gore-hounds, the producers and director are at pains to point out in a documentary accompanying the DVD that there is no extra footage, that this is the director's cut.

Tony Montana has become a legendary character. His lines, such as "Say hello to my lil' friend" and "Make way for the bad guy", have passed into folklore. Impersonating him is a party-piece favourite of many actors – apparently **Tom Cruise** does a very good impression. Pacino said he wanted to play Tony larger than life, which is one way of putting it – there's no gradual transformation à la Michael Corleone in *The Godfather* (1971). But it works in conjunction with the contributions of Stone and De Palma, neither of whom are known for their subtlety. *Scarface* is hyperreal and, yes, operatic: the blazing colours, the sumptuous sets, and the mountain of coke that Montana plunges his face into. It's all good.

Tony Montana: ultimate ghetto superhero?

The producers of *Scarface* were not allowed to film in Miami because the local Cuban community were worried that the movie would be defamatory. It's ironic then that the film has since become a favourite amongst many inner-city Latino and black communities, and that Tony Montana has become an icon. Or rather (as a documentary accompanying the DVD puts it) the "ultimate ghetto superhero". **Sean Combs** (aka P. Diddy, once known as Puff Daddy) has seen it no fewer than 63 times and has claimed that it "scared him straight": for him, and many other **hip-hop** artists, the fate of Tony Montana is a lesson to heed – a lesson with lots of violence and expensive jewellery.

Brother
dir Takeshi Kitano,
2000, Jap, 117m

It should have been the perfect match: Kitano comes to America; the Yakuza movie meets the gangster film. But the result – about a Yakuza member exiled to Los Angeles and trying to make a living (or, indeed, a killing) – doesn't work. Kitano's light touch has here become heavy-handed and Kitano's acting and directing style is a tedious parody of itself.

Sonatine

dir **Takeshi Kitano, 1993, Jap, 94m**
cast **Takeshi Kitano, Aya Kokumai, Tetsu Watanabe, Masanobu Katsumura, Susumu Terashima** *cin* **Katsumi Yanagishima** *m* **Joe Hisaishi**

In Japan, Takeshi "Beat" Kitano is less well known for his films than for his multi-faceted careers as a game-show host with seven programmes a week, a stand-up comedian, a political cartoonist and a painter; he once topped a poll as the public's choice for prime minister.

There, his movies are considered arthouse, and a bit of a side-project. In the West, however, critics go into raptures over his idio-syncratic, zen-like direction and the economy of his increasingly taciturn acting performances, in his trademark uniform of blue suit and crisp white shirt. The *noir*-leaning *Hana-Bi* (1997) is probably his greatest work, but *Sonatine* is the best of his gangster films.

Kitano plays Murakawa, a successful Yakuza boss who runs his own patch in Tokyo. He and his men are ordered by the don to go to Okinawa and help out in a gang war – a set-up Murakawa's boss has contrived to have the over-successful Murakawa killed. As soon as they get there they find themselves to be moving targets for local hoods and retreat to the coast, hiding out in a remote beach house, hoping for some kind of explanation from their superiors. There they just wait. And wait. And play Russian roulette, have firework fights and shoot frisbees. Murakawa also hooks up with a woman whose husband he killed. The gang are picked off one by one by a straw-hatted stranger, and Kitano exacts a bloody revenge.

And that's the plot. Very little happens, even less is said. The movie's colours are toned-down blues and greys, and its characters stare into the middle distance, almost as if they are having their portraits painted. *Sonatine*'s action scenes are practically *tableaux vivants* compared to those of its gangster-genre contemporaries. But the movie nevertheless has a hypnotic hold which racks up the tension. Its silence is punctuated by moments of disquieting violence, and this works to great effect in a scene that takes place in what must surely be the world's slowest elevator. Murakawa and his accomplices are ascending within it. It stops on every floor, people get in and out until a rival gangster enters and a gunfight ensues. The camera registers no change of dynamic, observing it all with a streadfast unanimity and consistent air of detachment.

They Live By Night

dir Nicholas Ray, 1948, US, 95m, b/w
cast Farley Granger, Cathy O'Donnell, Howard da Silva, Jay C. Flippen, Helen Craig *cin* George E. Diskant *m* Leigh Harline

Director Nicholas Ray's debut feature begins quite unexpectedly, with a soft-focus close-up of two lovers kissing. "This boy and this girl were never properly introduced to the world we live in..." goes the superimposed opening title. The titles continue, with the dramatic once-upon-a-time of "To tell their story...".

It then cuts to an aerial shot – Hollywood's first to be shot from a helicopter – of a car hurtling through the countryside, making a quick getaway. In it are three convicts on the run: Bowie, T-Dub, and "One-Eye" Chicamaw. Bowie (**Farley Granger**) is the movie's lover-boy, and it's quite apparent that he's very different from the two hardened criminals. He's sensitive – as T-Dub says, "he's got a soft heart and a head to match" – and he doesn't seem to be capable of the murder he was convicted for. The trio make their way to Chicamaw's brother's place, a farmhouse where they come across Keechie (**Cathy O'Donnell**), a young innocent who soon falls for Bowie. After they stage a succesful bank robbery, Bowie crashes his car, and Keechie tends to him as he recovers; it's not long before they hit the road together. Nicholas Ray then effortlessly changes the mood and lightens the tone as the couple get married in a quick, cut-price ceremony and even buy a car from the shady, mercenary wedding registrar. It's one of the many surprising comic moments that prick the collective, poetic gloom and is followed soon afterwards by another quirky example. The couple find a remote motel to lie low and ask to be placed in a cabin far away from anyone else. Misunderstanding their reasons, the motel-owner, who's teaching his son the tricks of the trade, says "Learn that, Alvin! Just-married people like to be alone!" "I should think so!" replies the boy. It's one of the movie's many leavening, light-hearted moments.

In the cabin, they find their Xanadu. Life is peachy until Chickamaw turns up, wanting Bowie to go back to work. Out of a sense of misguided loyalty he rejoins the gang, but both T-Dub and Chickamaw are killed after another bank job. Back in the cabin the two lovers are recognized by a plumber and they are forced back on the road, and to the city, where they can find no sanctuary. Realizing that she is better off without him, Bowie secretly leaves Keechie in the middle of the night, only for fate to intervene for the final time.

Rays of dark: the young lovers haven't a hope in hell in *They Live By Night* (1948)

They Live By Night is a great title, but the title of the novel on which the movie was based, *Thieves Like Us*, is more resonant of the overall theme: in the *noir* universe, everyone's a thief. (Maybe that's why **Robert Altman** used it for the re-make.) Regardless, *They Live By Night* is part of the holy trinity of "love on the run" movies which includes *You Only Live Once* (1937) and *Gun Crazy* (1949).

It's not difficult to see the lovers as forerunners of **James Dean** and **Nathalie Wood** in Nicholas Ray's most famous film, *Rebel Without A Cause* (1955): young people who feel they are at the margins of a society which doesn't understand them, who share a romantic belief that they are born to lose. The words of the introduction, "never properly introduced to the world they live in", apply to both couples. By the 1950s, teenage alienation was recognized and to an extent commodified. *They Live By Night* is a sign of where the culture was heading.

White Heat

dir **Raoul Walsh, 1949, US, 114m, b/w**
cast **James Cagney, Virginia Mayo, Edmond O'Brien, Margaret Wycherly, Steve Cochran** *cin* **Sid Hickox** *m* **Max Steiner**

James Cagney's triumphant return to the gangster genre, after ten years, revealed a very different actor playing a very different role to that of *Angels With Dirty Faces* (1938). In *White Heat* Cagney's face is puffier, he looks tired, and he's thickened considerably around the waist. During a heist on a mail train, the character he plays – Cody Jarrett – executes two train drivers because they've heard his name. The Cagney of old would never have played a role like this.

A lot has changed since the 1930s gangster film. After the train robbery we notice another genre development. Jarrett's mother is a long way from the naïve innocent played by **Beryl Mercer** in Cagney's *The Public Enemy*. She's more like Lady Macbeth – complicit and one of the gang. She gives her son pep talks and prompts him to kill a wounded colleague, just in case he's discovered by the police. And she helps him through his fits, the headaches that he describes as feeling like a buzzsaw in his brain.

After the robbery, the police track the gang down in Los Angeles. Following a narrow escape, Jarrett decides to give himself up, but for a different crime – a stick-up in a hotel on the same day as the train robbery, which means he'll only get two years rather than the electric chair. The cops play ball because they've put an undercover agent, Fallon (**Edmond O'Brien**) in the cell with Cody to find out where he's hidden the loot. While in jail, Jarrett's wife, a platinum-blonde Janus called Verna, does the dirty on him with his nemesis, Big Ed; they try to kill Cody in jail but, when it goes wrong, they shoot his mother. On hearing the news, Jarrett breaks down, before breaking out of jail with Fallon in tow, unaware that his new best friend is a cop.

Many critics have focused on Cody's psychosis, and observed how the same character traits that made a gangster successful in 1930s movies – ruthless ambition and a disregard for human

I blame the parents... Cody Jarrett (James Cagney, left), not quite "top of the world" yet

life – mark him out as a complete psychopath a decade later. The 1940s were the decade in which Hollywood had clearly started reading **Freud**: characters now had psychologies to be explained by a key incident revealed in flashback, most famously in *Citizen Kane*; or else they were given the full psychoanalytic treatment, as with **Gregory Peck**'s amnesiac suspect killer in **Alfred Hitchcock**'s *Spellbound*. Here, Cody is given an on-screen diagnosis (albeit by a police chief rather than a shrink). We're informed that Cody's father ended up in an institution, and that Cody pretended to have headaches to get his mother's attention – headaches that eventually became all too real. We discover that his mother is the only person he cares for (not even his wife can make a dent in him), that she is "the prop that held him up", and that he has "a fierce psychopathic devotion to her". It's all "dollar-book Freud", to quote a phrase Hitchcock once used, but it's nevertheless remarkable to see how the sociology of the 1930s has given way to the psychopathology of the 1940s.

Famously, the movie ends on top of a gas tank, with Cagney shooting at the cops down below who've got him cornered. Fatally wounded, he fires two bullets into the tank. Flames leap around him, and before the whole thing goes up, he utters the celebrated line "Made it, Ma! Top of the world!" As agent Fallon comments, he "finally got to the top of the world and it blew right up in his face". The film finishes with the fires (of hell?) licking the credits.

You Only Live Once

dir **Fritz Lang, 1937, US, 86m, b/w**

cast **Slyvia Sidney, Henry Fonda, Barton MacLane, Jean Dixon, William Gargan, Warren Hymer** *cin* **Leon Shamroy** *m* **Alfred Newman**

This film was the model for the "killer couple on the run" movies, a tradition that now includes *Natural Born Killers* (1994), *They Live By Night* (1948), *A bout de souffle* (1959) and *Bonnie And Clyde* (1967). Like *Bonnie And Clyde*, it took its inspiration from the story of Parker and Barrow; the difference with *You Only Live Once* is that it's only towards the end of the film that the couple are on the run and on the road.

In later films, the reasons behind the couple's descent into a life of crime are perfunctory: often the couple simply rob banks, and psychological or sociological explanation – if indeed there is any – is subordinate. *You Only Live Once*, however, spends most of its time explaining how the protagonists got there. Eddie (**Henry Fonda**) and Joan (**Sylvia Sidney**) are basically decent kids. Joan is the secretary of the city's public defender, loved by everyone – particularly her boss. Eddie has run into a series of troubles which have landed him in jail, but his essential goodness is emphatically demonstrated to us by his friendship with the prison priest. He's inside for the third time; a fourth misdemeanour and they will throw away the key. The parole he is granted is his last chance.

But when he gets out he's not given an even break. The only people who will give him a job are his old gang. Needing money for a house, it appears that Eddie has gone back to his old ways when a bank van is robbed and his hat found at the scene of the crime. Eddie is arrested, brought to trial and sentenced to the death penalty, all the while protesting his innocence. On the night before his execution, he escapes with Joan just as new evidence is found and a pardon granted; thinking it's a trick to give himself up, Eddie literally shoots the messenger, killing the jail's priest who tried to convince him that there really is no need to flee, and the couple hit the road. Holding up gas stations, they're soon blamed for practically every crime in the country.

In many ways, the pair are a classic *noir* couple. It seems that they have always been doomed, that he was knocking on the executioner's door the day he was born. But, apart from the coincidence of the pardon, it's not a savage god who is dictating their lives, or a fickle fate determining their destiny. It is the prejudices that surround them – of employers, authorities and property-owners – and an unforgiving society which has set them on their path. As Eddie says, albeit slightly disingenuously, "they made me a murderer".

The unthinking callousness of The Mob mentality was a theme in two of director **Fritz Lang**'s earlier films – *Fury* (1936) and *M* (1931). And many of his stylistic signatures are evident in *You Only Live Once*. Lang is renowned for bringing German expressionism to America, and its hallmarks are visible throughout the film, notably in shots such as the couple's car making its way through a landscape shrouded in rain, fog and doom, or the stark light from Eddie's jail cell casting lines of shadows on a wall. But there is one scene above all others that best displays Lang's visual flair. Eddie and Joan, fresh out of jail, are discussing their bright future together. We see their images reflected in a pond. A frog jumps in, the calm of the water is disturbed, and the image of the couple is distorted: what they say is undermined by what we see. Lang apparently spent a whole day trying to coerce the frog into jumping to exactly the right spot.

The Icons: dons of gangster cinema

Two gangster icons: Robert De Niro and Joe Pesci in
(iiconic director) Martin Scorsese's *Casino* (1995)

The Icons:
dons of gangster cinema

There are some actors, directors, producers and screenwriters who have bloodied the face of the gangster film in their own very special, unique way. Their influence upon crime cinema, upon cinema as a whole, and sometimes even upon popular culture in general, can be said to be truly iconic. Here's where we pay them the respect they deserve, from Bogie to Woo.

Humphrey Bogart
1899–1957

Humphrey Bogart "was as tough as Shirley Temple", according to James Cagney. The son of a doctor, he was brought up in a swankier district of Manhattan, and spent the first ten years of his career playing characters in top hat and tails.

He came by his trademark lisp during a stint with the navy in World War I: his ship was shelled and Bogart received facial injuries resulting in a paralysis of the upper lip and a permanent and distinctive speech impediment. The nickname "Bogie" was given to him by Spencer Tracy in his unsuccessful first Hollywood stint.

In 1934 Bogie was back in New York, broke and saddled with debts left to him by a father whose career had taken a sudden downturn before his death. Frequently drunk and depressed, it may well have been his pallid, hang-dog demeanour that landed Bogart the break-through role in the play *The Petrified Forest*. The clean-cut, upper-class Humphrey was certainly an unusual choice for the part of a desperado on the run, Duke Mantee.

From 1936 to 1941 he made 29 movies. In many of them he played gangsters who delighted in such names as Baby Face Martin (*Dead End*) and Rocks Diamond (*The Amazing Dr Clitterhouse*). In *Clitterhouse,* he was described by **Edward G. Robinson**'s psychiatrist as a "magnificent specimen of pure viciousness", which just about sums up most of his roles during the 1930s. In films such as *Angels With Dirty Faces, Brother Orchid, Bullets Or Ballots,* and *The Roaring Twenties,* Bogart came up against either Cagney or Robinson, and his function was to make them look good in comparison. The lead gangster had to be redeemable since the toughening of the Hays Code in 1934, and redemption often lay in the killing of the irredeemably bad Bogart (both Cagney and Robinson killed him twice).

In 1941 *High Sierra* gained Bogart a new drinking partner – John Huston – who co-wrote the script and was on set for much of the filming. Their friendship resulted in the film *The Maltese Falcon* and, in the role of Sam Spade, Bogie (like America that year) became the reluctant hero, provoked into action against his better judge-ment and his isolationist policy – a role Bogie made his own with Rick in *Casablanca,* Marlowe in *The Big Sleep* and Frank in *Key Largo.* However, Bogart never fully shook off the bad guy image during the 1940s and 1950s, playing a hood three more times in his career – in *All Through The Night, The Big Shot* and *The Desperate Hours.*

Bogart and the Rat Pack

A habitué of Legs Diamond's Hotsy Totsy club on Broadway during Prohibition, Bogart formed the legendary Rat Pack in 1955, with the original team of David Niven, Judy Garland, Lauren Bacall and Frank Sinatra (who took over the Pack and brought in new rats when Bogart died). They got their name after Bogie, Niven, Garland and Sinatra went on a historic binge in Las Vegas; when Bacall took one look at the giggling, dishevelled bunch, she proclaimed "you look like a goddamned rat pack". The Holmby Hills Rat Pack was formed.

James Cagney
1899–1986

James Cagney was a young street brawler from the Irish ghettos of New York who once broke his fist on another man's face, yet his first job in show business was as a chorus *girl*. This might seem to be a contradiction – the thug in drag – but this apparent dichotomy persisted throughout his career: Cagney was the dancer who played a gangster, and in many ways he was the sweetest gangster of them all.

Born in 1899 on the Lower East Side of Manhattan, he took every job under the sun in his teens until he landed *that* role. It was in a vaudeville production called *Every Sailor*, and every night he had to don a wig, tutu and high heels. It was because of the footwear that he had to leave the production – the heels were killing him.

There is a certain grapefruit that is almost as iconic as Cagney himself. The grapefruit, as is well known, did play its part in Cagney's success, walloped into the face of Mae Clark in *The Public*

A bona fide gangster movie icon, being squished by James Cagney into Mae Clark's face in *The Public Enemy* (1931)

Enemy. There are, unsurprisingly, many legends about that scene, including the story that Clark was genuinely shocked when Cagney shoved a grapefruit in her face, because nobody had apparently informed her about his intentions. Mae Clark was again on the receiving end in *The Lady Killer* when Cagney pulled her across the floor by her hair, thus cementing his screen reputation as a woman-beater.

For many, Cagney's greatest turn was as Cody

You dirty rat

The long-forgotten *Taxi!* (1931) is remembered only for the phrase "you dirty rat!", a line never actually spoken by Cagney. He actually said (to a man who's just killed his brother): "Come out and take it you dirty, yellow-bellied rat", making it the second greatest misquote in cinema history. (Bogie's "Play it again, Sam" is, of course, the first.)

Jarrett in *White Heat* – a sick, cold-blooded killer whose psychosis is clearly impressed upon us. But Cagney invested him with an aggressive vulnerability: the dancer's strength, delicacy and energy that he'd brought to all his tough guys. Significantly it was Cagney, according to biographer Richard Schickel, who insisted that Cody should have a medical condition to explain his psychosis.

It's closing time and the drinks are on Jack Carter (Michael Caine), as he finally wreaks his revenge in *Get Carter*'s sour climax

Michael Caine

1933–

Brought up in Camberwell, the son of a fish-market porter, Caine (aka Maurice Micklewhite) spent his formative years in the company of spivs, gangsters and professional assassins. The actor apparently never had any bother, however, because his family "were one of the ones you didn't mess with". His background came in handy when he played the three gangsters in his career: in *Get Carter, Mona Lisa* and *Shiner*, each is based on a different South London villain and each is the person Micklewhite could have been. To research *Get Carter* Caine returned home to the Elephant and Castle to seek the advice of old friends, asking them how he should play the character; in the end he based Jack Carter upon an old neighbour, stealing his clothes, his manner of speech, and the way he walked.

Apart from his kinship to the character, *Get Carter* seemed to be an unusual choice for Caine in 1971 (and writer/director Mike Hodges was surprised he'd agreed to play such a "shit"). Carter was a machine tooled for vengeance. But that was the attraction for Caine: he wanted to make *Get Carter* because "at the time, British gangster movies assumed that gangsters were stupid, silly and funny. I knew from my background that they were none of these three."

His second gangster role, as Mortwell in *Mona Lisa* (1987) was a Thatcher-era Flash Harry, a strip-lounge lizard who's gone legit with his porn empire; Carter's crisp, bespoke blue suit is replaced by an off-the-peg number whose cheap cut is punctuated by the full stop of Mortwell's stomach, the sharp good looks replaced by the bloat and jowls of middle age.

 Mona Lisa
dir Neil Jordan, 1987, UK, 104m

Bob Hoskins is magnificently pathetic as a very English Travis Bickle, a naïve ex-con called George who's employed by a reptilian porn magnate (Caine) to drive high-class prostitute Cathy Tyson to her appointments. Increasingly infatuated, George stumbles blindly into a demi-monde of hard-core porno and sadomasochism, a kind of Orpheus in the London underworld.

Chow Yun-Fat

1955–

"Chow represents everything I value in a person: morality, friendship, honour, love," said John Woo about his leading man. Sometimes an actor and a director just click, whether it's Robert De Niro and Martin Scorsese or Alain Delon and Jean-Pierre Melville, all of whom are Woo's heroes. The start of the Chow/Woo relationship is almost corny: the actor who was box-office poison and the director who had been exiled by his own studio came together and made the biggest film in Hong Kong history.

Chow Yun-Fat had worked as a postman, bellboy and camera salesman before he answered a newspaper ad for acting trainees at a television studio; a few years later he was a TV household name in series like *Shanghai Beach* and *Hotel*. He couldn't, however, make the transition to cinema, appearing in a number of box-office bombs.

But the success of *A Better Tomorrow* made Chow an instant icon, and teenagers donned dark glasses and the star's long duster coat, even in the colony's heat – there were a lot of sweaty teenagers in Hong Kong in 1986. The appeal was based not just on Chow's cool demeanour or baby-faced charisma, but on his choice of weapon. Chow's two-fisted use of Beretta 45s is the subject of the opening monologue in Tarantino's *Jackie Brown*. Gun dealer Samuel L. Jackson complains that all his customers want Berettas after seeing *The Killer*, even though the guns have a jamming problem: "*The Killer* had a 45. They want a 45." Woo gave it to Chow because of the unusual size of his hands: "when he's holding a small pistol, it looks like he's holding a toy. It's not solid. A special gun should be for a man with special qualities."

Francis Ford Coppola

1939–

Francis Ford Coppola isn't just a director, he's a *capo*. As many producers, particularly Robert Evans, have discovered, Coppola is the boss: he expects, and he gets total control. Almost as soon as he was making movies, Coppola created his own studio, and the financial failings of Zoetrope have been both the making and the downfall of the director. If Zoetrope had been self-sufficient, Coppola would never have made *The Godfather III*, but he would never have made *The Godfather* either.

His legendary attention to detail, his worrying over the minutiae even extends to his middle name. For a period during the 1980s he was known only as Francis Coppola, ditching the part of him that didn't seem Italian-American (he was named Ford after the programme that employed his musician father as musical arranger – *The Ford Sunday Evening Hour*). In fact it was his Italian-American ancestry that got him the job on *The*

Movie-brat auteur Francis Ford Coppola, on a *Godfather* set bed

Godfather. A graduate of UCLA film school, he cut his teeth working for Roger Corman, dubbing and editing Russian sci-fi films until he persuaded the producer to let him direct *Dementia 13* in 1963; he followed it up with *You're A Big Boy Now* (1966), *Finian's Rainbow*

(1968) and *Rain People* (1969). Within six years the Godfather-to-be had set up his own studio, with $300,000 from Warner Brothers. However, when the studio saw Zoetrope's first film – George Lucas' *THX 1138* – they wanted their money back. And this is where producer Robert Evans entered the picture.

Evans, the head of production at Paramount, had bought the rights to Mario Puzo's novel for a knockdown sum: even though the book was a bestseller, gangster films were box-office poison in the early 1970s. Evans approached almost every director in Hollywood before turning to Coppola, who had no track record at the box office, but was at least Italian-American. What Evans wanted more than anything was authenticity.

Coppola got to work on the script, stripping out most of the novel. And he insisted upon Brando, pleading with executives, even falling to the ground in one meeting and apparently faking a heart attack. Paramount finally gave way after the Method actor did a screen test, in which he famously inserted Kleenex in his cheeks.

But Coppola's problems did not end when the cameras rolled; if anything they intensified. The *capo*/director fought with everyone: with cinematographer Gordon Willis, with editor Aram Avakian, but mostly with producer Robert Evans. Over the course of the saga, they fought over Pacino, over Brando's mumbling (Evans wondered aloud whether the film would need subtitles), over the length of the film and over the music (Evans wanted *The Pink Panther*'s **Henry Mancini**, Coppola wanted Fellini's **Nino Rota**, and won). Coppola began to suspect Aram Avakian was angling to direct the film himself, and, in a Machiavellian manoeuvre worthy of Don Corleone himself,

Coppola fired Avakian and all those who had conspired against him.

The Godfather became the most commercially successful film of all time when it was released, but Coppola was not ready to make a sequel. He only agreed after Paramount accepted three conditions: that he would get a million-dollar fee, that Robert Evans would be nowhere near the set, and that the sequel would be called *The Godfather II*. The studio readily agreed to the first two, but haggled over the third condition: a sequel had never been named simply "part 2" before, as they believed it would only confuse audiences. But as with everything else in his career up until then, Coppola won. The filming of *Godfather II* was marginally less stressful than the first – with the exception of Pacino catching pneumonia and Brando refusing to make a reappearance in a final concluding scene.

The Godfather III was the one battle Coppola lost with the studios. In the DVD commentary he seems resigned to the fact that he shouldn't have made it, or at least should have made it his way. Whereas *The Godfather* was delayed until it was ready, the final part was rushed out, even though the sound mix wasn't ready and Coppola wasn't happy with the cut. In this sense, the *capo* was dead; as with the Italian-American Mob bosses of old, the individual had lost out to the corporation.

The Cotton Club
dir Francis Coppola, 1984, US, 128m

Loosely based on the career of George Raft, Richard Gere plays Dixie Dwyer, a cornet player who has a dangerous liaison with Dutch Schultz's moll, Diane Lane. A trawl through classic gangster clichés, including a montage of newspaper headlines, *The Cotton Club* lacks Coppola's personal touch, even though the director cast his nephew, Nicolas Cage, as Dixie's brother.

Charles Bronson, a long time before he developed his *Death Wish*, in Roger Corman's *Machine Gun Kelly*

Roger Corman

1926–

Corman's 1950s were largely spent directing mechanical creatures and papier-mâché crustaceans in films such as *It Conquered The World* (1956) and *Attack Of The Crab Monsters*, and girls in sweaters in *Sorority Girl* and *Teenage Doll* (both 1957). But in 1958 he moved on to the latest fad for the exploitation movie – gangster biopics.

His account of *Machine Gun Kelly*'s bank-robbing, kidnapping exploits and his subsequent simpering surrender to the police attempted something that had been somewhat lacking in his previous movies like *Not Of This Earth* (1957) – authenticity. Often even sticking to the facts, Corman added a large helping of Freud, and as a result *Machine Gun Kelly* was one of the few Charles Bronson movies ever to be admired by critics, particularly by the French. Corman immediately followed it up with *I, Mobster,* a fictionalized account of a Mob boss about to be questioned by the Senate, which set out to exploit the appeal of the television phenomenon of the Kefauver hearings (investigations by the Senate into organized crime) that had been screened from 1950 to 1951.

Some critics believe that *The St Valentine's Day Massacre*, made in 1967, is Corman's greatest achievement in the genre, and he would seem to agree: "I believe *St Valentine's Day* to be the most authentic gangster movie ever," he claims. He achieved that authenticity by employing a former Chicago news reporter from the 1920s, Howard Browne, as scriptwriter. With a documentary-style voice-over, the film has a forensic attention to detail. Corman had the freedom of Fox's back-lot; so the manor in *The Sound Of Music* became Capone's home and the set of *Hello, Dolly* made do for 1920s Chicago.

Bloody Mama, made in 1969, was an attempt to cash in on the phenomenal success of *Bonnie And Clyde*, and some critics regard it as a corrective to Beatty and Dunaway's beautiful good-time bandits. A retelling of the life and death of Ma Barker and her feral sons, *Bloody Mama* certainly didn't skimp on the psychosis. Corman employed two Method actors for the parts of the mother and her son Lloyd: **Shelley Winters** and **Robert De Niro**. Winters would listen to arias right up to the moment of shooting to get herself into character, and allegedly prepared for a burial scene by spending a night with a corpse in a funeral parlour. To look like a junkie, De Niro lost thirty pounds by surviving on just fruit juice and vitamins.

In 1970 Corman set up his own company, New World, and it was here as studio boss that he became the Yoda to a generation of movie brats. Making films such as *Night Call Nurses*, New World's ethos was to make movies which combined sex, action and liberal politics. Corman once gave Scorsese a valuable piece of filmmaking advice: "Martin, what you have to get is a very good first reel because people want to know

what's going on. Then you get a very good last reel because people want to hear how it all turns out. Everything else doesn't really matter."

Jules Dassin
1911–

Many people assume that the director of *Rififi*, who's made countless movies in Greece, must be French, or at least from continental Europe. In fact Jules Dassin was born in Connecticut, Jules is short for Julian, and the only reason he's made so many films outside America is that he was, effectively, in exile, blacklisted by HUAC.

His first film, *Nazi Agent,* was made in 1942, but prison drama *Brute Force* (1948) was the first identifiable "Jules Dassin film", in which claustrophobic settings loom large and characters are dwarfed and determined by their environments. This Dassin brand of *noir* worked to good effect in *Thieves Highway* (1949) and particularly well in his two city movies: *The Naked City* (1948) and *Night And The City* (1950) – no one has filmed London as well, or as "bad" (English critics were dismayed at the venal qualities that Dassin elicited from the capital).

The director came to London on the instructions of his friend Darryl F. Zanuck, the head of 20th Century Fox; Zanuck knew that Dassin was about to be blacklisted by HUAC and that the only way he'd make a movie (probably his last) was to start filming in London. Zanuck was right. Dassin eventually found work five years later with *Rififi* – and its centrepiece was a veritable *coup de cinéma*. The 25-minute heist without dialogue or music made film history – a much-imitated innovation with which his name will always be associated.

Alain Delon (right), ice-cool as the killer with the unlikely name (Jef) in Melville's masterpiece *Le samourai* (1967)

Alain Delon

1935–

The director **Michelangelo Antonioni** once said that Alain Delon's face was "harsh and pitiless". He unquestionably has a cruel beauty, which makes him the perfect angel of death, as demonstrated in his performance of Ripley in his debut, *Plein soleil* (1959), while Jean-Pierre Melville also elicited some of his satanic majesty in *Le samourai* (1967) and *Le cercle rouge* (1971).

Delon replaced Belmondo as Melville's favourite son, and he was much more of a natural choice. Jean-Paul Belmondo was a graduate of the *nouvelle vague*, and his vitality and improvisational style didn't chime with a director whose attitude to acting was "don't just do something – stand there!" Melville's actors were discouraged from betraying emotions or expressions, but Belmondo's face – with its cow eyes and boxer's nose – couldn't help but be expressive. Delon was different. His glacial good looks were perfect for the role of a contract killer who can't afford emotions in *Le samourai*. Even a moustache in *Le cercle rouge* couldn't disguise a lethal beauty which is expressed, ultimately, in his blue eyes. Or perhaps this lethal beauty is entirely in the eye of the beholder, wholly retrospective: that, after all, is the point of Delon — he's cinema's finest blank slate.

Borsalino
dir Jacques Deray, 1970, Fr/It, 126m

Delon and Jean-Paul Belmondo play rival gangsters who come together to rub out the opposition and take over the city in the 1920s. A homage to the 1930s gangster movies, the pulling power of Delon and Belmondo made this a phenomenal success and launched 1920s chic in France, in much the same way *Bonnie And Clyde* did in America.

Robert De Niro
1943–

When critics first saw Johnny Boy in *Mean Streets*, they'd never seen anything quite like it before. Director **Sydney Pollack** thought that Martin Scorsese had brought in a psychiatric patient on day release. De Niro was 30 years old when *Mean Streets* was released in 1973. A graduate of The Actors' Studio, he'd been in numerous movies before, including Corman's gangster flick *Bloody Mama* and three films for **Brian De Palma**, who introduced the actor to Scorsese. And after Coppola watched him in *Mean Streets,* he decided he'd found his young Vito Corleone for *Godfather Part II*; instead of an audition, Bobby was simply taken for a meal by the producers, who spent the evening examining his features to see if he could pass for a young Brando. It seemed the perfect casting, with De Niro hailed as the rightful heir to Brando, and to his title of "greatest American actor". He cemented this reputation with two more collaborations with Martin Scorsese — *Taxi Driver* (1976) and *Raging Bull* (1980) — forging a special relationship that's also produced *The King Of Comedy*, *Goodfellas*, *Cape*

Fear and *Casino*. It's a unique bond which actor **Ray Liotta** has commented upon in interviews: on the set of *Goodfellas*, Scorsese spent an hour in De Niro's trailer discussing which cufflinks his character, Jimmy Conway, should wear.

Something happened after *Raging Bull*, though — whether it was the effect of putting on weight for the role, De Niro has expended the energy he had in the 1970s. The critical cliché "electric performance" is entirely apt for

Robert De Niro as the affable, violent wiseguy Jimmy Conway in *Goodfellas*

Madness to his Method

There have been many anecdotes about De Niro's Method acting philosophy: putting on weight for *Raging Bull*, learning the saxophone for *New York, New York* and wearing the same style of silk underwear as Al Capone for *The Untouchables*. When he made *Bloody Mama* in 1969, he even seemed to be able to drive a car in character. With director Roger Corman and his cinematographer strapped to the fender of a jalopy, De Niro drove furiously down a dirt road with co-star Shelley Winters in the passenger seat. After the second perilous take, Winters told De Niro how much she admired his Method approach: "You're driving great, you're really looking like a guy driving out of control." "I am driving out of control," he said, "I have no idea how to drive."

1970s De Niro, whose performances generated a charge and *frisson* between screen and audience. There was a different, muted power to the best of his post-1970s performances – his role in *Goodfellas* being a case in point.

Ultimately, his range and versatility are demonstrable by the fact that he has played more than ten gangster roles and yet he has managed to avoid being stereotyped. Not only that, his screen performances have convinced audiences across the world (and the pop group Bananarama) that he is the quintessential Italian-American: he is, in fact, mainly Irish-American.

Ben Hecht

1894–1964

If *Underworld* is the first classic gangster movie, then it's writer Ben Hecht who – as much as

anybody – can claim to have invented the genre. Hecht certainly has the right credentials. He was a journalist and columnist for a number of Chicago newspapers in the 1920s, familiar with all the characters and stories that emerged from the crime capital of America. Hecht moved from Chicago, a city he mythologized in his autobiography *A Child Of The Century*, after his friend Herman J. Mankiewicz sent him a telegram: "Millions are to be grabbed out here and your only competition is idiots. Don't let this get around."

He made a serious mark on the gangster movie twice: first with the story for *Underworld* in 1927 and then with his script for *Scarface*, both of them borrowing heavily from the Al Capone mythology. And it didn't take long before the crime boss took notice. Before *Scarface* had started filming, two of Capone's henchmen approached the writer in his hotel room and brought out a copy of the script they'd somehow acquired. Wanting to know how much of the screenplay was about their boss, they were assured by Hecht that *Scarface* was about several other Chicago gangsters, but not Capone. According to Hecht, this was good enough for the heavies.

But then one of them turned and asked "If this stuff isn't about Al Capone, why are you calling it Scarface? Everybody'll think it's him." "That's the reason," Hecht reportedly replied. "Al is one of the most famous and fascinating men of our time. If you call the movie *Scarface*, everybody will want to see it, figuring it's about Al. That's part of the racket we call showmanship." And with that the gangsters left satisfied, though this tale of course could be another example of Hecht's fabled talent for storytelling.

Mark Hellinger

1903–47

"There are 8 million stories in the naked city. This has been one of them." It was the voice of producer Mark Hellinger, who concluded Jules Dassin's police thriller, and whose final words became the catchphrase of the subsequent TV series, *The Naked City*. He would, however, never know this as by the time the film was released in 1948, Hellinger had died of a heart attack at the age of 44.

Hellinger was responsible for either writing or producing *The Roaring Twenties*, *Brother Orchid*, *High Sierra*, *The Killers* and *The Naked City*. Most of his films were intended to have the punch and pith of a newspaper report – the trailer for *The Roaring Twenties* even had Hellinger at his typewriter knocking out the script as if it was a story hot off the wires. Hellinger was himself a journalist, but he wasn't a crime reporter – he was a Broadway columnist – but the reason he knew so much about crime was that he spent much of his leisure time in the company of criminals.

His circle of friends included **Bugsy Siegel**, **Lucky Luciano** and **Dutch Schultz**, who allegedly left him an armoured Rolls Royce in his will. And he wasn't shy about his connections or his ability: he was sacked from Warner Brothers after a personality clash with producer Hal B. Wallis; he returned again only to be sacked a second time for leaving the studio for six months to cover the war in the Pacific in 1944. On this occasion he formed his own production company, and made **Burt Lancaster** a star in *The Killers* (1946) and *Brute Force* (1947). When he died, a theatre was named after him; it still stands today.

John Huston

1906–87

"What I really like are horses, strong women and drink," said John Huston when asked if he had any sympathies with the Communist Party. Huston was a boxer, painter, member of the Mexican cavalry, writer and director. He was responsible for inventing the private-eye genre as we know it, and also changed the course of the gangster movie several times. In *The Maltese Falcon* he transformed Humphrey Bogart into an icon as Sam Spade; in his script for *High Sierra*, he made the gangster a hunted, haunted melancholic; and in *The Asphalt Jungle* he ushered in the heist movie. He made over sixty other films, including *The African Queen* (1951).

There's a consistency to the characters who crop up in his movies: dreamers and idealists who throw themselves into a project knowing they will ultimately fail. Whether in the Florida Keys, the Sierra mountains or the African jungle, Huston's characters are often on the margins of civilization – the frontiers which test and define them. There is no visual consistency between films, yet they are united by their slow pace. This deliberateness works in *The Asphalt Jungle*, in which the build-up has to be as painstakingly methodical as the robbery itself, but not in movies such as *The Maltese Falcon* or *Prizzi's Honor*, where the plot has to move at a lick.

If there was any continuity to the man himself, it was to be found in his renegade personality. He had undisputed courage: in the jungle, during the war or standing up against HUAC by organizing the Committee For The First Amendment and flying down to Washington to organize a star-studded protest. Yet he was also obsessed with gambling: while writing *Key*

Largo in a hotel on the Florida Keys, Huston lost almost all his cash on their roulette table and ended up betting the last of his money on the definition of "Immaculate Conception", ringing up a Monsignor in the small hours to win his bet.

But the most consistent theme in his life (apart from the women – three wives and countless mistresses) was his love of strong drink. The most telling story is told by cinematographer Jack Cardiff who recalled, in his autobiography, how everyone got terrible dysentery during the making of *The African Queen,* because the water they'd been drinking hadn't been filtered. Everyone was vomiting copiously, except Humphrey Bogart and John Huston who, needless to say, hadn't touched a drop of water. They'd been drinking nothing but whisky.

Harvey Keitel

1939–

"When I cast Harvey Keitel in my first feature I found him very much to be like me, even though he's a Polish Jew from Brooklyn," **Martin Scorsese** once wrote. Keitel was Scorsese's first muse, in *Who's That Knocking At My Door?* (1968) and then *Mean Streets* (1973), only to be eventually usurped by **Robert De Niro**. An ex-marine and graduate of The Actors' Studio, Keitel patiently spent four years working on (and off) *Who's That Knocking* while earning his corn as a court stenographer. Scorsese repaid his patience by giving him the lead role of Charlie in *Mean Streets*, which the director has admitted is the most autobiographical of all his characters. But this special relationship didn't last, and Keitel was relegated to playing a pimp in *Taxi Driver* (1976) and Judas in *The Last Temptation Of Christ* (1988). As David Thomson has said, Keitel's life would make a great film, but De Niro would probably get the lead role.

The irony is that

Bogie's drinking buddy, and legendary director, John Huston

Harvey Keitel in Martin Scorsese's *Mean Streets* (1973)

while De Niro formed his own studios, Tribeca, it's Keitel who, as producer, has had the biggest influence on American cinema. When Keitel received an unsolicited manuscript from a video-store clerk, he agreed to star in it and produce it, even though the writer had no experience. With Keitel's name attached to the project, Quentin Tarantino eventually got the funding he needed to make *Reservoir Dogs* (1991). Keitel was in *Pulp Fiction* (1994) and Tarantino's segment of *Four Rooms* (1995), only to see De Niro star in the director's next project, *Jackie Brown* (1997). Despite this, it's Keitel who completes the

spiritual lineage between Scorsese and Tarantino, although, when it comes to Scorsese "alter egos", it's another regular who sounds and looks most like the director: Joe Pesci.

Fingers
dir James Toback, 1978, US, 91m

Keitel plays a concert pianist who moonlights as a debt collector for his mobbed-up father in James Toback's emotion-racked melodrama, which venerable critic David Thomson hails as one of the great American movies. *Fingers* is an acquired taste, however: both Keitel and Toback are Method men who like to take things to the edge, and often fall off.

Takeshi Kitano

1955–

Takeshi "Beat" Kitano is a comedian, TV game-show host, poet, painter, writer, director and movie star. Or, perhaps, *silent* movie star: in his movies, he does little and says less. Like so

The taciturn Takeshi Kitano lets the firearms do the talking in *Sonatine* (1993)

many gangster directors (John Woo or Martin Scorsese, for instance) he was born into poverty. Kitano studied engineering at college but dropped out to form a comedy act, The Two Beats. By the early 1970s they were the most popular comedians on TV, thanks largely to Kitano's outspoken comments, which outraged a supposedly respectable and respectful Japanese society. His acting career began when Nagisa Oshima cast him as a prison guard in *Merry Christmas Mr Lawrence* in 1983; and it was as an actor that he was employed on *Violent Cop* in 1987. But when legendary Yakuza-flick director **Kinji Fukasaku** fell ill, Kitano took up the directorial reins and added another profession to the CV. Takeshi, with his zen-like direction, made a very different film to the one imagined by Fukasaku, and Takeshi subsequently refined his signature style to perfection in *Sonatine* in 1993. Even when all hell is breaking loose, which it sporadically does, Kitano's camera observes it all with calm detachment, and in interviews the director has explained that this actually has little to do with zen, but is how he has always seen the world, even when he was a child.

In August 1994, Kitano bought a scooter which he crashed into a telegraph pole on the same day; the impact almost killed him and left him with a partially paralysed face. This has only made his subsequent performances even more surreal: in some scenes the only thing that moves is the tic. After his near-death experience it's unsurprising that Kitano's most poignant, fully-realized film, *Hana-bi* (1997), was profoundly concerned with mortality. It was quintessential Kitano: the character he plays says virtually nothing; the compositions are flat, like a series of stills; and little happens, which makes the violence, when it does occur, all the

Iconic molls

Joan Blondell
1906–79

James Cagney used to complain about the number of films he had to make for Warner Brothers. He got off lightly compared to Joan Blondell, his co-star in the Broadway play *Penny Arcade*, who accompanied him to Hollywood to make *Sinner's Holiday* (1930). As well as playing a moll alongside Cagney in *The Public Enemy* (1931), she acted in 52 movies during the 1930s, including gangster flicks *Blondie Johnson* (1933) and *Bullets Or Ballots* (1936).

Mae Clarke
1910–92

Mae Clarke is probably best known as James Cagney's victim *du jour*: she received a grapefruit in the face in *The Public Enemy* and was pulled across the floor by her hair in *The Lady Killer*. Clarke reportedly blamed the grapefruit for the decline of her career – by 1950 she was playing "counter lady with change for a quarter" in *The Reformer And The Redhead* and in 1953 she played "happy shopper" in *Confidentially Connie*. Her penultimate role was "woman in the office" in *Thoroughly Modern Millie* in 1967.

Jean Harlow
1911–37

Even although Harlow only officially played a moll twice, in *The Public Enemy* and *Beast Of The City* (1932), she seemed to be playing the moll in almost every film she was in, most notably in **Frank Capra**'s *Platinum Blonde* (1931), in which she is a woman well aware of her own sexuality and the effect it has on men. It was a role she carried over into real life, dating mobster Longy Zwillman, who reputedly kept a lock of her pubic hair in his wallet. She was neck-deep in scandal in 1932 when her husband, Paul Bern, died in mysterious circumstances. Her own death was less mysterious but no less tragic. She died aged just 26, of acute nephritis.

more disquieting.

Only a few of his films are not about cops and mobs. Asked why he seems to be obsessed with gangsters, the director has argued that they are part of daily life in Japan: "You go out drinking, you will probably end up in a bar owned by the yakuza and if you work in the entertainment industry, you are bound to meet someone who is yakuza." In other interviews, the director has claimed that his father, Kikujiro, was a gang member, an inveterate gambler who was so badly in debt that the family once had to move house during the night.

Jean-Pierre Melville
1917–73

John Woo calls him his "spiritual idol" and Quentin Tarantino claims that *Le doulos* is the best script ever written. Melville's films–about–films have been a clear influence on both directors, and Melville would have been touched that his fascination with America has now been reciprocated. The writer/director wore a stetson, sunglasses and a trench coat, would drive around in open-topped, big-finned cars (just like his characters) and he even changed his surname from Grumbach in tribute to *Moby Dick* author,

Herman Melville. In his movies, he tried to make Paris look like Manhattan.

A member of the French Resistance during the war (a number of his films were about the conflict), he continued to fight all through his career – asserting his independence from his very first film by adapting *Le silence de la mer* (1947) without permission from either the author of the novel on which it was based, or the unions. He built his own film studios in Rue De Jenner, Paris, from where he laid down the law to actors: one of his rules stated that there were to be no affairs on set, as they were a distraction from the work.

Melville started his crime spree with *Bob le flambeur* (1956) and *Deux hommes en Manhattan* (1959). Both were as much about people as action. But, from 1963, his films were largely plot-driven. And even though they were filmed in France they existed in a never-never land which was neither France nor America, but a wasteland of Hollywood iconography: cars, bars, phone booths and clothes. The clothes in particular: almost every male lead wears the uniform of fedora and trench coat first seen on **Alan Ladd** in *This Gun For Hire* (1942). If Melville's characters can't express themselves verbally, they let their clothes do the talking. Volker Schlondorff, the assistant director of *Le doulos*, has revealed just how much time Melville would spend getting the brim of the fedora just right. He didn't want any gestures or facial expressions from his actors, they had to be more like screen icons than real people.

There are five films in the second phase of Melville's oeuvre, and they share striking similarities in theme and style. The films all start with a quotation, which is either totally made up or radically abbreviated. Famously, *Le samourai* begins with the words: "There is no deeper solitude than the samurai's, unless perhaps it be that of the tiger in the jungle." The quote is attributed to "The Bushido (The book of the samurai)". In fact, it's pure Melville. The movies invariably feature a game of cat and mouse between criminal and police inspector: even though they're on either side of the law, there is mutual respect between them. Melville's world is all about male bonding, and themes of loyalty and honour. Women are either duplicitous (*Le doulos*), will get you killed (*Le samourai*) or are absent (*Le cercle rouge*).

Despite these themes, loyalty is regarded as an impossibility; it's futile. The quotation that begins *Le doulos* states that "One must choose. To die … or to lie." Because this question of choice (which all his leading men wrestle with) is allied to a crushed fatalism, critics talk about Melville's existentialism. The director deliberately stripped his characters of any interior life, or any psychological motivations. We can only judge them by their actions, which is difficult in the case of *Le doulos* because we don't know what those actions are.

Melville's movies, particularly *Le deuxième souffle* and *Le cercle rouge,* were hugely popular but were sniffed at by critics, most notably those of *Cahiers Du Cinéma*, who accused him of making mere entertainment. The director's argument was that his films existed on two levels, like a *millefeuille* cake. There were those who only tasted the cream, but there were others who were much more discerning, who tasted the pastry.

Al Pacino

1940–

Michael Corleone in *The Godfather* and Tony Montana in *Scarface* are two landmark performances in gangster-film history. They are also defining moments in the phases of Al Pacino's film career. Michael and Tony are two sides of the same Al: Pacino part I and Pacino part II; little Al and big Al.

"A shrimp" is how Paramount executives described the actor when he screen-tested for the role of Michael Corleone. At the time, Pacino was a dishevelled thespian who'd studied so obsessively at The Actors' Studio in the mid- 1960s that **Lee Strasberg** had to tell him to take it easy; he'd won awards for his work on Broadway, but had only made two movies. The studios preferred **Warren Beatty** and even **Charles Bronson** but Francis Ford Coppola insisted upon having the shrimp. Even though the acting Oscars on *The Godfather* and its sequel went to the more obvious performances from Marlon Brando and Robert De Niro,

Make way for the bad guy

On January 7, 1961 a 21-year-old Al Pacino was arrested for carrying a concealed weapon. The fellow occupants of the car he was in were all wearing black ski masks and gloves and were apparently behaving in a suspicious manner, according to the police who arrested them. Pacino spent three days in jail, and was eventually fined. Legend has it that he talked his way out of a longer stretch by telling cops that he was rehearsing for a role.

Pacino's transmigration, or perhaps evacuation, of the soul of Michael Corleone over the course of three hours conveys the horror that

Late-period Pacino: on the run at the end of the paranoid, tense, unexpected triumph of a De Palma movie, *Carlito's Way* (1993)

Brando never quite captured in *Apocalypse Now*. What's most impressive is that there is no Jekyll and Hyde moment that signals the change in Michael; the closest *The Godfather* comes to a transformation scene is when Michael decides to personally take revenge on the men who made an attempt on his father's life. As he plots his vengeance, the camera draws closer to him, and we realize that Michael is his father's son after all. By the end of the scene his bible-black eyes have deadened.

The power of withdrawn, withheld emotion was characteristic of Pacino's 1970s screen persona. In *Scarface*, however, Pacino introduced us to his "little friend", Big Al. This Al was louder, his eyes popped out of their sockets, and veins bulged from his neck. As for his balls, he never broke them for anybody. The decision to go over the top with Tony Montana was a conscious one, to complement the heightened, operatic nature of **Brian De Palma**'s direction and Oliver Stone's script, and as such the performance was note-perfect.

By *Heat* (1995), Pacino wasn't delivering his lines, he was barking (in both senses of the word): bursting into song accompanied only by a roll of the eyes. Pacino was now a showman, and even his quieter roles, such as Carlito in *Carlito's Way* (1993) and Lefty in *Donnie Brasco* (1997), were still acts of showmanship. When he returned to *The Godfather* saga in *Part III*, Michael Corleone – a character whose life history, treacheries and complexities, was once all in the eyes – were now a riot of hand gestures, bared teeth, and unusual haircut decisions. It was as if Michael Corleone was aware of the Shakespearean dimensions of his character: the performance demonstrated that perhaps the difference between Little Al and Big Al is the difference between a screen and a stage actor.

Joe Pesci

1943–

When De Niro's wattage dimmed, it was left to Joe Pesci to fire up Scorsese's gangster films, to put us on edge. It's thanks to Scorsese and De Niro that Pesci is acting at all; he was managing a restaurant in the Bronx when they rang him asking if he'd like to audition for *Raging Bull*. They'd seen him in *The Death Collector*, a 1975

Unlikely gangsters

There are stars who have flirted with gangsterism early in their careers. **Spencer Tracy** starred in *Quick Millions* (1931). **Clark Gable** played the hood in *A Free Soul*, *The Finger Points* (both 1931) and *Manhattan Melodrama* (1934), and who knows how his career would have shaped up if he'd actually landed the lead role in *Little Caesar*. It's unlikely that he would have been chosen to play Rhett Butler. One trend, certainly in the UK, has been to cast comedians against type: **Freddie Starr** in *The Squeeze* (1977), Brian Conley displaying his serious side (and his backside) in *Circus* (2000), and Norman Wisdom doubling up in *Double X* (1991). **Sid James** would seem to be part of that tradition, but actually approached it the other way round; before he became a *Carry On* stalwart, he was part of the gang in comic and serious crime fare: attempting an American accent in *Joe Macbeth* (1955), aiding and abetting Alec Guinness in *The Lavender Hill Mob* (1951), and playing "Flash Harry" in *Dry Rot* (1956).

It's *that* pair again: Scorsese's favourite muses De Niro and Pesci take care of the gambling racket in *Casino* (1995)

low-budget stinker that sunk without trace, but which Scorsese had caught on TV. Pesci had left Hollywood soon after its release, after an explosive row with a casting agent, and had moved into catering. Previously he'd been a child actor on TV, a singer who released an album called *Little Joe Sure Can Sing*, and guitarist in a band called Joey Dee And The Starliters, who appar-

ently made a film called *Hey Let's Twist*.

After *Raging Bull*, Pesci appeared as a gangster in *Once Upon A Time In America*, a police informant in *Lethal Weapon II* and *III*, and a gangster once more in *Casino*, among other roles. But it's his Oscar-winning performance in *Goodfellas*, and his ability to explode on cue, that still burn the retina.

The hoods in the background

Richard Conte

1910–75

Conte's dark, Italianate looks increasingly made him fair game for Hollywood stereotyping as a gang boss. He was head of syndicate Mr Brown in *The Big Combo* (1955), hit man Nick Magellan in *New York Confidential* (1955) and an accountant for The Mob in *The Brothers Rico* (1957). But his greatest role came thirty years after his debut, as Don Barzini in *The Godfather*, when he was 62 years old.

Elisha Cook Jr

1903–95

"I've played rats, pimps, informers, hopheads and communists," said Elisha Cook Jr of his career that spanned over a hundred films. In most of them he played an unlikely villain, and it's not for nothing that he was dubbed "the lightest heavy". A small, unprepossessing figure, he would often play the sap's sap, most notably in Stanley Kubrick's *The Killing*, in which he's half man, half guppy, caught on the hooks of his duplicitous wife. But it's as a hood in a detective film that he's most famous, his unforgettable turn as Wilmer the punk in *The Maltese Falcon*, who wants to kill Bogart so much that he starts to cry.

Lawrence Tierney

1919–2002

When Lawrence Tierney was playing Joe, the mastermind behind the heist in *Reservoir Dogs*, the rest of the cast were a little wary of him, even though he was 73. Tierney didn't just *play* hard men: by 1955 he'd been arrested sixteen times. Over the course of his life he'd committed as many offences off-screen as on: kicking a student, strangling a cab driver, hitting a waiter in the face with a bowl, assaulting police officers and shop-lifting were just a few entries on his curriculum vitae. He made his film debut in 1943, became a B-movie star in the lead role of *Dillinger* in 1945, but never bettered himself as a killer on the road in *The Devil Thumbs A Ride* (1947), a landmark in brutalism. But by the 1950s the drinking and the fighting, and the headline-grabbing visits to prison and institutions, made him virtually unemployable: "I threw away about seven careers through drink," he once estimated. In 1973 he was stabbed in the abdomen and two years later he was questioned by police after a young woman had, apparently, thrown herself from her fourth-floor apartment: Tierney claimed that he got there just as she was going out the window. By the 1980s he was beginning to pick up work in television, and by 1992 he was leader of the pack in *Reservoir Dogs*. Not that he was particularly grateful to Quentin Tarantino – he spent most of the shoot complaining about the dialogue.

George Raft

1895–1980

There's a good reason why George Raft was stereotyped as a gangster. It was a role he knew very well. As well as appearing in dozens of movies, he's also been a character other actors have played in many others: **Richard Gere** has played him, so has **Joe Mantegna**, **Ray Danton** and **Douglas** Fairbanks Jr, though he's not always been named as George Raft. The actor even played himself in a fictional account of his dealings with the Mob in *Broadway* (1942), which recounts how he and his dancing partner were caught up with a hoodlum while working in a speakeasy. The later *Spin Of A Coin – The George Raft Story* (1961) was just as fictionalized and as sanitized.

In the 1920s Raft was a dancer and gun–carrier for the Mob and, like Gere's Dixie Dwyer in *The Cotton Club*, he left New York to become a screen hood. (And just like Dwyer, he couldn't act but he looked good.) His change of career allegedly became the inspiration for the character of Joe in *Little Caesar*, the best friend who leaves Rico to return to the world of dance. After playing the part of the best friend himself in *Scarface*, Raft went on to star or co-star in a roster of movies during the 1930s and 1940s – *The Glass Key* (1935), *Each Dawn I Die* (1939) and *They Drive By Night* (1940).

But it was his role in *Scarface* that most impressed mobster **Bugsy Siegel**; the two became firm friends, Bugsy moved into Raft's house, and Raft was guest of honour when Siegel opened the Flamingo hotel in Las Vegas in 1946. When Siegel was murdered, Raft took up with another gangster, **Meyer Lansky**, working with him on his casinos in Havana, which came to an abrupt end with the Castro revolution. Undaunted, Lansky and Raft moved to London, where Raft ran the Colony Club; realizing he was just a front for the Mob, the British authorities deported him in 1966. In the middle of all this activity, Raft continued to act, although less often, but he had one great role left in him: Spats in *Some Like It Hot* (1959). Although a parody, it was no less a joke than *The George Raft Story*.

Edward G Robinson

1893–1973

"He looked like a crustacean with its shell off" is John Huston's memorable description of Edward G. Robinson in the bath in *Key Largo*. At least "crustacean" makes a change from "toad" and "bullfrog", the

other animals that Robinson has frequently been compared to. "I may not have face value, but I've got stage value" is the phrase that the actor would use to convince theatre directors inclined to hiring leading men with classic good looks.

Born in Bucharest, his family moved to the lower East East Side of New York ten years later. He changed his name, **Emanuel Goldenberg**, when he started acting and toured around the States for over a decade, appearing in one silent movie, *The Bright Shawl* (1923), though he hated the way he looked on screen.

The "crustacean with its shell off" takes a bath in *Key Largo* (1948)

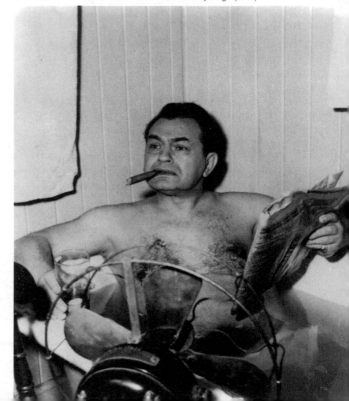

A Shakespearean actor, he finally became a star, much to his chagrin, when he played Al Capone (or rather "Nick Scarsi") in the play *The Racket*, a Broadway smash which toured the United States, except Chicago where it was banned (apparently for the production's own safety). Although Robinson didn't land the role in the film adaptation, he did come to the attention of the studios. His first part was, of course, as a gangster in *Hole In The Wall* (1928), in which he played a dandy underworld kingpin called The Fox. He transformed into Cobra Collins in *Outside The Law*, one of four more Mob-related films he made in quick succession including *The Widow From Chicago* and *Night Ride*.

The fourth was *Little Caesar*, cinema's first classic gangster movie and first classic gangster performance. Originally slated to play Rico Bandello's fawning new best friend Oreto, Robinson only got the main part after hectoring the producers. The original choice was **Clark Gable**, but the studios decided his ears were too big. It was possibly Robinson's crustacean/toad/bullfrog-like appearance that made him perfect for the most inhuman of all the classic gangsters, a man without qualities except the drive to succeed and an appetite for destruction.

His unusual appearance is exaggerated by the fact that his eyes are unnaturally wide open as he guns down his victims. This was never intended to be a character trait: the pacifist actor was so nervous about firing a gun, even a replica, that he kept blinking during the fight scenes. The producers' solution, to tape up his eyelids, only added to his subhuman demeanour.

A box-office phenomenon, *Little Caesar* led to minor riots in queues outside cinemas and to Robinson doing a lucrative tour of personal appearances "by Rico". And although he did play other parts, Robinson spent most of the 1930s in gangster roles or films. By 1940 Robinson had had enough; the Shakespearean thesp felt he had spent too long on Murderer's Row and wanted the freedom to act in the so-called prestige films of the type **Paul Muni** had been starring in. A deal was struck and Robinson agreed to appear in one more gangster flick, *Brother Orchid* (1940), as a mobster who hides out in a monastery, so long as he could star in his pet project *Dr Erlich's Magic Bullet* (1940), about the Jewish physician who discovered the cure for syphilis.

By 1947 Robinson had other things to worry about. When the **House Un-American Activities Committee** began in earnest in October of that year, Robinson was accused by actor Adolphe Menjou of having sympathies with the "Communist side" in recent disputes. A keen Democrat and proud Jew, the actor was one of the key members of the Hollywood Anti-Nazi League before and during the war. He was effectively persecuted for his various liberal associations – and for refusing to acquiesce to HUAC – leading to lack of acting work and the removal of his US passport.

In 1952 he finally capitulated and the work started to come in, including the inevitable gangster pic, *Black Tuesday* (1954). He made some notable films after that – *The Cincinnati Kid* and *Soylent Green* – but no great gangster movies; only a parody of his former self in the Rat Pack's *Robin And The Seven Hoods* in 1964.

Robinson died of cancer in 1973; he was awarded a Lifetime Achievement Oscar that year, even though (or probably because) he'd never even been nominated during his lifetime.

Robert De Niro and Martin Scorsese, on the set of *Goodfellas*

Martin Scorsese

1942–

A classic Scorsese film always begins with a quotation before the credits, the leading man setting out his stall. "As far back as I can remember I've always wanted to be a gangster," says narrator Henry Hill at the opening of *Goodfellas*. As far back as Martin Scorsese can remember, he wanted to be a priest. A short, asthmatic kid growing up in Little Italy, the director could never run with the gangs, and soon fell under the spell of a young priest who took him to the

pictures. It's not incidental that there's a tension between religion and crime in his gangster films, an antagonism best expressed in the character of Charlie in *Mean Streets,* who is equally drawn to God and the worldly, wild Johnny Boy.

Most of Scorsese's early life was spent amongst wise guys in the East Side of Manhattan. He would dedicate much of his time to avoiding trouble, to arriving at mass brawls late in the hope that they'd be finished by the time he got there. Another way to avoid trouble was to go to the cinema or watch films on TV (the Scorseses were the first family in the neighbourhood to get a set). And this sense of being both an insider and outsider is shared by Scorsese's characters: neither Charlie in *Mean Streets*, nor Henry in *Goodfellas* nor Sam in *Casino* is a made man, a full member of the Sicilian Mafia – they're all observers, both part of and apart from the family.

An NYU student from 1960 to 1965, Scorsese intermittently spent the next four years making *Who's That Knocking At My Door,* with court stenographer Harvey Keitel in the lead. He followed it up with *The Honeymoon Killers*, from which he was sacked for being too arty and insisting on shooting almost everything in master shots. Scorsese became an editor (notably on *Woodstock*) and was given a second chance to direct by **Roger Corman**, who offered him the job of *Boxcar Bertha* (1972) after seeing *Who's That Knocking*. Legend has it that Corman gave Scorsese free rein on the film as long as he kept to the schedule and the budget, and included nudity every fifteen minutes.

Scorsese duly obliged: the first love scene occurs exactly ten minutes in, but includes his own signature touch – a mural of Mary Magdalene on the back wall of a church. However, the most obvious example of Scorsese's religious iconography – the crucifixion of Bertha's lover – was already in the script. When the director read it, he saw it as a sign from God.

Scorsese abandoned his plans to make more exploitation movies. *Mean Streets*, originally titled *Season Of The Witch*, was a personal project – set on the streets he'd grown up on, about the friends that he'd known and the hoodlums he'd avoided, based on incidents he'd been party to (Scorsese once got out of a car that minutes later was struck by bullets fired from another vehicle).

Mean Streets was a critical success and conferred auteur status upon the director. A personal exorcism, Scorsese declared that he would never make another gangster movie again, and that he'd said all he had to say in *Mean Streets*. He's made three gangster movies since. His first change of heart happened in the late 1980s, when he read the reviews of Nicholas Pileggi's biography *Wise Guy* about Mafia foot soldier and FBI stool pigeon Henry Hill, and felt an immediate connection with the material. *Goodfellas* was a critical success whose reputation and influence continue to grow exponentially, celebrated as much for its dazzling formal innovations (such as the jump-cut frenzy of Henry's last coke-fuelled day as a wise guy) as for its story. Traces of *Goodfellas* can be detected in a whole decade of films under its influence.

Scorsese's second change of heart was not so well received. "Goodfellas II" is how the press cruelly dubbed *Casino*: it had two of its stars – **Robert De Niro** and **Joe Pesci** – essaying similar roles. It also had the same dizzying array of freeze-frames, slo-mo, fast-mo, and was mostly cut to a 1960s soundtrack. But there was a lot more of it – it was almost three hours long.

In terms of critical reception, it's been a law of diminishing returns for Scorsese's gangster output since the 1990s. *Gangs Of New York*, a personal project that was on the Scorsese back burner since 1976 received the most disappointing reviews of all four. The project was originally supposed to star De Niro, back in the early 1980s, and in 2000 a much older De Niro was offered the role of Bill The Butcher, but turned it down. **Daniel Day Lewis** was prised from his new profession of shoemaker to take the part, while the main role of Amsterdam went to **Leonardo DiCaprio**.

Gangs Of New York has many staggering set pieces (including a knife-throwing scene in which it's easy to forget to breathe) but is Scorsese's weakest film in terms of character development and emotional force. Interviews with the director are full of talk about film stock, and the suspicion remains that the director is now more interested in over-cranking a camera than telling a story.

Casino
dir Martin Scorsese, 1995, US, 178m

De Niro and Pesci largely reprise their roles from *Goodfellas*, though both are promoted from their roles in the previous film to take centre stage. Scorsese's cinematic chutzpah is dazzling but the effect of watching *Casino* is like witnessing a magic act for three hours: awe soon gives way to fatigue.

Shark Tale
dir Bibo Bergerson, 2004, US, 90m

No one could have forseen this career move: Martin Scorsese playing a blowfish in a children's cartoon. In fact, it's a gangster movie masquerading as a kiddies animation, even playing on the Darwinian nature of the genre. The first conversation that Scorsese's fish has with Robert De Niro's shark/don is an in-joke as they talk about how long they've worked together. And the references come thick and fast after that, including, of course, the predictable "sleeps with the fishes" gag.

Quentin Tarantino
1963–

Quentin Tarantino has a reference for a first name: he was named after the **Burt Reynolds** character in *Gunsmoke*, Quint Asper. It's entirely appropriate for a writer and director who spent his career referencing movies and old TV shows.

The man with Burt's name grew up wanting to be an actor, leaving school to pursue his dream, and ending up behind the counter of Video Archives on Manhattan Beach, Los Angeles. The video shop has since become the locus of slacker folklore: Tarantino got $4 an hour and as many free movies as he wanted, and spent his days with fellow clerk and future director **Roger Avary** discussing the merits of John Woo, Elvis Presley and Sonny Chiba. Together they wrote scripts and attended acting classes, which paid off when Tarantino sold *True Romance* for $30,000, and landed the part of an Elvis impersonator in an episode of *The Golden Girls*.

Tarantino was now able to make *Reservoir Dogs* on 16mm, and that was always the plan until a script found its way to Harvey Keitel. He rang Tarantino saying how much he liked *Reservoir Dogs* and explaining that he wanted to produce it. With the actor's name attached to the project, a studio executive called Richard Gladstein read the script and bankrolled the movie.

Reservoir Dogs was a cause célèbre at the Sundance Film Festival in 1991. Worries were expressed about its misogyny, racism and violence; and helped by Tarantino's own motor-mouthing the controversy became the best advertisement for the film. Even though it didn't even make a dent on the US box office, in Britain both *Reservoir Dogs* and its director became a cult. The PR blitz worked. As Roger Avary said, "after *Reservoir Dogs* Quentin could do whatever he wanted". What he wanted was to make the compendium film the two friends had always discussed.

The result, *Pulp Fiction,* was a phenomenon. It made over $100 million in the United States alone, and **Harvey Weinstein** has always claimed that its success saved Miramax. (And this is why Tarantino has never felt the sharp end of the man they call Harvey Scissorhands.) With its successor, *Jackie Brown,* the director paid a debt of gratitude to the first writer he'd ever read, the greatest influence on his own demotic – **Elmore Leonard**. In adapting Leonard's *Rum Punch*, the director acknowledged another key influence

– blaxploitation movies. He turned the white stewardess Jackie Burke into Jackie Brown, and cast the legendary star of *Foxy Brown*, **Pam Grier**, in the role. *Jackie Brown* was censured for its language by director Spike Lee. Samuel L. Jackson's character, the arms dealer Ordell is straight out of *Superfly* or *The Mack* and uses the word "nigger" like punctuation.

But it wasn't the race issue that stymied *Jackie Brown*'s success at the box office; it was just a little dull for most people. There were no exploding heads, less narrative fun and games, and except for a monologue about John Woo's *The Killer*, few conversations akin to the analysis of *Like A Virgin* or "The Royale With Cheese". It was a mature work and many critics hoped that the boy wonder had grown up. Instead he stopped. For six years he didn't direct another film and when he did return it was with his most juvenile work to date, the two instalments of *Kill Bill*.

Jackie Brown
dir Quentin Tarantino, 1997, US, 154m

In 1997 the movie had many hopes and expectations to measure up to, but now, without those preconceptions, *Jackie Brown* appears to be a work of great maturity, possibly the one Tarantino film that will get better with age. It's a typical Tarantino stew of influences – Elmore Leonard, blaxploitation, Melville's *Le doulos* and Kubrick's *The Killing*.

True Romance
dir Tony Scott, 1993, US, 119m

Even though Tarantino's own visual style may appear a little flat, even televisual, there may be a good reason: flashy visuals distract from the all-important dialogue. And the best evidence for that is Tony "Top Gun" Scott's *True Romance*. The skewed camera angles and MTV editing distract from Tarantino's script. Scott changed the original ending but also lost the essence of what makes a Tarantino film work.

Raoul Walsh
1887–1980

Raoul Walsh is the director who gave us three masterpieces: *The Roaring Twenties, High Sierra* and *White Heat*. He lived for 94 years, made films for 71 of them – often producing more than one a year – and yet none of his movies was nominated for the Best Picture or Best Director Oscar.

Starting out as an actor for **D.W. Griffith**, he played John Wilkes Booth in *Birth Of A Nation* and lost an eye during *In Old Arizona*. In 1916 he directed *Regeneration*, one of the earliest gangster films to survive. He would later tell tall stories about employing prostitutes as extras, who accidentally revealed on camera that they weren't wearing any underwear. Apparently Walsh was as good a storyteller in real life as he was on screen. After *Regeneration*, he made dozens of movies in almost every genre, including the minor work *Me, Gangster* in 1928. But it wasn't until he got a contract with Warner Brothers in 1939 that he established himself as a great crime director.

In an extraordinary (and extraordinarily short) relationship with producer **Mark Hellinger** he made *The Roaring Twenties*, *They Drive By Night*, *High Sierra* and *Manpower* – all in two years (Hellinger left Warners in 1941). All four films gave Walsh the reputation of being Warners' top action helmsman – someone whose films moved at a great lick but weren't afraid of wide open spaces. In a stage-struck Hollywood, Walsh's decision to film the climax of *High Sierra* in the real Sierra mountains (as opposed to a set with back projection) was genuinely revolutionary.

When James Cagney returned to Warners in 1949, it was Walsh who directed his next (and last great) film – *White Heat*. Even though Cagney's Cody Jarrett is clearly psychotic, Walsh managed to make the role into something with more pathos – just as he had done with Cagney in *The Roaring Twenties* and Humphrey Bogart in *High Sierra* – the hard man as lonely, human and doomed.

Richard Widmark

1914–

It was a laugh that launched Richard Widmark's career: a hysterical, psychotic giggle as he pushed a wheelchair-bound old lady down a flight of stairs in *Kiss Of Death* (1947). It's strange, then, that the director **Henry Hathaway** didn't originally want him for the role of Tommy Udo in the movie. His preference was for someone called Harry The Hipster, but the studios insisted upon Widmark, then an established stage actor. According to Widmark, in the first week of shooting Widmark confronted the director. He took him out to lunch, and although not a word was spoken during the meal, Hathaway didn't have a problem with him after that. Indeed, the pair became firm friends, and Widmark was a pall-bearer at Hathaway's funeral.

After *Kiss Of Death*, Widmark played a gangland mastermind in *The Street With No Name* (1948), a jealous psychotic in *Road House* (1948) and, by the time he made *Night And The City* (1950), he was established as a pioneer of the new breed of American gangster. Harry Fabian and, later, Skip McCoy in *Pick Up On South Street* (1953) are his stand-out performances in genre sleaze. Both are chancers and charmers, dreamers who

Richard Widmark (right) in one of the edgier, bad-guy roles few remember him for

snatch at the opportunity to make it big. Both Harry and Skip display a cocksureness which is undermined by the near-hysteria of their ambitions. Ironically, and unfortunately, it's for all the good cowboys, lieutenants and detectives that Widmark is now remembered rather than the psychotics and the spivs.

Kiss Of Death
dir Henry Hathaway, 1947, US, 98m, b/w

Sometimes a performance can be better than the film, a part greater than its sum, and this is true of Richard Widmark in *Kiss Of Death*. He has the intensity of early De Niro as Tommy Udo, the hood who's on the trail of Victor Mature, an ex-thief who unsuccessfully testified against him. Inexplicably remade in 1995 with Nicolas Cage (psychotic but not chilling) in the Widmark role.

Ray Winstone

1957–

Ray Winstone is synonymous with the British gangster movie (as in the phrase "not another gangster movie with Ray Winstone'), and yet he claims to have played only one gangster, in *Love, Honour And Obey* (1999). He argues that his other "gangster" roles in *Sexy Beast* (2001) and *Face* (1997) were thieves, and that's very different. Brought up in Hackney and Enfield, Winstone was a boxer and a drama student, until he was expelled from college, for reasons he doesn't like to go into. Winstone then got the kind of showbiz break that only happens in biopics: visiting the BBC to see some old friends, he was spotted by director **Alan Clarke** and given the role of Carlin in harrowing borstal drama *Scum*. It was in many ways his most gangsterly role, one that shared – more by accident than design – the rise-and-fall narrative of the classic gangster flick. It was here that Winstone uttered the sentence that's practically become his catchphrase: "I'm the daddy." After that, and a role in *Quadrophenia* (1979), little was heard of him bar the TV series, *Robin Of Sherwood*; the work dried up after his adventures in the forest.

Winstone was forcibly retired until his big-screen comeback in 1997 with his acclaimed, unsettling performance as Kathy Burke's vicious husband, Raymond, in **Gary Oldman**'s *Nil By Mouth*, which reminded critics that they'd once dubbed Winstone the British Cagney. From there he played Dave in *Face,* gave **Sadie Frost** and ex-public-schoolboy **Jude Law** some much needed credibility in their improvised, kara-oke gangster fare *Love, Honour And Obey*, and found his métier as Gal in *Sexy Beast* (2001), the ex-thief with the tight

Ray Winstone (left) and Ben Kingsley: the "thief" and the gangster of *Sexy Beast* (2001)

Chow Yun-Fat in a typically stylised Woo close-up from *The Killer* (1989)

yellow speedos and crisp, sunburnt flesh brought out of retirement by nerve-free gangster **Ben Kingsley**.

John Woo

1946–

John Woo reinvented Hong Kong cinema, brought gangsters back to life and initiated a set of movies known as "heroic bloodshed". He's king of

the face-off, the duel between the bad guy and the good guy who become mirror images of one another. In John Woo's films, polarities are illusory. Woo is himself a paradox: the director with the impossibly high body count (he's been described as "Count Body Count") and the Christian who abhors violence and loves musicals.

Born in mainland China, he fled with his parents to Hong Kong in 1951, became homeless in the fire of 1953, and moved to a Triad-dominated shantytown, where he frequently witnessed street killings and assumed he must be living in hell. Provided with an education by the Lutheran Church, Woo became a devout Christian and religion, chivalry and cinema became the three formative influences on his work. *The Killer* (1989) and *Face/Off* (1997) both have climactic shoot-outs in church.

Like Martin Scorsese, John Woo was a sickly child who spent much of his formative years in the cinema, watching American and European films, and he gained a particular affection for the movies of **Jean-Pierre Melville**. Woo is as interested as the French director in questions of brotherhood and loyalty, and refers to themes symbolically, through imagery and iconography.

However, it took the Hong Kong director thirteen years of filmmaking to begin making recognizably "John Woo" movies. *A Better Tomorrow* (1986) changed the fortunes of both Woo and his lead, the TV actor **Chow Yun-Fat**; it became the biggest commercial success in Hong Kong history. It was the first John Woo movie proper: here were the soon-to-be-familiar themes of brotherhood, idealism versus materialism, and the return of the knight errant in the shape of the gangster. He was an urban warrior who Woo believed was a new hero: "this kind of hero could be you, could be anybody – anybody who loves others, and can stand up and fight for what is right".

A sequel was made, with Chow Yun-Fat resurrected, and *The Killer*, envisioned as a homage to Melville, introduced the religious iconography and polished the Woo style, the gun battle-as-ballet, death in slo-mo, and the Berettas-in-both-fists with a seemingly endless supply of ammunition. The cop flick *Hard Boiled* (1992) proved to be the apex of the Hong Kong years, particularly the 45-minute climax: Chow Yun-Fat with a baby in one hand and a gun in the other, surrounded by villains with their own personal armoury, blasting his way out of a hospital. It made no sense but by then no one cared.

With the high priest of hip, **Quentin Tarantino**, paying public reverence, it was inevitable that Woo would move to America and when he did, he brought high expectations with him. However, his work in Hollywood – *Hard Target, Broken Arrow, Mission Impossible II, Windtalkers, Paycheck* – has been disappointing, but at least with John Travolta and Nicolas Cage in *Face/Off* he returned to his favourite theme of cop and villain who are (literally) interchangeable. By then John Woo was not just a director, he was a trademark, or to some, almost a cult.

Tools Of The Trade: the archetypes

Gloria Grahame, moll of molls, in
The Big Heat (1953)

Tools of the trade:
the archetypes

Gangster movies can sometimes be wildly inventive, breaking moulds and offering dazzlingly imaginative new ideas. However, there is only so far you can go from a basic template before things just ain't gangster no more. If the genre was a trench coat and you were to empty the pockets, here are some of the things you might find...

The "ascension killing"

Just to underline the Oedipal nature of the classic gangster narrative, many will invariably feature a moment when the Young Turk must kill his father figure and take his place, both behind his desk and in his bed. More often than not the older man is jealous of his protégé and is worried that he wants his job and/or his moll. Often he's right. As **Paul Muni** says in *Scarface*, "some day I'm gonna run the whole works".

And so the crime lord makes an attempt on the upstart's life, which he botches. Muni survives a gun battle and when he visits his employer, the old man quickly confesses to the murder plot and pleads for his life, offering his moll in return. Muni is unimpressed and walks away, leaving **George Raft** to do his dirty work for him. Pacino does it more memorably and in more extreme fashion in the remake. Robert Loggia is literally on his hands and knees, sobbing and offering him anything to stay alive. He reminds him of his paternal connection – he was the first one to bring him in, the first one to believe in him. Pacino turns away, and informs Loggia that he's not going to kill him. Loggia's relief is palpable until Pacino finishes his sentence: "Manolo, shoot that piece of shit."

The Godfather Part II has *the* most memorable ascension killing, by dint of a small fire. When De Niro's young Vito Corleone prepares to dethrone the neighbourhood boss Fanucci, he wraps a towel around his gun, which catches fire when he shoots. With a calm detachment that marks out the future don, Vito unwraps the towel, takes the gun and places it in Fanucci's mouth and squeezes the trigger. Fanucci hasn't been a father figure or mentor, but his crime was to ask for a

Vito Corleone (Robert De Niro) begins his ascent towards Don status in *The Godfather Part II* (1974)

share of Corleone's ill-gotten gains – "enough to wet his beak". Vito "makes him an offer he can't refuse" but Fanucci turns him down, and is probably the first and last refusenik ever to make that mistake.

The bent cop

When **Arnold Rothstein** took control of New York's underworld he knew that behind every successful criminal was a bent cop, and apparently he had most of New York's finest in his pocket.

Screen gangsters have taken their cue from Rothstein and co, and the bent cop is a familiar figure. Often he is a close companion, like Parky in *The Long Good Friday* (1980). Parky is another member of Harold Shand's corporation, and spends so much time with the London Mob boss that it's easy to forget that he has a day job with Scotland Yard. But this is not a relationship of equals, as is demonstrated in one key scene: Shand orders Parky to round up the usual suspects to find out "who's having a go" at him, but the copper refuses until Harold firmly puts him in his place with one of the best lines in the film, or indeed any film: "Bent law can be tolerated for as long as they're lubricating, but you have become definitely parched ... you're gonna wind up on one of those meat hooks, my son." When Parky acquiesces, it soon becomes clear who's the daddy.

But no matter how bent a cop is, he's still a cop, and therefore he's supposedly untouchable. Screen criminals generally understand that the full weight of the police force will come down upon them if one of their number is rubbed out. However, Al Pacino crosses the line twice, as Michael Corleone in *The Godfather* (1971)

and Tony Montana in *Scarface* (1983). There's a distinct look of surprise on Captain McCluskey's face when Michael shoots him in the neck and head in return for conspiring in the attempt to kill Michael's father. And when Tony Montana puts a bullet in the belly of Detective Bernstein for plotting against him, the policeman, again somewhat taken aback, reminds him of criminal etiquette: "you can't shoot a cop". Tony is no respecter of traditions, however, and shoots him again. It was, of course, Al Pacino who played the scourge of all bad apples in the New York Police Department in *Serpico,* the classic bent-cop movie, though here, it's good guy Pacino that gets shot.

The best friend

"That's what I get for a liking a guy too much," says Rico (**Edward G. Robinson**) after he's been betrayed by his best friend (**Douglas Fairbanks Jr**), who had accompanied him to the city to make it big, but has now had second thoughts about the life of crime and has returned to his first love, dance. He's fallen in love with a fellow hoofer and wants out; but Rico wants him to be his loyal lieutenant, to help him run the city. Rico can't bring himself to gun down his old pal – he looks at him misty-eyed, the camera goes into soft focus and we view Fairbanks' handsome face from Robinson's enchanted perspective. That, and the absence of a moll, prompted many people, including the novel's author **W.R. Burnett,** to claim that the movie had turned Rico gay – a sense underlined by the fact that Robinson is shot dead underneath a hoarding that advertises Fairbanks' and Farrell's significantly-titled new show, *Tipsy Topsy Turvy.*

Certainly every classic gangster movie has a

best friend who accompanies the gangster on his journey to power; less possessed by ambition, often more humane or even human, he's content to be the right-hand-man. There's a close bond between the two, they're like older and younger

The best friend: James Cagney as the bad apple in *Angels With Dirty Faces* (1938)

brothers – sometimes closer than the flesh-and-blood siblings (as in *The Public Enemy*). But only *Little Caesar* suggests there might be something more to the relationship.

There is, however, always a key moment when the mobster loses the friend, and this signals the beginning of the end. Often the loss is the result of a betrayal, when the best friend chooses love over money: in both versions of *Scarface*, the gangster kills his best friend when he discovers him with his sister. The sister is more like a lover to Pacino/Muni – she might as well be his moll – and when it comes to stealing the moll's affections, the best friend is often a repeat offender. **James Cagney** and **Clive Brook**, in *Doorway To Hell* (1930) and *Underworld* (1927) respectively, are both guilty of this crime of passion, leaving the mobster entirely on his own to fight either the police or his rivals. In *Once Upon A Time In America* (1983), **James Woods** takes it one step further, not only taking Robert De Niro's girl, but faking his own death. De Niro has to leave his old life behind and suffers a fate worse than death: a life in the suburbs. The loss of the best friend, therefore, equates to a loss of power, the loss of the gangster's better half and often the loss of the gangster's life.

The best friend became an even more important character after the toughening of the Production Code in 1934. Often representing the path that the criminal could have taken, the best friend, therefore, became not the loyal lieutenant but the moral conscience, and *Angels With Dirty Faces* (1938) has the ultimate: a priest. Pat O'Brien played the man of

God who effectively puts his childhood pal in the electric chair, and persuades him to redeem himself by dying "yellow". Before the Hays Code Cagney would have probably plugged him full of lead. *Angels With Dirty Faces* is thus the ultimate victory of the best friend.

Canaries

On The Waterfront (1954) begins with a "pigeon who cannot fly": an informant who was about to testify against the unions is thrown off a tall building. *The Doorway To Hell* starts with a gangster putting his Tommy gun in a violin case and heading off "to teach a guy a lesson". From the Yakuza to the Mafia's law of *omertà*, there is one rule: you don't squeal. The code of silence is universal. And those who break it face almost certain death. *The Godfather Part II* (1974) has a very subtle example: when Pentangeli goes to the Senate hearings to testify against the Corleone family, Michael walks into the room accompanied by Pentangeli's ageing brother. The implication is clear: you talk, your brother dies. Pentangeli suddenly loses his memory, and when he's visited later in prison by Tom Hagen, he's reminded of his duty. He duly cuts his wrists open in a warm bath.

In Mob mythology, the informer is the lowest form of human life – hence all the rat insults. In the 1950s, in the aftermath of the House Un-American Activities Committee, actors and directors themselves became informers – naming names of friends and colleagues they suspected of being Communist sympathizers. It's not surprising, then, that the informer was from then on viewed differently and often sympathetically in Hollywood movies. The most obvious example was *On The Waterfront*, obvious because director

and informer **Elia Kazan** consciously made the film as an explanation for his motives in getting several friends blacklisted. *Le doulos* (1962) has a title which references both the name of a hat and also slang for an informant; the *doulos* in this case was **Jean-Paul Belmondo** who may, or may not, have ratted out his friends and fellow thieves to the police. However, the *ne plus ultra* of the canary movie is of course *Goodfellas* (1990), the true story of Henry Hill, who informed on his friends and lived his "life like a schnook" under the Witness Protection Program.

Goodfellas is as far removed from *On The Waterfront* as can possibly be imagined: there's no soul-searching, no agonized monologues about being a contender, no tears. Henry's only concern about going into the protection programme is that he doesn't want to be relocated somewhere cold.

The cars

One of the first things that Al Pacino does when he comes into money in *Scarface* is buy a yellow, open-topped Cadillac with leopard-skin trim. As **Michelle Pfeiffer**'s moll adroitly remarks, it's like somebody's nightmare. The car, like the clothes, is a visible sign of the gangster's success, but it is more than just a signifier of status. It's often the instrument of death.

The classic gangster manoeuvre typically involves black sedans drawing up outside a restaurant and tearing it apart with machine-gun fire. Sometimes gangsters use the footrests as a handy platform from which to do their killing. *Little Caesar* was the first classic movie to use the car this way, when Edward G. Robinson gunned down one of his own gang as he made his way to church to confess his sins. Robinson himself almost loses his life when he is walking down the street and a dairy van draws close to him, from which rounds of ammunition are suddenly and anonymously fired. In the gangland wars of **Howard Hawks'** *Scarface*, gangs practically use the city as a race-track, cars firing upon each other in high-speed battles through the streets, which inevitably result in metal-crunching pile-ups. Far more "subtle" is the use of the *inside* of the car as a murder scene, and many films have borrowed Little Hymie Weiss' method of taking victims for a ride. Rocco and Clemenza show how it's done in *The Godfather*: they ask their victim Paulie to drive them out of the city; Rocco sits directly behind the driver and Clemenza holds

some cannoli (the cannoli is optional). Arriving at a remote spot, Clemenza tells Paulie to pull over because he has to take a leak, and while he's relieving himself, Rocco puts three bullets into the back of Paulie's head. Clemenza walks over and utters the immortal (and improvised) line: "Leave the gun, take the cannoli."

The city

"The gangster is the man of the city," wrote Robert Warshow in the most famous and most quoted piece of writing about the genre, *The Gangster As Tragic Hero*. "For the gangster there

HUAC

HUAC (The House Un-American Activities Committee) started operating in earnest in October 1947, but had been initially created in 1938 to investigate pro-Nazi organizations. Nine years later its remit had changed: Senate hearings were organized to look into alleged Communist infiltration of the Screen Writers' Guild. The initial hearing interviewed 41 so-called "friendly witnesses" including **Gary Cooper**, **Adolphe Menjou** and the president of the Screen Actors' Guild, **Ronald Reagan**, who between them named nineteen Hollywood employees they believed to be members of the Communist Party. The nineteen were subpoenaed to appear before HUAC and eleven were singled out. They became known as the Hollywood Ten when one of their number, **Bertolt Brecht**, skipped the country after giving his testimony.

The remaining dissenters were writers Ring Lardner Jr, Dalton Trumbo, Adrian Scott, Alvah Bessie, Albert Matz, John Howard Lawson, Sam Ornitz, Lester Cole, Herbert Biberman, and director Edward Dmytryck. They all cited the First Amendment and refused to answer the

committee's questions. Some of their Hollywood colleagues rallied behind them when **John Huston** set up the Committee For The First Amendment and chartered Howard Hughes' personal jet to organize a star-studded picket of the proceedings. Among the celebrity protesters were Danny Kaye, Sterling Hayden, Lauren Bacall and Humphrey Bogart (who, under pressure from Warner Brothers, later apologized for his presence there and claimed he had been duped by the Communist Party). The efforts of Huston et al were all in vain, as the Hollywood Ten were fired by their respective studios and each given twelve-month jail sentences for contempt (though none served their full term). When they came out of jail, they were put on a Hollywood blacklist – as, eventually, were over 300 other writers, actors and directors who refused to answer or to implicate others when they were asked "Are you now or have you ever been a member of the Communist Party?"

HUAC continued to exist, in name at least, until 1975, but 1950 is usually regarded as its high (or low) point, when **Senator Joe McCarthy** made his unique contribution. McCarthy, who was never a member of HUAC, claimed on February 9 that he had a list of 57 people in the State Department who were known to be members

is only the city; he must inhabit it to personify it." The mobster is very much defined by the modern world; he becomes who he is by taking over the city, and reaping its rewards by going to the most expensive nightclubs and the swankiest restaurants. But he makes his money by operating in the shadowlands of the city, the drug den or the speakeasy, the dank alley or the dive. Unlike anyone else, the gangster inhabits both high society and the underworld. As Colin McArthur has pointed out, the locale is so important that the word "city" appears in several titles: *Dark City, Cry Of The City, City Across The River, While The City Sleeps, The Sleeping City, Captive City,* and *The Naked City.* The latter was directed by **Jules**

Dassin, who evokes a city, with its sleazy bars and damp, lamplit streets, better than any other director: New York in *The Naked City,* London in *Night And The City* and Paris in *Rififi* have a real sense of place – the city is not just a character, sometimes it's the lead character.

This connection between the gangster and the city becomes apparent in films where the protagonist is on the run; in both *The Petrified Forest* (1936) and *High Sierra* (1941) **Humphrey Bogart** is no longer in the city that made him the man he is. Holed up in a remote gas station in the middle of a desert and trapped in the Sierra mountains, both Duke Mantee and Roy Earle are characters incapacitated by a sense of dislocation.

---

of the Communist Party. This speech, in addition to his witch-hunts into American public life – from the Senate to schools to the military – led to the Red Menace scare and to the HUAC investigations being pursued with renewed vigour. In June 1950 three ex-FBI agents published a pamphlet called *Red Channels*, which named 151 more writers, directors and actors who had not yet been subpoenaed.

It was in this fevered atmosphere that director **Elia Kazan** was called to testify in April 1952 and, even though he promised his friend **Jules Dassin** that he would never be a fink, Kazan named a number of colleagues including writers Clifford Odets and Lillian Hellman. Probably more than any other turncoat, it was Kazan's volte-face that rankled most with blacklistees, and old wounds were reopened when it was announced in 1999 that the director of *On The Waterfront* was to be awarded an honorary Oscar. A campaign was launched to persuade the Academy to change their minds, but it had little effect as Kazan was presented with his award by Martin Scorsese and Robert De Niro (who, ironically, had starred in one of the few Hollywood films about the horrors of the blacklist, 1990's *Guilty By Suspicion*). When the Oscar was handed over most of the audience

gave the veteran director a standing ovation, while others remained stubbornly seated.

Kazan, of course, continued to work in Hollywood after he testified, while some on the blacklist went into exile in Europe. Jules Dassin ended up in first Paris, then Greece, while Ring Lardner Jr found work in England writing the *Robin Hood* series for ITV. Edward Dmytryck fled to Britain until his visa expired in 1951; on his return to America he was jailed for six months, and testified to the House Committee as soon as he left prison. He got his old job back. Some writers who stayed in the US continued to work under pseudonyms, such as Dalton Trumbo, who won an Oscar for *The Brave One* (1957) under the nom de plume Robert Rich. Or else they used other scribes as fronts, as Abraham Polonsky did in borrowing the name of his friend and the novelist John O. Killens to write *Odds Against Tomorrow* (1959). A few weren't so lucky as Polonsky or Trumbo. **John Garfield**, the star of Polonsky's classic gangster film *Force Of Evil* (1948), was sacked by his studio when he refused to name names to the committee in 1951 and died a year later of a sudden heart attack at the age of 39. His friends always attributed his untimely death to the effects of the blacklist, and the pressures of HUAC.

Bogart (left) in limbo, out in the wasteland of *The Petrified Forest*

The three original couple-on-the-run films, *You Only Live Once*, *They Live By Night* and *Gun Crazy*, display a more ambivalent attitude towards the countryside. At first it seems like Eden – it's where all three couples spend their honeymoon and momentarily attain peace. But ultimately it's the place where they will be hunted down like animals: Henry Fonda, Sylvia Sidney, Peggy Cummins and John Dall all abandon their cars, the symbol of the modern world, and are immediately disorientated, lost in transition.

The clothes

Whether it's the dark shades and black suits of recent screen criminals, or the fedora, spats, diamond tiepin, and pinstripes of his classic counterpart, clothes maketh the gangster. Witness **Paul Muni**'s polka-dot suit in *Scarface,* George Raft's

footwear in *Some Like It Hot* (1959), or Edward G. Robinson's tiepin in *Little Caesar.* Even the choice of suit is significant: the ostentatious double-breasted cut of the gangster's attire versus the single-breasted jacket of the appropriately named plain-clothes policeman.

There's a rite of passage in many classic movies to mark the transition from man to gangster, and that's the purchase of the first suit. This sign of success, of conspicuous consumption, is shown in films from *The Public Enemy* to *Goodfellas*. When James Cagney makes it into the big time he gets measured up in a tailor's, insisting he gets plenty of room in his trousers; in *Goodfellas*, the young Henry Hill turns up on his mother's doorstep wearing a beige double-breasted suit and shiny black shoes that he's particularly proud of. His mother's horrified reaction sums it all up: "My God, you look like a gangster!"

Donning a tuxedo is another signifier of newly acquired wealth and status: when we first see the now successful Rico in *Little Caesar*, he's looking at himself in the mirror, worrying about how the tux looks on him, while his assistant suggestively alters his trousers and admiringly informs him that he's "getting up in the world". In *Quick Millions*, Spencer Tracy looks longingly at himself as he's about to spend a night at the opera, realizing that the tuxedo has completely masked his former profession of truck driver: "you could never picture me in overalls," he poignantly comments. The gang boss in *The Street With No Name* (1948) orders a young recruit "buy yourself a closetful of clothes. I like my boys to look sharp." And it's not just the sharpness of the clothes, it's the way they wear them, as in James Cagney's aggressive tilting of his cap in *The Public Enemy*.

By the 1960s the gangster is defined entirely by his clothes. It's not just a shorthand for violence, but for his character, his profession, and his ambitions. We know everything about him by what he's wearing. In *Le samourai*, we discover nothing about **Alain Delon** beyond his appearance; as Ginette Vincendeau comments, he wears his Alan Ladd trilby and raincoat like battledress; he's a walking dresscode. The film even hinges upon an identity parade where the key to identification is the hat. In *Point Blank* (1967) the sharp lines of **Lee Marvin**'s suit chime in with the minimalist decor to suggest a man with no characteristics other than the desire for revenge.

In the bad-taste decade of the 1970s, clothes were key: in blaxploitation "classic" *Superfly* (1972) **Ron O'Neal** sports a knee-length double-breasted coat with wings for lapels and a woollen-stitch pattern that's only ever usually seen on the skirts of little old ladies. Even the small-time hoods in *Mean Streets* take care of their appearance, albeit in mismatching suits and ties; but, crucially, they *think* they look good. Pacino proved in *Scarface* that though the gangster has money he has no style, no class. **Michelle Pfeiffer** lays into him like so: "You're an immigrant spic millionaire who can't stop talking about money." Wearing a Hawaiian shirt accessorized with gold jewellery and a fat cigar, he's a reminder that gangsters are wannabes, always aspiring to the thing they can never be. This is particularly true of the British spiv of 1940s cinema. The clothes are a little too loud, the jackets a little too checked, the ambition a little too obvious.

In the 1980s **John Woo**, a big fan of *Le samourai*, returned to the idea of letting clothes do the talking: in a long duster coat and sunglasses Chow Yun-fat became an instant icon in *A Better Tomorrow*. But his clothes do not signify social mobility or lack of class. They have nothing to say but "I know I look cool in this". Chow's style

set a trend for screen criminals, real-life Yakuza and ultimately, of course, *Reservoir Dogs*, which took the interest in sartorial concerns to its logical conclusion: the clothes have now become a uniform.

Comedy gangsters

Humour has always been part of the gangster genre. For instance, two years after *The Public Enemy* Cagney was already parodying his tough guy image in *The Lady Killer* (1933), playing a small-time racketeer who makes it big in Hollywood playing hard men. The number of comedies increased after 1934 and the tightening of the Production Code which put the squeeze on traditional gangster pics. Making light of the gangster was one way of circumventing the code and Edward G. Robinson played it for laughs many times, in John Ford's *The Whole Town's Talking* (1935), *A Slight Case Of Murder* (1938), *Larceny Inc* (1942) and *Brother Orchid* (1940). He even parodied his old screen persona in 1964 when he joined up with the Rat Pack for a comic cameo in *Robin And the Seven Hoods*.

By this time the gangster film was a period piece and its easily-identifiable iconography gave it large comic potential, which **Billy Wilder** mined successfully in *Some Like It Hot* (1959). Here **George Raft** played on his 1930s persona, and the movie included a famous in-joke. His character Spats walks past a hoodlum who's constantly flicking a coin. Annoyed, he asks him: "Where did you pick up that cheap trick?" The hood doesn't reply but the answer is, of course, from George Raft in *Scarface*.

The Mafia family have been easy targets: *Prizzi's Honor* took *The Godfather* as a model to base its humour upon, whereas Jonathan Demme's *Married To The Mob* (1988) took a similar premise that *Goodfellas* would. As author Jim Smith has pointed out, with the exception of **Al Pacino**, all the leading family members in *The Godfather I* and *II* have parodied their roles in it: **Marlon Brando** started it off by basically impersonating his own jowly Godfather self as "Jimmy The Toucan" in *The Freshman (*1990); **James Caan** taught son-in-law Hugh Grant how to speak the lingo in *Mickey Blue Eyes* (1999); and of course **Robert De Niro** did it the most (financially) successfully in *Analyse This* (1999) and *Analyse That* (2002), although the neurotic mob boss he plays, Paul Vitti, is less a version of Vito Corleone than a kind of remix of *Goodfellas*' Jimmy Conway and *Raging Bull*'s Jake La Motta.

The deaths

Noone dies like James Cagney; he had two of the greatest exit scenes in cinema history. Going out spectacularly in *White Heat,* Cagney's crazed Cody Jarrett stood his ground

Perhaps the funniest "gangster" comedy ever made: *Some Like It Hot* (1959)

Comedy hitmen

By 1969 the shocking revelations from the 1930s about the organized killers known as Murder Inc had sunk into public consciousness far enough to become material for a comedy, *The Assassination Bureau*, about a Victorian hit squad. The hit-man genre's potential for knockabout comedy was mined further in **John Huston**'s *Prizzi's Honor* (1987) with **Jack Nicholson** and **Kathleen Turner** as killers in love, and later in *Grosse Point Blank* (1997) with **John Cusack** playing a hit man at a high-school reunion, who has to carry out a job while romancing old flame **Minnie Driver**. In Billy Wilder's desperately unfunny final film *Buddy Buddy* (1981) Walter Matthau plays a hit man whose concentration is disturbed when Jack Lemmon keeps attempting suicide in the next hotel room, and **Aki Kurasmaki** warmed up the old chestnut about the man who arranges his own murder but changes his mind in *I Hired A Contract Killer* (1990).

on top of a gas tank surrounded by cops, opened the gas cylinders and started firing recklessly; and before the inevitable explosion he shouted one of cinema's most celebrated lines. Poignantly, in *The Roaring Twenties*, after a running battle with Humphrey Bogart's Mob, Cagney staggers back then falls onto the snow-covered steps of a church and dies in the arms of his lover. When she's asked who he is, she replies with another great gangster line: "he used to be a big shot".

This last death is more typical of the genre. As Colin McArthur has pointed out, it's significant that the gangster dies in the street: it's a public death, almost a public act of retribution dying on the streets where he brought so much chaos. Jean-Luc Godard understood the importance and the iconography of the public death and in *A bout de souffle* Jean-Paul Belmondo's demise

rivals Cagney's in *The Roaring Twenties*. As he staggers down the middle of the road, the camera trails behind him, almost gliding, and stops as he slumps; his moll (well, fellow traveller at least), Jean Seberg, catches up with him just as he utters his final words. She doesn't hear him properly and asks a cop what he said, who in turn appears to have misheard and tells her something she herself doesn't understand: Godard accompanies the gangster's screen death with misunderstanding, ambiguity and irony.

A "ballet of death" is how the final scene of *Bonnie And Clyde* has been described, and although it wasn't the first slow-motion death – the director Arthur Penn acknowledged his debt to **Akira Kurosawa** – it was certainly the most influential. Taking three days to shoot and four days to edit, the effect was created by shooting the scene with four cameras all running at different speeds. Beatty's and Dunaway's bodies seem to be jigging to the rhythm of the bullets, and that was exactly the effect desired by director Penn. He wanted to make Clyde's death look almost as if it had been choreographed to music, whereas Bonnie's supposedly gained its force from "the power of shock".

Francis Ford Coppola has admitted that James Caan's bullet-riddled death at a tollbooth in *The Godfather* was modelled on *Bonnie And Clyde*. But two directors have taken the slo-mo death and made it their own. After *The Wild Bunch* (1969) **Sam Peckinpah** slowed down almost all his shoot-outs. It works best in *The Getaway* (1972) when **Steve McQueen** is firing off a shotgun at a cop car. As the fender comes away and the lights shatter, the scene acquires a thematic resonance: the destruction of the modern by the primal.

Another notable exponent of the slo-mo "ballet of death" technique is John Woo – it has

Bonnie And Clyde (1967): the movie that set the trend for the "terpsichorean death scene"

become a critical cliché to talk about Woo's bullets-and-ballet style, his choreography of violence. But the director himself encourages such talk. In interviews he often mentions his love of musicals and how his fight scenes are choreographed like production numbers, the culmination of which was a gunfight in *Face/Off* (1997) accompanied by the strains of *Somewhere Over The Rainbow*. In films such as *The Killer* (1989) and *Hard Boiled* (1992) the shoot-outs quickly free themselves from the constraints of reality, with Chow Yun-fat effortlessly and accurately firing two Berettas at once with a seemingly endless supply of ammo, while his victims fall slowly through the air, bodies in rest and motion.

The heist

The robbery came into its own in the 1950s with *The Asphalt Jungle*, the first movie to be entirely dedicated to one job. In forensic detail it showed who to employ, the method of breaking into a bank, how to elude the electronic eye and more. The classic heist movie goes something like this. A criminal mastermind brings together a group of men from different parts of society to pull off one big job. The plans are meticulous, everyone knows their role, and the job is a success. Just when they think they've committed the perfect crime, it all goes wrong because one of the gang has spilled the beans, usually to a loved one, and the thieves fall out. No one lives to collect the money. *Rififi* and *The Killing,* in particular, fit this pattern, but it wasn't long before things changed.

In the caper movie that started in the 1960s the tone is lighter, the robbery is more outlandish and the thieves get away with the loot. And

Never get high on your own supply

Selling drugs is the line that screen gangsters don't, or shouldn't, ever cross. Because if they do, they often lose their lives or their liberty. It's a matter of pride to Harold Shand (**Bob Hoskins**) in *The Long Good Friday* that he doesn't sell drugs, and he suggests – with his typical blithe racism – that white men don't deal. Don Corleone (Marlon Brando) almost loses his life in *The Godfather* when he refuses to be part of Sollozzo's narcotics trade. Trevor Howard leaves the gang of spivs he's working for in *They Made Me A Fugitive* (1947) when he realizes they're selling more than just nylons and New Zealand mutton.

One of the two golden rules that Tony Montana (Al Pacino) is taught when he moves into the business is "don't get high on your own supply". He does of course. As with Ray Liotta's Henry Hill in *Goodfellas*, it proves to be his undoing.

the heist is not only carried out by professional criminals, often the thieves are either beautiful couples, raffish gentleman thieves, or even the wives of criminals. The booty would often be a priceless artefact in a museum or a diamond.

It was not long before real crooks began to use the heist movie as a training manual: *Rififi* was blamed for copycat crimes wherever it was shown. The British Board Of Film Classification still censors films on grounds of possible imitation – in the 1960s they would regularly take out shots of "slim Jims" (devices used to break into cars). Despite the censor's attention, however, heist movies can still instruct us how to pull off the perfect robbery:

• Synchronize watches (*The Getaway*)
Obviously. What would a heist be without watches being in synch?

• Cut the electricity supply (*The Getaway*)
First locate the source of the supply. In *The Getaway* the electricity lines run underneath the road. Drive the specially prepared van (with a hole in the floor) over the manhole-cover; take off manhole-cover and, armed with a large set of bolt-cutters, drop into the hole; walk along subterranean passage until the electricity lines become visible, and then cut them. This will disable the alarm.

• Wear a disguise (*Point Break, Charley Varrick*)
Wear a mask and be creative: you could disguise yourself as an old man, like Walter Matthau (*Charley Varrick*), or don the face of a US president (*Point Break*).

• Public relations (*Reservoir Dogs*)
According to Mr White (Harvey Keitel), if one is getting grief from a member of the public when carrying out an armed robbery, hit him on the bridge of his nose with the butt of your gun; if the manager himself is playing up, cut off his little finger and tell him that his thumb will be next.

• Bring an umbrella (*Rififi*)
When breaking into a bank or jeweller's, it's advisable to rent the building next door, or in the case of *Rififi,* break into the room upstairs. Burrow into the room that contains the safe without triggering the alarm – *Rififi* suggests making a small incision in the floor/ceiling, thrusting an umbrella into the available space, and opening it up. This will collect the debris from the digging. If you are going to drill into the building next door, make sure you know where the water pipe is (*Small Time Crooks*) and that you haven't mistaken a doughnut shop for the jeweller's (*Palookaville*).

• Trigger the alarm (*How To Steal A Million*)
A counter-intuitive move, but effective nonetheless. Find a closet to hide in, preferably next to the priceless artefact in the museum, run up to the aforementioned object and set off the alarm. Hide in the cupboard when the security guards investigate; when they have gone, repeat the action. They will assume the alarm is faulty and switch it off, particularly if they receive complaints about the noise from the French president, who lives nearby.

You never know when an umbrella might come in handy: ingenious heist tips courtesy of *Rififi* (1955)

Reel heists

There have been several films which have provided the inspiration for real thieves. They include:

• **Heat** On March 1, 1997 a bungled heist in Los Angeles bore a similarity to the final robbery in Michael Mann's drama. Armed robbers came out of a bank and started a running battle with police on the city streets. "These guys were ready for war," a local store-owner was reported as saying. "They had black masks with ammo belts around their waists." Just like De Niro and co. Whether the gang had based themselves on *Heat* is hard to tell, but the Dream Team certainly did. A band of armed robbers, they eluded police for four years, hitting security vans, vaults and airports in France and Spain. Police claimed that the gang hero-worshipped Robert De Niro, modelled themselves on the teams he led in *Heat* and *Ronin*, and named themselves after characters in the films (they even drove Audi 8s); they were finally caught in 2001.

• **Rififi** In many countries that showed Jules Dassin's groundbreaking, detailed account of a jewellery robbery, jewellers were robbed in exactly the same way as Dassin had documented. Dassin's standard line of defence was "I didn't show you how to commit a robbery, I showed you how difficult it was to commit a robbery." However, he concedes "no-one believed me".

• **The Ladykillers** The late British film historian John Huntley used to tell the story of his own unwitting contribution to British crime. As part of a film education programme, he would show films to prisoners in a jail in the South East of Britain. The one proviso was that he couldn't show crime movies, for obvious reasons, but he didn't think there was any harm in showing *The Ladykillers*, which after all was a farcical, far-fetched Ealing comedy. However, the film does contain a scene in which a bank van is held up by a road block near King's Cross and robbed of its contents. A few years later a near-identical robbery took place just outside the railway station… carried out by ex-convicts who had attended John's screening.

• Duck under the electronic eye (*The Asphalt Jungle, Topkapi*)

In *The Asphalt Jungle* the electronic eye was a single beam of light which was easy to duck under. But technology moved on. In *Topkapi*, the whole floor was alarmed, so the favoured method was to go in through the roof and abseil down to the priceless object. But watch out for birds. In *Entrapment*, the technology had become a lot more complex, and Catherine Zeta-Jones had to writhe through a cat's cradle of electronic eyes (in a tight-fitting garment, of course).

• Lock yourself inside the vault (*$*)

Warren Beatty breaks out of the bank, rather than into it.

• Buy a plane (*Rough Cut*)

Purchase a plane that looks exactly like one that's carrying a shipment of diamonds. Divert the real plane to an airport in a different country and land the dummy plane in its place. Take delivery of the jewels.

• Stop the van (*The Italian Job, The Ladykillers, Heat*)

If the loot is in a van, stop it in its tracks by either a) creating a traffic jam, b) staging an accident or c) taking a large articulated lorry and driving it at high speed at aforementioned van.

• Create a diversion (*The Killing*)

According to Stanley Kubrick's masterpiece, thieves need two diversions: one to steal the loot and the other to make the getaway. Distract the guards by staging a fight (a favourite of prison movies) and slip into the room they had been protecting. (In Peter Yates' *The Hot Rock*, the guards are distracted by a fake car accident outside the Brooklyn Museum.) When the loot is stolen, cause chaos and leave anonymously with the crowds who are hurriedly exiting; the suggested method is to shoot the favourite as it's making its way around the track, but this only works in racecourses.

• **Steal the bank (***The Bank Shot***)**
If none of the above works, steal the whole bank itself; pretend to be building contractors and move the entire premises to a more favourable location where the safe can be broken into at leisure.

The hitmen

This Gun For Hire (1942) is one of the earliest films to focus on the hit man as protagonist and is the start of a family tree that connects it to Jean-Pierre Melville's *Le samourai* and John Woo's *The Killer.* Alain Delon's choice of fedora and trench coat in *Le samourai* is a deliberate echo of Alan Ladd's uniform in the original; Delon's character is called Jef; Jeff is the name of Chow Yun-fat's character in *The Killer.*

But the similarities are not just superficial: Ladd's character is a man apart, with only his cat for company (Delon only has his bird and his bottles of water, but that's another story). For a hit man to be good at his job he has to be anonymous, unknown to anyone, sometimes even to the person who has supplied the contract. The loneliness of the long-distance hit man gives him an existential cool which is allied to a deep

Getting away with it

• **Cyclo** After being pushed further and further into the sleazy criminal underworld of Ho Chi Minh City, our pedal-cab child hero goes back to his day job

• **The Getaway** McQueen and McGraw make it to Mexico with the loot

• **Gloria** Gena Rowlands gets the hell out of New York

• **The Godfather Part II** Pacino servives while the rest of his family are killed; he dies of old age in *Part III*

• **Pulp Fiction** Samuel L. Jackson, one of the few gangsters to survive the movie, lives to go forth and walk the earth

melancholy, a pining for human contact other than a hit. In all three films, the hitman meets a woman who inspires feelings that induce a semblance of humanity in him, which threatens his profession since a killer cannot afford to have feelings – part of the job requirement is to be pitiless. In *This Gun For Hire*, Ladd, prompted by **Veronica Lake**, has to decide whether he will do something for a reason other than money, and work for his country against its wartime enemies. In *Le samourai* Delon has to decide whether to kill the only witness to his hit, a nightclub singer who's become the object of his affection. In *The Killer,* Chow pays for the operation of a young woman he has accidentally blinded. In a typically perverse Gallic move, it's a 12-year-old girl who unclogs the killer's heart in **Luc Besson**'s *Léon* (1994), and a conceptual artist (and potential victim), **Jodie Foster**, for whom **Dennis Hopper** changes his ways in *Catchfire* (1989).

The assassin's motives can only be economic. He's on the side of the highest bidder, and in that sense he's like a *ronin*, a samurai without a master, whose services are available to anyone with the right amount of money. It's not incidental that Melville's movie is titled *Le samouraï,* a connection Jim Jarmusch made even more explicit in *Ghost Dog* (1997), in which assassin **Forest Whitaker** works for the Italian Mafia but follows *hagukare,* the way of the samurai, the philosophies of which are used as chapter headings throughout the movie. Asian cinema has a seemingly endless fascination with hitmen, as titles such as *The Killer, Ichi The Killer, The Full-Time Killer,* and *Naked Killer* testify. A possible reason for the success of these amoral thrillers with Eastern audiences is that the rootless, friendless contract killer is the ultimate salaryman, an exaggerated embodiment of the alienation felt by a generation brought up in the anonymous, modernized, westernized high-rise cities of the tiger economies. Or possibly because killers look cool in slo-mo.

In America, hitmen, or "torpedoes", became a familiar figure after the Murder Inc trials of the 1940s, which uncovered a nationwide network of hundreds of contract killers with employees who went by such names as "Chicken Head" Gurino and "Blue Jaw" Magoon. The character became a regular feature of 1950s syndicate movies. Ususally taking a "supporting hood" position, they sometimes commanded their own films, as in *Murder By Contract* (1958), which documented the quotidian life of the average killer, a man who refuses to kill women because "it's hard to kill someone who's undependable". **Charles Bronson** played a hit man on the verge of retirement in *The Mechanic* (1972), **John Hurt** and **Tim Roth** tried to retire ex-villain and stool pigeon **Terence Stamp** in *The Hit* (1984); **Yvette Mimieux** played a part-time artist and assassin in *Hit Lady* (1987); and more recently a silver-haired **Tom Cruise** played a philosophizing hit man in *Collateral* (2004).

The changing depiction of the hit man, the most amoral of characters, is a good indicator of the shifting values of American cinema, and this is clearly signalled by the two different versions of *The Killers.* The 1964 version makes an important change from the 1946 *noir* incarnation, as the killers step out of the shadows and into the spotlight, moving from off-stage to centre stage. Both thrillers take as their starting point **Ernest Hemingway**'s short story in which a young man accepts his death at the hands of two assassins without complaint or putting up a fight. Both films try to explain the motives for the victim's curious indifference to his imminent demise. In **Robert Siodmak**'s 1946 re-imagining, an insurance investigator is introduced as a narratorial device, and he pieces together the life of "the Swede" (**Burt Lancaster**). The heavies who make such an impression in the first scene disappear into the night, only to reappear in the last scene, and they are shot dead before they can say another word. In **Don Siegel**'s 1964 version it's the hitmen themselves (**Lee Marvin** and **Clu Gulager**) who investigate the reasons for the victim's puzzling fatalism; Marvin gets tangled up with **Angie Dickinson** and discovers to his cost just how *fatale* a *femme* she is.

This substitution of the killers for the investigator is significant. *The Killers* anticipates a time when murderers will replace cops in the audience's affections, as in *Bonnie And Clyde,* or when cops will behave like criminals, as in Don Siegel's *Dirty Harry.* As such it presages the death of the Motion Picture Production Code as Hollywood knew it. Siegel himself had fired the first shots with the release of *Baby Face Nelson,* which violated the code's ban on the depiction of real criminals. And even though **Lee Marvin** doesn't get out alive in *The Killers,* the film heralded a near future. In the cynical 1970s the hitmen, the Mafia and the armed robbers all get away with it – as in *Charley Varrick,* which, of course, was directed by Don Siegel.

The Killers

dir Robert Siodmak, 1946, US, 105m, b/w

In the very first shot we're travelling with the killers as they drive into Brentwood; at a diner Charles McGraw and William Conrad start to intimidate the owner. They rattle off dialogue straight from Hemingway's short story and, using only words as weapons, they tie up the chef and a customer and wait for "the Swede" to arrive. When they realize he's not coming, they walk away to kill Burt Lancaster in his bed. And that's the last we hear of them, until the final reel. In between the dialogue is sub-Hemingway, but the sinuous flashback structure is pure *noir*.

The Killers

dir Don Siegel, 1964, US, 93m

Siegel's shadow-free version both adds and subtracts from the original; by focusing on the hitmen, it gains from Lee Marvin's performance, but loses it all in the telling of victim John Cassavetes' story. Not only is the acting not up to scratch (this applies equally to Ronald Reagan's last film appearance), but Siegel clearly loses interest when the killers are not on the screen.

Léon

dir Luc Besson, 1994, Fr/US, 133m

Jean Reno plays a lonely assassin whose life changes when he protects 12-year-old Mathilda (Nathalie Portman) from the deviant cop who murdered her family. Voted second in a poll of screen anti-heroes (*Taxi Driver*'s Travis Bickle came first), *Léon* has clearly touched a nerve with a number of people, even though the relationship between hit man and tweenie is halfway between heart-warming and extremely dodgy. Scenes which shifted the balance to the latter were removed, including one in which Mathilda asks Léon to sleep with her, and reinstated later in a director's cut.

Ghost Dog: Way Of The Samurai

dir Jim Jarmusch, 1999, US, 116m

Professional assassin Forest Whitaker works anonymously for the Cosa Nostra but when he kills the wrong person, his employers decide to retire him, Italian-style. A typically cool Jarmuschian mix with hip-hop, samurai philosophy and references to Seijun Suzuki's *Branded To Kill*, it is slightly let down by a few tired old Italian Mafia clichés.

Collateral

dir Michael Mann, 2004, US, 120m

Silver fox Tom Cruise plays a contract killer who pays innocent cabbie Jamie Foxx to chauffeur him around Los Angeles and keep his appointments with death. Foxx has to decide whether he's going to be an accessory to murder or lose his life, and a battle of wits and ethics plays out amongst the gunfire. Mann leaves behind the portentousness of *The Insider* and *Heat* to go back to his *Starsky And Hutch* roots, delivering that rare thing, a genuinely good Hollywood thriller.

The "honour killing"

The honour killing differs from all the other various "of-necessity" murders that every self-respecting screen hoodlum takes on; it's a result of a slight against the family or the murder of a relative. *The Godfather*, which introduced the importance of the family to professional criminals, naturally has the best honour killings. In the first part, the honour killing is the turning point for Pacino's character Michael Corleone. It's the moment he joins the family business. Afterwards there is no way back for him; he can never be a civilian again. A parallel moment in *The Godfather Part II* sees De Niro returning to Sicily to take revenge on the man who was responsible for his father's murder, some thirty years on. He visits the villa of Don Ciccio, an old man who can hardly move out of his chair. On the pretext of a business meeting, De Niro introduces himself and tells him who his father was; when the old man cannot hear him, De Niro moves closer, says it again, "my father's name was Antonio Andolini … and this is for you". And with that he plunges a knife into Ciccio's belly, sticks him like a pig, drags the blade up towards his chest, and lets it rest there.

The lawyer

William J. Fallon, dubbed by the press "the attorney of the damned" and legal adviser to Mob boss **Arnold Rothstein** and assorted other thieves, pimps and murderers, is the basis for that habitué of courtroom dramas, the shyster lawyer who will stop at nothing to get his client off. Fallon's speciality was getting a no-trial or hung jury, and he would win cases by a combination of court histrionics and old-fashioned bribery. He was the subject of three *films à clef* in 1932 alone: *Lawyer Man*, *Attorney* and *The Mouthpiece*. Fallon died in 1927, so it was up to his son to sue the producers of *The Mouthpiece* for libel, in a case that was settled out of court. This didn't stop the film being remade twice, in the form of *The Man Who Talked Too Much* (1940) and *Illegal* (1955). The latter starred **Edward G. Robinson**, and repeated the stand-out moment in the original in which the lawyer dramatically drinks some poison to prove it's not lethal, and very soon afterwards vomits it all up.

It wasn't long before the lawyer became a part of the Mob: in *Angels With Dirty Faces*, **Humphrey Bogart** crosses the line when, as lawyer Frazier, he betrays James Cagney and goes into business with crime lord and club-owner **George Bancroft**; in *The Asphalt Jungle* Mob lawyer **Louis Calherne** decides to become a criminal himself when the high cost of keeping his mistress **Marilyn Monroe** is too much for him. In *The Firm* (1993), Tom Cruise realizes that his whole company is intimately tied up with the Mafia.

The most famous Mob lawyer, though, is **Robert Duvall**'s Tom Hagen in *The Godfather*. He seems to be the most thoughtful and reasonable member of the Corleone clan. His motto is "it's not personal, it's business". He seems to be both a part of it and apart from it, and doesn't get his hands dirty. But there are three key moments which reveal that Hagen is truly one of the family. It's Hagen who suggests that the Corleones move into narcotics. It's Hagen who goes to see film producer Jack Woltz and asks for singer Johnny Fontane to be given a break in his new war film – Woltz famously wakes up next day with the head of his favourite horse beside him. And it's Hagen, in *Part II*, who visits stool pigeon Pentangeli and has a quiet word, reminding him of what happened to people who betrayed the emperor in Ancient Rome. After his visit, Pentangeli opens his veins in a warm bath.

The best example of the blurring of what's

Shakespearean gangsters

A "gutter Macbeth" is how novelist W.R. Burnett described his creation Rico Bandello in *Little Caesar*, and there's always been an element of Shakespearean tragedy to the gangster's tale. Possessed by an ambition that will be both his making and undoing, he's both Macbeth and his missus. And the British film *Joe Macbeth* (1955) made those links quite explicit in the story of a gangster spurred on by his wife to usurp his boss, Duce.

Where the musical *West Side Story* famously borrowed the plot of *Romeo And Juliet* for its tale of teen gang warfare, **Baz Luhrmann** went the whole hog, turning the ill-fated lovers into the offspring of two warring Mob families: swords are replaced by guns, Verona becomes Verona Beach, and the Montagues and the Capulets become Latino and Caucasian gangsters. With its choreographed gunfights and MTV-style editing, Luhrmann's *Romeo + Juliet* (1996) could easily have been renamed *John Woo's Romeo + Juliet*.

legal and illegal is to be found in *Force Of Evil* (1949). This is not just because the lawyer (John Garfield) is working for the Mob, but because he's found ways to use the law to make money for his client: by creating a semi-legal scam involving the numbers rackets and by "merging" their rivals rather than wiping them out. As his grateful gangster boss tells him, once upon a time he would have resorted to violence to get the same amount of money. It's a refection of what really happened in America in 1931 in the creation of the Combination. When The Mob became corporate, the individual gave way to the syndicate, and organized crime became dominated by lawyers and accountants.

The Mob(s)

When it was announced that a film was going to be made of **Mario Puzo**'s bestselling novel *The Godfather*, the Italian-American Civil Rights League immediately protested. They organized mass demonstrations in New York, and called for a boycott of the movie both from audiences and from union members working on the set. The production company also received bomb threats and producer **Al Ruddy** noticed he was being followed by a sinister figure wherever he went. The League claimed that *The Godfather* perpetuated the stereotype that all Italian-Americans were gangsters. The irony is that the League itself was run by the head of a notorious New York crime family, **Joseph Colombo**. Whatever methods he used against the production team evidently worked – the words Mafia and Cosa Nostra never appear in the finished film. Colombo never got to see the fruits of his hard work, however. He was shot in the head in

1971, slain by other Mafia members who were allegedly unhappy about the attention and publicity he was bringing to the families.

After the success of *The Godfather*, its sequel dared to use the term Mafia, as have many other gangster movies since – so much so that the term has lost its historical and geographical specificity. With the exception of *The Black Hand* (1949) and *The Brotherhood* (1968), movies never mentioned the Mafia, possibly out of fear, possibly because little was known about the workings of the clans, but largely because FBI director **J. Edgar Hoover** denied that the Cosa Nostra even existed. That was until 1957 when the Feds stumbled upon an underworld conference in Apalachin, New York and arrested over sixty mobsters. After the Apalachin "accident", even Hoover could no longer deny the Mafia's existence, although it took the movies another decade.

In place of Mafia, the words "syndicate" and "organization" were used, but even they were not exactly commonplace until the 1950s. Before then, organized crime was seen as consisting of a handful of warring gangs: in **Howard Hawks**' *Scarface*, Paul Muni's gang seems to number about ten, as does that of his rivals on the North Side. In *Angels With Dirty Faces*, apparently it's only three people who are responsible for the crime and corruption in the city: James Cagney, Humphrey Bogart and George Bancroft. And when they are disposed of, everything is right in the world again. As *The Public Enemy* concludes, "the end of Tom Powers is the end of every hoodlum". This individualization of the gangster, making the crime story the rise and fall of one person with a psychological flaw, created the sense that order was restored with their death, and that crime was ring-fenced: corruption was corruption of

How they met their end: some novel deaths

- **Black Caesar** Fred Williamson is shot by the Mafia but, having survived, is ironically mugged by kids from his own neighbourhood

- **Bullets Over Broadway** Hood Chazz Palminteri is bumped off by his own boss for bumping off the moll who was ruining Chazz's play

- **High Sierra** Bogie is shot by cops in a shoot-out on a plateau in the Sierra mountains, with a dog named Pard

- **King Of New York** Walken dies in a cab held up by traffic after being fatally wounded in a shoot-out on a subway train with a cop

- **The Ladykillers** Thieves fall out after interference from little old lady

- **The Long Good Friday** Bob Hoskins is escorted off to execution by Pierce Brosnan, playing an IRA hit man

- **Mean Streets** De Niro is shot by none other than director Martin Scorsese, here a hit man for an old friend to whom De Niro still owes money and whom he has insulted

- **Performance** Is it James Fox or is it Mick Jagger in the back of that car, being driven off to be rubbed out?

- **Pulp Fiction** John Travolta is shot by Bruce Willis while reading a comic book on the toilet

- **Some Like It Hot** George Raft is killed by a cake (okay, okay, it's a gunman in a cake...)

were employed by the national crime syndicate. As in *The Killers*, hit men would go to a small town or city, rub out their victim, and leave without a trace. The second was the **Kefauver hearings** of 1950–51, which revealed the extent of organized crime to a television audience. The Senate enquiries were so popular that they became a public event. People without televisions – the majority of the country – would crowd outside shops that sold TVs to see the testimony of 600 Mob leaders, hoods, corrupt politicians and police officers. Hollywood immediately took notice and a slew of films about all-powerful syndicates followed: *The Enforcer*, *Phenix City Story*, *The Racket*, *Hoodlum Empire*, *New York Confidential*, *Chicago Confidential* and many, many more. Some, like *Chicago Confidential* (1957), were about state attorneys who carried out investigations into racketeering in their city, others were about cops who discover to their cost the extent of organized crime when they refuse to close a seemingly open-and-shut case. Two of the best are *The Big Heat* (1953) and *The Big Combo* (1955); even though crime is embodied in one entity in both films, a Mr Big, the latter's power is all-pervasive. In *The Big Heat,* the police commissioner himself is a paid-up member of The Mob, and in both movies the cop hero has to work outside the law to bring the criminals to natural justice. And even when he wins, the message is clear: crime is routine and doesn't end with the death of a Mob boss.

the soul, not the paying-off of civic officials, politicians and policemen.

Two events changed both public perception and the movies. The first was the so-called **Murder Inc** trials of the 1940s, which revealed the existence of a company of assassins who

The molls

In the early 1930s molls were in many ways another status symbol, another sign of the gangster's success. Often the moll is a society girl seduced by the trappings of power and wealth, such as **Karen Morley** in *Scarface,* **Marguerite Churchill** in *Quick Millions* and **Norma Shearer** in *A Free Soul.* Sometimes she's the victim of his violence (Mae Clark on the wrong end of a grapefruit in *The Public Enemy*) but more often she's cradling him in her arms when he dies.

However, there are exceptions to the moll-as-doormat rule, notably **Jean Harlow** in *The Public Enemy.* In her one key scene, she's lying luxuriantly in the foreground, dominating the frame, while Cagney is behind her, dwarfed by her, fretting that she's giving him the run-around. It's a sign of things to come, with the arrival of the *femme fatale* in the 1940s.

Before, both **Gladys George** in *The Roaring Twenties* (1939) and **Ida Lupino** in *High Sierra* (1941) had devoted themselves to a man who admitted he didn't love them. Both knew they were second-best to a younger woman. In the former film, Cagney is infatuated with a singer, whom he puts on in his club and pays the audience to applaud. In the latter, Bogart is similarly obsessed, by a teenager with a club foot whose operation he pays for. When the girls turn out to be duplicitous, both gangsters turn pragmatically and unromantically to the older woman, and they become companions until the gangsters' deaths.

The Roaring Twenties and *High Sierra* are transitional; the older and younger female leads represent the past and the future of the genre respectively. Lupino and George are the old-fashioned moll, whose motto is "stand by your man". The younger woman, however, is a beautiful, youthful Janus, who becomes the focus of the protagonist's obsession. A few years later, the lover will become responsible for the gangster's death in films such as *Out Of The Past* (1947) and *Criss Cross* (1949). The reasons for the transformation from moll to *femme fatale* have often been attributed to a postwar disillusionment, when soldiers returned home to discover that women had been doing their jobs, and doing them just as well. In *film noir* the

Down but definitely not out: the scarred pickled pixie Debbie (Gloria Grahame) in *The Big Heat*

female of the species is deadlier than the male, a threat to life and livelihood, and the movies' plots were a way of putting women back in their place or, failing that, in the grave.

When molls did make a comeback, in a return to the classic genre, they had of course changed. In *Machine Gun Kelly* (1958) **Susan Cabot** is part moll, part *femme fatale*, but mostly a mother figure who leads the gang and who dominates **Charles Bronson** so much that he ends up crying like a small child. "I never wanted to be Public Enemy No. 1," he bawls. In *The Godfather* **Diane Keaton** is much more passive but her role is much more complex. Ultimately she's the film's conscience and in the last scene, when Pacino shuts the door on her, he's shutting out the part of him that was idealistic and incorruptible.

In the 1980s the moll of the 1930s was resurrected, unsurprisingly, in films directed by men whose work had previously been tagged as misogynistic. **Sergio Leone**'s *Once Upon A Time In America* returned to the *Public Enemy* representation of moll as victim of the mobster's violence: **Elizabeth McGovern** is savagely raped by Robert De Niro. In Brian De Palma's *Scarface* Michelle Pfeiffer is nothing more than appendage, a token of success who literally comes with the territory when Al Pacino kills her Mob boss husband. She's the ultimate trophy wife.

This is not to say that there is no place for assertive women in the gangster genre. Often their presence, no matter how minor, can have a subversive appeal, like Jean Harlow's effortless toying with Cagney. Billy Wilder wrote an entire film about the appeal of the moll in Howard Hawks' *Ball Of Fire* (1941), in which seven cloistered academics fall for a wisecracking **Barbara Stanwyck**, who is on the run from her gangster boyfriend. But the greatest moll of all is **Gloria Grahame** in *The Big Heat*. As pickled pixie Debbie she steals the film from Glenn Ford's dull introverted cop. She has the best lines in the film, the greatest presence and, when she gets her own back on Lee Marvin, one of the greatest acts of revenge in film history.

Moral panics

Moral panics have been as much a feature of the genre as guns, cars and molls; in fact they preceded many of the other component parts. These fears go as far back as 1913 when three real-life criminals starred in *The Wages Of Sin* and Moving Picture News was concerned that "all the worst elements in the youth in our cities will flock to see this film". *The Racket* (1928) was banned in some cities and censored in others, but only because gangsters themselves were worried about the film's effect on their business.

But moral panics really began with talking pictures, when the gangster moved centrestage. *Scarface* was held up for two years while censors fretted about the lifestyle that the film was advertising; eventually new scenes were added and another ending was bolted on, in which justice is seen to be done. *Scarface* also had a disclaimer at the beginning of the film, as did *The Public Enemy*, both claiming that they were some sort of public service. And when *The Public Enemy* was re-released it had a prologue to the prologue, as did *Little Caesar,* explaining the historical context of both movies.

By the time of their re-release, the Motion Picture Production Code was in full force and every film had to be approved by the Hays Breen Office. By 1934 pressure had built up against the major studios: the Catholic Church formed the **Legion Of Decency** and threatened eternal damnation on those who had seen films condemned by the church. The FBI had also taken an interest in movie production, and sociologists produced studies of prisoners which claimed that they had been lured into a life of crime by the prospect of the luxuries and easy money acquired by their screen equivalents. And a book called *Our Movie Made Children* was published which claimed that *Little Caesar* had inspired three murders. By 1935 there was a short-lived moratorium on the production of gangster movies.

Then it was a whole genre under attack; often it was just one film that suddenly became the focus for concern. In 1948 *No Orchids For Miss Blandish*, a cheap British adaptation of **James Hadley Chase**'s novel, felt the brunt of the press and politicians' outrage. The *Monthly Film Bulletin* described it as "the most sickening exhibition of brutality, perversion, sex and sadism ever to be shown on a cinema screen". Dr Edith Summerskill, Parliamentary Secretary to the Ministry Of Food, told the Annual Meeting of the Association Of Married Woman that the film would "pervert the minds of the British people". Questions were asked in the Houses Of Parliament, and the movie was banned by many local councils. The cinemas that did show *No Orchids For Miss Blandish* were packed out.

In the 1990s two films associated with **Quentin Tarantino** were the subject of anguished censorship in Britain. *Reservoir Dogs* was refused a video certificate in the aftermath of the James Bulger case, in which the press blamed the horror movie *Child's Play III* for influencing two child-killers (who were themselves minors). It was at least three years before Tarantino's debut was released on video, and in that time the Conservative government changed the law, requiring the British Board Of Film Classification to judge the psychological *harm* a video could do before granting it a certificate. In 1994 the Home Secretary,

The best lines

"Made it Ma – top of the world"
James Cagney, *White Heat*

"I'll make him an offer he can't refuse"
Al Pacino, *The Godfather*

"All I have in this world is my balls and my word and I don't break them for no-one"
Al Pacino, *Scarface*

"You dirty yellow-bellied rat"
James Cagney, *Taxi!*

"You're a big man but you're in bad shape"
Michael Caine, *Get Carter*

"Out of the way – I'm gonna spit"
Paul Muni, *Scarface*

"Bent law can be tolerated for as long as they're lubricating, but you have become definitely parched."
Bob Hoskins, *The Long Good Friday*

"Luca Brasi sleeps with the fishes"
Richard Castellano, *The Godfather*

"Let's go to work"
Lawrence Tierney, *Reservoir Dogs*

"We're sisters under the mink"
Gloria Grahame, *The Big Heat*

Michael Howard, demanded that more cinema films should be refused a video classification, and it looked like the movie would never be available for home entertainment in the UK. At least *Reservoir Dogs* was in cinemas; for a while it seemed that *Natural Born Killers* would never be seen in the UK in any form. Its problems were compounded by press reports that **Oliver Stone**'s film had spawned ten copycat killings in America and France. Eventually both films were released on video, even though 200 MPs called for the BBFC chief to resign in 1996 when *Natural Born Killers* finally got a certificate. A few years later a *Natural Born Killers* special-edition DVD came out, which contained even more violence than the cinema version. There was no moral panic.

When Britain's chief censor James Ferman retired in 1998 he said he had only one regret about his career, that he didn't cut a scene from *Pulp Fiction*. But it wasn't a scene of violence, it was the shooting-up scene. The shot of a glistening syringe against a black background, set to the surf music of **Dick Dale**, and the smile on John Travolta's face after he has injected himself, was, Ferman claimed, "practically an advertisement for heroin".

The mothers

The mother of the hoodlum started out as an innocent who could think no ill of her son. In *The Public Enemy*, the mom seems blissfully unaware of her offspring's profession. Even when James Cagney brings home a barrel of beer and plonks it on the dining table, his mother doesn't cotton on that he may be involved in

bootlegging. When the eldest son points out that his younger brother is not only not in politics, but he's a murderer, she not only doesn't believe him, but assumes that he must be mentally disturbed, that "he ain't himself, he doesn't know what he's talking about". And this may have been based on reports of **Al Capone**'s mother, who was similarly disposed to her beloved son: "Al's a good boy," she would insist, especially when he moved her into his fifteen-bedroom mansion.

The notion of gangster as mummy's boy reached its logical Oedipal conclusion in *White Heat* (1949), in which the mother is no longer an innocent, but part of the gang. And she dominates her son, James Cagney, helping him through his bouts of psychosis, reminding him not to leave a potential witness alive. He means it when he says

Ma Grissom and her gang count their loot, in Robert Aldrich's *The Grissom Gang* (1971)

he doesn't know what he'll do without her. In one telling moment he throws himself on her lap as if he's diving back into the womb.

When Cagney goes to jail in *White Heat*, his mother takes temporary charge of the gang; a year earlier in 1948, Ma Grissom had already taken control of her bunch of hoods in *No Orchids For Miss Blandish*. She masterminds a plot to swipe kidnap–victim Miss Blandish from the original kidnappers and take the ransom for themselves, but the plan falls apart when her son falls for the captured heiress. In **Robert Aldrich**'s 1971 remake, *The Grissom Gang*, Ma Grissom is far more of a vicious harpy. But even she doesn't compare to **Shelley Winters** in *Bloody Mama* (1970). In Roger Corman's delirious take on the exploits of 1930s bank robber Ma Barker and her gang of sons, she bathes and goes to bed with her offspring. The success of the film led Corman to produce a trilogy of "bad mother" movies: *Big Bad Mama* (1974) and *Crazy Mama* (1975) with **Angie Dickinson** and **Cloris Leachman** respectively as the unsuitable parents.

This mother love theme reappears typically (and stereotypically) in tales of gay gangsters, particularly in two Kray Twins–related movies: *Villain* (1971's Richard Burton vehicle, modelled on aspects of Ronnie Kray) and **Peter Medak**'s 1990 biopic. In *The Krays,* **Billie Whitelaw** is as much the star as Martin and Gary Kemp, and the title refers as much to her as it does the twins. Unlike Margaret Wycherly in *White Heat* she doesn't take part in any villainy, but she does bring tea and biscuits to their meetings, and everything they do – the nightclubs they open, the monogrammed shirts they wear – is all designed to impress her. But just how much she knows about their modus operandi is open to question, a grey area the film skilfully leaves unresolved. She's a combination of the naïve and the complicit mother, neither saint nor sinner. But like all the representations of a gangster's mum, Freud is never far away.

Musical gangsters

Every Bollywood gangster movie is a gangster musical by default: even in their urban realism *Agneepath* (1990), *Satya* (1998), and *Vaastav* (1999) have musical interludes. When the gangster takes his girl to the countryside in *Satya*, song and dance breaks out as it often does in the countryside in Bollywood cinema. Apart from the presence of the lead actors it has no relation to what has gone on before, as if a mischievous editor had spliced in a reel from another production: there's light where there was darkness, sun where there was rain, and the camera that was once hand-held now swoops and circles the couple as they sing their hearts out. And when the music's over, both the lovers and the film return to the grime and crime of the city.

Guys And Dolls (1955) is the most famous western gangster musical, with **Frank Sinatra** as inveterate gambler Nathan Detroit who bets that **Marlon Brando**'s Sky Masterson can seduce Salvation Army goody-two-shoes **Jean Simmons**, while the cast intermittently break out into numbers like "Luck Be A Lady Tonight". But the ultimate musical gangster is **James Cagney**, who was originally a vaudeville song-and-dance man. Ironically, he only combined song and crime once, in the forgettable *Never Steal Anything Small* (1959), which was, disappointingly, one of the bum notes of his career.

Bloody Mama
dir Roger Corman, 1970, US, 90m

Corman's roadkill movie begins uncompromisingly with a young girl being held down by her brothers while her father rapes her. The next time we see Kate Barker, she's a stone-hearted bandit. Ma and her brood proceed to head out onto the highway, robbing and snuffing out life as they go. Bloody Mama is often hailed as a much-needed antidote to *Bonnie And Clyde*'s beautiful-people-as-bandits light-heartedness; and it's certainly an odyssey of incest, rape and sadomasochism. But that doesn't necessarily make it a better film.

Big Bad Mama
dir Steve Carver, 1974, US, 83m

Neither big nor particularly bad, Angie Dickinson is a concerned mother who only wants to feed her two daughters. At first she tries bootlegging, then robbery, and finally kidnapping; the three of them jaunt across America, meeting bank robber Tom Skerrit and gigolo William Shatner, and along the way all their clothes fall off. There's an attempt at addressing some feminist issues, which is undermined somewhat by the frequent female nudity.

Crazy Mama
dir Jonathan Demme, 1975, US, 83m

Mother, daughter and grandmother rob and con their way across the US to take back the farm that was stolen from them. Jonathan Demme's film is more genuine in its politics and feminism than *Big Bad Mama*, but as the most respectable of the Mama trilogy, it's also the least interesting.

Newspapers

The advent of talking pictures brought an influx of journalists into the industry, answering Hollywood's need for writers who could do dialogue. Two of the most talented and influential were **Ben Hecht**, who wrote the screenplay for the first *Scarface,* and **Mark Hellinger**, who wrote and produced *The Roaring Twenties.* It's natural, then, that many films featured scenes in newspaper offices, in which hacks comment on the preceding events, or that crusading newspaper men were seen to make a difference in many a movie. The most obvious righteous journo

propaganda features in *Angels With Dirty Faces*, in which the publisher of *The Morning Press* tells zealous priest Pat O'Brien that "the press will back you to the limit". Headlines from his paper scream "Priest Declares War On Underworld Vice" and the editor is seen handing out assignments to eager hacks, ordering them to investigate the shady backgrounds of Humphrey Bogart and James Cagney. The press campaign against the gangster and his duplicitous lawyer forces cracks in the uneasy truce between them, and results in an inevitable gunfight: Bogart is shot dead and Cagney ultimately executed. Thanks to the press, the city streets are now safe.

Another use of newspapers is the classic montage device that informs us of events through the passing of time: spinning headlines relate the gangster's rise to power, the war between gangs, the end of Prohibition et al. For a couple of years after silent films Hollywood still relied upon inter-titles, and newspaper headlines were the most effective method of relaying information without seeming like a return to the silent age. Even the credits of the 1930 film *Doorway To Hell* are printed on newspapers which spill out of the printing press.

But the most creative use of this cinematic shorthand came from **Fritz Lang** in *You Only Live Once.* **Henry Fonda**'s Taylor has been captured and put on trial for murder. We cut to a headline of *The Daily Bulletin*, which announces "Taylor Freed…". The camera moves to the left, showing the paper pinned up on a wall; next to it is another headline –"Taylor Jury Deadlocked". Then the camera pans back to reveal *another* headline – "Taylor Guilty". Looking at the three possible front pages are the editor and his assistant, waiting for the verdict to come through. The phone rings, the editor listens carefully and slowly points to the headline they will use: "Taylor Guilty".

The speakeasy

Once the gangster has bought his new suit, his next stop is the nightclub. It's where he can show off his fancy threads, take his moll or meet a girl, and mix with the high society that has benefited from his bootlegging. The importance of the club is evident in films such as *Conflict* (1930), in which the key location is Club Palmer, *Murder On The Roof* (1930), featuring Club Corsair, and most importantly *Broadway* (1929), in which almost all the action takes place in the Paradise, a sort of Art Nouveau cathedral – it's as if Fritz Lang had built a nightclub in *Metropolis*. As David E. Ruth says, these films introduced "movie viewers to an extravagant world of sensuous consumption", where they could vicariously experience new pleasures: dancing girls, jazz bands and champagne. It's the place where consumption truly became conspicuous.

But gangsters don't just patronize the club. Often they own it, as was true in real life. **Larry Fay** managed several nightclubs, as did **Arnold Rothstein**, and his employee **Legs Diamond** owned the Hotsy-Totsy on Broadway, the back room of which was the venue for many of his slayings. In *The Finger Points* the gang run the Sphinx Club; in *Beast Of A City* (1932) a nightclub is The Mob's HQ; in *Little Caesar* Sam Vettori runs the Palermo and does all his shady dealings in the office behind the neon sign, while his rival Archie Lorch bankrolls a much classier joint called the Bronzed Peacock.

What's striking is how *open* these clubs are. They don't hide behind bolted doors or peepholes, and alcohol is readily available. There are actually relatively few speakeasies in cinema, which is odd as there were estimated to be 32,000 in New York alone in 1929. In *The Roaring Twenties* James Cagney's club is behind Hartners Paints and Varnishes and to gain entrance customers have to go through a door behind the counter. In *Some Like It Hot* a funeral parlour is the front for the jazz bar owned by **George Raft**'s Spats. *Once Upon A Time In America* also uses the funeral business as a cover, but the speakeasy itself is in a warehouse behind the official saloon, Fat Moe's, and alcohol pours out of the radiators.

In more recent films, the nightclub has been replaced by the disco, and champagne by cocaine. But the function remains the same: it's still a cathedral of conspicuous consumption, where the gangster displays his wealth. The movie brat directors understood the importance of the club to the gangster genre. Most of **Martin Scorsese**'s *Mean Streets* centres around Tony's bar which is permanently bathed in a hellish red. **Brian De Palma** makes that connection even more explicit in *Scarface* by naming the disco the Babylon, and much of the key action takes place in this mirror-decked palace of excess. It's where Pacino attempts a clumsy seduction of Michelle Pfeiffer on the dance floor, where he's taught the golden rule of drug dealing (don't get high on your own supply), where the corrupt cop demands his share of Pacino's takings, and where his best friend meets his sister. And it's in the nightclub that masked hit men try to gun down Al Pacino's Tony Montana, who's an easy target because his enemies always know where he'll be: in Babylon.

The technology

In what must be one of the most bizarre pieces of technology committed to celluloid, the chief of police explains how his tracking device will

Taking a dive

It's one of the clichés of sporting movies: the boxer who's under orders to throw a fight. And it's been a staple plot device ever since the early days of the talkies, in films like *The Big Fight* (1930), in which a prizefighter is drugged by his girl because her brother is in debt to the Mob. **Marlon Brando** could have been a contender in *On The Waterfront* if he hadn't gone down under orders from his mobbed-up brother Rod Steiger; in *It Always Rains On Sunday* (1948), a boxer promises to "go down in the second, and make it look artistic"; **Bruce Willis** makes a run for it after defying Ving Rhames' orders to hit the canvas in *Pulp Fiction*; and *Raging Bull* (1980) doesn't pull its punches about boxing's Mob connections.

But the acknowledged champion of taking-a-dive movies is *The Set-Up* (1949). Robert Wise's immaculate drama focuses on just one fight, in which over-the-hill punchbag Robert Ryan has one last crack at victory, unaware that his trainer has taken money from hood Little Boy for him to take a dive.

work in *White Heat*. He's placed an oscillator underneath James Cagney's automobile, which sends a high-pitched whine to transmitters in two police cars. If one transmitter picks up an impulse bearing 210 degrees and the other picks up a signal bearing 45 degrees, then using a map and two pieces of ribbon the police can plot Cagney's exact whereabouts. That's the theory, anyway. The cars themselves are fitted with a silver hoop on their roofs which twitches back and forth, giving them the appearance of low-budget B-movie UFOs.

There are other examples of less bizarre but equally primitive technology in early movies: in 1936's *Bullets Or Ballots*, Humphrey Bogart places a rather conspicuous bug in Edward G.

Robinson's room, which is about as subtle as using a large microphone. Inexplicably, in 1967's *Le samourai* the police place a bug the size of a family-size matchbox behind Alain Delon's curtains; unsurprisingly he discovers it within seconds of returning to his flat. In 1949's *Force Of Evil* lawyer **John Garfield** knows his phone is being tapped because there's a buzz on the line.

Gadgetry really came into its own in the heist or caper movie. Yet in 1950's *The Asphalt Jungle* all **Sterling Hayden** and his team have to do is duck under the electronic beam which is in front of the bank's safe. However, things have got a little more complicated recently with an increasing use of computer wizardry, where the electronic eye has become a cat's cradle of blue neon, the floor is mined with pressure pads, the room has to be at a constant temperature, or a fingerprint or retina scan is required to unlock the steel doors. This requires the obligatory scene wherein the thieves have to recruit a boffin character who has to get into the system's mainframe and disable the alarm. Almost always the boffin is an eccentric or loner who has one unusual tic or trait and lives in some unlikely dwelling, often a warehouse.

The possible originator of this character is **Benny Hill**. In *The Italian Job* **Michael Caine** decides to approach Benny because he is the only man for the job. However, Benny is residing in a mental home because of his unfortunate obsession with big women. Once sprung from the institution he has to create a new computer programme which will replace the huge reel of computer tape in the Turin traffic centre and thus crash the system, creating the traffic jam that will provide them with the necessary heist distraction. In the cases of *The Good Thief* and *$*, both hit upon the same ingenious idea: the boffin recruited is the same boffin who created the software in the first place.

The Tommy gun

When Paul Muni receives a shipment of machine guns in *Scarface*, he cannot disguise his glee. Like a child in a toy shop, he picks up one of the weapons, shouts "Out of the way – I'm gonna spit!" and peppers the room with bullets. The gun he was deliriously firing was a Thompson, otherwise known as the Chicago Piano, the tommy or the Typewriter. It was named after its inventor, Brigadier General **John T. Thompson**, who had developed it for trench warfare. The army had no use for it, but the criminal underworld did. Weighing only eight pounds, the weapon could fire up to a thousand cartridges a minute. And it wasn't even banned by legislation such as the New York 1911 Sullivan Law (which prohibited the purchase of small firearms). The Thompson was fairly cheap and easily available by mail order or from a sporting-goods shop. All you had to do was supply your name and address.

The tommy gun became synonymous with both the real and the screen gangster. With its unusual barrel it didn't look like any other gun: it was a ready-made icon. And it made the holder look good. For unlikely gangsters such as Mickey Rooney in *Baby Face Nelson* or George Segal in *The St Valentine Day's Massacre,* the gun provided a lethal cool that their screen personas don't suggest.

Paul Muni in *Scarface* (1932), with iconic firearm, preparing to "spit"

The World Is Yours: global gangsters

The sharply-dressed gangster and moll of *Tokyo Drifter* (1966)

The World Is Yours: global gangsters

While the archetypal movie mobsters are Tommy-gun-toting Americans (with the occasional dodgy British geezer from across the Pond), they have organized-criminal cousins in whole other hemispheres. And, even in countries whose cinema doesn't really do the gangster film per se, there are often movies that offer too many of the genre's singular, visceral thrills not to merit a mention. It's a mob, mob world...

Australia

For a continent whose white population was once almost wholly made up of cops and felons, it's not surprising that Australia has an established tradition of crime movies.

The story of the most celebrated outlaw in the ex-penal colony has been made into two well-known biopics: both **Mick Jagger**, in 1970, and **Heath Ledger**, in 2003, have starred as Ned Kelly. But they weren't the first. *The Story Of The Kelly Gang* (1906) was, at the time of its release, the longest film in the world, at a record-breaking 70 minutes. Kelly, the antipodean Robin Hood, was one of the very first subjects of Australian cinema, and he was soon joined by other outlaws in a genre known as "bushranger movies": the likes of Captain Thunderbolt, who was immortalized in the appropriately named *Thunderbolt* (1910), and Mad Dog Morgan, who was the subject of the rather more soberly-titled *Dan Morgan* (1911). This neo-Western genre accounted for 13 percent of all Australian films made in the 1910s. Ten were made between 1910 and 1912 alone, until the films were banned in 1920 by the government of the state of New South Wales, concerned about cinema's increasing glamorization of criminals. The bushrangers made the occasional comeback, with *Captain Thunderbolt* (1953) and *Mad Dog Morgan* (starring an unlikely Dennis Hopper) in 1976, while wacky auteur **Yahoo Serious** updated the Ned Kelly legend with *Reckless Kelly* (1993), about a bucket-headed hero who saves an island paradise from developers.

In the 1970s and 1980s Australian cinema was dominated largely by bawdy comedies and political thrillers, but in the post-Tarantino world order the criminal began to muscle his way back into the Aussie movie. And for the first time, they were bona fide gangsters, rather than their country cousins. **Heath Ledger** resorted to bank robbery after finding himself in debt to local gangster **Bryan Brown** in *Two Hands* (1999). Brown played a bigger fish in *Dirty Deeds* (2002) – a 1960s Sydney mob boss who has to fight off the Chicago Mafia, out to steal his slot-machine empire from him. *The Hard Word* (2002) starred a bearded and greasy **Guy Pearce** as one of three convicts who are pulled out by corrupt cops to stage a heist or two. **Eric Bana**, an Aussie comedian, gave a career-altering performance as real-life career criminal Mark Brandon Read whose dubious achievements he catalogued in Andrew Dominik's *Chopper* (2000). No matter how good some of these films were, there was little distinctive about them, and little to distinguish them from the American originals. It's a lamentable phenomenon that can be witnessed in Russia, Ireland, South Korea, United Kingdom, and most places on the filmic map – the global franchising of the Tarantino brand: hipster killers accessorized with the patina and patter of cool, queasy violence cut to a breezy retro soundtrack, and directors who clearly want to be part of the gang and can't or won't maintain a distance between themselves and their playful psychopaths. Welcome to the new world cinema, where all the films are alike, and only the accents are different.

Eric Bana plays an unlikely "hero" in one of Australia's few crime movies, *Chopper* (2000)

Chopper
dir Andrew Dominik, 2000, Aus, 94m

In a star-making performance, Eric Bana (pre-*Hulk*) did the full De Niro and bulked himself up to play self-mythologizing career criminal, Mark Brandon Read. The film took the criminal's own stories of life inside and outside jail as its source material, but Dominik's admittedly impressive film is a little too in awe of its subject to do what needed to be done and cut Brandon down to size.

Dirty Deeds
dir David Caesar, 2002, Aus, 110m

Sydney hood Bryan Brown, king of the slot machines, takes on the Chicago Mafia, in the shape of John Goodman. It's a typically uneasy modern mix of unreasonable behaviour and broad comedy. The American mob are ultimately defeated by the plucky Aussie gangster but, disappointingly, the film's derivativeness doesn't quite win a similar victory for the Aussie gangster flick.

Brazil

With all the fuss and column inches that *City Of God* (see p.89) provoked – even Brazil's president wrote a front-page article about it – you'd be forgiven for thinking that this was the first film ever to be made in the *favelas*.

In fact the slums of Brazil had long been a prime location for filmmakers, dating as far back as the Cinema Novo movement of the late 1950s with movies such as *Favela Five Times* (1961), *The Big City* (1966) and, most famously, **Hector Babenco**'s *Pixote* (1981).

The unflinching story of a street urchin who leaves a detention centre to sell drugs on the violence-plagued streets of São Paulo, *Pixote* turned the spotlight on the predicament of thousands of street children in Brazil. The movie made a star of 11-year-old urchin **Fernando Ramos da Silva**, who left his former life in the hope of becoming an actor. His career was seriously blighted by his illiteracy; although he appeared in one other film, his inability to read his lines meant that his attempt at a starring role in a daily soap opera went disastrously wrong. His miserable return to the *favelas* is documented in the biopic *Who Killed Pixote?* (1996), which showed how da Silva's brothers coerced him back into a life of crime, leading to his death at the age of 19 – shot by police officers in his home.

Da Silva's death sent shockwaves through the Brazilian film industry. "Everyone in Brazil was traumatized," said *City Of God* co-director **Katia Lund** who, significantly, set up a charity to help the street kids who acted in *City* to continue their education and to receive proper training, having learned from *Pixote*'s lesson.

In terms of gangster movies Brazilian cinema has been a bric-a-brac of filmic oddities, such as the disturbing, lurid *Devil Queen* (*A rainha diaba*, 1973) which its director described as "pop-gay-black thriller": the film's title referred to a razor-wielding homosexual mobster who ran Rio de Janeiro's drug and vice rackets. *The Amulet Of Ogum* (*O amuleto de Ogum*, 1974) was a fabulist tale from director **Nelson Pereira dos Santos** that blended myth with realism to provide a state-of-the-nation allegory. It was about a boy whose mother performs the *umbanda* ritual upon him – which renders him immortal while she is alive. She sends him off to join a gang, but when he defects to a rival set of gangsters, his former employers try to kill his mother in order to vanquish him.

The Day Of The Professionals (*O dia das profissionais*, 1976) had a *noir*ish plot about a diamond smuggler who hires a hit man to kill the thief who stole his stash, only to lose both the jewels and his wife to the hired killer. The hit man subject was explored more recently in *Belly Up* (*Os matadores*, 1997) centred on two hired killers

– one grizzled veteran and one new kid on the block. They are waiting for their target at a town on the Brazilian/Paraguayan border and pass the time reminiscing about the country's most renowned gunslinger – cue dramatic flashbacks. *City Of God* was just around the corner.

 Pixote (Pixote a lei do mais fraco)
dir Hector Babenco, 1981, Braz, 127m

While cinematic pyrotechnics were clearly never part of the director's overall vision of the movie, this harrowing slice of Brazilian realism is never less than tense, and became an international arthouse *cause célèbre*.

China

While Hong Kong has witnessed a boom in gangster movies, their growth has been somewhat steadier on the mainland. This is not unconnected to the fact that, when the Communists took power in 1949, they waged a highly successful war on organized crime.

Up until then the country, and Shanghai in particular, had been dominated by gangs that delighted in names such as **The Elders And Brothers Society**, **The Red Gang** and **The Heaven And Earth League**. With so little source material, it's not surprising that the contemporary gangster movie has not flourished. According to a report in *The Independent* newspaper in 1995, the advent of the Chinese crime cinema genre has paralleled the return of organized crime to

the mainland.

According to **Chris Berry** in the book *New Chinese Cinemas*, the country's first detective movie, *Desperation* (*Zui hou de feng kuang*) was made as late as 1988, and was the first film in China to pursue the age-old Western theme of cop versus killer. *Black Snow* (*Ben mingnian*), made a year later and directed by **Xie Fei**, featured another well-worn Western trope, the ex-con who returns home in the vain hope of going straight. When gangs appeared in more recent Chinese cinema, they took the disappointingly non-violent form of a rock band in *Beijing Bastards* (1993) or bike-riding juvenile delinquents in *In The Heat Of The Sun* (1995).

So Close To Paradise (*Biandan, guniang*, 1998)

comes closer to what we think of as a traditional gangster movie. It was a tale of just-about-getting-by in the city, and it featured a small-time hustler who kidnaps a Vietnamese bartender, unaware that she is the girlfriend of the area's most ruthless crime boss. Meanwhile in Taiwan, one of the country's most prestigious directors, **Hou Hsiao-Hshien** made *Goodbye, South, Goodbye* (*Nanguo zaijan, nanguo*) in 1996, about a pair of small-time hoods and their molls which "proved to be quite popular with Taiwan's visibly tattooed set", as **Jeff Yang**, author of *Once Upon A Time In China*, put it. Hou's critically-acclaimed, languorous road movie follows the adventures of a retired gangster and his sidekick, Flathead, who decide to pull off one final scam, involving the transfer of pigs (an indigenous variation on a theme), and head south to pull off the deal, only to be thwarted at the last by a rival set of mobsters.

The most famous and most recognizable mainland gangster movie, however, was directed by one of China's international stars, **Zhang Yimou**. *Shanghai Triad* (*Yao a yao dao waipo qiao*) was the last bloom of the on- and off-screen relationship between the director and his leading lady, **Gong Li**, who had been lovers since their first collaboration, *Red Sorghum* in 1987. *Shanghai Triad* also signalled the end of the affair between Yimou and the critics, until he became their darling once again with *Hero* (*Ying xong*, 2002) and *House Of Flying Daggers* (*Shi mian mai fu*, 2004).

Yimou's films before *Triad* were set in rural, feudal China and offered viewers an insight into a world rarely glimpsed – they were the best kind of armchair tourism. Many critics who had swooned over the charged erotic atmosphere in *Ju Dou* (1990) and the stately, painterly melodrama in *Raise The Red Lantern* (*Da hong deng long gao gao gua*, 1991), claimed that Yimou had

sold out to genre. Despite the presence of all the usual Zhang touches – blazing reds and rapturous close-ups of Gong's visage – *Shanghai Triad* is a melodrama rarely discussed in the hushed tones reserved for Zhang's other work, possibly because its generic roots are showing.

It wasn't as if the director hadn't had enough problems getting the film made in the first place. The Chinese authorities had halted production just as it was about to begin shooting, in effect to punish Yimou for sending his previous film *To Live* (*Huozhe*, 1994) to the Cannes Film Festival

Gong Li, the moll of Zhang Yimou's *Shanghai Triad* (1995)

without the permission of the state film bureau. *Shanghai Triad* was finally made in collaboration with the official studio and its script was passed by the censor who approved of the fact that it was set in the 1930s and depicted the country's criminal, capitalist past before the Communist revolution got rid of both criminals and capitalists. The Ministry Of Radio, Film And Television backed its entry in the Cannes festival, where Yimou believed it would win the top prize, the Palme D'Or. Instead most critics (and the judges) turned their back on the film, claiming that unlike his previous films, which were allegories about bureaucracy, *Shanghai Triad* had little to say about modern China.

In fact, in 1995 the authorities had arrested a number of important gangsters, including an extortionist called "the Dwarf", while Chinese newspapers reported increasingly hysterical news of bank robbers, grave robbers and "vampire gangs" who would cut their victims open and sell their blood to the local hospitals. Even though *Shanghai Triad* was set seventy years earlier, it couldn't have been more relevant. As state control weakens and the market economy begins to take hold in China, we can confidently predict more gangsters and, of course, more gangster movies.

Shanghai Triad (Yao a yao dao waipo qiao)
dir Zhang Yimou, 1995, HK/China/Fr, 108m

The last bloom of the love affair between star Gong Li and director Zhang Yimou. A teenage boy is paid by a don to look after his moll, a bewitching chanteuse called Bijou. As the boy becomes increasingly obsessed, he begins to spy on her and things take a turn for the gangsteristically promising when he overhears a plot to kill his inamorata.

France

The villains in French crime cinema are often the cops. Whether they are routinely abusing their suspects, as in Bertrand Tavernier's searing *L.627* (1992), or routinely accepting bribes like Gérard Depardieu in *Police* (1985) or Philippe Noiret in *Le Cop* (1984), it's generally a case of "bad cop, bad cop".

Gallic cinema has also always been fascinated by the criminal exploits of youth, whether in **Bertrand Blier's** *Les valseuses* (1974), **Matthieu Kassowitz's** *La haine* (1995), or the post-Tarantino, comic-book, hyper-realism of *Dobermann* (1997), with its ultra-violent armed gang, led by the ubiquitous **Vincent Cassell**.

It's a long way from **Jean Gabin** and *Pépé Le Moko* (1937), anointed "the initiator of the French gangster movie" by Ginette Vincendeau in her BFI Classics book on the movie. *Pépé* was a film that played to the tastes of French audiences who had lapped up *Little Caesar* (1930) and *Scarface* (1932). The noun "le gangster" had only been coined twelve years earlier, in 1925: one critic complained that *Pépé Le Moko* had "no other ambition than to transpose the American gangster to another country". In fact, a decade later Hollywood would be transposing *Pépé* to the United States – his love for a femme fatale would soon become a character trait for almost every *film noir* hero.

Pépé also cemented the star power of former vaudeville singer Jean Gabin, who became the most popular screen idol of the 1930s and, in Vincendeau's words, the "good bad boy" of French cinema. Gabin tended to be cast as either an ordinary person driven to crime, as in *La belle equipe* (1936) and *Gueule d'amour* (1937), or a criminal with a heart of gold as in *Pépé, la bandera* (1935) and *Les bas-fonds* (1936). But the films that sealed Gabin's reputation as the crestfallen romantic loser were Jean Renoir's *La bête humaine* (1938) and two masterpieces by Marcel Carné – *Quai des brumes* (1938), in which Gabin played an army deserter who falls for a young woman and is forced to kill when she is threatened, and *Le jour se lève* (1939), as a good man turned bad by the lure of a temptress.

Gabin was celebrated as the great working-class hero of the 1930s which is, from a modern perspective, not the first conclusion you would draw, especially as the striking thing about him is not his ordinariness or famed proletarian solidity but his sartorial elegance. Jean Gabin was no chav. (Although, to a 1930s audience, his scarves and his silk ties in *Pépé Le Moko* wouldn't have signalled class, they would have screamed "pimp".) There always an inner grace to his performances so, when the movies changed in the 1950s, Gabin easily re-invented himself as a man of style and sophistication. That sea-change is identified by Susan Hayward in her book *French National Cinema*: "the new breed of gangster lives in luxu-rious apartments, wears tailored suits and drives ostentatious American cars". The three films that defined the style-conscious era were *Touchez pas au grisbi* (1954), with Gabin as a wearied thief who wants to collect his money from a gold bullion robbery and leave behind his life of crime, Jean-Pierre Melville's *Bob le flambeur* (1955) and *Rififi* (1955), in which the decision not to smash-and-grab but to take the more stylish path – breaking in through the ceiling of the jewellers – crystallizes the move from old-school thuggery to the new urbanity.

In the 1960s **Jean-Luc Godard** took a grinder both to cinema and to the gangster film. Godard stole creatively, magpie-like, from the plots and iconography of the genre, and not just in *A bout de souffle* (1959 – see p.71). *Bande à part* (1964) was described by **Pauline Kael** as a "reverie of a gangster movie", and **Quentin Tarantino** was so impressed that he named his film company after

Gallic screen icon Jean Gabin in *Pépé Le Moko* (1936)

the idiosyncratic heist movie. He showed the scene in which the three lovers are dancing in a café to Uma Thurman and John Travolta before their twist in *Pulp Fiction*. Tarantino's astute observation of the three was that "they're not dancing well, but they're actually dancing *great*".

Actually, heist movie is far too generic a tag for *Bande à part*: the plot, such as it is, concerns two minor hoods – played by **Sammi Frey** and **Claude Brasseur** – and their starry-eyed friend, played by **Anna Karina**, who plot to rob her aunt's home. There is a sense, though, that they are just "playing" at being gangsters, just as the director is "playing" at making a gangster movie. Frey dresses in the archetypal trilby-and-trenchcoat uniform, the two men often stage shoot-outs with their fingers, play Pat Garrett and Billy The Kid on the streets of Paris, and dream of being racing drivers. Even when one is eventually killed, he staggers comically all over the place, like a small child acting in a school playground. As the film's narrator says of Franz, he was "uncertain if reality is becoming dream, or dream reality".

In *Pierrot le fou* (1965), Jean-Paul Belmondo managed to achieve what he singularly failed to do in *A bout de souffle*: to leave Paris with his lover (in this instance, Anna Karina). As they drive down south, they ape Hollywood's couples on the run, robbing and killing as they go.

Jean-Paul Belmondo was already a star by the time he made *A bout de souffle* and he increased his wattage in commercial gangster films like Claude Sautet's *Classe tous risques* (1960), *Le casse* (1971) and, most impressively, in Jean-Pierre Melville's *Le doulos* (1962). Whereas Godard said that a film needed a beginning, a middle and an end but not necessarily in that order, Melville kept the pieces together. He did, however, share Godard's interest in American iconography – snap-brim hats, raincoats, guns – and made style the successful substance of his movies. *Le samourai* (1967) was a match made in heaven between two men obsessed with image – director Melville and star Alain Delon – and they continued their profitable relationship in *Le cercle rouge* (1970) and *Un flic* (1972).

The 1960s ended

Delon and Belmondo, wearing the borsalinos that gave the 1970 movie its name

with summit meetings, in various combinations, of the screen- actor superpowers of French crime cinema in *The Sicilian Clan* (1969) and *Borsalino* (1970).

Even though Jean Gabin and Alain Delon had already both starred together in *The Big Snatch* (1963), *The Sicilian Clan* is regarded as their finest ensemble moment. It was certainly their most commercially successful. Delon is sprung from prison by crime lord Gabin to take part in an audacious mid-air heist, while hotly pursued by a third French screen icon, **Lino Ventura**. *Borsalino* (1970) united Delon and Belmondo on screen. It was phenomenally popular, not just because of their buddy–buddy act but because of its 1930s setting. At the time, according to critic Robin Buss, France "was enjoying a passion for *le retro*, which extended to styles of dress, furniture, architecture, literature, art and design". The borsalino (the type of hat the two idols wore) became an instant fashion icon on the film's release. *Borsalino* was directed by Jacques Deray, who enjoyed a fruitful relationship with Delon, making a number of movies with him in the 1970s, including the inevitable sequel, and *Le gang* (1974), in which Delon played master thief Robert "*le dingue*" ("the nutter").

In the 1980s, the police became the staple anti-heroes of French crime cinema, outdoing the bad guys in every department. The 1960s now appear to have been the golden age for *le gangster français*, despite more recent efforts such as *Dobermann* to re-energise the genre. Even Vincent Cassell's violently, gleefully amoral bank robber in that film cannot compare with **Philippe Noiret**'s cop, out of control in colonial Africa, in Bertrand Tavernier's superb adaptation of Jim Thompson's novel, *Pop. 1280*, *Coup de torchon* (1981). An unconscionable killer who blithely has sex with his victim's widow, who

doesn't care about the crimes in his jurisdiction but dispenses his own justice at night, Noiret is happily, venally corrupt. No gangster could ever compete with such a monster.

Le doulos
dir Jean-Pierre Melville, 1962, Fr/It, 108m, b/w

While *Le samourai* is often regarded as the masterpiece of Melville's gangster films, *Le doulos* is much more entertaining, and pulls off one of the great narrative coups in cinema history. Jean-Paul Belmondo plays a police informer who appears to betray his best friend, steal his jewels, and kill the rest of the gang: only 20 minutes from the end do we find out what's going on, and even then we still don't know if we can really believe our eyes.

Bande à part
dir Jean-Luc Godard, 1964, Fr, 95m, b/w

The generic moments are, unsurprisingly, not the most memorable or astonishing elements of Godard's playful tribute to the heist movie; rather, it's the moments when we want to *be* the characters, or at least be their friends, as in the record-breaking mad dash through the Louvre and the rightly-famous sequence in which the three lovers dance, barely in step with one another, to a café jukebox.

The Sicilian Clan
dir Henri Verneuil, 1969, Fr, 120m

With ingenious use of a metal-cutter, hit man Alain Delon escapes from a prison van to join Jean Gabin in the heist of a lifetime. Gabin's much commented upon youthful solidity matures into a gravitas that is perfectly suited to a mob boss, while Delon is his usual inscrutable self.

Le cercle rouge
dir Jean-Pierre Melville, 1970, Fr/It, 150m

A newly released convict (Alain Delon), a man on the run (Gian-Maria Volonte) and an alcoholic ex-police sharpshooter (Yves Montand) come together to pull off a jewellery heist that owes much to *Rififi*. Muted in its colours and style, this was Melville's most conventional and most commercially successful film, but it's difficult to see how it differs from a work of pure commerce, such as *The Sicilian Clan*, which is at least more entertaining.

Germany

German crime cinema has traditionally been more obsessed with serial killers, arch-villains and perverts than Mob bosses: the dastardly Dr Caligari, the criminal mastermind with psychic powers Dr Mabuse and the child-murderer played by Peter Lorre in *M* (in which, admittedly, gangsters do feature – helping to hunt Lorre down because all the police activity is bad for their business).

The detective novels of King Kong creator Edgar Wallace held an almost inexplicable fascination for German audiences and filmmakers before and after the war. Five were adapted between 1927 and 1934, none appeared during the Nazi years in which crime fiction was almost taboo, and 32 were made between 1959 and 1972, with titles such as *The Man With The Glass Eye* (1969) and *The Mark Of The Frog*. These Wallace films

Rainer Werner Fassbiner (right) and his fellow meanderers in his Godard-inspired debut, *Love Is Colder Than Death* (1969)

nearly always featured a Scotland Yard detective who plumbs the depths and the fog of a London underworld (albeit a London of the imagination) which is almost entirely populated by the cast of a Dickensian pantomime. Every instalment would have an arch-criminal (often played by Klaus Kinski), revelling in a name such as The Snake or The Shark, who left his calling card with his own unique brand of murder (though decapitation proved to be a favourite).

Only once were gangsters the villains, in *The Secret Of The Red Orchid* (1962), in which dubiously dubbed FBI agent **Christopher Lee** aided Scotland Yard in defeating two rival gangs from Chicago, who had moved their operations to London. Lee wasn't the most famous FBI agent in German cinema, though: Fed **Jerry Cotton** was the fictional hero of eight films alone between 1965 and 1969. In the first, *Schüsse aus dem Geigenkasten* (*G-Man Jerry Cotton*, aka *Operation Hurricane: Friday Noon*), the James Bond-style hero infiltrated a gang of heist merchants.

The end of the decade saw the debut feature film from **Rainer Werner Fassbinder**. *Love Is Colder Than Death* (1969) was the cold, clammy side of *A bout de souffle*'s coin in which Franz, played by Fassbinder himself, is a lowlife pimp who refuses to join a crime syndicate. On the sleazier side, the 1960s also witnessed the rise of exploitation cinema in Germany. The erotic thriller was the B-movie sub-genre of choice: movies that were cheap cocktails of violence and sex for connoisseurs of sleazy eurotrash. The best-known are the *St Pauli* series – *Der Arzt von St Pauli* (*Street Of Sin*, 1968) and *Der Pfarrer von St Pauli* (*Priest Of St Pauli*, 1970), among others – directed by one **Rolf Olsen**. In the world of cult movie directors, Olsen can be seen as on a par with, say, Italy's Fernando Di Leo. His finest

92 minutes were undoubtedly *Blutiger Freitag* (*Bloody Friday*, 1972), a hard, gory, ridiculous and often repellent contribution to the heist-gone-wrong sub-genre. *Freitag*'s gang of bank robbers is led by the psychopathic Heinz Klett (**Raimund Harmstorf**), a hirsute, 1970s fashion casualty in aviator shades who bears a disorientating resemblance to the bearded **Ewan McGregor** of the *Star Wars* movies.)

In the 1990s, of course, Quentin Tarantino left his mark upon crime cinema right across the globe. There was amoral, jokey violence aplenty in films such as *Sexy Sadie* (1996), about the last days of Edgar, an escaped serial killer. *Run Lola Run* (1998) was a huge hit, depicting the rescue mission of its heroine Lola (**Franka Potente**) – she has twenty minutes to raise the money her boyfriend owes his gangster boss, and get it to him – in three very different ways. Its slick techno soundtrack and camera-friendly lead actress targeted it perfectly at the bull's-eye of the MTV-generation demographic.

 ### Dr. Mabuse: The Gambler
dir Fritz Lang, 1922, Ger, 231m, b/w

Usually regarded as an early example of German Expressionism, *Dr Mabuse* is considered by some to be a gangster movie. And not just because the protagonist is an arch-villain with a gang, but because he uses his magical powers for pecuniary rather than supernatural ends. Just like every grasping mobster, he's in it for the money. However, it must be noted that he is nevertheless a madman with a psychic eye who can hypnotize his victims with a well-aimed stare. Gangster movie or not, it is indubitably a masterpiece.

 ### The Testament Of Dr. Mabuse
dir Fritz Lang, 1933, Ger, 122m, b/w

There's more gang activity in Lang's sound sequel – one of Mabuse's crew even sports a fedora and a pair of spats. But Mabuse himself is still more like a character from a comic book. With his shock of white hair, ability to summon up ghostly spirits, and dastardly plan to bring about a criminal reign of terror, he's like Lex Luthor, or any of those other arch-villains with extra-sensory powers that superheroes have to battle on a regular basis.

Love Is Colder Than Death (Liebe ist kälter als der Tod)
dir Rainer Werner Fassbinder, 1969, Ger, 88m, b/w

Featuring all the hallmarks of the European existential gangster movie – chain-smoking, battered leather jackets, and louchely arbitrary human interaction – it's also a

mysteriously engrossing movie (if you're patient enough to allow it to be so).

Blutiger Freitag (Bloody Friday)
dir Rolf Olsen, 1972, Ger/It, 97m

An irrepressibly funky soundtrack, a lead villain who appears to have dressed for a Scandinavian porn movie, and every shot unmistakeably of its early-1970s time – "Krautsploitation", anyone?

Hong Kong

"Hong Kong is the world capital of *heishehui* ('black societies')" writes David Bordwell in his book *Planet Hong Kong*. "Since the end of World War II triad gangs have controlled extortion, gambling, heroin smuggling and prostitution … Triad members, many of them martial artists, have long been involved in filmmaking."

It's not surprising, then, that there have been so many Triad movies since the mid-1980s, that gangsters are unequivocally represented as heroic and honourable, and that the biggest star in Hong Kong (possibly the world), **Chow Yun-Fat**, became a national treasure by playing a Triad member. Bey Logan, author of *Hong Kong Action Cinema*, goes so far as to say that the glamorization of gangsters led to an increase in membership of Triads in the 1980s, which might explain why the mobs moved into filmmaking, and why one star, **Andy Lau**, "found himself being pressurised by real gangsters to make appearances, sometimes only cameos, in their productions".

The so-called "heroic bloodshed" genre began with *A Better Tomorrow* (1986), an alchemical meeting of star Chow Yun-Fat and director John Woo (who are both discussed in detail on pp.185 and 286). But there are other producers and directors who have made Hong Kong a world cinema superpower, such as Tsui Hark, the producer of *A Better Tomorrow*, whose Film Workshop company gave Woo his big break with *A Better Tomorrow*. After directing its sequel, Woo refused to direct the mooted prequel. It was Hark who directed *A Better Tomorrow III* (1989), putting his own stamp on the trilogy. As a director, Hark, unlike Woo, is known for his strong female characters. Apparently Hark made the radical suggestion that the original *A Better Tomorrow* could be about three women, and he introduced the previously unmentioned character of Mark's lover, Chow Kit-ying (**Anita Mui**), and the plot revealed somewhat controversially that it was she who had given Mark (Chow Yun-Fat) his much-imitated look. The duster coat, sunglasses and two-fisted Beretta stylings were borrowed wholesale from her. This news didn't go down too well with many of the series' macho fanboys, who were somewhat piqued to discover they were dressing like a girl. Hark and Woo teamed up again on *The Killer* (1989) and allegedly fell out over who should take the story credit when the rights were sold to Hollywood. They haven't worked together since.

A testimony to Chow Yun-Fat's popularity among HK action movie audiences is the fact that he's been the favourite of not just one but two Hong Kong directors, starring in five Ringo Lam productions including the so-called *On Fire* series, the first of which, *City On Fire* (1987), provided **Quentin Tarantino** with the plot of *Reservoir Dogs*, with Chow playing an undercover cop who infiltrates a gang of armed robbers.

The inspiration behind the film was a newspaper article about a shoot-out between police and thieves during a botched jewellery robbery, and much of Lam's early work had a ripped-from-the-headlines quality. *Prison On Fire* and its sequel (1987 and 1991) were condemnations of jail conditions wrapped up in the packaging of an action movie, while *School On Fire* (1988) concerned an education establishment overrun by Triads. Much has been made of Lam's docudrama approach, but this is a long way from the social realism that has gritted British screens for the last forty years. Ringo Lam is no Ken Loach. What Lam did was to remove the gloss from Hong Kong action thrillers – Chow Yun-Fat's lack of sartorial cool in *City On Fire* is apparently one of the reasons the movie never repeated the phe-

nomenal success of *A Better Tomorrow* – before putting it all back on again for *Full Contact* (1992). This directorial volte-face amped up the violence, and the striking primary colours, with washes of yellow flooding the screen. He out-Wooed Woo with one set piece in which the camera follows the trajectory of a bullet on its fatal journey from gun to flesh.

Still in Hong Kong, but on another planet entirely, **Wong Kar Wai** created his own brand of artfulness, having started out in genre. His debut, *As Tears Go By* (1988), was unusual for Wong in its complete adherence to a script (something he hasn't

Chow Yun-Fat, as an undercover cop, in Ringo Lam's *City On Fire* (1987)

done again), and even a linear plot – a bloodthirsty story starring Andy Lau as a gang member who tries to leave the life, but who is brought back in by the dallying and ambition of his younger brother. The movie closely parallels Scorsese's *Mean Streets*: Lau is akin to the Harvey Keitel role, while Jacky Cheung's character resembles Robert De Niro's, a firebrand who always gets into fights and debts, and who will bring his brother down with him. Despite its uncharacteristically coherent narrative, *As Tears Go By* had distinct Wong touches: the use of uniform colour-coding, scenes shot in lollipop reds and blues, and application of the slowest of slo-mo.

Chunking Express (1994) showcased the Wong we all know and scratch our heads over. The most successful of his "inaction" movies, it starts with drug smuggler **Brigitte Lin** in blonde wig and sunglasses looking for the courier who stole her stash and cash; as she wanders into a café she bumps into "Cop 233" who has just decided to fall in love with the next woman he meets. A fragmentary narrative about parallel lives produces a profound film about superficiality. Lin is an icon in an empire of neon signs advertising Coke, McDonalds and Del Monte pineapples. Wong used similar formalist and narrative devices in *Fallen Angels* (1995), a fragment of which is about a dapper, posturing contract killer and his personal secretary, who harbours masturbatory fantasies about him. A visionary meditation on time and surface, it's often described as being either the stunning epitome or excessive pastiche of the Wong style.

Wong Kar Wai is sometimes slighted as being a director for the MTV generation. **Andrew Lau,** the director of the *Young And Dangerous* (1996) series, would probably take that as a compliment. With its rock soundtracks and pop idols, obligatory fast-cutting and furious camera work, the six films succeeded in selling the Triad members as rock stars (and the movies led to inevitable rip-offs, with 1996 producing *Mongkok Story* and *Sexy And Dangerous*, about an all-girl gang). All six were phenomenal hits (especially with the Triads) and most pitted the hero,

A blonde-bewigged Brigitte Lin in Wong Kar Wai's *Chungking Express* (1994)

gang leader Chan-Ho Nam (singer **Ekin Cheng**), against the old order, which he both defeats and humiliates; the first two films even had comic-book sections to highlight the cartoon origins of the series. It's not coincidental, then, that in the first scene of *Once Upon A Time In A Triad Society* (1996) the protagonist wipes his bum on a comic book. *Once...* is a rejoinder to the *Young And Dangerous* movies and the glamorization that's an essential and lucrative ingredient of the series. The "hero", gang boss Kwan, relates his story in flashback from a hospital bed. His sympathetic story, in which he's portrayed as a victim of circumstance stops suddenly halfway through the film, and Kwan admits that we've been watching a lie. His life story is then re-viewed, but now Kwan is the bully and not the victim, his violent career in crime a result of his choice, greed and ambition.

Similar narrative tricksiness was employed to great effect by the director **Ka-Fai Wai**'s *Too Many Ways To Be No.1* (1997). Made before Germany's *Run Lola Run*, *Too Many Ways* deployed the same device of rewinding and replaying the plot's basic scenario with different outcomes: just one crucial choice by the protagonist decides the entire direction of the story. The result in each case was bleakly and blackly comic. It was but one of several startlingly innovative techniques the maverick director used – one shoot-out in the film is conducted entirely in the dark.

Since the handover to mainland China, Hong Kong's film industry has been in recession but, at its lowest ebb, in 2002 fortunes were reversed by the phenomenal success of *Infernal Affairs*. Directed by Andrew Lau, it's certainly a more mature affair than his *Young And Dangerous* series, though that's possibly due to co-director **Alan Mak**. The first part of *Infernal Affairs* took to its logical conclusion Hong Kong cinema's obsession with doubles, parallel lives and mirror images. Telling the stories of a cop who infiltrates the Triads and a Triad member who infiltrates the police, it was another case of Hong Kong's cinema of split personality, with its emphasis on brothers both real and surrogate in a world where cops and criminals are doppelgängers, where heroes go undercover and lose their identity. It may not be coincidental that these films have emerged from a place which had a similar identity crisis, that once belonged to both Britain and China, but was part of neither. Whether the *Infernal Affairs* trilogy will save Hong Kong cinema is by no means guaranteed. Critic Tony Rayns believes its success "defers collapse rather than rescinds it".

Rich And Famous (Gong woo ching)
dir Taylor Wong, 1986, HK, 104m

An earlier outing for the now well-worn two brothers scenario, with Andy Lau as the adopted good seed and Alex Man as the bad seed, a loose cannon whose impetuosity always leads Lau into trouble. When the two come under the patronage of kindly don Chow Yun-Fat, Lau's loyalties are split as his brother is always angling for a fight in this routine (and routinely successful) drop of heroic bloodshed.

Tragic Hero (Ying hung ho hon)
dir David Lai and Taylor Wong, 1987, HK, 96m

The sequel to *Rich And Famous* has Lau return to the colony to help Chow fight Man, whose impetuous nature has now given way to psychotic behaviour. The final reel of *Tragic Hero* is a particular favourite of HK fans because of its money shot – the two Hong Kong icons Andy Lau and Chow Yun-Fat, standing side by side, armed to the gills, taking on all the bad guys.

City On Fire (Longhu fengyun)
dir Ringo Lam, 1987, HK, 110m

Ringo Lam's influential thriller doesn't exactly boast the documentary realism that some critics claim for it; it's just a little less style-conscious than most of Hong Kong cinema. Its main claim to fame is the direct influence it had on Tarantino, but it's only the bare bones of the last fifteen minutes or so (and one identical shot) that are identifiable elements of *Reservoir Dogs*. In many ways it's the acorn to *Dogs*' oak tree.

As Tears Go By (Wangjiao jiamen)
dir Wong Kar Wai, 1988, HK, 100m

Wong Kar Wai's partially successful debut could be seen as a kind of reworking of Scorsese's *Mean Streets*. Occasionally Wong moves out of Scorsese's shadows to produce spurts of the Kar Wai we know – slo-mo, splurges of blues and reds, the theme of forlorn love – but these are just exceptions to a film that plays too much by the rules.

Young And Dangerous (Guhuozai zhi ren zai jianghu)
dir Andrew Lau, 1995, HK, 99m

Ushering in a second wave of Hong Kong cinema, *Young And Dangerous* was hailed, at least by the film company, as an *A Better Tomorrow* for the nineties. The luxuriously coiffured Nam and his fun-loving criminals take on the older, meaner, short-haired Kwan and co. Andrew Lau's hand-held realism sits uncomfortably with the unapologetic glamorization of his subjects – they're a sort of Triad version of S Club 7.

Too Many Ways To Be No.1 (Yi ge zi tou de dan sheng)
dir Ka-Fai Wai, 1997, HK, 90m

Brother Kau and his amateur thieves bungle badly and bloodily through every situation they enter into. Hailed at the time as one of the most singular movies ever made in Hong Kong, almost every scene boasts some form of delirious invention, whether in the story-telling or the camera-work – when, for instance, a whole fight scene is shot upside down.

Full Time Killer (Chuen jik sat sau)
dir Johnny To and Ka-Fa Wai, 2001, HK, 102m

"O" (Takashi Sorimachi) is Asia's number one assassin, a haunted, alienated hitman who regrets the lack of intimacy that his profession necessitates. Tok (Andy Lau) is a flash, leather-clad upstart who loves action movies, but above all, loves his work. Tok stalks and challenges O in a bloody game of cat-and-mouse in this partly inventive, partly derivative Andy Lau star vehicle.

India

Amongst all the high camp and technicolour spectacle of singing princesses and their suitors, there wouldn't seem to be much place for gangsters in India, yet it is often alleged that if it wasn't for *real* gangsters (and their finances) there would be no Bollywood at all.

In recent years numerous press reports have alleged that producers, faced with spiralling costs and with no assistance from the government, had to look elsewhere to pay for their stars' wages and those big production numbers, and were welcomed with open wallets by the **Mumbai Mafia**. There have been accusations in court that *Chori chori chupke chupke* (2001) was financed by the *bhais* (brothers or dons) of the Mumbai underworld; in August 2002, Indian police investigated allegations that *Devdas* (2002), the most expensive Bollywood movie ever, received similar funding. Meanwhile, film producer **Gulshan Kumar** was assassinated in broad daylight in 1997, stars have been hired and fired by the **Mumbai Mafia**, while others have become targets for extortion rackets: in January 2003, actress **Preity Zinta** claimed in court that she had received threats from a gangster called Chota Shakeel. Thirteen other witnesses from the film industry were also going to testify, but quickly and mysteriously retracted their claims.

In a parallel universe, gangsters have become just as visible on screen in films like *Satya* (1998), *Vaastav* (1999) and *Company* (2002). It's a tradition which started with *Kismet* in 1943, the first Hindi film to focus on an anti-hero, in this case a smuggler – a popular pastime for Indian anti-heroes. Rural bandits (or *dacoit*) are our main focus of attention for this period of Indian "gangster" cinema, the most famous exponent of which, in the West, was *Bandit Queen* (1994). A dramatization of the life of the legendary Phoolan Devi, it is hardly representative of the genre.

Far more typical is *Gunga jumna* (1961), about a young man who turns to crime when he's forced out of his village, and who comes into conflict with his policeman brother. The character of the good son, the brother on the side of the law, is, according to Travis Crawford in *Film Comment* magazine, *de rigueur* for the bandit movie: he's the audience's screen surrogate and a provides a way of redeeming the anti-hero. Hollywood hit upon the same tactic in the aftermath of the Hays Code, the self-regulatory code of ethics created in 1930 by the Motion Picture Producers and Distributors of America (MPPDA).

In the 1950s there was a move from the village to the city in Bollywood movies, and a new villain began to emerge from the shadows. Embodied first by the urbane **K.N. Singh** and then by the actor known simply as **Pran**, they felt at home in drinking dens, restaurants, fast cars and nightclubs, usually accompanied by a moll, in Hollywood-influenced, John Huston-inspired movies such as **Raj Kapoor's**

Awaara (1951*)* and Guru Dutt's *Baazi* (1951).

The real breakthrough, however, came in 1975. This was the year when Emergency Rule was declared which, like Prohibition in the United States, seemed only to succeed in uniting and organizing criminals. Coincidentally or not, 1975 was also the year when two films changed the face of crime in Bollywood movies, and both starred **Amitabh Bachchan**. *Sholay* and *Deewaar* were true phenomema: *Sholay* was in cinemas for five years, while *Deewaar* hung around for fifty weeks. Curry Western *Sholay,* in which ex-policeman **Sanjeev Kumar** hires two fun-loving criminals, played by Amitabh Bachchan and Dharmendra, to fight a nefarious bandit who mercilessly killed Kumar's entire family. It introduced a new level of villainy – an arm-lopping psychopath called **Gabbar Singh**. Despite, or possibly because of, his penchant for torture and unconscionable, cold-blooded murder, the villain became more popular than the hero with Indian audiences for the first time.

Deewaar, on the other hand, featured a new type of hero. His name was Vijay (aka Victory). The part was the third in a long line of Vijays for Amitabh Bachchan (in all he's played someone called Vijay some seventeen times) and, whether he was a smuggler or a cop, Vijay always took the law into his own hands. This attribute was apparently the key to his appeal in post-Emergency Rule India. Ever since *Zanjeer* in 1973, Bachchan was Bollywood's angry young man. His other significant Vijays were in movies such as the blaxploitation-influenced flares-and-funk camp-fest, *Don* (1978) – in which he played both the head of an international smuggling ring and his exact double – and the thriller *Agneepath* (1990), in which he played Mafia don Vijay Dinanath Chavan. The latter is regarded by many as one of the greatest of his 150 or so performances.

By the 1990s Indian gangsters were their own

men, distinct from the *dacoit*, their country cousins. They looked and behaved like their western counterparts: *Agneepath* nodded in the general direction of De Palma's *Scarface*, while many more, such as *Dharmamatma* (1975) and *Dayavan* (1988) tipped their fedoras to *The Godfather* (1971), which was a huge hit across the continent. The two most successful examples of this cross-cultural fertilization were the Tamil film *Nayakan* (1987) and the Hindi *Parinda* (1989).

Nayakan, by acclaimed director **Mani Ratnam**, has a classic rise-and-fall narrative with a twist: a young boy kills the policeman who murdered his father, and flees to Mumbai; there he makes his way up in the underworld, only to be knocked off by his own bodyguard, who turns out to be the son of the policeman he offed in the first reel. *Parinda* not only paid homage to *The Godfather* and *Nayakan* but also to *On The Waterfront* (1954), with its repeated motif of pigeons in flight (*Parinda* translates as "bird"). A self-conscious attempt to make art out of a genre, Vidhu Vinod Chopra's film has the classic two brothers narrative, the good and the bad seed: Kishan is forced to work for mob boss Anna to pay for his brother's education; when Karan discovers his brother's profession, he is killed and Kishan has to redeem and purge himself through the act of revenge.

In the 1990s there was a virulent strain of smiling violence, and a gaggle of villains who were direct descendants of *Sholay's* Gabbar Singh. *Vaastav* (1999) centred on a boastful young thug who shows off his guns and gold to his parents and forces his girlfriend at gunpoint to have an abortion. It was a thriller which, in the words of Travis Crawford, "integrates ruthless cruelty and musical episodes in deft and surprising ways". But the benchmark was set by *Satya* (1998), which introduced a new level of brutality (scenes of torture) and realism (a documentary approach to the

slums of Mumbai) to Mumbai cinema, and gang members are depicted as real people, with real domestic issues. Like all these *dacoit* and gangster movies (with the exception of 2002's *Company*), it wasn't so committed to realism that it didn't contain the usual incongruous musical interludes, however. Tellingly, *Satya* reveals the extent of the underworld's influence on the Mumbai film industry – one *bhai* boasts how he used both his influence and his gun to get a friend a part in a movie, while in an early scene a Bollywood film director is assassinated in broad daylight.

Deewaar
dir Yash Chopra, 1975, India, 174m

Deewaar means "wall" and refers to the barrier between the two brothers who, exiled from their village, grow up determined to fight the injustice heaped upon them. One becomes a policeman, the other becomes the leader of a smuggling ring and enters a world of penthouse suites, hotel bars and louche women. Yash Chopra's melodrama is oddly compelling despite moments that defy parody, such as the appearance of thunder and lightning in dramatic situations.

Sholay
dir Ramesh Sippy, 1975, India, 188m

Playing Gabbar Singh, this really is Amjad Khan's film. It's a truly reptilian performance – he even looks like an iguana (with a beard). Mere words cannot sum up the experience of watching the deranged, genre-defying *Sholay*, which is like a Mumbai mix of the films of Monty Python, Cliff Richard and Sergio Leone, De Palma's *Scarface*, and those speeded-up bits in TV's *Benny Hill*.

Satya
dir Ram Gopal Varma, 1998, India, 170m

Like James Cagney in *The Roaring Twenties* (1939), Satya is a decent man who only becomes a gangster out of economic necessity. His bravery makes him the perfect right-hand man for Mumbai mob boss Bheeku, while his quiet charm wins over his unsuspecting neighbour, wannabe singer Vidya. This epic thriller has the raw verve and vitality of Latin American films such as *Amores perros* (2000), and the musical numbers sit both surreally and poignantly amongst the documentary realism.

Vaastav
dir Mahesh Manjrekar, 1999, India, 145m

The English title of *Vaastav* is *The Reality*, but there's little evidence of reality in this camp-fest. Sanjay Dutt plays the irrepressible Raghu, who kills the brother of a criminal overlord and has to seek protection from the overlord's rival, One-Eyed Vittal, discovering that he has an aptitude for murder. The extraordinary thing about *Vaastav* is that rather than dying in his mother's arms, as Bollywood criminals often do, the hero's loving mum shoots him at point-blank range, arguing that he'd "died" years ago. It's a long way from *Mother India*.

Ireland

The Irish gangster movie has only come into its own in the late 1980s and early 1990s with films like *The Courier* (1988), *I Went Down* (1997) and *The General* (1998).

Just why there has been a late flowering of crime movies has been the subject of much discussion. In the book *Keeping It Real* Lance Pettitt argues that the country's capital has only recently become a suitably iconic location: "by the mid 1990s, Dublin was able to boast a cityscape that was sufficiently photogenic for the cinematic requirements of the gangster genre; modern buildings jostled with dockland warehouses and rundown areas of inner city". The reason why Dublin now had the prerequisite mix of high and low life was the development of the country's tiger economy, and it's this sudden upturn in the country's fortunes that many critics have pinpointed as the reason for the parallel upturn in gangster movies.

Whether it's in South Korea, Thailand or Ireland, the gangster film seems to be the flip side, if not a by-product, of the tiger economy. The free market after all provides the right con-

ditions for the mobster to blossom – the emphasis on individual opportunity, the lack of state intervention, and the equation of success with material gain. And, for any filmmaker who wants to address the state of the entrepreneurial nation, the gangster is a handy metaphor. Coincidence or not, there have been numerous crime movies since the economic boom, such as the **Richard Harris** film *Trojan Eddie* (1996), while *High Boot Benny* (1994) and *The Informant* (1997) showed that it wasn't just the British film industry – with films such as *Odd Man Out* and *The Long Good Friday* – which could make powerful thrillers about the IRA.

This new interest in Irish crime was signalled by a whole slew of movies about two real-life figures from either side of the law: investigative reporter and would-be gangbuster **Veronica Guerin** and legendary bank robber **Martin Cahill**. There have been two movies about Guerin, the journalist who tirelessly and possibly obsessively, sought to expose the movers and shakers of the burgeoning Dublin underworld and was allegedly murdered by a drug baron whom she'd named and shamed. She was fictionalized, albeit barely, when **Joan Allen** played "Sinead Hamilton" in the low-key *When The Sky Falls* (2000), made by *The Long Good Friday*'s director **John Mackenzie**. The threat that the gangs still posed was marked by the fact that the crew had to employ security guards on set while they filmed on the streets of Dublin. Although the Hollywood production *Veronica Guerin* (2003) was more upfront in naming its sources, its realistic edge was blunted by the gloss and the upbeat ending that director **Joel Schumacher** imposed upon the material.

Meanwhile, Martin Cahill has been the subject of three movies in as many years – *The General* (1998), the pointless *Ordinary Decent Criminal* (2000) and the TV movie *Vicious Circle* (1999). Cahill was a legendary Robin Hood figure, a bank robber who was "bigger than *Riverdance*" (according to *Vicious Circle*), but who found himself on the wrong side of not just the law but also the IRA when he refused to get involved in drug running. **John Boorman** won the Best Director prize at Cannes for his visually impressive *The General*. Boorman was inspired to make the film when Cahill broke into his home and stole, amongst other valuables, a gold record that the director received for the sales of the *Deliverance* soundtrack (Cahill can be seen with a stolen gold record in the movie.) All three films reveal the making of the Cahill myth by the local media, but are themselves willingly seduced by the outlaw's charisma and have become part of the process of his unlikely promotion to folk hero status.

Another modern international phenomenon is the Tarantino effect – films that try to emulate his sparkling collision of graphic violence and hipster humour. The Irish symptom was *I Went Down* (1997), a self-conscious attempt to locate the imagery and iconography of the genre in rural Ireland resulting in a mix of seamy bars, gunplay and quirkiness that nudges the viewer too often in the ribs to be an entirely pleasurable experience.

I Went Down
dir Paddy Breathnach, 1997, Ire/GB/Sp, 107m

Written by Conor McPherson, the award-winning playwright best known for *The Weir*, *I Went Down* is a quirky – sometimes too quirky – comedy about two misfits. Bunny and Git have to track down a man called Frank who owes money to a gangster called Tom. As with *The Actors*, McPherson doesn't quite manage to translate his undoubted theatrical talents to the cinema screen.

The General
dir John Boorman, 1998, Ire/GB, 124m, b/w

Filmed in colour but screened in black and white so as not to "romanticize poverty" according to Boorman, the lush monochromatic photography not only succeeds in romanticizing Martin Cahill but gives the chase scenes a distinctly *Keystone Cops* feel.

Ordinary Decent Criminal
dir Thaddeus O'Sullivan, 2000, Ire/Ger/US/GB, 94m

Ordinary Decent Criminal is a thinly veiled version of the same story as *The General*, with Kevin Spacey wincingly miscast as "Michael Lynch", the story's legendary Dublin bank robber. A limp embarrassment.

Italy

The Italian Mafia actually consists of four different gangs with different power bases: the Cosa Nostra in Sicily, the Camorra in Naples, the 'Ndrangheta or Calabrian Mafia, and Sacra Corona Unita or United Sacred Crown.

It's fair to say that the Mafia are part of everyday life in Italy and it's equally fair to say that the national cinema does not reflect this fact. For example, books about Italian films rarely, if ever, feature the word "Mafia" in their index. There have been directors such as **Carlo Lizzani** who made docudramas about real, but very much independant, gangsters such as Luciano Lutring in *Svegliati e uccidi* (1966). And there has been an abundance of heist movies. *Big Deal* was one of the first films, in either Europe or America, to parody *Rififi* and make a joke out of the heist genre, thus ushering in the comedy variant, the caper movie. The Italian crime movie continued to develop, with a spate of 1970s B-movies, many of them directed by **Fernando Di Leo**.

The Mafia have occasionally broken cover in Italian B-movies such as *We Still Kill The Old Way* (1967), a murder mystery set in Sicily; *Stick 'Em Up Darling* (1974); *Napoli spara* (1977), an effective drama about the impossible task of investigating the Camorra; and *Italian Graffiti* (1973), which is set in 1920s Chicago and is best described as a spaghetti gangster movie. **Ricky Tognazzi** dramatized the story of the judges

Mobster *con fuoco*: the movies of Fernando Di Leo

Often shot and edited in two weeks, and dismissed at the time as "eurotrash", the works of cult auteur Fernando Di Leo were finally taken seriously after a prestigious retrospective at the 2004 Venice Film Festival. They were introduced by long-time fan Quentin Tarantino, who first saw Di Leo's *Boss Of The City* (1976), a Mob thriller featuring **Jack Palance** as "Mr. Scarface", when he was a video-store clerk. Immediately hooked, he watched every Di Leo VHS he could get his hands on. He has gushed that "there's always an underlying irony, even in the grimmest things shown, and this makes his films truly unique" and that "I owe Fernando a great deal in terms of passion and filmmaking."

Of all these lurid, violent thrillers involving hitmen, cops and mafia dons, Leo's "Milieu" trilogy is of particular interest to us: *Milano calibro 9* (1972) is about a small time criminal who leaves prison to find himself up to his neck in intrigue when he's accused of stealing $300,000 and comes up against sadistic gangster **Mario Adorf**; *La mala ordina* (1972) focuses on a pair of New York hitmen, Frank and Dave (who QT paid homage to in the form of Jules and Vincent in *Pulp Fiction*) with an Italian pimp in their sights (not realising that he is the wrong man); and *Il boss* (1973) concerns a killer who ignites a Mob war when he wipes out a Mafia clan, was based on real events and temporarily left behind the genre universe to expose corruption in contemporary Italian society.

However, not of all Di Leo's oeuvre has been critically reclaimed. Time hasn't been kind to *Stick 'Em Up Darlings* (1974), a dire sex comedy with **Ursula Andress** as a Mob boss who moonlights as an air hostess. Warning: Di Leo's films are only intermittently interesting, they have their moments and that's it. In the memorable phrase of critic Nigel Floyd "they would make a great set of stills". Recommended for lovers of retro-kitsch who like to watch their movies with an air of ironic detachment.

Ugo Piazza (Gastone Moschin), an unlikely gangster in *Milano Calibro 9*

who risked their lives bringing Mafiosi to trial in the powerful drama *La scorta* (1993). *To Die For Tano* (1997), directed by **Roberta Torre**, was the first – and will in all probability remain the only – musical about the Mafia. It told the true story of the mobster Tano Guarrasi, but in a garish high-camp way **Baz Luhrmann** would be proud of. Torre also shot the docudrama *Angela* (2002), a straight and sober tale of the trials and tribulations of a mobster's wife. Apart from these and a few others it seems that *omertà*, the code of silence, applies as much to the film industry as it does to the Mob lifestyle.

The work of director Fransesco Rosi has persistently flouted this rule. Rosi has spent his career critiquing the power, corruption and lies of Italian society. His debut *La sfida* (1958) told the story of young gun Nino Vingelli, and the challenge he posed to the old order of the Camorra, particularly his boss, José Suárez. Typically, Rosi was as interested in the stratified Neapolitan society and its shifting power relations as he was in the psychology of the two main characters.

Rosi's films try to render the seemingly invisible forces that determine human action. In *Salvatore Giuliano* (1961), the legendary Sicilian bandit of the title is presented as a pawn both of the Mafia and the far right. His contingency is underlined by the fact that he is never granted a close-up, and is never the centre of attention or the author of his own actions. He is always filmed as part of the background, as just another figure in the Sicilian landscape, which emphasizes the external factors that have made him the outlaw he is. In other words, Rosi shows us the bigger picture. Similarly, when an apartment block collapses in *Hands Over The City* (1963), the director investigates the social forces that have led to its destruction: civic corruption, the insidious relationship between politicians and the Camorra that has eroded the foundations of Neapolitan society. Rosi's films credit the viewer with some intelligence. We're trusted to make up our own minds – although the director doesn't unmediatedly present the facts, he understands that facts are the hardest things to come by, particularly in a secret society. *Exquisite Corpses* (1975) is an investigation without conclusions – Inspector Rogas (**Lino Ventura**) investigates the murders of a series of judges who themselves have been investigating the Mafia and left-wing terrorists; just as he believes he has exposed government cover-ups and uncovered the truth, Rogas is shot dead. His death results in another lie and another cover-up.

The closest Rosi has come to making a recognizable piece of genre fiction is *Lucky Luciano* (1973), but this is no straightforward biopic. Starting with underworld kingpin Charles Luciano's infamous deportation from America to Naples, it's a forensic analysis of the collusion between the American army and organized crime that allowed the Mafia to regain political power at the end of World War II (Mussolini had all but destroyed the Mafia) and ensured that Luciano only served nine years of his forty-year jail sentence. The film boasts a superbly composed, fast-cut shoot-'em-up set piece in its **Night Of The Sicilian Vespers** scene, which jars deliberately with the documentary approach that Rosi utilizes for the rest of the movie. (The best example of the latter is a particularly long scene in a United Nations committee meeting, which informs us that most of the heroin flooding into America was produced by Italian pharmaceutical corporations.) It shares its disconcerting, almost surreal, clash of styles with *Salvatore Giuliano*, a defiance of expectations both for those seeking genre thrills and for those who prefer neo-real-ist naturalism. Rosi's films are a heady mix of authenticity and artifice.

How Rosi has made a career defying the Mafia without being discovered at the bottom of a river wearing concrete boots remains a mystery. *La sfida* was allegedly originally going to be made in Sicily, rather than Naples, until the producers got cold feet. But the production of *Salvatore Giuliano* had few problems filming in Giuliano's home town of Montelpre where the bandit is still regarded as a folk hero. Journalist **Tullio Kezich** was even employed to help out with any local difficulties and, though Giuliano's family did threaten to sue, that was the extent of the aggravation that Rosi got. Which makes other filmmakers' silence on the subject of organized crime even more puzzling.

But perhaps times are changing. In *The Consequences Of Love* (2004), a business consultant named Titta Di Girolamo, has lost 220 million dollars of the Cosa Nostra's money and in retribution has been exiled to Geneva where he acts as a glorified delivery boy. Once a week for eight years, he has deposited suitcases full of cash into a local Swiss bank. In between drops he sits in his hotel room, injects heroin, eavesdrops on the neighbours, masturbates, accommodates hitmen and conducts a relationship, of sorts, with a barmaid. And that's pret-

Francesco Rosi's debut movie, *La Sfida* (1958)

ty much it, until one of the money bags is stolen and Girolamo is brought to account, Mafia–style. The film's essentially mundane story and dry, dispassionate tone are a riposte to *Goodfellas* et al, which director **Paolo Sorrentino** believes have "mythologised organized crime".

La sfida (The Challenge)
dir Francesco Rosi, 1958, It, 95m

Francesco Rosi hit upon his trademark style of neo-realism and theatrical artifice with his debut, a potent drama about the rise and fall of an ambitious hood. Vito challenges the authority of his boss Aiello with initially sucessful results, marked out by the gaining of a luxury flat, a fast car and the local beauty Assunta. The dream life doesn't last long, and when the organization catches up with Vito, Aiello extracts his inevitable revenge.

Big Deal On Madonna Street
dir Mario Monicelli, 1958, It, 111m

Cosimo, the bungling leader of a gang of inept thieves, is arrested just before he's about to pull off a major robbery; he reveals his ambitious plans to his friend Peppe, who decides to carry out the job for himself. The ensuing chaos plays merrily with the newly-minted clichés, including a pin-sharp joke about synchronizing watches.

Milano calibro 9 (Milano Calibre 9)
dir Fernando Di Leo, 1972, It, 97m

Tarantino rather excitably called it the greatest Italian *noir*. It is, at least, the best of the trilogy, with a dynamism that the others lack. Di Leo even pauses for breath to stage an unlikely discussion, a sort of Socratic dialogue, between two cops who debate whether all property is theft. And he tops it all off with a couple of satisfying twists. But don't believe what you read about Di Leo being the Italian Jean-Pierre Melville – he's not fit to touch the brim of the great man's fedora.

La mala ordina (Manhunt)
dir Fernando Di Leo, 1972, It, 92m

Well-scrubbed and brightly lit, this displays all the aesthetic values of an unsuccessful TV pilot from the early 70s. With his overheated use of the zoom lens, Di Leo here has the visual sophistication of a tourist with a camcorder, only coming into his innovative own with a climactic shoot-out at a scrapyard. The rest is a depressingly familiar mix of corny dialogue, stilted performances, tacky décor and nude, abused women. Less a movie, more a cheese platter for those who aren't yet fed up with kitsch.

Il boss (The Boss)
dir Fernando Di Leo, 1973, It, 100m

Hit man Henry Silva gets caught up in a turf war between the Calabrian Mafia and the Cosa Nostra (run by his Machiavellian boss Richard Conte). Fans claim that it's an exposé of corruption in Italian society and it's true that, via some clunky expository dialogue, the hierarchy of the Mafia is revealed and links to the church and government alluded to. However, this is all mixed up in the usual Di Leo blend of spirited set pieces, narrative longueur, dubious dubbing and even more dubious sexual politics – this is a film for people who think that shots of a man slapping a naked woman is transgressive cinema.

La scorta
dir Ricky Tognazzi, 1993, It, 92m

Ricky Tognazzi's powerful dramatized account of a true story. Judge De Francesco uses his bodyguards as an unofficial team of investigators, but things go awry when they uncover corruption and Mafia collusion in the justice department. The Mafia never make an appearance, but their presence is constantly felt with car bombs and assassinations.

The Consequences Of Love (Le conseguenze dell'amore)
dir Paolo Sorrentino, 2004, It, 100m

One of the few major Italian movies about the Mafia, *Consequences* is oddly tangential rather than forensically polemical. Sorrentino's matter-of-fact approach suitably reflects the commonplace, prosaic presence of the Mafia in Italy. But if the subject matter is atypical, then in other respects *Consequences* is very much an Italian film. Its glacial pacing and theme of bourgeois alienation are highly reminiscent of early Antonioni.

Japan

As director Takeshi Kitano has said, the Yakuza are a part of everyday life in Japan but, unlike the case of the Mafia in Italy, this fact is recognized in Japan's national cinema.

Perhaps this is partly due to the fact that the Yakuza are shrouded in a Robin Hood mythology and represent a continuity with a past that was ruptured by the white heat of post-war technological advance. Both the history and the cinema of Japanese crime have been expertly and succinctly documented by Mark Schilling in his highly recommended *Yakuza Movie Book*.

The modern Yakuza began to evolve in the middle of the eighteenth century. They operate by a strict code of chivalry (called *jingi*) and are structured like a traditional family, with all the notions of hierarchy and community that the term implies. The pre-war Yakuza movies, in particular, played upon the mythological aspects of bandits such as Kunisada Chuji. In 1952, when the occupation of Japan ended, a new breed of screen Yakuza began to emerge, and by 1963 the sun had risen on a golden age.

The film of this halcyon period either focused on modern, contemporary gangsters or were set in the seventy-year period between the end of feudalism and the beginning of World War II. The so-called *ninkyo-eiga* chivalry films centred around the concept of *giri-ninjo*: the choice the hero had to make between self-interest and an obligation to others that might cost his life. The basic premise involved two gangs: the good gang which represented the old world order of morality and loyalty, and the bad gang, typically thieves without honour who had sold out to big business. When the head of the good gang was murdered, the hero would seek revenge by entering the modern headquarters of his rivals and confronting the villain, armed only with a sword (significantly refusing to arm himself with a gun). The other archetypal story line, as in *Gang tai gang* (1962), would have the hero emerge from prison to discover that society and the syndicate had changed for the worse and given into greed. *Jinsei gekijô: hisha kaku* started the boom that became a cultural phenomenon for Japanese males of a certain age. Critic **Tadao Sata**, himself a young man in the 1960s, believes the films appealed to the hordes of lonely bachelors who'd moved to the city from the provinces and who dreamt of belonging to a gang.

With its espousal of traditional values and rejection of modernity the *ninkyo-eiga* genre inevitably appealed to the right wing of Japanese politics, such as writer Yukio Mishima, who declared that *Sochu tobaku* (1968), about a hit man whose sense of honour drives him to kill his corrupt boss, was a masterpiece of Japanese cinema.

Most of these films, however, were factory fodder – products churned out mainly by the Nikkatsu and Toei studios (Toei making 37 Yakuza movies in 1967 alone). The key player in the Toei studios was the producer Koji Shundo, while his daughter **Junko Fuji** became one of the genre's major stars, alongside **Ken Takakura** and **Koji Tsuruta**.

Takakura was the star of two long-running film series, *An Account Of The Chivalrous Commoners Of Japan* (in eleven parts) and *Remnants Of Chivalry In The Showa Era* (in nine parts), and starred alongside Robert Mitchum in Hollywood's take on Japanese gangs – the Paul Schrader-scripted *The Yakuza* (1975). Koji Tsuruta was an ex-juvenile delinquent who volunteered for the suicide squadron during World War II and for years afterwards suffered survivor guilt when many of his colleagues perished (an interesting parallel wartime experience to Lee Marvin's). Both Takakura and Tsuruta starred in the film that's been credited as starting the *ninkyo-eiga* wave, *Jinsei Gekijô: hisha kaku*, in which Tsuruta loses out to Takakura when they fall for the same courtesan. The outcome of *Jinsei Gekijô* was par for the stoic course for Tsuruta. His characters were marked by their suffering, sacrifice, loneliness, but above all duty – a quality he himself embodied by volunteering for the kamikaze squadron. As Schilling says, "he was living out the central drama of his youth".

The other star, the third man of Yakuza movies, was the inexpressive ex-mobster **Noburo Ando**; once a leader of 300 gang members, he went on the run in the late 1950s until his arrest and eventual imprisonment. He was released in 1964 and starred in a film about his life a year later, *Blood And Rules*; he went on to star as other people, notably in Fukasaku's *Street Mobster* (1972), but went back to his roots in *The True Story Of The Ando Gang* (1973) and *Noburo Ando's Record Of Flight And Sex* (1979), about his love life on the run.

Given the predictable, derivative nature of the studio produce, it's not surprising that the films that have stood out, such as **Masahiro Shinoda's** *Pale Flower* (1964) and **Nagisa Oshima's** *The Sun's Burial* (1962) are the ones which did something different with the formula, and questioned Japanese cinema's obligation both to *giri-ninjo* and generic formulae. Which is why the films of the distinctly individual **Seijun Suzuki** are now regarded as the classics of the period. Suzuki, who didn't wash or change his clothes while he was shooting a movie, had made over twenty films for Nikkatsu before he discovered his métier with the cartoon-like *Yaju no seishun* (*Youth Of The Beast*, 1963), a style which he perfected in *Tokyo Drifter* (*Tôkyô nagaremono*, 1966), a primary-coloured odyssey for a gangster in a powder-blue suit. With *Branded To Kill* (1967), Suzuki left reality behind altogether. Ostensibly, its plot concerns Japan's "third-best hit man", who himself becomes a target after failing to complete an assassination due to an errant butterfly blocking his gun's sight. The president of Nikkatsu found the movie so incomprehensible that he sacked the director on the spot. Suzuki did not make another film for ten years.

By 1973, the *ninkyo-eiga* movies were all played out; according to author Donald Ritchie, the codes of chivalry meant nothing to the new youth market, while Mark Schilling blames the genre's demise on the retirement of actress and icon **Junko Fuji**. The death of the traditional gangster was heralded by the newly cynical *Battles Without Honour And Humanity* (*Jingi naki tatakai*, 1973), directed by a man who was responsible for many of the *ninkyo* movies, the late **Kinji Fukasaku**,

Seijun Suzuki baffled the studio execs with his idiosyncratic *Tokyo Drifter*

now better known for *Battle Royale* (2000).

In his 1960s films, such as *Gang domei* (1963) there was always one lone wolf who still believed in upholding the traditional values. Those values came to be regarded as outmoded hogwash and the Robin Hood myth was cruelly exposed in *Battles* and its four sequels (which were followed by another series, *New Battles Without Honour And Humanity*), and what was for many the director's finest work, *Graveyard Of Honor* (*Jingi no habaka*, 1975). They were part of a new trend called *jitsuroko rosen*, or "line of realism", and introduced a new star, **Bunta Sugawara**, who was employed explicitly because of his anti-heroic qualities. When the series finished in 1976, the Yakuza had been declared dead – at least on screen – and it was the end of the line for realism.

When **Takeshi Kitano** took over the directorial reins of *Violent Cop* (1989) after Kinji Fukasaku left the project, he revived the Yakuza genre with the explicit intention of making something that was definitely not *ninkyo*. Kitano had been brought up amongst gangsters in South Tokyo and knew the banal truth behind the Yakuza. Kitano's films, such as *Sonatine* (1993) and *Brother* (2000) are distinctly *sui generis*, and bear little comparison with those of any other director in cinema. Except, perhaps – and even then purely by virtue of the idiosyncrasy they share – to the works of **Takashi Miike**. His first feature film was *The Third Gangster* in 1995, but Miike properly started to make his mark with *Shinjuku Triad Society* (1995), the first of his Triad trilogy about the relationship between Chinese and Japanese gangsters, completed by *Rainy Dog* (1997) and *Ley Lines* (1999). *Fudoh; The Next Generation* (1996) brought him to the attention of an international audience, while *Dead Or Alive: Hanzaisha* (1999) is widely regarded as a watershed, the moment Miike's stock rose. That film's

The weird world of Takashi Miike

Best known in the West for the outré horror film *Audition* (1999), Miike averages five films a year in the director's chair, and his output has included musicals, sci-fi and a star vehicle for Speed, Japan's equivalent of The Spice Girls. Miike, whose films are part of the V-Cinema (ie straight-to-video) phenomenon in Japan, often have Yakuza as heroes, but any resemblance between his films and *ninkyo-eiga*, or any other genre for that matter, is purely coincidental.

attempts at realism, however, were abandoned by its sequel, *Dead Or Alive 2* (2000), whose surreal qualities (and scene of necrophilia) are far more representative of the Miike style. *Ichi The Killer* (2001), for example, featured a hit man who comes when he murders, whilst *Gozu* (2004) was about a junior Yakuza member who is haunted by the ghost of a man he accidentally killed.

The body is often under attack in Miike's world. Eyes are gouged, men and women are routinely and casually raped, the "hero" of *Ichi The Killer* has a blade at the end of his boot which slices and dices his victims, and the plot of *Shinjuku Triad Society* focuses on the trade in body parts. When Thai director **Pen-ek Ratanaruang** cast Miike as a Yakuza in *Last Life In The Universe* (*Ruang rak noi nid mahasan,* 2003), he discovered that it was a role Miike was very familiar with. As the director explained to *Sight And Sound* magazine, it was Miike who had ended up "dealing with the Yakuza when we shot in Tokyo, because in Tokyo you don't ask permission from the police, you ask the Yakuza".

Pale Flower (Kawaita hana)
dir Masahiro Shinoda, 1963, Jap, 96m, b/w

Its debt to *A bout de souffle* (1959) is occasionally burdensome: some of the dialogue towards the film's close is portentous and embarrassing in its attempts to be deep and "existential" (if the subtitles can be trusted). But *Pale Flower* remains extraordinary for its angular, monochrome cinematography, for its rigorous soundtrack, and for the self-conscious patina of cool it lacquers its cast with. The movie's whimsical moments, and the mechanical capriciousness of its protagonists, may well have given Wong Kar Wai a few ideas.

More madness from Seijun Suzuki: *Branded To Kill* (1967)

Tokyo Drifter (Tôkyô nagaremono)
dir Seijun Suzuki, 1966, Jap, 81m

Tetsu, a gangster in an extremely striking suit, has to leave the city of yellow nightclubs and purple discos after witnessing a double murder. Heading south, with no particular place to go, he's hunted by the police and a rival gang. Seijun Suzuki's sense-defying spectacle is 81 minutes of colour-saturated delirium.

Branded To Kill (Koroshi no rakuin)
dir Seijun Suzuki, 1967, Jap, 98m

Jo Shishido plays a chipmunk–cheeked, boiled-rice-obsessed hit man who fights his own Mob (and his frequently naked wife) when he fails to carry out a job after a butterfly settles on the cross-hair of his rifle. The plot is more or less irrelevant – at least, it certainly appears to take second place to style for the movie's director. It's as if *Point Blank* had been directed by Buñuel and re-edited by Godard.

Battles Without Honour And Humanity (Jingi naki tatakai)
dir Kinji Fukasaku, 1973, Jap, 99m

Within the first five minutes a woman is savagely raped and two men have their arms hacked off. The arterial spray spurting towards the camera sets the tone for this unflinching examination of the bloody and futile world of the Yakuza. Between the numerous battles without honour and humanity (but plenty of ketchup), Fukasaku's iconoclastic thriller tracks the rise of Bunta Sugawara, whose reckless bravery and unlimited capacity for violence propel him through the ranks of the Yakuza in post-war Hiroshima.

Dead Or Alive: Hanzaisha
dir Takashi Miike, 1999, Jap, 105m

This conservative Miike offering begins with a celebrated montage of buggery, blood-letting, stripping, carnage, cunnilingus and dancing, before calming down to tell the story of a successful hit man whose younger brother returns from the US and is dismayed to find how his education has been funded. Almost disappointing in its narrative cohesion, just when the film seems to have settled down, Takashi inserts a moment of bestiality, a scene where a woman is drowned in a paddling pool of her own excrement, and an apocalyptic sci-fi finale to top it all off.

Mexico

Mexico has had a curious, often synchronous relationship with Hollywood. In the 1930s films were remade for the Spanish-speaking market at exactly the same time as the original was being produced.

The same sets and story lines were employed, only the actors and the director were different. Or else, Mexican studios would simply copy what was popular beyond the border: hence the appearance of *El terror de Chicago* in 1934. The 1940s was the golden age of Mexican cinema, when its film industry was among the biggest in the world, and the gangster melodrama came into its own. Numerous movies were produced with titles like *El gangster* (1947), *Cabaret Shanghai* (1949) and *Paco el elegante* (1950).

The head honcho of Mexican gangster movies was **Juan Orol**. He wrote, directed and starred in a vanity project called *El reino de los gangsters* (1947) about a man, Johnny Carmenta, who has to form a gang to save the nation from political corruption. Orol quickly followed it up with two sequels, *Gangsters contra charros* (1947) and *El Charro del Arrabal* (1948) and later returned to the genre in 1954 with *Bajo la influencia del miedo*, about an innocent man framed for murder who becomes a vengeful mob boss after he leaves prison. Not one of these films is worth watching, according to author Eduardo de la Vega Alfaro in his book *Mexico's Cinema* – not even for their admittedly high-camp value. Eduardo singles out only one example from the gangster melodramas that is worth bothering with: *El suavecito* (1950). It concerns a dandy hood – "that's not a man, that's a barber shop sample" is his father's opinion of his dress sense – and the fateful spiral towards

his eventual death in a bus station.

The new wave of Mexican cinema, sparked by the phenomenal success of films such as *Amores perros* (2000) and *Y tu mamá también* (2001), has been credited to a renaissance in the country itself, following the end of 71 years of governance by the Institutional Revolutionary Party. The movies' emphasis on wild youth, dog-fighting gangs et al was nothing new however. There's long been a tradition in Mexican cinema of teenage criminality, most famously in **Luis Buñuel**'s *Los olvidados* (1950), which shocked many with its portayal of juveniles as being seriously delinquent, rather than just boisterous scamps. And testament to its continuing influence was *De la calle* (2001), the directorial debut of **Gerardo Tort**. Described as "*Los olvidados* meets *Amores perros*", it tells the story of a teenage street kid who steals drug money from the corrupt cop who runs the neighbourhood.

The caper movie triumphed in the form of 2003's *Nicotina* (its tag line being "I'm *dying* for a smoke") which was a huge success at Mexican box offices and won several international awards. Directed by **Hugo Rodriguez**, it was a very post-Tarantino affair concerning a geeky, mumbling computer hacker (played by *Y tu mamá*'s **Diego**

Post-Tarantino hi-jinks and problems with the Russian Mafia in the much-hyped *Nicotina* (2003)

Luna) who steals Swiss bank passwords. He gets into trouble with the Russian Mafia when he delivers them the wrong disk. At the time of publication, *Nicotina* had not had an English-language release, and a DVD is apparently pending. Rather worryingly, reports so far have suggested that it's closer in temperament to **Guy Ritchie**'s *Snatch* than Tarantino's *Pulp Fiction*. Still, its real-time action (meaning that the film's 92 minutes are 92 minutes of the characters' lives on screen) sounds an intriguing enough gimmick to deserve a wider audience.

Poland

Crime films were not at a premium during the Communist regime, partly because the authorities claimed that organized crime did not exist in a socialist republic, but also because genre films were frowned upon.

According to author Marek Holtof in his book *Polish National Cinema*, "film's task was to communicate, educate and perform other social duties". Entertainment was certainly not regarded as a social duty. Since the introduction of the free market, however, action movies have prospered, including *The Private Town* (1993), about a town terrorized by small-time gangsters. In such movies, criminals were typically dressed in black suits and dark ties and – according to Holtof – resemble "stereotypical businessmen". Holtof points out that "According to Polish folk wisdom, gangsters and businessmen have a lot in common in the post 1989 period."

Psy (1992), regarded as the first action movie of the new era, explicitly looked at what had changed since the collapse of Communism, and the answer is – fundamentally nothing much. *Psy* translates as dogs (the Polish soubriquet for policemen) but has been given the title *Pigs* for the English-speaking market, and focuses on two members of the former security police who have to answer to the verification committee. One, Franz, has remained with the force but refuses to apologize for his old behaviour, while the other, Olo, is using his police training in the employ of a drug dealer. As Franz remarks, the old force "are members of the best organized Mafia in the world". And this is not a case of good cop, bad cop. Franz is merely marginally less evil than Olo; *Psy* reveals an unbroken line of corruption

between Poland's two regimes. The only difference between Communism and capitalism is a matter of economics – it costs more to bribe a state attorney these days.

Psy was a phenomenal success on its release, which was only eclipsed at the box office by its sequel. It made a star of its lead actor **Boguslaw Linda**, who was soon given the nickname Bogie. Of the crime films that followed in its wake, *Kiler* (1997) in particular has emulated its box-office success, although the two have little in common. *Kiler* is a broad comedy directed by Juliusz Machulski, who previously made the Russian co-production *Déjà vu*. What's noticeable about *Kiler* is that it hasn't taken long for the gangster to become a figure of fun in Poland. Siara, the chief gangster, has money but no class. He lounges around all day in his shellsuit or in one of his two indoor pools, while his wife wears three dead animals at a time, the stripes of each fur clashing badly with the other. The message is clear: the nouveau riche gangster is another product of the free market.

Psy
dir Wladyslaw Pasikowski, 1992, Pol, 104m

Boguslaw Linda plays Franz, an unrepentant member of the former security police, while his friend Olo now works for a cop-killing mob boss. The two remain close and help each other out until Olo is ordered to kill his old colleague. The film was criticized at the time for its American influence, its amorality and cynicism. But it is not the smiling violence of Hollywood's moral vacuity, more a product of a world-weary recognition that organized crime did in fact exist in the days of the socialist republic, and that capitalism has only made it more prominent and more profitable.

Kiler
dir Juliusz Machulski, 1997, Pol, 104m

Cezary Pazura plays an innocent cab driver called Kiler
who's mistaken for one of Europe's deadliest hit men by
both the mob and the cops. Having been imprisoned, he
is sprung from jail by one hairy, lardy don to take out an
investigative reporter who's getting too close for his liking.
Machulski's dark farce soon gives way to knockabout
comedy that wouldn't look out of place on Hollywood's
production line.

Kilerów 2-óch
dir Juliusz Machulski, 1999, Pol, 127m

Kiler is now a bona fide celebrity who mingles with
presidents and royalty, but whose fame has angered mob
bosses Siara and Lipski, who covet his money. This sequel
starts out as a social satire in which Poland is in the grip of
a moral malaise, where personality is more important than
politics, boasting the telling line: "Do you think a Pole can't
make the big time? What about the Unabomber?" Trouble
is, *Kiler 2* soon descends into a broad, unfunny farce about
doubles.

Russia and the Ukraine

The Russian Mafia is beginning to replace
Colombian drug barons as the villain *du jour* in
Hollywood. These are the new bad guys whose
motives don't need explaining – they are just
plain bad.

British films such as *Rancid Aluminium* (2001)
and *Spivs* (2004) have employed the Russian
Mafia in a similar way, as has Mexico's *Nicotina*
(2003). In the homeland, however, they see things
slightly differently.

Brat (*Brother*, 1997), the most celebrated
example of Russia's crime cinema, was criticized
for its sympathetic portrayal of a young hit man,
and its amorality was blamed on the influence of
Hollywood, the films of **Quentin Tarantino** in
particular. *Brat* was the work of arthouse film-
maker **Alexei Balabanov**, famous in the West
for the highly stylized and kinky *Of Freaks And
Men* (1998). In *Brat* he eschewed artfulness for
naturalism, observing rather than condemning
(or even commenting upon) a hero who, from
the very first scene, in which he stumbles into a
music video shoot, seems oblivious to the dangers
around him, as if shell-shocked by his experiences
as a soldier in the Chechen war, but he survives
through a simple (albeit warped) moral precept of
keeping his word. In the opinion of many critics, including Birgit Beumer in the book *Russia
On Reels*, *Brat* introduced a new character into
Russian cinema: "a hero who defends his own
'moral code' without following a social or legal
normative pattern: the killer". This killer hero
became an icon for a new cinema audience,
"a representative of a post-Soviet generation
unexpectedly released from the cage of moral
and social certainties" according to Professor
Julian Graffy in his review of the film in *Sight
And Sound*. If the "heroic" nature of its protagonist wasn't immediately obvious in *Brat*, then its
sequel left us in no doubt: the hit man was a
folklore hero, a Russian Robin Hood, fighting
for truth which, the hero concludes, will always

be more powerful than money.

The fact that *Brat* is the best-known Russian Mafia movie in the West may have something to do with the fact that Balabanov is an arthouse director: genre films rarely make their way out of their own country to the world cinema market. *Kings Of Crime* (1988), for instance, was the most successful Russian film ever on its release, attracting an audience of 70 million, but is still unavailable in any form outside the federation. Officially the first thriller about the Mafia, its success launched a new genre cinema in Russia, and author Anna Lawton argues in her book *Kinoglasnost* that its popularity was due to the fact

that "the genre has been a longtime favourite of the Soviet audiences who have enjoyed foreign movies".

Kings Of Crime was steeped in the iconography of foreign movies: the *femme fatale*, the dapper crime lord, the car chase and so forth. And it also didn't skimp on the requisite violence: an iron is placed on the stomach of one victim and switched on, while another unfortunate has to saw his own arm off to escape the handcuffs that are keeping him in a room that's filling up with carbon monoxide. The film wasn't so successful with critics who awarded it the "Three Ks" for "konjuncture, kommercialism and kitsch"

The late Sergei Bodrov Jr, star of *Brat* (1997)

Sergei Bodrov Jr

The charismatic star of *Brat* first acted in a film for his famous director dad in *Prisoner Of The Mountains* (1996). Junior made his own directorial debut with *Sisters* in 2001, a gangster movie in which he played a Mob boss whose daughters are threatened when he refuses to pay a debt. Tragically, Bodrov Jr was killed in an avalanche in 2002, while filming his next movie in the Caucasus mountains. He was 31.

at the Odessa Festival. Set in an unnamed Soviet republic, *Kings Of Crime* related the story of two warring Mafia families and treated police corruption as a mundane reality, with that old generic stand-by, the bent cop.

It was made during the period of *glasnost*, but since the fall of the Soviet Union, the meteoric rise of the Russian Mafia has only been matched by the rise of the Russian gangster film. A slew of tough-guys-and-torture movies have been produced in the last decade, including *Lifeline* (1996), a vicious crime drama in which the Mafia kidnaps a Frenchman to finalize a deal with Central Asian criminals. It was directed by Pavel Lungin, who also made *Tycoon* (2002), the most successful film in Russian film history – a classic rise-and-fall story of an ex-maths professor with a killer instinct for making money when the free market opens up. It was apparently based on the life of Russian billionaire **Boris Berezovsky**, and exposes institutionalized corruption at the heart of the federation's political system. The criminal himself seems disappointingly innocent in comparison, and *Tycoon* was one of many films, like *24 Hours* (2000), that romanticized the "new Russian".

The other strand that dominated post-Soviet cinema was the polar opposite: the vigilante movie. Movies such as *Anti-Killer* (2002), *The Refuse Collector* (2001), and *Riflemen Of The Vorishlov Regiment* (1999) starred Russian Charles Bronsons whose mission it was to clean up a town and take out the trash. What all these films shared was an apparent love of Tarantino, who was "devoured whole in Russia" according to writer Julian Graffy. They all suffered from the same complaint – Americanization (a common ailment whose symptoms are a rash of cars, guns and molls). There is one honourable exception, according to Graffy. *Bumer* (2003) dealt specifically with the problems of imports. The title referred to the Mercedes car driven by four gang members as they leave Moscow; significantly, and with more than a hint of an allegory, the import soon breaks down when it can't deal with the Russian roads.

The films that have stood out have often played with generic expectations, such as the arthouse hit *Moscow* (2000), which begins with a lecture about minks, a voice-over informing us that the European mink is weaker than its American counterpart, and why mating the two spells disaster. Director **Aleksandre Zeldovich** is clearly talking less about minks and more about movies. He consciously – sometimes over-consciously – avoids the hallmarks of the American genre, and tries to produce something indigenously Russian. As did director Sergei Solovev with the *glasnost*-era *Assa* (1988), a bizarre, burlesque tale about a rock group taking on the Mafia, in which a musician becomes part of a dangerous love triangle with a mob boss and his moll. Similarly strange was *Country Of The Deaf* (1997), director Valery Todorovsky's moving tale of a deaf girl, Ya Ya, and her friend, Rita, who become involved with the deaf Mafia (yes, really!) so that Rita can pay off her boyfriend's gambling debts. Another oddity was Polish director Juliusz Manchulski's comedy *Déjà vu* (1989) about a Chicago gangster who, in 1925, is requisitioned to Odessa to carry out a hit. He finds himself in all sorts of mistaken-identity escapades, particularly when he lands a part in the Odessa steps sequence of Eisenstein's *Battleship Potemkin*.

Ukrainian cinema has also reflected a new criminal reality, most notably in *A Friend Of The Deceased* (1997), a lugubrious hitman drama, in which contract killers are as freely available on the black market as dried milk. As one underworld figure pointedly comments "Friendship disappeared with our glorious Soviet past. Today, there's no friendship, there are only business relations." On the subject of the black market, a genuine oddity was thrown up in 2003, when Russia produced a gangster version of *Lord Of The Rings*, in a manner of speaking. **Dmitri Puchkov**, a former policeman, replaced the subtitles on pirated films with his own translations, turning the good characters, such as Frodo, into cops, and the bad orcs into Russian gangsters. Copies are now available on DVD at a knockdown price, but only on the black market, of course. Try eBay, if your Russian's up to scratch.

A Friend Of The Deceased (Priyatel pokoynika)
dir Vyacheslav Krishtofovich, 1997, Russ, 100m

Aleksandr Lazarev plays an unemployed translator whose wife leaves him. In a fit of depression he hires a hit man to take his life. When he falls in love with a prostitute and rediscovers his *joie de vivre*, however, he finds out that he can't cancel the contract and employs another killer to bump off the first one. Sounding like a recipe for a farce, *A Friend Of The Deceased* is a potent, mournful drama about the state of a nation where everyone is for sale.

Brat (Brother)
dir Alexei Balabanov, 1997, Russia, 96m

Danila Bagrov can find no work after leaving the army, and finds temporary employment with his older brother as a novice hit-man. The film hinges upon the performance of Sergei Bodrov Jr – charismatic, credible and childlike almost to the point of being autistic. As the young man who readily accepts the job of a part-time killer, he somehow manages to retain the audience's sympathy throughout. Everything about Bagrov is simple: he loves music, he keeps his word, he protects the weak and he, ahem, kills bad people. He's a metonym of a generation on auto-pilot.

Country Of The Deaf (Strana glukhikh)
dir Valery Todorovsky, 1997, Russ, 105m

A deaf stripper, Ya Ya, leads wide-eyed innocent, Rita, into an underworld entirely populated by the hard of hearing. A deaf don soon offers Rita a deal: "I need ears and you need money", and persuades her to accompany him on a perilous drug deal, to act as his early warning system. Quirky and painterly, *Country Of The Deaf* is a decidedly singular work of art.

Brat 2 (Brother 2)
dir Alexei Balabanov, 1999, Russ, 122m

There's more plot in the first five minutes than there was in the whole of *Brat*: an old war buddy of Bagrov's, Konstantin, is killed when he tries to help his big-league hockey-player brother, who's in trouble with the Chicago and Russian Mafia. Seeking revenge, Bagrov goes to the US. The sequel lacks the original's subtlety, often giving way to a cartoonish inelegance. It can't, or won't, maintain the distance between character and audience. Bagrov is unequivocally presented as a knight errant, and as such the film itself seems to endorse his xenophobic nationalism.

Moscow (Moskva)
dir Aleksandre Zeldovich, 2000, Russ, 139m

Plot is eschewed for a study of characters who populate the demi-monde of piano-playing, ballet-loving gangster Mike, in a film that lingers long in moments of meditative, narrative stasis, and is shot in a series of painterly frames, dominated by blazing scarlets and marine blues.

There are some generic elements, not least the moments of torture when a victim is buried in a mound of black-market food and produce, and another has his internal organs inflated by an air pump.

 Tycoon: A New Russian (Oligarkh)
dir Pavel Lungin, 2002, Russ, 128m

A detective investigates the apparent murder of one of Russia's powerful oligarchs, Plato Makovski, and his life is pieced together à la *Citizen Kane*. That's where the comparison ends; although it's no masterpiece, *Tycoon* does at least have the same *film à clef* fascination as *Scarface* (1933). It lacks the violence we expect from modern gangster movies: Plato is nothing more than a man with a scam, and the real villains are the corrupt bureaucrats in the Kremlin. This has led some critics to speculate exactly who financed *Tycoon* – maybe the answer lies in the title.

Scandinavia

The Danish film *The Olsen Gang* (1968) was such a huge hit on its release that it was remade in both Sweden and Norway.

However, there were important cultural changes made to the scripts, according to the book *Nordic National Cinema*. For instance, in a scene in the Danish original, one of the thieves is distracted by a porn mag, while in the Norwegian version his attention is grabbed by a bag of sweets – apparently that says a lot about the differences between the two countries.

The film was about a gang who bungle all attempts to steal a Bavarian work of art from a Danish museum, and it spawned six sequels in Sweden, and twelve in Denmark, including the most recent addition, *Olsen Gang Junior* in 2001. The basic pattern is that the gang comically fail in their mission each time and in each sequel the leader, Egon, emerges from prison with a new get-rich-quick scheme. Highlights of the series include *The Olsen Gang Sees Red* (1976) involving the theft of a Chinese vase for a baron who double-crosses them, *The Olsen Gang Outta Sight* (1977), where they steal from parking meters, and *The Olsen Gang Goes To War* (1978), where Egon and his gang steal plans by the EU to turn Denmark into a theme park called Daisy Land.

Denmark has also churned out a few 21st-century gangster flicks – marked by the inescapable Quentin Tarantino influence (surely the Esperanto of the world's cinema languages). **Lasse Spang Olsen**, founder of Denmark's first stunt-school, directed *In China They Eat Dogs* (1999), a comedy heist flick. It told the story of Arvid, a bank clerk, who enlists his criminal brother Harald to pull off a robbery in order to fund an IVF operation (needed by the wife of a bank robber whose attempted robbery Arvid had previously foiled). The movie was followed by a quirky but more formulaic prequel, *Old Men In New Cars* (2002), which upped the violence and gave Harald, the gangster brother, more of a star billing. The mooted heist, this time, is to fund a liver transplant. Are waiting lists on the Danish health service really that bad?

Released in between these two was another

comic gangster film, *Flickering Lights* (2000). Four small-time hoods – friends since childhood – go on the run after cheating a Copenhagen gang boss named Faroe (he comes from the Faroe Islands) out of a lot of kroner. Whilst hiding out in an old forest inn in the countryside, the good life gets to them: they are seduced by such bourgeois pleasures as house renovation, and open a restaurant. Directed by the screenwriter of *In China,* **Anders Thomas Jensen**, the film contained both violence and whimsy, and had something of the Dogme school to it.

Lilya 4 Ever
dir Lukas Moodyson, 2002, Swe/Den, 109m

Granted, this is not a gangster movie by anyone's definition. But Lukas Moodyson's follow-up to *Together* (2000) does concern one brutal aspect of organized crime. Lilya meets a young man in a small depressing town in Estonia. He persuades her to run away to Sweden, but when she gets to Stockholm she discovers that she's been sold into the white-slave trade. As she's locked up in a tower-block flat and forced into prostitution, *Lilya 4 Ever* becomes a sobering assessment of a grim reality behind the mythical façade of sexual liberation that has routinely been projected onto Sweden.

Swedish spivvery in the gangster comedy *Flickering Lights* (2000)

South Korea

In recent years South Korea has usurped Hong Kong as the powerhouse of Asian cinema, its home-grown product regularly defeating Hollywood blockbusters at the box office.

Its genre cinema is making a name for itself internationally, a fact underlined by the awarding of the Cannes jury prize to **Park Chan Wook**'s revenge tragedy *Old Boy* in 2004.

A number of theories for its cinematic domination have been mooted: the end of military dictatorship and censorship in 1992 has obviously played a large part, but author Kyung Hyun Kim believes that the upturn in Korean cinema was due, perversely, to the downturn in the Korean economy in 1997, which meant that venture capitalists replaced conglomerates like Daewoo and Samsung in funding Korean cinema. This in turn added a new edge and energy to the product itself. Tony Rayns points to the fact that South Korea is the only country in the world which has had an active filmmaker as its

Minister of Culture – **Lee Chang Dong**.

The government minister wrote and directed one of the first gangster films in the South Korean new wave – the decidedly unglamorous *Green Fish* (1997). The movie's hero, Mak–Tong, returns from national service to find that Seoul has changed beyond recognition and that his family is falling apart. As a way to make ends meet, he becomes a chauffeur for a mob boss whose moll becomes a source of increasing temptation. Set in one of the Korean cities that turned into a boom town seemingly overnight, Lee's expressed intention was to examine what happens to people in the midst of an economic "miracle". The answer, according to *Green Fish,* is only bad things.

As well as Park Chan Wook, the other auteur beloved by Western film distributors is **Kim Ki-Duk**, of whom writer Kyung Hyun Kim remarked "there has never been in the history of Korean cinema anyone whose body of work has been as controversial". Kim would earn that reputation for one shot alone in his S&M drama *The Isle* (2000), a shot which involved fish-hooks and female genitalia. However, it's not because of that squirm–inducing moment that the film is banned in Britain, but for a scene in which a fish is flayed alive and thrown back into the water. And just when critics thought they had got the measure of Kim as Korean cinema's resident sicko, he made *Spring, Summer, Autumn, Winter … And Spring* (2003), an almost wordless visionary meditation on nature, set in a Buddhist temple.

Kim is an ex-Marine who went to France to look at art and claims to have seen his first-ever film there – *Silence Of The Lambs*. He

The South Korean Minister of Culture's gangster movie, *Green Fish* (1997)

has described his approach to cinema as "kidnapping viewers and thrusting them into my world", which is not a dissimilar fate to the one that befalls the female lead in Kim's gangster movie *Bad Guy* (2002). She's a fresh-faced innocent coerced into prostitution by a besotted gangster who spies through a one-way mirror as she has sex for money. Kim himself explains things thus: "people look at the world of prostitutes and hoodlums and say 'this is trash, we need to clean this up'. But these people's lives deserve to be treated with respect."

The espionage thriller *Shiri* was the beginning of the Korean cinema boom in 1999; the most popular film ever made in Korea, it was soon usurped by **Park Chan Wook**'s *Joint Security Area* (2000) which lost the title a year later to the gangster film *Friend* (2001), seen by eight million people in Korea alone. Based on the experiences of writer/director Kwak Kyung-Taek, *Friend* documents the lives of four school buddies as their friendships fragment and turn ultimately to enmity when two go to college and the two who stay behind get caught up in the underworld battle for the local shark's-fin market.

According to an article in the *International Herald Tribune*, *Friend* was taken up by the so-called "386 generation", thirtysomething Koreans, who were born in the 1960s, went to college in the 1980s and who are more interested in family and friends than geopolitics and nuclear proliferation. The film's key lines – "what are friends for ?" and "am I just your servant ?" – became catchphrases amongst the cognoscenti in Seoul and other large cities. The film's popularity, according to Kwak, was because the audience had undergone similar experiences to his characters: "this is about friendship among Koreans".

There are very few female directors in the South Korean new wave, and the female characters of its movies are often seem being stripped,

raped or mutilated. So at least *My Wife Is A Gangster* (2001) was a refreshing change. Here the hobnail boot is on the other foot, as a foul-mouthed female Mob boss called Mantis abuses her new, hapless husband. He doesn't have a clue about her day job – despite the black eyes she regularly administers. A knock-about farce with sudden jolts of violence, *My Wife Is A Gangster* saw off *Shrek* at the Korean box office. Hollywood took notice and stuck

My Wife Is A Gangster (2001)

to its policy of "if you can't beat 'em, re-make them": Miramax bought the rights on the first day it was shown in Cannes. Reports of **Cameron Diaz** playing the potty-mouthed mobster are still, thankfully, unconfirmed.

Green Fish (Chorok mulgoki)
dir Lee Chang-Dong, 1997, South Korea, 111m

A low-key yet elegant directorial debut from Lee Chang-Dong, *Green Fish* maps a world of disappointment, bewilderment, powerlessness and moral ambiguity.

Friend (Chingoo)
dir Kwak Kyung-Taek, 2001, South Korea, 113m

"Memories are flashing in my mind like islands scattered in the sea. From now on, my rowing memories will visit the islands one by one." The first words we hear are from director Kwak Kyung-Taek, which signal his intention: this is not going to be another Asian action movie chock-full of cool, neon-lit hit men. Instead Kwak's film is a sincere examination of the meaning and keeping of friendship over the decades. Despite its lush photography, impressive themes and epic timescale, *Friend* is not quite the "Once Upon A Time In Korea" it promises to be.

My Wife Is A Gangster (Jopog manura)
dir Jin-gyu Cho, 2001, South Korea, 107m

A gang boss and confirmed spinster, Mantis, agrees to her dying sister's wishes to find a husband, and eventually settles on an unwitting civil servant. It's easy to see which elements Hollywood will hang onto in the mooted remake: the basic premise, the broad comic scenes as the gangster has a Pygmalion-style make-over to woo suitors, and the husband's continuing ignorance of his wife's day job. What Hollywood won't keep is the attempted eye-gouging and the moment when Mantis miscarries after a rival deliberately and repeatedly kicks her pregnant belly.

Bad Guy (Nabbeun namja)
dir Kim Ki-duk, 2002, South Korea, 100m

A minor hood, Han-gi, becomes obsessed with a girl he sees sitting on a bench, and engineers a situation in which she falls into his debt, owing him $10,000. The only way she can get the money is to sell her body, and Han-gi watches her through a one-way mirror as she plies her trade. Significantly, it's *his* pain the audience is meant to feel: he's persistently filmed in hues of envious green, as he watches the ruin of a woman he worships. Despite the lurid packaging, there's little sex or violence for fans of extreme cinema to gawp over – not a fish-hook in sight.

Thailand

It was a gangster film that reversed the fortunes of the ailing Thai film industry. *Dang Bireley And The Young Gangsters* (1997) became the most popular film ever made in Thailand and led a renaissance that saw a Thai film being released in the UK for the first time – the campathon *Iron Ladies* (2000) about a volleyball team entirely composed of gay men, transvestites, and trans-sexuals.

Hot on its high heels was the kitsch cow-boy spectacular *Tears Of The Black Tiger* (2000). **Wissit Sasanatieng**, the director of *Black Tiger*, was the screenwriter of *Dang Bireley,* while *Black Tiger*'s producer, **Nonzee Nimibutr**, directed it.

However, the two films would seem to have little in common – *Dang* is a violent, camp–free

retelling of the life of a 1950s gangster and James Dean lookalike, who had a photo of his hero in his locket and who named himself after his favourite soda, Bireleys. And just as Dang himself looked to America, so too does director Nimibutr, who brought his advertising background to bear on the film's visual stylings.

Apart from the US, the chief influence on Asian filmmakers is, of course, Hong Kong, and, as such, the **Pang Brothers** – Danny and Oxide – are the exemplars of current Asian cinema. The identical twins were born and brought up in Hong Kong but worked for twelve years in Thailand before they made their debut *Bangkok Dangerous* (2000), which they followed up with their internationally acclaimed horror movie *The*

Eye (2002). *Bangkok Dangerous,* about a deaf hit man, shows what can happen to Asian films that try too hard to ape the success and style of Hong Kong cinema – they lose their identity in the process. Even though it is one of only a few Thai films widely available in the West, its Hong Kong stylings render it instantly recognizable. Shot in familiar colours against familiar backdrops, peopled by familiar gunmen and punctuated by familiar violence, *Bangkok Dangerous* is edited so hard and so fast that it loses all sense of space and place, and the Thailand it reveals is a sort of Wong Kar Wai theme park, a neon-lit never-never land. It is not so much evidence of a national cinema as of simply another brand of the pan-Asian experience, like an indistinct restaurant which fuses recipes and ingredients from around the continent and produces a gloop of unknown origin that somehow manages to be both spicy and bland.

A fragment from the beautifully shot, floating world of *Last Life In The Universe* (2002)

A far more original movie came from the Thai director **Pen-ek Ratanaruang** in the form of the 2003 Thai/Japanese/Hong Kong co-production *Last Life In The Universe* (2003). Anyone familiar with Chris Doyle's impressionistic cinematography for Wong Kar Wai will instantly recognise his imprimatur, although Doyle forsakes the blurry neon he brings to Wong's Hong Kong in favour of washed-out airy blues and greens. The film's pace is carefully measured and tense. **Tadanabu Asano**, star of Takashi Miike's *Ichi The Killer,* plays Kenji, a Clark Kent type who works in a library and suffers from an allergy to fish.

Miike himself makes a late cameo in the movie, and Asano's acting career is referred to via an in-joke. In a nightclub, Kenji's blasé gangster brother assures a friend that he is not in any trouble for sleeping with his (Yakuza) boss's daughter: "You've seen too many Yakuza movies", he teases. Then, in the next scene, the camera briefly takes in a poster of *Ichi The Killer* in the library where Kenji works. Needless to say, Kenji's brother's confidence is horribly unfounded.

Dang Bireley And The Young Gangsters (2499 antapan krong muang)

dir Nenzee Nimibutr, 1997, Thai, 110m

It's difficult to tell why this film was so phenomenally popular in Thailand: it looks almost exactly like a Hollywood movie. Or maybe that's exactly the reason. There's very little that's involving or innovative in this biopic of Dang Bireley and his deadly rivalry with "Pu". The final scene tries to be Peckinpah-esque but ends up tacky. Not even good tacky.

Bangkok Dangerous
dir Pang Brothers, 2000, Thai, 105m

This Wong Kar Wai-inspired tale is about the impossibility of romance for a contract killer. A deaf-mute blows his big date when he can't control his killer instincts after a romantic interlude in a park is interrupted by muggers. His colleague Joe rashly and single-handedly takes revenge when his girlfriend is raped. Hong Kong cinema's tics and tropes – stylized slo-mo, the ties of brotherhood, scenes bathed in one primary colour – translate almost too easily to Thailand, with little sense of an indigenous cinema beyond something vaguely "pan-Asian".

Last Life In The Universe (Ruang rak noi nid mahasan)
dir Pen-ek Ratanaruang, 2003, Thai/Jap/HK, 92m

Arguably more Chris Doyle's film than Ratanaruang's, it's as if the movie is taken at such a slow pace purely to luxuriate in Doyle's beautiful desaturated colours and perfectly-proportioned frames. Not much gangster business, but there's a masterfully placid turn from Tadanobu Asano as a quiet librarian (with Yakuza credentials) which will surprise anyone familiar with his roles in *Ichii The Killer* or *Zatoichi*.

Wiseguy Wisdom: the information

James Gandolfini and crew in *The Sopranos*

Wiseguy Wisdom:
the information

You can't keep a good gangster down. The irrepressible ambition of the self-made mobster has made him a near-universally recognizable archetype of popular culture. This chapter – while by no means exhaustive – measures how far the tentacles of the gangster film have wrapped themselves around television, video games, the Internet, music and other media rackets.

Audio-visual

Gangsters on TV

Cold, sadistic violence is the oil that fuels the Mob-flick machine. This is hardly the sort of thing that attracts advertisers to TV networks; perhaps this is the reason why there have not been all that many gangster TV series.

Other movie genres have generated TV spin-offs aplenty – think *Buffy The Vampire Slayer* or *M*A*S*H*, or the hundreds of sci-fi shows that followed in *Star Trek*'s wake. Maybe the Tony Montanas and Al Capones of this world are just too big for such a small box (with the notable, triumphant exception of one **Tony Soprano**). Nevertheless, here is a selection of television's finest gang-related programmes (plus a few that aren't that great, but that you ought to know about).

City Of Men
2002

Featuring all the familiar faces from *City Of God* (2002), albeit with subtly reshuffled personalities and names, this is one of those rare instances of TV spin-off from a big-screen movie that actually works. Visually, it's a lot more inventive than the average TV series, with interpolated Super 8 moments, and even some animation. The violence of the movie has been turned down a notch or two, and the nine episodes (each a complete story in itself) concentrate more on personal relationships and teenage rites of passage. But there are still enough of the post-*Goodfellas* shocks and jolts to make the return to these *favellas* a very satisfying trip.

Gangsters
1975-78

This rare foray into the British underworld is a television landmark for a number of reasons: the explicitness of its violence, which led to a national debate; its precedent-setting casting of a member of an ethnic minority as its leading man; and its postmodern *coup de TV* of a conclusion.

Ahmed Khali played agent Khan who, in return for getting ex-SAS hardman and former nightclub-owner John Kline (**Maurice Colbourne**) off a manslaughter rap, facilitates Kline's infiltration of the Birmingham underworld. Set up as manager of the Maverick nightclub, Kline is drawn into drug wars and eventually Triad activity. This bemused Birmingham City Council, who took exception to the venal depiction of their fair city. The series has now become famous, or infamous, for a final episode that baffled and upset many viewers but which now seems like a precursor to *Twin Peaks*-style weirdness. Writer **Philip Martin** turned up

playing a number of characters, including a deadly W. C. Fields look a like called The White Devil, who killed Kline with magical powers. But things really took a turn for the postmodern when Kline was buried in a grave next to one reserved for Martin himself and "for all those who perished during the making of *Gangsters*". And even though that's the end of the hero, it wasn't the end of the episode, which piled twist upon twist until actress **Elizabeth Cassidy**, who played Kline's wife, seemed unable to take it any more. When she was told that mobster **Saeed Jaffrey** was actually an FBI agent, she laughed uproariously, looked straight into the camera and said "that's got to be the end"; with that she walked off. The scene cut quickly to another camera which was perched high in the gantries of a TV studio, and revealed that we'd been looking at a set all along (it wasn't that hard to guess). But even that was not the end of it. The real self-reflexive *coup de grâce* arrived when we cut to another scene, in Pakistan, where Martin was playing himself – a writer dictating his script to an elderly Asian gentleman sitting at a typewriter and to a group of enchanted youths who had evidently been listening to the story all along. With a flourish, Martin gathered his scripts and threw them into the crowd. At which point the frame froze and a caption appeared across the screen: "That's all folks". This was primetime television in the 1970s.

Gangbusters
1952

Before there was *The Untouchables,* there was *Gangbusters*. Originally starting out as a radio show in the 1940s, *Gangbusters* was introduced by hosts such as "Special Agent Clifton of the FBI". The TV series would relate the stories of public enemies such as **John Dillinger**, "who could bluff his way out of jail with a block of wood but was stopped by a lady in red". The cheap, stagey reconstructions would dramatize events like Dillinger's escape from jail and boasted some priceless dialogue:

> *Dillinger: What's for chow?*
> *Prison Guard: Stew.*
> *Dillinger: Again? It's that chef that ought to be hung.*

Lock, Stock And...
2000

To give it some credit, the movie *Lock, Stock And Two Smoking Barrels*, from which this spin-off was spun, was at least a lot more confident than the average Brit-flick of the time. If it's possible to leave aside the trying-too-hard screenplay, it did at least have intelligent editing, an interesting use of colour (a sort of neo-sepia) and a few slo-mo effects. But there's not much you need to know about this spin-off series. Looking like a flick-book edition of *FHM* magazine, it took the sentimental spivvery of *Only Fools And Horses* and steroidally inflated it into a tumescent, noisome and geezerly monster. Amazingly, there are six whole episodes (plus a pilot) of this RADA cockney rubbish.

The Long Firm
2004

The publication of **Jake Arnott**'s debut novel coincided with the *Lock, Stock*-inspired boom in British gangster fiction and fashion, but was very different from other manifestations of British geezer chic, and not only in its superior quality.

The Long Firm exposed the homoerotic subtext of machismo, pointing out what was really hard

Mark Strong, as Harry Starks, in *The Long Firm* (2004): as shadowy and slippery as the 60s London underworld that spawned him

about hard men. As **Quentin Crisp** once put it, "some roughs are really queer; some queers are really rough". The rough queer in Arnott's novel was a 1960s Kray-a-like flash by the name of Harry Starks, whose story was told from the perspective of five people who had come in contact with him and, occasionally, his white-hot poker.

Four of the novel's five different chapters were filmed: Harry's brush with the gentry in the form of gay aristocrat Lord Thursby (**Derek Jacobi**); his involvement with a fading starlet with a big mouth, Ruby Ryder (**Lena Headey**); and the start of his downfall when he becomes embroiled with drug dealer Jimmy (**Phil Daniels**); and, while in jail, Starks' scamming of naïve sociologist Lenny (**Shaun Dingwall**). The only chapter that didn't make the cut was the first one, involving a rent boy and the aforementioned poker. Apparently it wasn't excised because of censorship issues, but simply because only four parts had been commissioned.

The difficulty for award-winning playwright **Joe Penhall** and actor **Mark Strong** was to put flesh and bones on an elusive character who was something to everybody. The fact that the televised version of Harry was both man and monster, snake and charmer, set on his own slightly pathetic trajectory, is testimony both to the dexterity of Strong's acting and Penhall's writing.

The Sopranos
1999–

With Italian-American gangsters all played-out and washed-up in the cinema, having been organizing crime for almost as long as the movies have existed, it was a young pretender of a TV series that taught Hollywood a lesson in how to deal with the Mob. *The Sopranos* started with a jokey premise: a *capo*, Tony Soprano (**James Gandolfini**) visits a psychiatrist, Dr Melfi (**Lorraine Bracco**) because he has panic attacks and a mother who despises him.

The series, however, went deeper into the woods very rapidly. Dr Melfi was drawn into Tony's orbit after she was raped in a car park and sought revenge; she ended up having to see a

shrink herself (an occasional cameo role played by the director **Peter Bogdanovich**). Tony's long-suffering wife Carmela finally threw him out of the house, after almost giving into temptation herself with local priest Father Phil. Tony's mother, Livia, tried to have him killed; Tony's nephew became a junkie psychopath (with aspirations to be a writer); and worse still, his daughter, Meadow, wanted to be a lawyer. And that's only half the family…

The initial idea of the show's creator **David Chase** was to write about his own relationship with his late, formidable mother, but he transferred his neuroses to a gangster when he realized there would be very little interest in a series about a television executive and his mum. Chase had been a fan of Mob movies ever since seeing *The Public Enemy* on television, and *The Sopranos* is littered with references intended to bring out the film detective in the clued-up viewer.

The most obvious connection is with *Goodfellas*, which Chase has described as the last great gangster film. He borrowed a few of its actors: Lorraine Bracco, of course, played Henry Hill's wife, Karen, while **Michael Imperioli** (Tony's nephew Christopher) played Spider, the bartender who gets shot in the foot by Joe Pesci's Tommy De Vito, and eventually shot dead. (In a satisfying moment for reference-checkers, Christopher shot a bakery assistant in the foot in one stand-out *Sopranos* episode). Even Ray Liotta was asked to take part in the first series, but refused the offer, worried that he'd be stereotyped.

The Sopranos wouldn't be the same without its *Godfather* influence, however; it's a movie that's referred to, discussed and imitated right through all five series. The wiseguys of *The Sopranos* employ the term "sleeps with the fishes", re-enact scenes from the movie, and debate the

---

"Sopranalysise this"

Which came first: *Analyse This* or *The Sopranos*? Both came out at around the same time, and both have the same premise of a gangster visiting a shrink – played in *Analyse* by Robert De Niro and Billy Crystal respectively. The sequel, *Analyse That*, even featured a *Sopranos*-like TV show about a suburban Mob boss, which is so unauthentic that De Niro has to give the cast lessons in realism. However, both De Niro and Crystal maintain that any resemblance to *The Sopranos* is entirely incidental. *Analyse This* had its funny moments. *Analyse That* didn't.

Tony Soprano (James Gandolfini; left) shows us exactly what kind of tasteless patterned shirt you wear if you're a New Jersey Mob boss

merits of DVD over laserdisc. Hitman Silvio Dante does a "Moe Greene special" – he shoots a victim through the eye (as seen in the climactic murders in *The Godfather*).

With pleasing symmetry, it transpired that Mafiosi themselves were regular viewers of the TV series after the FBI taped a conversation between a New Jersey *capo* and his enforcer. **Joseph "Tin Ear" Scalfano** and **Anthony Rotondo** were recorded having a discussion about the realism of the series. "Is that meant to be us?" asked Scalfano. "Where do they get their information from?" To which his boss replied: "Every show you watch, you pick up somebody.

One week it was Corky. One week it was – well from the beginning – it was Albert G." "Tin Ear" and Rotondo are not alone in their appreciation of *The Sopranos*' authenticity. Henry Hill himself is an admirer and has only one major reservation: he didn't buy the episode in which the Mob tried to help Christopher with his heroin problem by staging an intervention. In real life, he would have been "whacked". The only people who are not so keen on *The Sopranos* are the **National Italian American Foundation**; in an echo of the problems *The Godfather* had with the Italian-American Civil Rights League, the Foundation have claimed the series perpetuates damaging

The harshest critics

"Tin Ear" and Rotondo are not the only mobsters who have passed judgement on their fictional counterparts. From **Humphrey Bogart** to **Chow Yun-Fat**, young hoods have always tried to ape the style and dress sense of their screen idols, although **Al Capone** was not so impressed, claiming that gangster movies were a useless influence that only made young people want to act tough.

Michael Caine has recalled discussing *Get Carter* with a South London villain who liked the film but complained that Carter didn't have a family life, and that family was important in gangland. Caine gently explained that Carter wasn't seen with his family because his brother had just been killed, and that was the point of the movie.

However, there is one firm favourite with wise guys, according to a report in *The Independent* newspaper in 2001, which quoted ex-Pennsylvania cop Frank Friel as saying that every mobster's house that he'd raided all had the same video... a cherished copy of *The Godfather*.

called *The Scarface Mob* (1959) and based upon **Eliot Ness'** autobiography; but as the series progressed it soon left the reality behind. While the real Untouchables disbanded after **Al Capone**'s prosecution, their fictional counterparts, led by **Robert Stack**, stayed together to fight Capone's successor **Frank Nitti** and then almost every villain who'd been dubbed Public Enemy No.1: Ma Barker, Mad Dog Coll and Dutch Schultz, to name just three criminals that the real Ness never investigated.

With its **Walter Winchell** voice-over and shocking-for-its-time violence, *The Untouchables* was popular with audiences and unpopular with the FBI and sections of the Italian–American community. In answer to their critics, the series added a disclaimer and reduced the number of villains of Italian extraction. **Barbara Stanwyck** joined the series briefly as a member of the Bureau Of Missing Persons, as did original moll Joan Blondell (of *The Public Enemy*) and future stars **Lee Marvin**, **Harry Dean Stanton**, **Robert Duvall** and **Robert Redford**. The success of the 1987 film version led to an ill-advised new series in 1993 that was untouched by either success or interest.

stereotypes, and called for a boycott in 2001.

In 2004 *The Sopranos* won the prestigious Emmy award for Best Drama – the first cable show ever to do so. Some critics, however, argue that the success of the self-referential *Sopranos* heralds the end of Rico, Capone and the traditional gangster: when TV gangsters refer ceaselessly to movie gangsters, where is there left for the genre to go, other than down the postmodern plughole in ever-decreasing circles?

The Untouchables
1959–63

In its first manifestation *The Untouchables* was a two-part drama (and eventually a feature film)

Wacky Races
1969–70

In car number seven, The Bulletproof Bomb, racing against Professor Pat Pending, Peter Perfect, Penelope Pitstop and, of course, Dastardly and Muttley, were the smallest gangsters ever to grace a sedan – Clyde and **The Ant Hill Mob**, in Hanna Barbera's unique homage to Blake Edwards' **The Great Race** (1965).

Video games

Are the movies just that little bit too "vicarious" for you? Well, thanks to the wonders of bits, bytes and pixels you can now indulge your inner hoodlum without leaving your couch...

The Getaway: Black Monday
PlayStation

"She's had more pricks than a second-hand dartboard" is the ear-catching opening line of this video game – a clear signpost that we're in mockney territory and are with the Jack the Lads who populate **Guy Ritchie**'s febrile imagination. However, as the camera pans out we discover who we're not in the company of thieves, but inside a police car. It's a knowing, witty moment, from a team of designers who've probably seen every bad British gangster film of the 21st century.

As the scene ends we take on the character of Sergeant Mitchell (a possible reference to the *EastEnders* hardmen?) as he raids a housing estate armed to the gills; as the game progresses we shift into the shape of Eddie, an ex-boxer who's taking a beating after a failed heist, and petty thief Sam. Each level has its own scenario, played out by actors, filmed on motion-capture and animated (or rather re-animated, as motion capture still has the (black) magical powers to transform humans into zombies). The most impressive part of *The Getaway* (and its prequel) is the virtual London which players can drive or walk through: almost every landmark, building and retail outlet on major roads is present and correct, from Nelson's Column to The Sock Shop. Just don't expect many side-roads, though.

The Godfather
PC; PlayStation; Xbox

Marlon Brando's last acting role wasn't in a movie at all, it was in a video game. Reprising the role of Don Corleone, or rather supplying Corleone's voice, Brando was joined by most of the original cast, with the notable exception of Al Pacino, who apparently refused to have any part in the enterprise. The executive producer of the game, David DeMartini, insisted that he had met Francis Ford Coppola, who gave not only his support, but also access to his private library. Yet according to a report in *The Observer* newspaper, **Francis Ford Coppola** claimed that he knew nothing about the interactive adaptation of his masterpiece. The problem of just how a stately paced epic like *The Godfather* can be turned into a fast and furious shoot-'em-up has been solved by using only key elements from the original. The game has characters and a story of its own which interact with the movie's narrative. So the game includes key episodes such as Sonny's murder, while minor roles such as Paulie are given back stories but, just as importantly, players can roam freely in the *Godfather* universe.

Grand Theft Auto: San Andreas
PC; PlayStation; Xbox

Heavily criticized for its violence, *Grand Theft Auto* made more money on its first day of sales than the opening of any film in the UK ever. Whereas its prequels, *Grand Theft Auto* and *Vice City*, were loosely based on *Goodfellas* and *Scarface* (1983 vintage), *San Andreas* is straight out of Compton, like an interactive version of *Menace II Society*.

And if the movie connections weren't obvious enough, one of the first voices we hear is that of **Samuel L. Jackson** as a cop who takes our protagonist for a ride. He's joined later by **James Woods**, **Peter Fonda** and **Chris Penn**, who voice just some of the 500 speaking parts, with 100,000 lines of dialogue between them. They usually make an appearance in the scenes that interrupt the play, interludes of high melodrama as, for instance, two brothers fighting in the shadow of their mum's grave. The cussing we expect from a gangsta movie is also present. *San Andreas* is entirely populated by mother-fuckers, it appears.

The game is set in a virtual South Central LA called Los Santos and we play Carl Johnson, a member of the Grove Street Crew, embroiled in a deadly turf war with the gangs of Ballaz. Cue the predictable drive-by shootings and armed robbery. But what's most impressive about *San Andreas* is the right to roam: players have the freedom of the city, and not just Los Santos but San Fransisco-clone San Fierro and Vegas-alike Las Venturas. Each city is virtually perfect, a scale model that invites total immersion.

Which means we can hijack cars, beat employees of a fried-chicken emporium (slogan: "Taste The Cock") to a bloody pulp, talk to/abuse strangers on the street and gain weight. On the positive side, we can go for a swim, have a haircut, get a girlfriend, learn to fly a plane and parachute from it. *Grand Theft Auto* is about the closest the industry has come to attaining the holy grail: a movie you can both watch and play. It's a shame that so much time, talent and design has been spent on a game which is essentially about car-jacking, cussing and killing people.

Mafia
PC; PlayStation; Xbox

It's not surprising that someone has made a game from the archetypal 1930s gangster film. After all, a simple story such as *Little Caesar* plays out like a video game itself, presenting its hero with a series of obstacles and opponents that he must overcome to get to the top. Starring the original Super Mario Brother, **Edward G. Robinson**'s mission is to progress to the next level: level one is to go to the city, level two is to join a gang, level three is to take over the gang and level four is to take over the city. *Mafia* is set in the same milieu as *Little Caesar*, wherein every man wears a fedora and every car is a jalopy. But it starts with a different scenario.

Our screen surrogate is Tommy, a hard-working taxi driver who is forced at gunpoint by two hoods to help them flee from the police and take them back to their boss, Salieri. When Tommy, with a little help from us, has completed his mission, he's made the inevitable offer he can't refuse. After ferrying passengers around the city of Lost Heaven, Tommy joins the gang and gets up to all sorts of mischief – rubbing out the opposition and being chased by police across rooftops. However, unlike *Grand Theft Auto* and *The Getaway*, *Mafia* feels like an old-fashioned arcade game, has no stars making cameo appearances, and despite its filmic influences, is the least movie-like of the three. We'll just have to wait until *Little Caesar* is available on Playstation.

Film soundtracks

Here are ten examples of the best background music a wiseguy could wish for to accompany his extorting, threatening, bootlegging or whacking. As dodgy East End don Harry Flowers said in *Performance*, "I like that. Turn it up."

City Of God
EastWest

Director **Fernando Meirelles** deployed samba and funk thrillingly over montages of gang wars (which arguably serve only to fuel the vicarious thrill of watching the street fighters in action). Most of the CD is made up of new material from **Antonio Pinto** and **Ed Cortez**, whose vibrant cod-Seventies funk is in keeping with both the period setting and the director's hyperactive editing rhythms. For the rest of the soundtrack Meirelles took the Scorsese route of re-energising classic tracks with selections from **Wilson Simonal** and Brazilian funk legend **Tim Maia**.

However, the most interesting inclusion is a song, "Convite Para Vida", by sometime actor **Seu Jorge**. Jorge had spent a few years on the streets of Rio until he was spotted in a nightclub and invited to join a theatre troupe. In 1993 he formed a band called Farofa Carioca, whose live shows became the talk of the town thanks to the innovative participation of jugglers and trapeze artists. Their first, and last, record *Moro No Brazil* was a hit both in Brazil and the Far East (Jorge really was big in Japan). Even though his follow-up, a solo album called *Samba Esporte Fino*, was hailed as a classic, it was only when he played Knockout Ned in *City Of God* that Jorge came to worldwide attention. This led directly to a role in **Wes Anderson**'s *The Life Aquatic With Steve Zissou*, in which he stole the film with his soulful renditions of David Bowie classics in Portuguese. His latest, also highly acclaimed, album *Cru*, contains an Elvis cover, "Don't", and a song, "Mania de Peitão", which warns about the perils of breast implants.

Get Carter
Cinephile

Number one with a bullet. Composed by **Roy Budd** when he was just 24, it wasn't even his first soundtrack. Budd was something of an early starter: he'd given his first public performance on the piano at the age of 6. He supplied the music to over fifty film and TV productions, and spent the last months of his life working on a soundtrack to **Lon Chaney**'s silent masterpiece *The Phantom Of The Opera*, which he'd spent £350,000 of his own money to buy and restore. He died of a brain hemorrhage a month before he was due to conduct its world premiere, at the age of 46.

The main theme is an oddly effective mix of a few haunting notes and a funky, almost rickety rhythm, which perfectly sums up the experience of taking a British Rail train in the early 1970s. Which was the point, as the music was composed to accompany Carter's rail journey to Newcastle. Those few baleful notes were only intended to be used once, over the main theme, but when director **Mike Hodges** heard the track, he realized that he could use them as a motif all the way through. They add a level of melancholy to the brutal proceedings and provide a subtle reminder to the audience about Carter's motives, the sad events that propel him onwards. Hodges has since credited Budd with making his protagonist more sympathetic, and that simple, spare refrain certainly evokes a humanity which Carter cannot, or will not, reveal. Members of the audience with keen ears will notice a slight variation to the theme – the title track was played on piano strings which had been plucked and then treated with reverb; but for the motif, Hodges asked his composer to play the same notes on a harpsichord, to create a more poignant, resonant effect. It's a small thing, but it's that astute attention to detail that distinguishes *Get Carter* as both a soundtrack and a movie – it's why both are classics.

The Godfather
Silvascreen

Nino Rota and his theme tune, with its plaintive solo trumpet, is arguably as responsible for *The Godfather*'s success as Coppola, Brando and Pacino. And, just like them, the composer came close to being sacked. Would *The Godfather* be the phenomenon it is today if producer **Robert Evans** had won the day and replaced Rota with the *Pink Panther* composer Henry Mancini?

Goodfellas
WEA

Inspired by the use of "I'm Forever Blowing Bubbles" in *The Public Enemy*, Martin Scorsese alchemically fused popular music and film imagery in a way that no one – not even Quentin Tarantino – has since. *Mean Streets* boasts probably the greatest, most electrifying use of rock songs on a film soundtrack: there is nothing in cinema history to rival the *frisson* induced by the opening bars of "Jumping Jack Flash" which accompany De Niro's cocksure, slow-motion entry into Tony's bar. Sadly, the soundtrack is unavailable, but at least *Goodfellas* is on CD, with

Bobby Darin's "Beyond The Sea", Tony Bennett's "Rags To Riches", and Cream's "Sunshine Of Your Love", but unfortunately none of the medley that provides the jittery, heady soundtrack to Henry Hill's coke-fuelled, nerve-jangled last day as a wiseguy.

Guys And Dolls
Intersound

It's a close-run thing between this and *Bugsy Malone* for the title of best gangster musical in the West, but any soundtrack that has **Marlon Brando** singing "Luck Be A Lady" has to be a winner.

The Italian Job
MCA

Worthy of merit just for the maddeningly catchy "Get A Bloomin' Move On" with its singalong chorus of "We're The Self Preservation Society", **Quincy Jones**' song is as memorable and as iconic as the line "you were only supposed to blow the bloody doors off".

Once Upon A Time In America
Rykodisc

A rare example of the score preceding the filmmaking. **Ennio Morricone**'s music was so integral to Sergio Leone's concept for *Once Upon A Time* that the composer was asked to complete the soundtrack before filming had begun, so that the director could play the score while the scenes were being shot. The result is one of the most elegant examples of cinematic symbiosis. Morricone's themes are as elegiac and dreamy as Leone's images and, vital for a film about memory, extremely memorable.

Reservoir Dogs
MCA

Taking his cue from Scorsese, Tarantino's use of the breezily inoffensive "Stuck In The Middle With You" as a counterpoint to the grotesque torture on screen was a stroke of genius. The director once claimed that he wouldn't have made *Reservoir Dogs* if he hadn't got permission to use the Steelers Wheel track. QT would have made a great DJ, so it's not surprising that the retro-chic soundtrack album sold by the bucket-load. But the CD also came with some welcome extras. Track one features Steve Wright laconically introducing *Little Green Bag,* while track eight is the considered discussion about the true meaning of Madonna's "Like A Virgin".

After *Dogs* it soon became very modish for hip films to include snatches of dialogue on their CD soundtracks. The albums for *Natural Born Killers, Clerks, Higher Learning,* and of course, *Pulp Fiction* all boasted key lines from their respective movies. *Reservoir Dogs,* though, wasn't the first soundtrack to do this, nor was QT entirely responsible for it here. The credit must go to **Kathy Nelson** who supervised the album's production and had first used dialogue on the *The Fisher King* CD, which included the rantings of DJ **Jeff Bridges**.

Satya

Broadway and Hollywood have nothing on Bollywood in terms of churning out musicals, and many Indian DVDs have a menu that allows the viewer to jump straight to the musical numbers, which has the effect of making it a DVD which doubles as a soundtrack CD with pictures. *Deewar* and **R. D. Burman**'s score for *Sholay* are both recommended, but *Satya* is the pick of the bunch, if only for "Gholi Maar", a rousing, Rabelaisian chorus of drunken gangsters, and a plaintive solo number, "Bheega Pani", that is mournfully in keeping with the tone of **Ram Gopal Varma**'s epic, and inventively uses rain as a percussion instrument. The songs are not available on CD, but are easy to download via the numerous websites that sell music from Bollywood hits.

Superfly
Rhino

The soundtrack was often the only authentic element of many blaxploitation flicks, and the true legacy of this wave is the music of artists such as **James Brown** and **Curtis Mayfield**, who combined soul, politics and pleasure in a way that the films rarely did. This is particularly true of *Superfly*.

It's said that **Curtis Mayfield** watched a rough cut of the film and was so unhappy with what he saw that he decided to write songs that would act as a counter to **Gordon Parks Jr**'s lurid, glamorized images, which he regarded as an advert for cocaine. The result is two songs, "Pusherman" and "Freddie's Dead", which according to playwright Caryl Phillips "remain to this day among the most potent anti-drug anthems to the sickness near the heart of American life".

But there is no Nancy Reagan-style, just-say-no worthiness. Lyrics like "Another junkie plan/ Pushin' dope for the man" were accompanied by groovesome, low-slung bass licks and kicking guitar riffs. Coming from the gospel tradition, Mayfield understood that a message always needs a good tune. *Superfly* is not just the greatest instance of a soundtrack being far better than the movie, but one of the most savvy, potent and groovy examples of agit-pop.

Websites

The Internet is a film buff's paradise. There are thousands of general cinema-related sites, of course, but also a few shady back-alleys, where you'll find all sorts of arcane gangster-related goings-on.

General film sites

Action Web
www.geocities.com/Hollywood/6648/index.html

John Woo and Tsui Hark are royally served here, with filmographies, biographies and all the latest news, including the results of the Chow Yun-Fat lookalike competition.

Bugsy's Club
www.bugsysclub.com/club/community/info_glossary.html

Poker site with an amusing glossary of gangster slang. Elsewhere on its pages is a surprising amount of historical information about real-life gangsters Bugsy Siegel, Al Capone, John Dillinger, Bonnie and Clyde, John Gotti and more.

Crime Culture
www.crimeculture.com

A good starting place with links to other sites and a particularly authoritative article about the origins of the genre.

eBay
www.ebay.com

Where would we be without eBay? Perfect not just for

discovering classics that have only been committed to VHS and since deleted, it's also the place to find the latest DVD releases from Hong Kong, Korea and Thailand.

Film Site
www.filmsite.org/crimefilms.html

An excellent overall cinema site, it also has a good introductory essay about the origins of the gangster flick.

Gangster Slang
www.sginc31.narod.ru/humor/slang.htm

Learn how to speak wise guy. Soon you too could be slipping phrases such as "Tell your moll to hand over the mazuma" into everyday conversation.

The Hong Kong Movie Database
www.hkmdb.com

A comprehensive resource for information on over 10,000 films and 15,000 people, it also offers a forum and review section. Essential.

Original Gangsters
www.dirtysquatters.com/evocrim/og/

Dedicated to classic gangster movies, this site offers a Top 10 and appreciations of star gangsters, support gangsters, molls and directors.

The Ultimate Gangster And Crime Film Website
www.geocities.com/~mikemckieman/

Features an A–Z of movies, a section on films that focus on Prohibition, a list of famous actors who played gangsters and a handy links page.

The Unofficial Tommy Gun Page
www.nfatoys.com/tsmg/

Here the story is told of General John Thompson's deadly invention. It comes complete with appropriate sound effects.

Movie sites

The Godfather Trilogy
www.jgeoff.com/godfather.html

...or "the website you can't refuse". A work of true fandom, each part of the trilogy gets its own site, with an array of quotes, trivia, photos, transcripts, scene descriptions, location details, and "the don's office floor plan". It also has a page entitled "What's with the ghostly image at Don Vito's funeral?", which features a video capture of a woman's face which appears inexplicably and quite spookily on Michael Corleone's suit. See for yourself.

The Miller's Crossing Home Page
www.geocities.com/%7Emikemckiernan/mcfrontpage.html

Includes the full script, a glossary, a shot-by-shot analysis of the tommy-gun scene, and of course, a page about trivia – which informs us that five hats were worn by Gabriel Byrne during the making of the film.

Scarface
www.scarface1983.com

The first thing you notice is the Latino panpipe music, which assails you every time you enter a new page. There are clips from the soundtrack, trivia, quotes, and an inventory of the differences between the cinema release and the TV version; it also offers us a chance to buy *Scarface* action figures.

People sites

The Humphrey Bogart Website
www.bogart-tribute.net/index.shtml

Features audio clips, trivia games, urban legends, and a gallery of all the cartoon characters that have been based upon Bogie.

James Cagney: One Of A Kind
www.meredy.com/cagney/

Has a trivia game, biography, filmography and MP3s of the star singing "Yankee Doodle Dandy".

Henry Hill
www.goodfellahenry.com

The official website of Henry Hill proves that the real-life protagonist of *Goodfellas* is no longer living like a schnook under the Federal Witness Protection Program. The site gives us the opportunity to buy his book, read his bio, catch up on the latest Mob arrests in a news section, and see his recent photos. We're also invited to e-mail Henry.

Jean-Pierre Melville
www.jeanpierremelville.com

As you might expect, JPM gets a stylish, grey-hued website, which has the standard-issue biography and filmography (and is in French).

A Tribute to Edward G. Robinson
www.moderntimes.com/egr

Does exactly what it says on the tin, with a biography, a filmography and photographs.

Martin Scorsese
www.scorsesefilms.com

Martin Scorsese gets the web treatment with a well-designed compilation of articles, quotes and photos. There's a similar experience offered by www.martin-scorsese.net.

Quentin Tarantino
www.godamongdirectors.com

You'd think that Tarantino, and the obsessive interest he generates, was made for the Internet. However, many of the pages/shrines are now out of date or defunct, which tells you a lot about either the Internet boom or the Tarantino boom, or both. Godamongdirectors seems to have official approval from the man himself as being "the coolest" website and is mainly a compendium of interviews, forum discussions, and screenplays. www.tarantino.info has all the latest news, but disappointingly refers to www.imdb.com for the information on individual films. Tarantino's own company's site www.abandapart.com hasn't even updated its information on their boss, informing us that he's currently shooting a film called *Kill Bill*.

Left: the so-called "Godamongdirectors" Quentin Tarantino, in one of his forays in front of the camera (and in *Reservoir Dogs* suit), during the shooting of Robert Rodriguez's *From Dusk Til Dawn* (1996)

Festivals

Cognac Festival Du Film Policier
France, April

Created in 1982 to showcase any film from the mystery/thriller genre, "a four day event which promises a lot of whodunits" and, possibly to prove that there's more to the town than a warming spirit. Films are screened in and out of competition, both long and short, American and European, old and new.

Crime Scene
UK, July

Organized by Adrian Wootton, who created the Shots In The Dark Festival, this annual London shindig has the same mix of novelists and filmmakers, retrospectives and premieres, but has yet to have the defining moment that graced Shots In The Dark, and it is unlikely ever to have, unless Wootton unearths the new Tarantino.

Michinoku International Mystery Film Festival
Japan, October

Based in the city of Morioka and boasting a mixture of local and foreign films, a competition for first-time directors, and a retrospective based on a theme, eg spy movies.

Mystfest (International Mystery Film Festival)
Italy, June

Centred around the city of Cattólica, Mystfest is "open to mystery, crime, detective and thriller films".

Noir In Festival
Italy, December

Based in the ski resort of Courmayeur in the Italian Alps. Since the 1990s, it has been dedicated to the best of cinema and literature in thriller, mystery, spy, science fiction and *noir*. Twelve of the year's best films are shown and prizes are awarded for best film and best performance. There is also a short-film season and a retrospective of the works of directors such as Hitchcock, John Woo and Sam Raimi.

The Quentin Tarantino Film Festival
US

For five years, the Austin Film Society annually showed movies programmed by QT – the now familiar blend of Hollywood B-movies, Eurotrash, martial arts and blaxploitation; evenings were often given themes, like 2001's "Bunch-of-guys-on-a-mission war movie" night.

Shots In The Dark
UK

The now sadly defunct crime festival became legendary for one evening in May 1994. Quentin Tarantino had shown *Reservoir Dogs* for the first time in the UK the previous year and had programmed a blaxploitation bill for the festival. He was due to make a guest appearance and introduce a film of his choice, though prospective punters were told that the movie in question was definitely not going to be the director's latest offering. Of course, this was a fib. Shots In The Dark was the first place to show *Pulp Fiction* outside the Cannes Film Festival, and Tarantino conducted a Q&A session afterwards that continued until the small hours of the next morning, and has become folklore amongst film nerds.

Books

Biographies

Capone
John Kobler (Penguin, 1976)

Kobler's superlative book is not just a biography of the most famous gangster of the twentieth century, but also one of a city. With a novelist's eye for detail, Kobler gives each supporting player a life of his own: Dion O'Banion, Little Hymie Weiss, Big Jim Colosimo and their brethren are all given due back story and a set of facts and statistics to support their case studies. Kobler devotes a similar forensic attention to his leading man, documenting Capone's political connections, modus operandi, public image and neuro-syphilis, leaving no stone unturned. All written in the vernacular of the genre, *Capone* is a hard-boiled biography.

Francis Ford Coppola: A Film-maker's Life
Michael Schumacher (Bloomsbury, 1999)

Exhaustively researched, particularly the section on *The Cotton Club*, this book covers areas which are not extensively detailed in Peter Cowie's *The Godfather Book*, such as the reason why Marlon Brando was given a belt by the rest of the cast with the words "Mighty Moon King" engraved on the buckle.

Humphrey Bogart: Take It And Like It
Jonathan Coe (Bloomsbury, 1991)

Ever since his novel *What A Carve Up*, it's been clear that Jonathan Coe is a film lover, and even though this biography of Bogie is a slim volume, Coe cherry-picks the most relevant anecdotes and stories, and presents a cogent argument about the contradictions in Bogart's public and private personae throughout the photo-packed pages.

James Cagney: A Celebration
Richard Schickel (Little Brown, 1985)

Not intended as a straightforward biography, but as "an essay that intends to analyse a screen character", the veteran critic of *Time Magazine* thankfully strikes the right balance between Cagney's life story and his own opinion.

Jean-Pierre Melville: An American In Paris
Ginette Vincendeau (BFI, 2003)

The first major study of the French director in the English language could easily be dry as dust, but Vincendeau's comprehensive (and easily comprehensible) analyses of Melville's movies are shot through with biography, on-set stories and the director's public spats with François Truffaut.

How I Made A Hundred Movies In Hollywood And Never Lost A Dime
by Roger Corman (Random House, 1990)

Corman's brief but entertaining co-written autobiography averages one good anecdote for each film. The self-effacing Corman is more interesting when discussed by others; Corman manages to make the production of exploitation movies like *Night Call Nurses* seem so bloody sensible.

Little Caesar: A Biography Of Edward G. Robinson
Alan L. Gansberg (New English Library, 1983)

Gansberg's introduction focuses on Edward G. Robinson's appearance at the House Un-American Activities Committee, and the part that Ronald Reagan played in his downfall. It's the HUAC section that's the strongest part of this well-researched biography.

An Open Book
John Huston (Knopf, 1980)

When a friend read Huston's autobiography they allegedly remarked, "That's great, John, but who's it about?" Huston's memoir not only skimps on the more colourful aspects of his life, but his contribution to the gangster genre scarcely gets a look-in. *High Sierra*, *Key Largo*, and *The Asphalt Jungle* get about half a page each.

Scorsese On Scorsese
Ian Christie & David Thompson, eds (Faber, 1989)

The quintessential book about Scorsese. Everything you want to know, from his early years – replete with alarming anecdotes such as his watching a baby fall from a high building in Little Italy – to how he created a set the size of a small town in Rome for *Gangs Of New York*. Judiciously edited (a real feat considering how much the director talks), the interview is accompanied by plot synopsis and cast and crew details of every film Scorsese has made up to 2003.

Sergio Leone: Something To Do With Death
Christopher Frayling (Faber, 2000)

The one book to buy about Sergio Leone. Frayling's passion, humour, intelligence and friendship with Leone are in evidence on every page of this critique/biography. The planning, production and the different versions of *Once Upon A Time In America* are meticulously detailed, and there's an astute analysis of the film's relation to the 1930s classics. A labour of love.

General

Aurum Encyclopedia Of Gangsters
Phil Hardy, ed. (Aurum, 1998)

The *Aurum Encyclopedia* provides a capsule review for every film that includes a gangster in a major role from 1927, so even *Batman* gets its own entry. Editor Phil Hardy supplies a neat summary of each decade as well as an introduction outlining themes and parameters. The only quibble is that there hasn't been an updated reprint, and that even though there's an index of film titles, there's no other index to cross-reference actors or directors. Still, an essential text.

Behind The Mask Of Innocence
Kevin Brownlow (Knopf, 1990)

Kevin Brownlow has made silent films his domain.He is the world authority on the subject, and this book is a matchless study not just of early gangster pics, but of white-slave films, Red-scare movies, political exposés and drug warnings.

The BFI Companion To Crime
Phil Hardy, ed. (BFI, 1997)

Edited by Phil Hardy (of *Aurum Encyclopedia* fame), the BFI companion cherry-picks the best gangster and detective films, discusses sub-genres in mini-essays and provides thumbnail sketches of influential figures from writer W.R. Burnett to bandit John Dillinger (whose penis gets a lot of attention from contributor Kim Newman). Though there are no entries on stars and directors, the *BFI Companion* is a fine complement to the *Aurum Encyclopedia*.

BFI Modern Classics series
Various authors (BFI)

As a rule *BFI Classics/Modern Classics* are indispensable guides to landmark films. Though each book is different in its treatment, a successful formula has begun to emerge: a movie is broken down scene by scene, which brings together analysis, interviews, biography, on-set reports, critical reactions and the cultural forces which may have informed the film-maker's decisions. *Bonnie And Clyde*, *Heat*, *Pépé Le Moko* and *Once Upon A Time In America* are particularly good examples of this style; unfortunately the series can also get a little over-academic.

British Crime Cinema
Steve Chibnall & Robert Murphy (John Wiley, 1999)

A much-needed series of essays about the neglected history of the British crime-movie spree: spivs, *Performance*, *Get Carter*, *The Squeeze,* and *No Orchids For Miss Blandish* all get a chapter each, and about time too.

City On Fire
Lisa Oldham Stokes & Michael Hoover (Verso, 1999)

John Woo's favourite book on Hong Kong cinema is strong on biographical detail but is let down by its academic pretensions: Stokes and Hoover are convincing when they analyse the Chinese codes of honour that inform the narrative of Woo's movies, but a lot less so when arguing that *The Killer* is a searing indictment of late capitalism.

Crime Movies
Carlos Clarens (Norton, 1980)

Even though it was published in the 1980s, Clarens' book has not been bettered as the set text on the subject. Never hiding behind jargon to make his arguments, Clarens writes in a muscular prose style and with passionate authority, striking a precise balance between biography and analysis. Confining himself to the American crime movie, Clarens is particularly strong on the early half of the century: the neglected silents, Cagney's "hoofer alertness" and "slightly bruised sensitivity", and the FBI's contribution to cinema.

Chow Yun-Fat in *The Killer* (1989): is this movie really a searing indictment of late capitalism?

Gangster Films
Jim Smith (Virgin, 2004)

Concentrating on 25 "classics", including *Kill Bill* and *Robin And The Seven Hoods*, Smith divides his analysis up into sections on cast, summary, players, director, visual interest, quotes, sources-to-screen, contemporary reaction, trivia, sex/money/death and his own critical verdicts.

The Godfather Book
Peter Cowie (Faber, 1997)

Peter Cowie has enviable, unrivalled access to Francis Ford Coppola, which renders *The Godfather Book* the last word on *The Godfather* trilogy. The first part of the book is rich with behind-the-scenes stories – the threats, the feuds, the triumph of Coppola's will. In part two, themes of family and power are adeptly explored, Coppola's style is rigorously explained, and characters are expertly dissected.

The Immediate Experience
Robert Warshow (Doubleday, 1962)

Only seven pages long, Warshow's essay *The Gangster As Tragic Hero* is surely the most quoted piece of writing about the genre – so much so that it's practically illegal not to make reference to it in a gangster book. Written in 1948, when Hollywood movies were dismissed by right-thinking critics, Warshow took both the gangster movie and the Western seriously, regarding the crime film as "a consistent and astonishingly complete presentation of the modern sense of tragedy".

Inventing The Public Enemy
David E. Ruth (University of Chicago, 1996)

Less about the gangster movie and more about its place in the popular mythology of Capone and co, David E. Ruth's treatise locates the mobster in the society that made him. The jazz age, the new consumer culture and the growing city come to life with all their shiny new playthings: cars, guns and nightclubs.

The Mafia Encyclopedia
Carl Sifakis (Facts on File, 1987)

Exhaustive, instructive and entertainingly written, Carl Sifakis' encyclopedia is an impressive piece of research. From Al Capone to John Gotti, the author documents all the major players in American organized crime during the twentieth century, as well as members of the supporting cast like Murray Llewellyn Humphreys, the only Welshman in the Mafia. There's an explanation too of preferred methods of murder (such as the Italian Rope Trick), mob argot such as "taking for a ride" and "the no-hands rule", and the reason why Mafiosi keep pigeon coops. Despite the tacky cover, this is highly recommended.

Planet Hong Kong
David Bordwell (Harvard University Press, 2000)

Leading film prof Bordwell manages to be both intelligent and intelligible and, unusually for an academic, conveys his genuine passion for the subject. His readings of movies, particularly those of Wong Kar Wai, and the phenomenon of "Woo-ness", are dexterous, astute and not without humour (again, another rarity for an academic).

Pump 'Em Full Of Lead
Marilyn Yaquinto (Twayne, 1998)

Yaquinto's book is the natural successor to Carlos Clarens' *Crime Movies*; focusing on American cinema, she starts the crime story before D.W. Griffith and ends in the age of Tarantino. Her book has an edge in its unravelling of the movies' ties to real life, for instance its comparison of the fact and the fiction of *Bonnie And Clyde*.

Underworld USA
Colin McArthur (Viking, 1972)

Possibly the first book to take the genre seriously, the word seminal is one often applied to Colin McArthur's 1972 iconoclastic textbook. Without relying upon jargon, McArthur applied the auteur theory to "B-movie" directors like Robert Siodmak and Don Siegel, identified the iconography of the genre, and expounded its themes and its development from gangster to syndicate. A slim volume, the only problem is that it's too darn short.

The Yakuza Book
Mark Schilling (Stone Bridge, 2003)

Schilling is one of the leading authorities on Yakuza movies, a man who has sat through hundreds of hours of an often derided genre. A labour of love, his book provides a succinct introduction to Yakuza both real and imagined, while *ninkyo-eiga* is comprehensibly explained, and the major players are interviewed and profiled, including Takashi Miike, Kinji Fukasaku, Seijun Suzuki, Takashi Kitano, Ken Takakura, Junko Fuji and Koji Tsuruta.

Novels

The Asphalt Jungle
W.R. Burnett (Knopf, 1949)

John Huston was well known, in his screenwriter capacity, for being faithful to the original novel. Almost everything that appears in his iconoclastic heist movie happens in Burnett's hard-boiled classic: the forensic details of how to pull off a caper, who to employ, and how much they should be paid, as well as the carefully-drawn characterizations, the excoriation of the secret hearts of the hardmen, and the melancholy that hangs over the film.

High Sierra
by W.R. Burnett (Knopf, 1940)

Raoul Walsh's thriller has attained iconoclastic status because of its melancholic, introspective portrayal of Roy Earle as the last gangster standing. This anomie haunts

Sterling Hayden (foreground) shows that meticulous planning pays dividends in *The Asphalt Jungle* (1950)

the novel from page one. It begins with Earle reminiscing about his grandfather's porch, and continues in lyrical vein until Burnett, ever the cynical novelist, reminds the reader of all the unpleasantness that Earle has forgotten about from his idyllic childhood. Burnett co-scripted the film with John Huston, so it's not surprising that whole chunks of dialogue from the novel were transferred to the screenplay (though the film omits the ironic part that Pard the dog plays in Earle's downfall): Burnett's writing style is such that the novel was almost a blueprint for a movie to begin with.

The Hoods
Harry Grey (Crown Publishers, 1953)

Harry Grey (aka Harry Goldberg) wrote the novel, upon which *Once Upon A Time In America* was based, when he was in Sing-Sing. According to Christopher Frayling's superb biography of Leone, Grey – who looked every bit the ageing gangster – only agreed to sell the film rights to the novel if Leone met up with him; and he stipulated they could only meet if there were no witnesses. Grey was a minor hoodlum who ran with the likes of Meyer Lansky, Bugsy Siegel, Dutch Schultz and Frank Costello in 1920s New York. *The Hoods* is semi-autobiographical, but as Sergio Leone used to say, it reads like the script of a B-movie: "This was the big brain behind the Boss and the Combination ... He was modest. He kept in the background. He was the power behind the throne."

Jack's Return Home
Ted Lewis (Michael Joseph, 1970)

Ted Lewis was an illustrator and animator who worked on The Beatles' movie *Yellow Submarine* and gave up to work full time on this, his second novel, the basis of the movie *Get Carter*. And it's interesting to see how much of his work survived in the film: the plot, characters and even the line "you're a big man, but you're in bad shape" (though it was, admittedly "you're a big bloke – you're in bad shape"). The main difference is that *Jack's Return Home* was set in Scunthorpe (even though it's never named), while *Get Carter* was only relocated to Newcastle after writer/director Mike Hodges had first considered Hull and then Nottingham.

The other major change is that the book is narrated in the first person – there's no equivalent voice-over in the film, of course. It gives Jack Carter a semblance of humanity – although "humanity" may be stretching it a bit. Introduced to his niece who he hasn't seen for eight years, the gangster's first thoughts are "she was older than her fifteen natural years. I could have fancied her myself if she hadn't been who she was." The novel fills in many details that the film leaves out, particularly his fractious relationship with his brother, and delivers a classic *noir* narrative coup – the entire book is Carter's dying thoughts.

Little Caesar
W.R. Burnett (McVeagh/Dial Press 1929)

As soon as they turn the first page on Burnett's debut novel, fans of the film will notice something's up. Rico is not a friend of Joe's. In fact Rico hates Joe. The best friend narrative that's a key to the movie genre was not Burnett's invention: Joe only grasses on Rico when he's banged up inside and facing a lengthy jail sentence.
Written with pace and precision, everything else from the movie is present and correct, however, including the last line "Mother of God, is this the end of Rico?". Burnett complained vociferously to the producers that they'd made his character gay, by adding the line "that's what I get for liking a guy too much", but Rico's sexual preference is equally apparent in the book, with lines like "Joe couldn't figure Rico out. Women didn't seem to interest him."

Scarface
Armitage Trail (1930, Edward Clode)

Any resemblance between this novel and either of the *Scarface* films is almost coincidental. Apart from sharing a couple of names, Tony Camonte and Johnny Lovo, Trail's novel has little or nothing to do with Howard Hawks' movie, which proves that the screenwriting genius Ben Hecht was really the creator of *Scarface*. Which is not to say that the novel is uninteresting: one day someone might make a good movie from it.
Armitage Trail was the pseudonym of 23-stone writer Maurice Coons, who died of a heart attack at the age of 28, leaving only two novels and several detective stories.

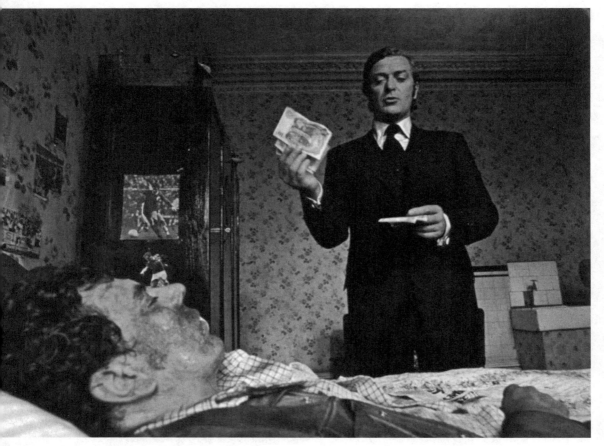

With friends like these... Jack Carter (Michael Caine), "hero" of the novel *Jack's Return Home*, in Mike Hodges' *Get Carter* (1971)

Like Hecht, Trail lived in Chicago and also based his Scarface on the legends of Al Capone. There's a *frisson* of authenticity about many of the insights, such as the character of the Gun Girl, who carries the gangster's gat for him in case he is frisked by the cops, and there's an exuberant gusto to the writing which skirts the edges of

parody. This is the opening line, which sets the scene and tone for the rest of the novel:

"Tony Guarino, destined to be the greatest of all America's notorious gang leaders, was eighteen when he committed his first serious crime. And the cause, as is so often the case, was a woman. But what a woman!"

Picture credits

The Publishers have made every effort to identify correctly the rights holders and/or production companies in respect of the images featured in this book. If despite these efforts any attribution is incorrect, the Publishers will correct this error once it has been brought to their attention on a subsequent reprint.

Cover Credits

ITV.com-Carlton International/LFI (Christopher Walken in *King Of New York*)

Illustrations

BFI (24) Biograph Company American Mutoscope & Biograph Co. General Film Company Image Entertainment (26) Fox Film Corporation William Fox Image Entertainment (27) Eminent Authors Pictures Inc Goldwyn Pictures Corporation Fright Video Goldwyn Distributing Company Grapevine Video LS Video Kino Video (186) (190) CICC Filmel TC Productions New Yorker Films Prodis BFI(224) Ashton Productions The Mirisch Corporation MGM Home Entertainment United Artists MGM/UA Home Entertainment Criterion Collection BFI(239) American Broadcasting Company (ABC) Anchor Bay Entertainment BFI(269) Cinecittà Lux Film Suevia Films S.A Vides Cinematografica Interpeninsular BFI(274) Nikkatsu Corporation Home Vision Entertainment Criterion Collection BFI(279) Gorky Film Studios Kinokompaniya CTB Roskomkino Kino International Corp Video Project Corbis (1) Kobal (32) Walter Wanger Productions Inc United Artists Corporation Columbia/Tristar (36) King Bros. Productions Inc Pioneer Pictures Corporation United Artists CBS/Fox Warner Home Video (42) Vanguard Productions United Artists New Concorde Home Entertainment (51) Superfly Ltd., Warner Bros. Warner Home Video (53) Palladium Productions Warner Home Video MGM/UA Home Entertainment (83) Tatira-Hiller Productions Warner Brothers/Seven Arts Warner Home Video (124) Harris-Kubrick Productions MGM Home Entertainment The Criterion Collection United Artists (129) Black Lion Films Limited Handmade Films Ltd. Calendar Productions The Criterion Collection (222) Warner Bros. The Vitaphone Corp Key Video MGM/UA Home Entertainment Warner Home Video (253) Paris Film Rialto Pictures LLC Criterion Collection Pathé Cinéma Moviestore (10) American International Pictures MGM/UA Home Entertainment Inc. MGM/UA (14) Tristar Pictures Columbia/Tristar Buena Vista Home Video (21) Miramax Initial Entertainment Group Miramax Buena Vista International (29) First National Pictures Inc. MGM/UA Home Entertainment Warner Bros (30) The Vitaphone Corporation Warner Bros. Warner Home Video (46) Dorcheste Warner Bros. Javelin Films Ltd Warner Bros (48) Oakhurst Productions Paramount Pictures Paramount Pictures United International Pictures (UIP) Paramount Home Video (57) Film Workshop Ltd. Golden Princess Film Production Ltd Magnum Entertainment Buena Vista Fox Lorber Criterion Collection (60) New Line Cinema (64) Miramax Initial Entertainment Group Miramax Buena Vista International (70) Indusfilms Prima Film Société Nouvelle Pathé Cinéma StudioCanal Image Iberia Films Societe Nouvelle de Cinematographie Gaumont Buena Vista International Fox (75) Metro-Goldwyn-Mayer (MGM) Loew's, Inc. MGM/UA Home Entertainment Inc. Criterion Collection Warner Home Video (80) Columbia Pictures Corporation Columbia/Tristar Studios (86) Associated British Picture Corporation Charter Film Productions Ltd Warner Home Video Movies Unlimited (90) O2 Filmes VideoFilmes Lumiere Productions Studio Canal 02 Filmes Curtos Ltda e Hank Levine Film GmbH Miramax Buena Vista International (95) David Foster Productions First Artists Tatiana Films National General Pictures Solar Productions National General Pictures Warner Bros. (99) Columbia Pictures Columbia Tristar (103) Paramount Pictures Corporation Paramount Home Video Paramount Home Entertainment (105) Paramount Pictures Corporation Paramount Pictures, The Coppola Company Paramount Home Entertainment (110) Warner Bros Inc. Warner Home Video (114) Warner Bros. Regency Enterprises Forward Pass Monarchy Enterprises B.V. (120) Basic Pictures Media Asia Films Ltd Miramax Films Mega Star Video Distribution (127) First National Pictures Inc. MGM/UA Home Entertainment Warner Bros. (132) Taplin-Perry-Scorsese Productions Warner Bros Inc. (136) 20th Century Fox Circle Films Inc. (140) Embassy International Pictures PSO International Rafran Cinematografica Warner Bros Regency Entertainment The Ladd Company Warner Home Video (142) Columbia Pictures Corporation Horizon Pictures Columbia/Tristar Studios (146) Goodtimes Enterprises Warner Bros Warner Studios (150) Metro-Goldwyn-Mayer (MGM) Warner Studios (153) Warner Bros MGM Home Entertainment (155) A Band Apart Jersey Films Miramax Films Buena Vista Int Miramax Films Criterion Collection (162) Warner Bros. MGM/UA Distribution (169) The Caddo Company Silver Screens United Artists Universal Pictures (174) RKO Radio Pictures (176)

Key Video Warner Bros Warner Home Video (179) Universal Pictures De Fina-Cappa Syalis D.A. & Legende Enterprises Universal Pictures MCA (183) Warner Bros MGM Home Entertainment (185) Metro-Goldwyn-Mayer (MGM) BFI Films Warner Home Video Warner Studios (188) American International Pictures (AIP) El Monte Productions (190) Warner Bros Warner Home Video (192) (195) Taplin-Perry-Scorsese Productions Warner Bros Inc. (196) Bandai Visual Co. Ltd. Shochiku Films Ltd. Yamada Right Vision Corporation Miramax Home Entertainment Buena Vista Home Video (199) Epic Productions Inc. Universal Pictures (201) Universal Pictures De Fina-Cappa Syalis D.A. & Legende Enterprises Universal Pictures MCA (203) Warner Bros. Key Video MGM/UA Home Entertainment Inc. Warner Home Video (205) (209) Twentieth Century Fox Fox Video (210) FilmFour Kanzaman S.A. Recorded Picture Company (RPC) Sexy RPC Ltd Twentieth Century Fox FilmFour (211) Film Workshop Ltd. Golden Princess Film Production Ltd. Magnum Entertainment Buena Vista Fox Lorber Criterion Collection (213) Columbia Pictures Corporation Columbia/Tristar Studios (216) Paramount Pictures Corporation The Coppola Company Paramount Home Entertainment (218) First National Pictures Inc. Warner Bros. Pictures Inc. CBS/Fox MGM/UA Home Entertainment Inc. (236) Columbia Pictures Corporation Columbia/Tristar Studios (244) The Caddo Company Silver Screens United Artists Universal Pictures (245) Nikkatsu Corporation Criterion Collection (248) Australian Film Finance Corporation (AFFC) Mushroom Pictures Pariah Entertainment Group Image Entertainment Inc First Look Pictures Releasing Beyond Films (251) Alpha Films La Sept Cinéma Ministère des Affaires Étrangères Shanghai Film Studios UGC Images Sony Pictures Columbia/Tristar Studios (254) Adel Productions Marianne Productions S.A. Mars Film Paramount Pictures (259) Buena Vista Home Video Rim Dimension Home Video (260) Jet Tone Production Co. Rolling Thunder Miramax Home Entertainment Miramax Ent (272) Nikkatsu Corporation Criterion Collection (289) HBO (295) HBO (304) (308) Film Workshop Ltd. Golden Princess Film Magnum Entertainment Buena Vista Fox Lorber Criterion Collection (310) Metro-Goldwyn-Mayer (MGM) Loew's, Inc MGM/UA Home Entertainment Inc Criterion Collection Warner Home Video Warner Home Video (312) Metro-Goldwyn-Mayer (MGM) BFI Films Warner Home Video (34) Paramount Pictures MGM/UA Home Entertainment Inc Paramount Pictures Universal Home Entertainment UMVD Ronald Grant (40) Antares Produzione Cinematografica Del Duca Films Rialto Pictures LLC Criterion Collection (67) Los Altos Productions Twentieth Century Fox (78) Cinema City Film Productions Rim Tai Seng Video (160) Indusfilms Prima Film Société Nouvelle Pathé Cinéma Rialto Pictures LLC Criterion Collection UMPO (164) Los Altos Productions Twentieth Century Fox (226) Tatira-Hiller Productions Warner Brothers/Seven Arts Warner Home Video (228) Indusfilms Prima Film Société Nouvelle Pathé Cinéma Rialto Pictures LLC Criterion Collection UMPO Grabs (256) Antiteater-X-Film e-m-s the DVD-Company Wellspring Media (268) Cineproduzioni Daunia 70 (276) Altavista Films Cacerola Films Videocolor Lightning Entertainment Arenas Entertainment (283) M&M Productions Danmarks Radio (DR) United International Pictures (UIP) (284) East Film Company The Klock Worx Company Ltd. (285) Hyun Jin Films Korea Pictures Suh Se-Won Production Co. Ltd. (287) Bohemian Films Cinemasia Artificial Eye Palm Pictures BBC Drama Group(293)

Index

Page references to films discussed in the Canon chapter, people or things described in the Icons chapter, and specific feature boxes are indicated in **bold**.

A

A bout de souffle 44, **69**, 111, 112, 144, 177, 225, 253, 254
Albino Alligator 58
Al Capone 9, 20, 38, 43
Four big-screen Al Capones **9**
Allen, Woody 87–88, 134
Altman, Robert 50, 167, 174
The American Friend 53
The Amulet Of Ogum 250
Analyse This 88, 294
Analyse That 294
Ando, Noburo 272
Angels With Dirty Faces 32–33, 50, **73**, 81, 162, 175, 182, 218, 219, 233, 234, 241
As Tears Go By 120–121, 259–260, 262
The Asphalt Jungle 18, 19, 40, 41, 43, 46, 48, 50, 64, **75**–76, 123, 193, 227, 229, 233, 243, 306, 309
Atlantic City 56
Attenborough, Richard 47, 85–87
Avary, Roger 58, 154, 207

B

Baby Face Nelson 8, 38, 43, 44, 231, 244
Bachchan, Amitabh 263–264
Bad Guy 65, 284, 286
Badlands 33, 50, 52
Balabanov, Aleksei 64, 278–279, 281
Ball Of Fire 38, 237
Bande à parte 74, 251–252, 253
Bangkok Dangerous 287, 288
Barker, Ma 16–17, 189, 296
Barrow, Clyde 17–18, 45
Battles Without Honour And Humanity 272, 274
Beatty, Warren 14–15, 17, 45, 82–84, 200, 229
Belmondo, Jean-Paul 56, 71–74, 190, 191, 219, 225, 254, 255
Benton, Robert, 14, 45, 82
The best lines **238**
A Better Tomorrow 55–56, 57, **77**–78, 2011, 223, 258–259
Big Bad Mama 49, 240, 241
The Big Combo 41, 112, 198, 235
Big Deal On Madonna Street 267, 270
The Big Heat 41, **79**–80, 99, 152, 235, 237, 238
Billy Bathgate 11, 13, 14, 54
Bindon, John 149–150
Black Caesar 50, **80**–82, 159, 235
The Black Hand 4, 49, 234
Blondell, Joan 151, 197, 296
Bloody Mama 16, 49, 189, 190, 240, 241
Blue Velvet 56
Blutiger Freitag 257, 258
Bob le flambeur 41, 43, 65, 195, 253
Bodrov Jr, Sergei **280**, 281

Bogart, Humphrey 13, 19, 32–35, 38, 41, 43, 73, 98, 117–118, 121–123, 161–163, **181**–182, 193, 194, 220, 221, 233, 234, 241, 243, 296, 303, 306
Bonnie and Clyde 17–18, 45, 302, 308
Bonnie And Clyde 17, 18, 33, 45, 49, 50, 59, 74, **82**–84, 102, 154, 163, 177, 189, 225, 307
Boorman, John 48, 149–151, 167, 266
Borsalino 191, 255
Il Boss 267, 270
Boulting Brothers 85–87
Boxcar Bertha 49, 205
Boyz N The Hood 59, 60, 62, 66, 136
Branded To Kill 47, 272, 274
Brando, Marlon 49, 101–103, 133, 141–143, 187, 191, 200, 224, 227, 240, 243, 297, 300, 306
Brat 64, 278, 279, 281
Brat II 278, 281
Breathless 56
Brighton Rock 37, **85**–87
Brother 174, 273
The Brotherhood 47, 49, 234
Budd, Roy 95–96, 299–300
Bullets Or Ballots 31, 33, 182, 196, 243
Bullets Over Broadway **87**–88, 235
Bugsy 14, 15, 54
Bugsy Malone 52, 64, 300
Bullet Boy 66
Bunker, Eddie 158
Burnett, W. R. 18–19, 117–118, 217, 233, 307, 309–310
Buscemi, Steve 156
Buster 50, 61

Carlito's Way 62, 200
Casino 190, 206
Cassavetes, John 99–100, 232
Le cercle rouge 189, 190, 195, 198, 254, 255
Charley Varrick 49, 52, 228, 232
Chinatown 50, 52
Chopper 248, 249
Chungking Express 260
Circus Boys 56
City On Fire 56, 120, 157, 259, 261
City Of God 63–64, **89**–91, 249–250, 292, 297
City Of Lost Souls 65
City Of Men 292
Clarke, Mae 52, 182–183, **197**
The Coen Brothers (Joel and Ethan Coen) 135–136
Cohen, Larry 80–82
Collateral 231, 232
Colors 57
Comedy hitmen **225**
The Consequences Of Love 269–270
Conte, Richard 112, 202
Cook Jr, Elisha 123–125, **202**
The Cook, The Thief, His Wife And Her Lover 55
Coppola, Francis Ford 47, 49, 62, 82, 101–106, 108, 140, **186**–187, 225, 297, 305
Corman, Roger 9, 16, 44, 163–164, **188**–189, 205, 241, 242, 306
The Cotton Club 11, 13, 54, 59, 187, 202
Country Of The Deaf 280–281
Crazy Mama 240–241
Criss Cross 36, 39–40, 236
Cummins, Peggy 111–113, 222
Cyclo **92**–93, 230

C

Caan, James 101–103, 224, 225
Cagney, James 7, 15, 30–35, 42–44, 54, 74, 81, 117, 118, 135, 151–153, 161–163, 175–176, 181, **182**–184, 208, 218–225, 233–243, 264, 303, 306–307
Caine, Michael 46, 49, 51, 95–97, **185**, 238, 243, 296
Calhern, Louis 75–76
Cammell, Donald 51, 61, 147–150
Capone 9
Capone, Al 4–9, 15, 19, 20, 23, 26, 27, 28, 43, 63, 163, 170, 192, 296, 302, 305, 308, 310

D

Dall, John 111–113, 222
Dang Birely And The Young Gangsters 65, 286, 288
Dassin, Jules 37, 41, 46, 48, 137–138, 143, 159–160, **189**–190, 221
Dead Or Alive 62, 273, 274
Deewaar 263–264
Delon, Alain 74, 135, 166–167, 185, **190**–191, 223, 243, 254–255

Demme, Jonathan 55, 242
De Niro, Robert 63, 104–110, 113–116, 130–133, 138–140, 185, 189, **191**–192, 200–201, 205, 206, 218, 221, 224, 232, 237, 260, 294, 300
De Palma, Brian 5, 9, 54, 55, 62, 126, 191, 200, 237, 242
The Departed 123
Le deuxième souffle 47
Dickinson, Angie 151, 231, 240, 241
DiCaprio, Leonardo 64–65
Di Leo, Fernando 257, **267**, 268, 270
Dillinger (1945) 38, 44
Dillinger (1973) 11, 30, 49
Dillinger, John 8–11, 18, 19, 117, 293, 302, 307
Dirty Deeds 248, 249
Dr Mabuse: The Gambler 258, 259
Donnie Brasco 62, 200
The Doorway To Hell 5, 33, 218, 219, 241
Le doulos 44, 55, 157, 196, 199, 219, 254, 255
Doyle, Christopher 119, 121, 287, 288
Dunaway, Faye 17, 45, 48, 82–84
Duvall, Robert 57, 101–106, 233, 296
Duvivier, Julien 33, 146–147

E–F

The Enforcer 4, 43, 235
Evans, Robert 101, 186–187, 300
Face 61, 210
Fassbinder, Rainer Werner 256, 257
Ferrara, Abel 125–126
Fingers 195
Floyd, Nigel 267
Fonda, Henry 33, 177–178, 222, 235
Force Of Evil 38, **93**–95, 234, 243
Fox, James 51, 61, 147–150
Frears, Stephen 56, 62, 125
The French Connection 52
Friend 65, 285
A Friend Of The Deceased 281
Fuji, Junko 271, 272, 309
Fukasaku, Kinji 56, 196, 272, 273, 274, 309
Full-Time Killer 262
The Funeral 126

Fuller, Sam 42, 43, 48

G

Gabin, Jean 33, 41, 43, 144–145, 252–253, 255
Gable, Clark 15, 30, 32, 204
Gangbusters 292–293
Gangs Of New York 3, 63, 65, 206, 305
Gangster No.1 61, 148
Gangsters 292
Gangsters on stage **19**
Garfield, John 93–95, 118, 221, 234, 243
The General 265, 266
The Getaway **95**–96, 125, 225, 228, 230
The Getaway: Black Monday 297, 298
Get Carter 50, 51, 52, 60, 85, **97**–98, 148, 238, 296, 299–300, 307, 309
Getting away with it **230**
Get Shorty 59, 62
Ghost Dog 231, 232
Gloria **99**–100, 230
G-Men 31, 33
Godard, Jean-Luc 17, 44, 45, 58, 71–74, 83, 111, 112, 225, 253–254
The Godfather 27, 47, 49, 50, 54, 65, 81, 100, **101**–103, 108, 138, 140, 154, 171, 186–187, 199–200, 217, 220, 224, 225, 227, 232, 233–234, 237, 238, 264, 294–297, 300, 303, 306
The Godfather Part II 13, 54, 63, 103, **104**–106, 113, 154, 187, 215, 219, 230, 232, 234, 303
The Godfather Part III 62, 106, 186, 187, 200, 303
The Godfather (video game) 297
Goodfellas 63, 91, **107**–110, 133, 134, 154, 191, 192, 201, 204, 205, 206, 219, 222, 224, 227, 270, 292, 294, 297, 300
The Good Thief 65, 242
Grahame, Gloria 38, 79–80, 99, 237, 238
Grand Theft Auto: San Andreas 297–298
The grapefruit **152**
Green Fish 284, 285
Greene, Graham 19, 37, 39, 86
Griffith, D.W. 23–25, 28, 208, 308
The Grifters 62, 125

The Grissom Gang 16, 17, 38, 49, 240
Gun Crazy 33, 35, 36, **111**–113, 154, 174, 222
Guys And Dolls 12, 240, 300

H

Hana-Bi 61, 172, 196
Harlow, Jean 151, 153, **197**, 236, 237
Hark, Tsui 258–259, 302
The harshest critics **296**
Hawks, Howard 38, 54, 168–170, 220, 234
Hayden, Sterling 75–76, 101, 123–125, 220, 243
Heat 106, **113**–116, 200, 229, 307
Hecht, Ben 20, 26, 28, 168, 170, **192**, 241, 310
Heist 58
Hellinger, Mark 20, **193**, 208, 241
High Sierra 8, 18, 19, 34, **117**–118, 193, 192, 205, 221, 235, 236, 306, 309
The Hit 55, 56, 231
Hodges, Mike 51, 52, 95–97, 299–300, 309
Hopper, Dennis 53, 56, 57, 230, 248
The horse **7**
Hoskins, Bob 128–130, 185, 227, 238
The Hot Rock 48, 230
How To Steal A Million 228
HUAC **220**
Hughes Brothers (Allen and Albert Hughes) 60, 107, 133–134
Hung, Tran Anh 92–93
Huntley, John 229
Huston, John 19, 52, 55, 56, 75–76, 117, 121–123, 145, 182, **193**–194, 203, 220, 263, 306, 309

I–J

Ichi The Killer 273, 287
Iconic molls **197**
I, Mobster 188
Infernal Affairs 65, **119**–121, 261
Infernal Affairs II 66
Infernal Affairs III 66

The Italian Job 46–49, 60, 229, 243, 300
It Always Rains On Sunday 37, 39, 243
I Went Down 265, 266
Jackie Brown 59, 81, 124, 186, 193, 204
Jackson, Samuel L 153–156, 204, 230, 298
Jagger, Mick 145–148, 247
James, Sid 204
Jorge, Seu 89, 299

K

Kar-Wai, Wong 119–120, 259–260, 262, 308
Kazan, Elia 42, 102, 141–143, 221
Keitel, Harvey 14, 130–133, 153, 156–158, **194**, 202, 203, 260
Kelly, Gene 4, 49
Key Largo 11, 35, 118, **121**–123, 145, 193, 306
Ki-Duk, Kim 284–285, 286
Kiler 277, 278
Kilerow 2-och 278
The Killer 55, 57, 78, 120, 204, 207, 208, 227, 230, 235, 259, 307
The Killers (1946) 36, 40, 191, 231, 232
The Killers (1964) 231, 232
The Killing 41, 46, **123**–125, 198, 227, 229
Killing Zoe 58
King Of New York **125**–126, 235
Kings Of Crime 279–280
Kiss Of Death (1946) 36, 205–206
Kitano, Takeshi 56, 58, 61, 172–173, **196**–197, 271, 272, 273, 309
The Krays 61, 240
Kray twins (Reggie and Ronnie Kray) 49–52, 95, 147
Kubrick, Stanley 41, 116, 123–125

L

L.A. Confidential 63
The Ladykillers (1955) 37, 44, 229, 235
Lam, Ringo 56, 119–120, 259, 261
Lancaster, Burt 36, 39, 56, 193, 231, 232

Lang, Fritz 33, 79–80, 136, 177–178, 235
Lansky 13
Lansky, Meyer 11, **13**, 14, 15, 54, 191, 309
Last Life In The Universe 273, 287, 288
Lau, Andrew 65, 66, 119–121, 260–261, 262
Lau, Andy 119–121, 258, 260–262
Layer Cake 61, 66
The League Of Gentlemen 45–47
Leonard, Elmore 59, 62, 207
Léon 230, 232
Leone, Sergio 54, 140–142, 237, 264, 300, 306, 309
Leung, Tony 92, 119–121
Lewis, Joseph H. 111–113
Li, Gong 251, 252
Lilya 4 Ever 283
The Limey 63, 64
Jake Lingle 19–20
Ray Liotta 107–110, 191, 227, 294
Little Caesar 4, 18, 23, 27, 28, 30, 32, **127**–128, 134, 151, 202, 203, 217–218, 219–220, 222, 233, 237, 242, 252, 298, 310
Lock, Stock And… (TV series) 293
Lock, Stock And Two Smoking Barrels 25, 57, 60, 61, 63, 66, 96, 293
The Long Firm 293–294
The Long Good Friday 54, 55, 60, 64, **128**–130, 215, 227, 235, 238, 265
Love Is Colder Than Death 256, 257
Luciano, Charles "Lucky" 11–12, 54, 59
Lucky Luciano 11, 12, 49, 268–269
Lund, Katia 63, 89–91, 250

M

Machine Gun Kelly 38, 43, 44, 163, 188, 237
Mackenzie, John 128–130, 266
Madness to his Method **192**
Mafia 298
Mak, Alan 65, 66, 119–121, 261
La Mala Ordina 267, 270
Malick, Terrence 50, 52
Mamet, David 13, 58
Manhattan Melodrama 10, 30, 32

Mann, Michael 106, 113–116, 230
Married To The Mob 55
Marvin, Lee 79–80, 149–151, 223, 231, 232, 296
Mayfield, Curtis 50, 301
McQueen, Steve 48, 97–98, 225, 230
McVicar 55
Mean Streets 49, 62, 66, 74, 109–110, **130**–133, 191, 194, 204, 205, 223, 235, 242, 260, 300
Meirelles, Fernando 63, 89–91, 299
Melville, Jean-Pierre, 4, 41–44, 47, 65, 71, 74, 157, 166–167, 185, **197**–198, 211, 254, 255, 303, 306
Menace II Society 59, **133**–134, 297
Miike, Takashi 61, 62, 64, 65, **273**, 274, 287, 309
Milano Calibro 9 267, 270
Miller's Crossing 54, **135**–136, 303
Mona Lisa 55, 185
Monroe, Marilyn 75–76, 233
Morricone, Ennio 138–140, 300
Moscow 280, 281
Muni, Paul 19, 30, 118, 168–170, 200, 215, 222, 238, 244
Musical gangsters **240**
The Musketeers Of Pig Alley 23–25, 27, 28
My Wife Is A Gangster 65, 285, 286

N

Natural Born Killers 33, 58–59, 62, 177, 239, 301
Nayakan 264
Ness, Elliot 8, 296
Never get high on your own supply **227**
New Jack City 60
Nicotina 275, 276, 278
Night And The City 37, **137**–138, 189, 208, 221
No Orchids For Miss Blandish 16, 38, 238, 240, 307
Novel deaths **235**

O

Ocean's 11 (1960) 19, 45–46, 47, 75
Ocean's 11 (2002) 64, 65
The Olsen Gang 282

Olsen, Rolf 257, 258
Once Upon A Time In America 54, 63, **138**–140, 141, 199,
218, 237, 242, 300, 306, 307, 309
Ong-Bak 66
On The Waterfront 42, 102, 133, **141**–43, 219, 243
Orol, Juan 275
The Outfit 149
Out Of Sight 59, 63, 64
Out Of The Past 36, 38, 39, 236

P

Pacino, Al 54, 62, 101–106, 113–116, 126, 170–171, 187,
198–200, 215, 217, 223, 224, 227, 232, 237, 238, 242,
297
Pale Flower 47, 272, 274
Palminteri, Chazz 87–88
Palookaville 58, 228
Pang Brothers 287, 288
Parinda 264
Park, Chan-Wook 66, 284, 285
Parker, Bonnie 17–18, 45
Pasta alla Mafiosi **108**
Peckinpah, Sam 97–98, 125, 225
The Penalty 26, 28
Penn, Arthur 18, 45, 50, 82–84, 102, 225
Penn, Christopher 126, 156, 158, 298
Penn, Sean 57, 62, 88
Pépé Le Moko 33, **144**–145, 252–253, 307
Performance 25, 51, 60, 61, 85, **145**–148, 235, 307
Pesci, Joe 107–110, 133, 195, **200**–201, 206, 294
The Petrified Forest 8, 19, 32, 221
Pfeiffer, Michelle 54, 55, 170–171, 223, 237, 242
The Phenix City Story 11, 41, 44
Pick-Up On South Street 42, 43, 209
Pixote 249
Point Blank 11, 48, **149**–151, 163, 167, 223
Point Break 218
Polonsky, Abraham 38, 41, 93–95, 221
Pop goes the gangster **61**
Powell, Michael 133
Prime Cut 131
Prizzi's Honor 55, 56, 224, 225

Prohibition, speakeasies and bootlegging **6**
Psy 277
The Public Enemy 6, 7, 15, 28, 30, 32, 33, 132, 135,
151–153, 175, 182–183, 197, 218, 222, 223, 234, 235,
237, 239, 296, 300
Pulp Fiction 54, 58, **153**–156, 195, 207, 230, 235, 239,
243, 276, 301
Puzo, Mario 49, 101, 108, 187, 234

R

The Racket 8, 19, 27, 203, 237
Raft, George 15, 30, 54, 118, 169–170, **202**–203, 215,
222, 223, 242
Ratanaruang, Pen-Ek 273, 287, 288
Ray, Nicholas 50, 173–174
Reel heists **229**
Regeneration 24, 25, 28, 205
Reservoir Dogs 8, 25, 38, 52, 56, 58, 75, 79, 124, 153,
154, **156**–158, 195, 198, 207, 223, 228, 238, 259, 301
Rich And Famous 261
Richardson, Charlie 51, 61,147
Rififi 41, 46, 75, 138, **159**–160, 189, 221, 227, 228, 229,
253, 255
The Rise And Fall Of Legs Diamond 12, 13, 38, 43, 47
Ritchie, Guy 60, 63, 66, 96, 276
Road To Perdition 64, 65
The Roaring Twenties 13, 32, 33, **161**–163, 182, 193, 208,
224, 236, 241, 242, 264
Robbery 48, 50
Robin And The Seven Hoods 48, 204, 223, 308
Robinson, Edward G. 19, 27, 30–35, 48, 74, 118, 121–
123, 127–128, 182, **203**–204, 217, 219–220, 222, 223,
233, 243, 303, 306
Roeg, Nic 145–148
Romeo+Juliet 233
Rosi, Francesco 11, 49, 165–166, 268–270
Rota, Nino 81, 101–102, 104, 300
Rothstein, Arnold 12, 54, 216, 233, 242
Rowlands, Gena 38, 99–100, 230

S

St Valentine's Day Massacre 9, 43, **163**–164, 189, 244
Salvatore Guiliano 12, **165**–166, 268, 269
Le samourai 44–45, 58, 74, 135, 151, 163, **166**–167, 190, 198, 223, 230, 231, 243, 254–255
Satya 240, 263, 264, 301
Scarface (1932) 5, 9, 15, 19, 23, 25, 28, 30, 32, 33, 49, 128, 151, **168**–170, 191, 199, 215, 220, 222, 223, 234, 236, 237, 238, 241, 244, 310
Scarface and the censors **168**
Scarface (1983) 5, 54–55, 62, 115, 126, **170**–171, 196, 197, 215, 217, 219, 223, 227, 237, 238, 242, 252, 264, 297, 303
Schultz, Dutch 11–14, 20, 54, 59, 296, 309
Scorsese, Martin 3, 49, 61–65, 74, 82, 93, 107–110, 121, 130–134, 185, 191, 192, 194, 195, 200–201, **205**–206, 211, 221, 242, 260, 301, 304, 306
La scorta 268, 270
Seberg, Jean 56, 71–74
The Set-Up 243
Sexy Beast 61, 65, 96, 148, 210
La sfida 268, 270
Shakespearean gangsters **233**
Shanghai Triad 251, 252
Shark Tale 206
Shiner 61
Shinjuku Triad Society 61, 62, 273
Sholay 263, 264
The Sicilian Clan 255
Siegel, Bugsy 14–15, 54, 192, 202, 302, 309
Siegel, Don 44, 52, 162, 231–232, 309
Sinatra, Frank 12, 45, 47, 48, 101, 182, 240
Singleton, John 59, 60, 62, 134
Smart Money 31
Soderbergh, Steven 59, 63, 64, 65
Some Like It Hot 200, 222, 223, 235, 242
Sonatine 61, **172**–173, 194, 273
Sonnenfeld, Barry 59, 62, 135
"Sopranalysise this" **294**
The Sopranos 55, 294–296
The Squeeze 52, 54, 307
Starr, Freddie 52, 204
Stone, Oliver 59, 171, 197, 239
Stormy Monday 55, 57, 61
Sugawara, Bunta 273, 274

Superfly 50, 223, 301
Suzuki, Seijun 47, 272, 274, 309
Sweet Sweetback's Baadaass Song 50
Sympathy For Mr Vengeance 66

T

Takakura, Ken 271–272, 309
Taking a dive **243**
The Taking Of Pelham 1-2-3 52, 157
Tarantino, Quentin 56, 58–62, 74, 124, 153–158, 166, 167, 193, 195, 198, 203–205, **207**–208, 238, 253, 257, 259, 266, 275, 276, 280, 282, 300, 301, 304, 305, 308
The Testament Of Dr Mabuse 257
They Live By Night 18, 33, 35, 50, 59, 156, **173**–174, 177, 222
They Made Me A Fugitive 37, 39, 227
Thieves Like Us 50, 176
The Third Man 37, 39
This Gun For Hire 19, 35, 39, 44, 167, 195, 230
The Thomas Crown Affair 48, 160
Thompson, Jim 97–98, 123–125, 255
Tierney, Lawrence 38, 44, 157, 158, **202**, 238
To Die For Tano 268
Tokyo Drifter 47, 272, 274
Too Many Ways To Be No.1 261, 262
Topkapi 46, 48, 160, 229
Touchez Pas Au Grisbi 41, 43, 253
Tracey, Spencer 12, 30, 181, 204, 222
Tragic Hero 261
Travolta, John 59, 62, 153–156, 208
True Romance 203, 205
Truffaut, François 44, 45, 61, 73, 83, 160
Tsuratu, Koji 271–272, 309
Tycoon 280, 282

U

Underworld 6, 23, 26, 28, 191, 218
Underworld USA 11, 48
Unlikely gangsters **200**

The Untouchables 5, 6, 8, 9, 20, 54, 190, 296
The Untouchables (TV series) 292, 296
The Usual Suspects 58, 62

V–Z

Vaastav 240, 263, 264, 265
Van Peebles, Melvin 50
Veronica Guerin 266
Villain 52, 240
Viterelli, Joe 87–88
Wacky Races 296
The Wages Of Sin 25, 237
Walken, Christopher 57, 125–126
Walsh, Raoul 24, 25, 28, 117–118, 161–163, 175–176, **208**, 309
Warner Brothers 18, 30, 31, 48, 51, 144, 153, 163
Warner, Jack 19, 45, 84

Wellman, William 132, 151
Weiss, Little Hymie 4, 6, 7, 15–16, 152, 220, 305
When The Sky Falls 266
White Heat 16, 35, 44, 128, **175**–176, 184, 207, 224, 238, 240, 243
Who Killed Pixote? 249, 250
Widmark, Richard 36, 37, 42, 43, 137–138, **209**
Wilder, Billy 38, 223, 225, 237
Winstone, Ray 61, 65, **210**–211
Withers, Googie 37, 137–138
Woo, John 4, 55–56, 57, 74, 77–78, 119–120, 166, 185, 186, 194, 195, 203, 204, 211–212, 223, 227, 258–229, 302, 305, 307
Woods, James 138–140, 218, 298
Yimou, Zhang 251, 252
Young And Dangerous 120, 260–261, 262
You Only Live Once 17, 33, 35, 59, 73, 136, 154, 174, **177**–178, 222, 235
Yun-Fat, Chow 55–56, 57, 77–78, 157, **185**–186, 208, 258–259, 261, 296
Zanuck, Darryl F. 19, 137, 152, 189

Rough Guides travel...

UK & Ireland
Britain
Devon & Cornwall
Dublin
Edinburgh
England
Ireland
Lake District
London
London DIRECTIONS
London Mini Guide
Scotland
Scottish Highlands &
 Islands
Wales

Europe
Algarve
Amsterdam
Amsterdam
 DIRECTIONS
Andalucía
Athens DIRECTIONS
Austria
Baltic States
Barcelona
Belgium & Luxembourg
Berlin
Brittany & Normandy
Bruges & Ghent
Brussels
Budapest
Bulgaria
Copenhagen
Corfu
Corsica

Costa Brava
Crete
Croatia
Cyprus
Czech & Slovak Republics
Dodecanese & East Aegean
Dordogne & The Lot
Europe
Florence
France
Germany
Greece
Greek Islands
Hungary
Ibiza & Formentera
Iceland
Ionian Islands
Italy
Languedoc & Roussillon
Lisbon
Lisbon DIRECTIONS
The Loire
Madeira
Madrid
Mallorca
Malta & Gozo
Menorca
Moscow
Netherlands
Norway
Paris
Paris DIRECTIONS
Paris Mini Guide
Poland
Portugal
Prague

Provence & the Côte
 d'Azur
Pyrenees
Romania
Rome
Sardinia
Scandinavia
Sicily
Slovenia
Spain
St Petersburg
Sweden
Switzerland
Tenerife & La Gomera
 DIRECTIONS
Turkey
Tuscany & Umbria
Venice & The Veneto
Venice DIRECTIONS
Vienna

Asia
Bali & Lombok
Bangkok
Beijing
Cambodia
China
Goa
Hong Kong & Macau
India
Indonesia
Japan
Laos
Malaysia, Singapore &
 Brunei
Nepal

The Philippines
Singapore
South India
Southeast Asia
Sri Lanka
Thailand
Thailand's Beaches &
 Islands
Tokyo
Vietnam

Australasia
Australia
Melbourne
New Zealand
Sydney

North America
Alaska
Big Island of Hawaii
Boston
California
Canada
Chicago
Florida
Grand Canyon
Hawaii
Honolulu
Las Vegas
Los Angeles
Maui
Miami & the Florida Keys
Montréal
New England
New Orleans
New York City

New York City
 DIRECTIONS
New York City Mini Guide
Pacific Northwest
Rocky Mountains
San Francisco
San Francisco
 DIRECTIONS
Seattle
Southwest USA
Toronto
USA
Vancouver
Washington DC
Yosemite

Caribbean
& Latin America
Antigua DIRECTIONS
Argentina
Bahamas
Barbados DIRECTIONS
Belize
Bolivia
Brazil
Caribbean
Central America
Chile
Costa Rica
Cuba
Dominican Republic
Ecuador
Guatemala
Jamaica
Maya World
Mexico

Rough Guides are available from good bookstores worldwide. New titles are published every month. Check www.roughguides.com for the latest news.

...music & reference

Peru
St Lucia
South America
Trinidad & Tobago

Africa & Middle East
Cape Town
Egypt
The Gambia
Jordan
Kenya
Marrakesh
  DIRECTIONS
Morocco
South Africa, Lesotho &
  Swaziland
Syria
Tanzania
Tunisia
West Africa
Zanzibar

Travel Theme guides
First-Time Around the
  World
First-Time Asia
First-Time Europe
First-Time Latin America
Skiing & Snowboarding in
  North America
Travel Online
Travel Health
Walks in London & SE
  England
Women Travel

Restaurant guides
French Hotels &
  Restaurants
London Restaurants

Maps
Algarve
Amsterdam
Andalucia & Costa del Sol
Argentina
Athens
Australia
Baja California
Barcelona
Berlin
Boston
Brittany
Brussels
Chicago
California
Corsica
Costa Rica & Panama
Crete
Croatia
Cuba
Cyprus
Czech Republic
Dominican Republic
Dubai & UAE
Dublin
Egypt
Florence & Siena
Florida
Frankfurt
Greece
Guatemala & Belize

Iceland
Ireland
Kenya
Lisbon
London
Los Angeles
Madrid
Mallorca
Marrakesh
Mexico
Miami & Key West
Morocco
New York City
New Zealand
Northern Spain
Paris
Peru
Portugal
Prague
Rome
San Francisco
Sicily
South Africa
South India
Sri Lanka
Tenerife
Thailand
Toronto
Trinidad & Tobago
Tuscany
Venice
Washington DC
Yucatán Peninsula

Dictionary Phrasebooks
Czech

Dutch
Egyptian Arabic
European Languages
  (Czech, French,
  German, Greek, Italian,
  Portuguese, Spanish)
French
German
Greek
Hindi & Urdu
Hungarian
Indonesian
Italian
Japanese
Mandarin Chinese
Mexican Spanish
Polish
Portuguese
Russian
Spanish
Swahili
Thai
Turkish
Vietnamese

Music Guides
The Beatles
Bob Dylan
Cult Pop
Classical Music
Elvis
Hip-Hop
Irish Music
Jazz
Music USA
Opera
Reggae

Rock
World Music (2 vols)

Reference Guides
Books for Teenagers
Children's Books, 0–5
Children's Books, 5–11
Cult Fiction
Cult Football
Cult Movies
Cult TV
The Da Vinci Code
Ethical Shopping
iPods, iTunes & Music
  Online
The Internet
James Bond
Kids' Movies
Lord of the Rings
Muhammad Ali
PCs and Windows
Pregnancy & Birth
Shakespeare
Superheroes
Unexplained Phenomena
The Universe
Weather
Website Directory

Also! More than 120 Rough Guide music CDs are available from all good book and record stores. Listen in at www.worldmusic.net

ROUGH GUIDES GOES TO THE MOVIES

THE ROUGH GUIDE TO
comedy

1843534649

THE ROUGH GUIDE TO
gangster m

1843534231

THE ROUGH GUIDE TO
horror m

1843535211

1843535203

gh Guide to
sci-fi movies
John Scalzi

WITHDRAWN

Available from all good boo